Quest *for the*
HISTORICAL
APOSTLES

Quest *for the* HISTORICAL APOSTLES

✳

Tracing Their *Lives* and *Legacies*

W. BRIAN SHELTON

𝕭
Baker Academic
a division of Baker Publishing Group
Grand Rapids, Michigan

© 2018 by W. Brian Shelton

Published by Baker Academic
a division of Baker Publishing Group
PO Box 6287, Grand Rapids, MI 49516-6287
www.bakeracademic.com

Printed in the United States of America

Library of Congress Cataloging-in-Publication Data
Names: Shelton, W. Brian, author.
Title: Quest for the historical Apostles : tracing their lives and legacies / W. Brian Shelton.
Description: Grand Rapids : Baker Publishing Group, 2018. | Includes index.
Identifiers: LCCN 2017052479 | ISBN 9780801098550 (pbk. : alk. paper)
Subjects: LCSH: Apostles. | Church history—Primitive and early church, ca. 30–600.
Classification: LCC BS2440 .S47 2018 | DDC 225.9/22—dc23
LC record available at https://lccn.loc.gov/2017052479

18   19   20   21   22   23   24   7   6   5   4   3   2   1

To Bill Shelton,
whose paternal love and faith in Christ
have blazed a path for my own faith journey.

His influence and support have ranged from rearing his children
in church to an appreciation for my theological career.

He positioned me to complete confirmation at a young age,
where the pastor realized a coincidence that day:
"Twelve confirmed. Like the twelve apostles.
Perhaps this is no coincidence."

Contents

Acknowledgments

J ust as the apostolic college was an assembly of individuals with a common cause, this book had its own writing college that deserves mention. The fellowship of Clarkesville United Methodist Church provided the initial impetus for this work when they reached for insight beyond what a book on the apostles could offer. Thanks are due to David Nelson, Wells Turner, and the Baker editorial and production professionals for their generous support. Thanks to Torri Beck and the Seby Jones Library staff at Toccoa Falls College for endless research support. President Robert Myers and five school deans offered understanding to their provost to pursue a meaningful outlet amid numerous other administrative responsibilities. Special thanks to Kent Rothwell for laboring through a draft from a layman's perspective simply out of a love for learning and a contribution to friendship. Finally, the work would not have been possible without initial recommendations by Drs. Robert Yarbrough, Joel Green, Bryan Litfin, and Kenneth Steinhauser, as well as their influence on me.

Particular thanks go to Sally Shelton, whose interest in biblical studies continues to mature alongside my own. Her dedication to dialoguing about apostolic journeys, tying together pieces of the New Testament, and sacrificial supporting of writing projects is invaluable. It is my hope that Annie, Katie, and Maggie Shelton will follow in her footsteps and someday profit from the journeys of the apostles presented here.

While it seems idealistic, expressing acknowledgment to thirteen apostles long gone seems fitting. My respect for these fellow believers deepened as their journeys and sacrifices slowly unfolded to me. I realized the profound inspiration that they continue to offer those who journey and sacrifice for the same kingdom cause generations later. Although the church is regularly criticized, I think the apostles would be proud that the message instrumental to their own lives continues to be perpetuated among Christians around the world.

Rome, Lent 2017

Abbreviations

General and Bibliographic

†	death (at a place or date)
ANF	*The Ante-Nicene Fathers: Translations of the Writings of the Fathers down to A.D. 325*. Edited by Alexander Roberts and James Donaldson. Revised by A. Cleveland Coxe. 10 vols. New York: Christian Literature, 1885–87. Reprint, Peabody, MA: Hendrickson, 1994.
AT	author's translation
ca.	*circa*, about
Cain	Jerome. *Commentary on Galatians*. Translated by Andrew Cain. FC 121. Washington, DC: Catholic University of America Press, 2010.
CE	Common Era
chap(s).	chapter(s)
d.	died
Elliott	J. K. Elliott. *The Apocryphal New Testament: A Collection of Apocryphal Christian Literature in an English Translation*. Oxford: Clarendon, 1993.
fl.	flourished
FC	Fathers of the Church
Hills	Julian V. Hills, trans. *The Epistle of the Apostles*. Early Christian Apocrypha 2. Salem, OR: Polebridge, 2009.
Holmes	*The Apostolic Fathers: Greek Texts and English Translations*. Edited and translated by Michael W. Holmes. 3rd ed. Grand Rapids: Baker Academic, 2007.
James	*The Apocryphal New Testament: Being the Apocryphal Gospels, Acts, Epistles, and Apocalypses*. Translated by Montague Rhodes James. Oxford: Clarendon, 1924. Reprint, 1972.
KJV	King James Version
Lienhard	Origen. *Homilies on Luke*. Translated by Joseph T. Lienhard. FC 94. Washington, DC: Catholic University of America Press, 1996.

Malan	Abdias. *The Conflicts of the Holy Apostles*. Translated by Solomon Caesar Malan. London: BiblioLife, 2015.
NICNT	New International Commentary on the New Testament
n.p.	no page number available
NPNF¹	*A Select Library of Nicene and Post-Nicene Fathers of the Christian Church*. First series. Edited by Philip Schaff. 14 vols. New York: Christian Literature, 1886–89. Reprint, Peabody, MA: Hendrickson, 1994.
NPNF²	*A Select Library of Nicene and Post-Nicene Fathers of the Christian Church*. Second series. Edited by Philip Schaff and Henry Wace. 14 vols. New York: Christian Literature, 1890–1900. Reprint, Peabody, MA: Hendrickson, 1994.
r.	reigned
Robinson	James M. Robinson, ed. *The Nag Hammadi Library in English: The Definitive Translation of the Gnostic Scriptures Complete in One Volume*. San Francisco: HarperSanFrancisco, 1990.
Schneemelcher	*New Testament Apocrypha*. Edited by Wilhelm Schneemelcher. Translated by R. M. Wilson. 2 vols. Philadelphia: Westminster, 1963–66.
TNTC	Tyndale New Testament Commentaries
trans.	translated by
v(v).	verse(s)
vol(s).	volume(s)
Williams	Epiphanius. *Against Heresies*. In *The Panarion of Epiphanius of Salamis*, book 1. Translated by Frank Williams. Boston: Brill, 2009.

Old Testament

Gen.	Genesis	2 Chron.	2 Chronicles	Dan.	Daniel
Exod.	Exodus	Ezra	Ezra	Hosea	Hosea
Lev.	Leviticus	Neh.	Nehemiah	Joel	Joel
Num.	Numbers	Esther	Esther	Amos	Amos
Deut.	Deuteronomy	Job	Job	Obad.	Obadiah
Josh.	Joshua	Ps(s).	Psalm(s)	Jon.	Jonah
Judg.	Judges	Prov.	Proverbs	Mic.	Micah
Ruth	Ruth	Eccles.	Ecclesiastes	Nah.	Nahum
1 Sam.	1 Samuel	Song	Song of Songs	Hab.	Habakkuk
2 Sam.	2 Samuel	Isa.	Isaiah	Zeph.	Zephaniah
1 Kings	1 Kings	Jer.	Jeremiah	Hag.	Haggai
2 Kings	2 Kings	Lam.	Lamentations	Zech.	Zechariah
1 Chron.	1 Chronicles	Ezek.	Ezekiel	Mal.	Malachi

New Testament

Matt.	Matthew	Luke	Luke	Acts	Acts
Mark	Mark	John	John	Rom.	Romans

1 Cor.	1 Corinthians	2 Thess.	2 Thessalonians	1 Pet.	1 Peter
2 Cor.	2 Corinthians	1 Tim.	1 Timothy	2 Pet.	2 Peter
Gal.	Galatians	2 Tim.	2 Timothy	1 John	1 John
Eph.	Ephesians	Titus	Titus	2 John	2 John
Phil.	Philippians	Philem.	Philemon	3 John	3 John
Col.	Colossians	Heb.	Hebrews	Jude	Jude
1 Thess.	1 Thessalonians	James	James	Rev.	Revelation

Old Testament Apocrypha

2 Esd.	2 Esdras
4 Macc.	4 Maccabees
Sir.	Sirach
Wis.	Wisdom of Solomon

Other Ancient Works

Ant.	Josephus, *Jewish Antiquities*
Conflicts	Abdias, *Conflicts of the Holy Apostles*
Ep. Apos.	Epistle of the Apostles
Gos. Thom.	Gospel of Thomas
Haer.	Irenaeus, *Against Heresies*
Hist. eccl.	Eusebius, *Ecclesiastical History*
J.W.	Josephus, *Jewish War*
Life	Josephus, *Life of Flavius Josephus*
Ps.-Abd.	Apostolic History of Pseudo-Abdias
Strom.	Clement of Alexandria, *Miscellanies*
Twelve	Hippolytus, *On the Twelve Apostles*
Vir. ill.	Jerome, *Illustrious Men*

Introduction

The Quest

Turning to the disciples, He [Jesus] said privately, "Blessed *are* the eyes which see the things you see, for I say to you, that many prophets and kings wished to see the things which you see, and did not see them, and to hear the things which you hear, and did not hear them."

Luke 10:23–24

While Jesus was saying this, Thomas, Andrew, James and Simon the Canaanite were in the west, with their faces turned east, but Philip and Bartholomew were in the south turned towards the north, but the other disciples and the women disciples stood behind Jesus. But Jesus stood beside the altar.

Pistis Sophia[1]
late third century, Egypt

The lives of the apostles deeply intrigue us. For Christianity's faithful, these historic figures are pioneers, heroes, and saints. They are models for the faith and sources of firsthand knowledge of the Christ. They walked with Jesus, beheld his marvels, wondered at his conversations, and reflected deeply on his teaching. They sat at the Last Supper table, grew weary

---

1. Schneemelcher, 1:258.

at Gethsemane, witnessed the crucifixion, and marveled at the resurrection. Not knowing what their individual futures held, they were shaken at Pentecost, grew into church leaders, and watched the church rise to a level of indelible competition with religions in the Roman Empire. Most apostles passed into obscurity, but all died without any thought that generations to follow would herald them as icons of the faith and personifications of religious ideals. In their time these figures were stones in the historic foundation of early, expanding Christianity, and now their stories are inspirational and interesting to us. Even atheist Tom Bissell, writing about the history of the apostles, declares, "I have long believed that anyone who does not find Christianity interesting has only his or her unfamiliarity with the topic to blame."[2]

Interest in the apostles extends to some of the greatest believers in church history. Seven years before her death, Corrie ten Boom shared a story with the congregation at McLean Presbyterian Church in Virginia. Her account was imaginary, but it provides a powerful perspective on the contribution of the apostles. She described how angels gathered around Jesus at his ascension into heaven, and these guardians inquired how the world would know about the redemption he had accomplished. "I have trained my men," he explained to his heavenly audience. "To evangelize the whole world?" the angels asked. "Every corner of it," he responded. "How many men did you train for such a mammoth task?" they inquired. "Twelve men," he asserted. "Just a handful? But what if they fail?" "If they fail," said Jesus, "I have no other plans." Puzzled, the angels insisted, "But is that not a great risk to take?" "No," said the Lord, "because they will not fail."[3] Ten Boom's being a Holocaust survivor makes the illustration more profound: both she and the apostles embody a profound sense of overcoming.

In the immediate generations after the apostles, their legacy was enhanced through oral tradition and fabled writings. Unbeknownst to Corrie ten Boom when she told her story, a parallel legacy existed from a second-century writing that underscored her picture of the apostles' success. In the Epistle of the Apostles, Jesus says of Paul, one of the apostles: "Upon him will be the perfection of my testimony."[4] Yet no early church scholar believes that the twelve apostles wrote this second-century epistle bearing their name. With uncertainty about what information concerning the apostles is historical and what is fictional, historians are now left to apply critical skills to make these determinations. While any embellishment always represents an effort to honor

2. Bissell, *Apostle*, xx.
3. Ruffin, *The Twelve*, 175.
4. Ep. Apos. 31 (Hills, 60).

the apostles, the calculation of authenticity is more challenging for scholars who research from a position of faith. Such a task is intimidating since an objective scholar desires to graciously permit the voices of early Christian history to speak for themselves yet is compelled to weigh and filter their stories. A comprehensive collection of reliable information about the twelve apostles is not easily available, but such a collection as this book offers can benefit the church in understanding its early history.

For those who are familiar with the New Testament, knowledge of the lives of the apostles beyond Acts is likely limited to the epistles that bear apostolic names. Those familiar with early church history may comprehend the influence of the apostles across the empire and in the formative structure of the church without knowing their historical lives and the unique contributions they made. Graduate students who construct bridges between the New Testament and early Christian studies likely discern the collective influence of the apostles without knowing the individual paths of mission that the Twelve took. The apostles dispersed geographically in Acts before legends about their ministry and martyrdoms emerged in the annals of church history. Even then, the legends are sometimes treated as apocryphal literature and thus ignored without considering the possibility of a historical core or are viewed as Catholic saint stories with unsubstantiated sites of miracles and burials.

The stories and contributions of the apostles provide an important entrée to church history and thus *should* be available to a wider audience. The episodes of their lives and legacies are curious and valuable to many Christians. But books about the apostles are commonly written for a popular audience, focusing on personality analysis and quick summaries of their final ministry and death places, while analyses of their legacies are often limited to background information in biblical commentaries solely related to epistles bearing their name. Historically sound books on the topic are often obscure, produced by minor or confessional publishers. A recent, single, comprehensive work is not available as a historical assessment of both the lives and the legacies of the apostles in church history.

This work takes on the legends and legacies of the apostles from the New Testament, extant primary source material, contemporary veneration practices remaining from lost information, and secondary research theories. At the same time, our historical knowledge of the apostles is limited to a dispersed set of sources, so the contemporary images of the apostles are as significant as the discernment of their ancient stories. This book combines the historical data with iconic and theological developments concerning the apostles in the immediate and the distant generations that followed.

The Character of a Quest

This book employs the theme of "quest" to search for the apostles on two levels. The reader and the author travel through the annals of time and ancient sources in search of the historical apostles. Like the quest theme that figures prominently in literature across many cultures, we inquire through a process termed *historia* for the paths of the eleven original disciples and two additional disciples.[5] The legends of the apostles seem only to whisper from the shadows of the pages of early church texts, originally scattered across the ancient world. We struggle to hear them clearly as we seek to overcome the obstacles of competing traditions, unbelievable legends, and missing data that compete with our objective efforts toward veracity. While seeking the apostles, we wish not only to discover their journeys but also to enhance our faith, hoping for evidence at one turn while cringing at the loss of evidence at another. In this sense, the quest shapes us.

On another level, the apostles themselves were on a quest to deliver the message of Christ through travel and encounters in lands foreign to them. Like the heroes of journey fables of various cultures, these men were driven by belief and characterized by their own human passion. Vladimir Propp suggests that quests stem from either an external act that creates an insufficiency or an internal act that reveals an insufficiency. In both instances, a quest is provoked to address a situation of insufficiency.[6] In the case of the apostles, an external event such as the final commission of Jesus at his ascension (Matt. 28:19–20) or the empowering of the disciples at Pentecost (Acts 2:1–4) clearly identified evangelism as a task that needed to be undertaken, externally provided by God. At the same time, the psyches of this circle of twelve who witnessed miracles and struggled to make sense of their perceptions had undergone a transformation. The apostles came to recognize their own potential contribution to the furthering of the kingdom introduced by Christ, realizing that they could not keep silent about the gospel (Acts 5:40–42). Motivated externally by Christ's command and internally by their own love for the message of Christ, the apostles embarked on a quest. Through their struggles, encounters, successes, failures, and even supernatural acts, they advanced the cause of the kingdom by their preaching and teaching. Their quest shaped them. This book is thus a quest for a quest.

The title of this work deserves further qualification. While *Quest for the Historical Apostles* captures the intent of the work, for biblical scholars the cadence of the title echoes the 1906 work of Albert Schweitzer, *The Quest*

---

5. Cairns, *Christianity through the Centuries*, 17–18.
6. Propp, *Morphology of the Folk Tale*, 35.

of the Historical Jesus. Schweitzer's work is recognized as more than a mere historical evaluation of Jesus, as it seeks also to penetrate the identity of the historical Messiah figure through a complex theological analysis of the figure and a higher-critical biblical assessment of the authenticity of the Gospel texts shaping his image. *The Quest of the Historical Jesus* participated in a movement in response to nineteenth-century German Protestant liberalism, whose influences Schweitzer claims had "marked out the ground which is now occupied by modern critical study. And they filled in the death-certificates of a whole series of explanations which, at first sight, have all the air of being alive, but are not really so."[7] From the influence of liberal theology as well the response of Schweitzer and others, biblical studies lost sight of the ability of Scripture to foster faith. Eta Linnemann describes the situation: "This ideology was at first intermixed with the Christian faith; but in the course of its refinement it rejected the Christian faith as essentially incompatible."[8] Schweitzer himself was a French-German scholar and alumnus of the University of Tübingen, the symbolic seat of critical studies of the New Testament. He articulated a highly idealized but higher-critical portrait of Jesus, attributing psychological and political qualities to him that extended beyond the Gospel histories in order to posit a Christ redeemed from modernism but still different from the one the premodern church had offered.

This quest is akin to Schweitzer's quest, but with a different approach. This expedition limits attempts at discovering answers to identity questions about the apostles themselves and focuses on their journeys. These men were confident in the resurrection and focused on transforming unbelievers into Christians. Although the title of this book evokes the higher-critical biblical quest, it does not represent a critical reading that calls into question the basic existence of the apostles or the veracity of the biblical accounts. From the biblical accounts it builds a profile of each apostle and his legacy. Similarities to the First Quest of the Historical Jesus, characteristic of Schweitzer's efforts, may be seen here in my filtering and weighing the claims of gnostic or pseudepigraphical writings rather than of the biblical writings. Any reader who expects a reconstruction of the basic apostle stories in the spirit of Schweitzer will be disappointed since this work is not critical in this way but assumes a positive motive behind the apostolic mission.

Furthermore, this present work constructs in faith the historicity and legacy of the apostles in the spirit of Augustine's instruction for study, "Except ye

7. Schweitzer, *Quest of the Historical Jesus*, 84.
8. Linnemann, *Historical Criticism of the Bible*, 39.

believe, ye shall not understand," leading to the dictum *crede, ut intelligas*.[9] Augustine meant that faith guides a quest, providing a foundation of belief that extends into new realms of reason and understanding. Ryan Topping explains, "Faith is never something Augustine sets *against reason*; indeed, insofar as there is a contrast to be made it is not between reason and faith, but between *reason and authority*."[10] Authority is the primary challenge in the approach of this quest, as it weighs the veracity of numerous works among the early church testimonies of the journeys of the apostles. Primacy is given to Scripture, while extrabiblical works are bridled for analysis before automatically ascribing historicity to their claims. This is a work of pursuit, a quest to discover and explain the roads of these traveling individuals according to church history. I hope this work is not only insightful and interesting but will also strengthen readers in their Christian faith, not necessarily by reinforcing dogmatic expectations of miracles and myths but by clarifying, complementing, and critiquing the confusing legacy of the apostles.

Layout

This book shares and analyzes the background stories and legacies of the apostles as they advanced from the New Testament into early church history. Each chapter presents the biblical data on an apostle; explores and weighs the relevant extrabiblical material; identifies theological, geographical, and symbolic significance; and combines these into a structured image that the church permanently inherits. This examination includes Matthias and Paul. Matthias is treated because of his replacement of an original disciple, that "one of these *must* become a witness with us of his resurrection" (Acts 1:22). Paul is treated because of his significance in the New Testament and early Christianity, although he described himself as "the least of the apostles, and not fit to be called an apostle, because I persecuted the church of God" (1 Cor. 15:9). The chapters also occasionally consider medieval and modern reports of the apostles. An overall conclusion on the evidence discovered will close the quest.

The research approach to the chapters is fivefold. First, (1) biblical sources, with brief interpretation, will provide information on each apostle. Next, (2) extrabiblical early Christian sources will reveal a range of meritorious or legendary material about the biography of an apostle. Here, judicious treatment of legends includes assessing each source, determining the viability of its claims through correspondence with biblical and extrabiblical sources,

9. Augustine, *Homilies on the Gospel of John* 29.6 (NPNF[1] 7:184).
10. Topping, *Happiness and Wisdom*, 177.

and measuring the permanent influence of the stories. (3) A synthesis of the overall image of each apostle will be established, more or less congruent with the impression of him perpetuated through time in the life of the church, but hopefully more expansive. (4) Symbolic analysis will explain the permanent representations of the life or contribution of the apostle. Finally, (5) a report on the possible sites of the apostle's tomb will be provided.

The biblical material for each apostle ranges from significant attention to mere mention in lists. Peter receives the most attention of all the disciples in the Gospels and second most in Acts; he can serve as an illustration for how the material will be presented. Occasionally in apocryphal teaching literature, Peter dialogues with Jesus, yet usually the text provides neither bibliographical data nor particular insight into the disciple. The Acts of Peter gives narrative attention to Peter, while also providing attention to Paul as background, which will inform the chapter on that apostle. Church historian Eusebius reports that Peter came to Rome, and the testimony of other early church writers is marshaled to confirm his presence there. An early medieval writer describes how he came to the house of Peter in Capernaum during the late sixth century, while a modern scholar ties together two strands of Peter's journey through archaeological and literary evidence.

The extrabiblical material on the apostles chronologically follows their journeys from the book of Acts. This material is generally grouped into two types here: historical and apocryphal. The historical data include passing comments by early fathers such as Clement of Alexandria or Tertullian about an individual apostle, as well as specific biographical paragraphs such as those of Hippolytus or Eusebius in dedicated works that summarize the apostles' lives and ministries. On the other hand, apocryphal works are less verifiable sources, coming in the form of acts and teachings. The Acts of Peter reports Peter healing his daughter and then returning her to disabled status, while the Acts of John affirms the apostle's ability to command bedbugs. The Acts read as historical biographies, but the fable-like content and the mysterious teaching almost disqualify them from serving as credible sources of information for our quest. Each source must be weighed independently. Likewise, teaching books, such as the gospel of Thomas and the book of Thomas the Contender, often augment the canonical Gospel teachings of Jesus with mysterious sayings that range from incomprehensible to ascetic exhortations to suffer as part of the gnostic worldview of salvation. Just as the early church did, this book treats these teaching manuscripts as not particularly helpful in providing insight into apostolic biographies. But unlike the heresiological treatises of the early church, these works are examined for a historical core that might help guide our quest.

Finally, all of this historical material is accompanied by the developed image of each apostle, which leads to the church's perspective on the figure today. Each apostle's various symbols, the legends around his possible resting places, and his use in ritual practices are analyzed to conclude the treatment. Thus, this book will provide a comprehensive, historically centered, and critical evaluation of the stories and early Christian literature on all of the apostles, as well as our inherited contemporary understanding of these men. It could also function as the centerpiece to a literature set that resourcefully employs the apostolic figures as models for the faith.

Purpose and Style

When one contemplates how the successful promotion of Christ's original mission was dependent on the first generations of disciples, one begins to grasp how the message of the gospel must have been immensely convincing. The achievement of advancing the teaching of one Galilean prophet to become the official religion of the Roman Empire and the cornerstone of Western civilization indicates how miraculously impressive and powerful that subject matter was and still is. Philip Schaff puts it this way: "The rapid success of Christianity under the most unfavorable circumstances is surprising and its own best vindication."[11] As people of faith, entertaining a supernatural history, we recognize the Holy Spirit in action; as people of earth, recognizing a natural history, we realize that the disciples were the sacrificial and transformed agents responsible for the expansion of Christianity. Our purpose is to explore the transformative power of this message that drove thirteen disciples across the ancient world on a quest to share the hope that this message offers.

This book's characteristic style will be to provide content that is not too critical but addresses the most critical issues, not densely scholarly but is still historically insightful, not overtly evangelical but is still respectful of the figures, and readable but is also a resource for research. I hope the audience will be broad; I aim to appeal to evangelicals, mainline Protestants, Catholics, and Orthodox alike, seeking neutrality on perspectives of the apostles that place these traditions in conflict. Pedagogical aids in the form of maps are plentiful and necessary.

This study of the apostles could be interesting to any Christian, but students are particularly in view for this book. The work is designed to link New Testament studies with church history, imagined in an undergraduate or a graduate setting, bridging from the New Testament to a study of early Christianity.

---

11. Schaff, *History of the Apostolic Church*, 1:197.

Church history, early Christianity and patristics courses, and New Testament courses focusing on Acts could employ this work. Secondarily, the work can function for individual research in part or whole when an apostolic legacy needs elaboration. It can function as a contextual aid in studies of martyrs, cultic reverence, or historical influence. Examination of the lives and contributions of the twelve apostles through the combination of historical and literary scholarship aims to provide a foundation that is intelligent, informed, and useful. Third, the work can function to inform the nonstudent about the narrative story of each apostle, perhaps answering questions of curiosity as well as of the veracity and meaningfulness of the Christian faith.

Biases should be conceded up front. I write as an orthodox Christian, maintaining a faith in the canonical Scriptures and the potential historical usefulness of the Apocrypha but rejecting the gnostic writings as generally not informative for the Christian faith. Yet all provide insights into the early church's perspective on Christ and salvation in varying degrees. This position is a combination of faith presupposition and analytical evaluation of the writings of the early church; the foundational position of the book stems from a faith in Scripture that has been reinforced by decades of evaluative consideration of the differences between canonical, apocryphal, and gnostic sources. I seek to hold in tension (1) a belief in the inspiration of the Scriptures that does not necessarily extend to the Apocrypha and certainly not to the gnostic writings and (2) a willingness to evaluate the meaning and shape of Scripture through early extrabiblical sources. While the extrabiblical sources are not treated as Scripture, the historical information they provide has a profound potential for the faith.

In this approach, Augustine is again marshaled as cited above. His words *crede, ut intelligas*, "believe that thou mayest understand,"[12] find fulfillment in Anselm's *credo ut intelligam* when he appeals to God to think well, "I believe so that I may understand."[13] This principle is at work here for this author and potentially for the reader: we study the lives of the apostles with an admitted bias toward the Scriptures in the hopes that we may strengthen our faith and find merit in the historicity of early church records. Anselm's maxim *fides quaerens intellectum*, "faith seeking understanding," will also be adopted as a posture to possible belief in legends in congruence with known faith.

This faith-based approach to apostolic history finds its methodology further reinforced by R. G. Collingwood in his influential *The Idea of History*, in which he describes how the second great crisis of European historiography

---

12. Augustine, *Homilies on the Gospel of John* 29.6 (NPNF[1] 7:184).
13. Anselm of Canterbury, *Proslogion* 1, in Davies and Evans, eds., *Anselm of Canterbury*, 87.

occurred when Christianity began expressing itself through historical writing in the fourth and fifth centuries. Accordingly, "It is inevitable that man should act in the dark without knowing what will come of his action. . . . From this follows that the achievements of man are due not to his own proper forces of will and intellect, but to something other than himself, causing him to desire ends that are worth pursuing."[14] This statement is as true for the boldness of the apostles as it is for the approach to confronting the dubious historical sources that will be encountered in this book. This is the core of Christian historiography: recognizing divine providence in the actions and the recording of history as well as in our own assessment of that history.

I expect some to read this work in its entirety, while for others it will serve as a resource for historical and literary information on one apostle of particular interest. It is set apart from other books in its expanse of history, its use of lesser-known primary literature of the early church, and in its synthetic focus on the image of each apostle.

Challenges

The challenges to such a task are many. Since the decline of the premodern era, few contemporary writers indiscriminately accept early church historical writings as fact. More notably, in the decline of the modern era, premodern historiography is treated dismissively by biblical scholars such as Bart Ehrman and early church scholars such as Candida Moss. Ehrman insists, "The New Testament is a historical construct, not a 'given.' . . . It is not fully representative of the views and writings of early Christians."[15] Moss insists that the martyrdom accounts from the first two hundred years of the faith mostly "aren't historical accounts; they are religious romances written and intended to be read for moral instruction and entertainment."[16] The postmodern attitude (if the moniker is permitted) is a critical outlook extending beyond skepticism to distrust and uncertainty of sources that must be overcome to learn about the apostles. While scholars such as Ehrman and Moss have made important contributions to the study of the early church, their approach at best establishes equity between various sources and at worst risks dismissing the sources altogether. Several challenges in the contemporary era are

---

14. Collingwood, *Idea of History*, 46–47. He elaborates: "Thus the plans which are realized by human actions come about not because men have conceived them, decided on their goodness, and devised means to execute them, but because men, doing from time to time what at the moment they wanted to do, have executed the purposes of God" (47).

15. Ehrman, *New Testament and Other Early Christian Writings*, 4.

16. Moss, *Myth of Persecution*, 88.

explained here to help the reader recognize the obstacles to a study of the apostles such as this one.

As a first challenge, ancient sources by their very nature come from a period of *different historical standards*. Writers of early church history often championed their own agenda, used unreliable sources, stated uncertainties with certainty, and reported material in the hopes of its veracity. For example, critical historian Walter Bauer remarks of Eusebius, known as the father of church history, "We cannot establish any firm foothold on the basis of what Eusebius himself contributes," mainly because he champions the cause of the church.[17] Yet Collingwood has already made clear that a Christian historiography will ascribe providential causes to human agency as part of its ethos.[18] At the same time, the ancient writings are still full of valuable material that can be discerned and mined for authenticity. In a work dedicated to confronting historian Walter Bauer's dismissal of the heresiological writings of the church fathers, I write, "The question of reliability and legitimacy is a real one, but not an insurmountable one nor a disqualifying one."[19] Still, one needs to treat early church writing cautiously because of its tendency to report its own perspective.

In the case of the apostles, there is a second challenge in that the *stories are limited* and information is lost. Access to sources is limited, assuming there ever were written sources available on certain apostles. This makes us prone to embrace any story that fills the gap, making apocryphal works appealing, even if we reject the ridiculous and provide a historical opportunity for the normal. For example, there are several possibilities concerning the imprisonment(s) and release(s) of Paul in Rome. Two sites claim his imprisonment, which suggests two imprisonments. Descriptions of his captivity experiences range from a liberal house arrest to a miserable dungeon. Legends exist that he traveled to Spain, leading historians to entertain a period of freedom after his arrival in Rome in the book of Acts and before his execution in Rome. We are right to explore the possibilities, but those options sometimes must remain tentative when the full story of even Paul has been lost. As another example, accompanying the difficulty of establishing the apostles' resting places is the seeming fact that the bones of the apostles are fragmented and scattered across churches. Eckhard Schnabel notes the residual effect of the incomplete histories of the apostles: "It is a fact that no early Christian text that reports or claims to report historical events attempts to provide a complete

---

17. Bauer, *Orthodoxy and Heresy in Earliest Christianity*, 192.
18. Collingwood, *Idea of History*, 50.
19. Shelton, "Patristic Heresiology," 202.

historical account. It is precisely the missing 'coherence' that may indicate
that Christian authors of the second and third centuries had information
about the ministry of the apostles. Since they did not write a comprehensive
history of the early church, they passed on information that they had in a
selective and uncoordinated manner."[20]

By the time these biographies were written, they came *steeped in religious
myth*, a third challenge for this task. Their function was to testify to both the
natural and the supernatural work of the men whom the faith championed.
Thus arose a sort of apostle historiography, writings intended to promote the
ministry of the apostles and perpetuate the signs and wonders of the New
Testament. For example, on one hand Bartholomew is recorded as ministering
in India in natural fashion in the Apostolic History of Pseudo-Abdias. On
the other hand he is also recorded as healing the demonized daughter of the
Indian King Polymius, which created opportunity to preach the gospel. Peter
Berger explains how religions try to impose order and purpose on wicked
and destructive human experience, particularly the phenomena of evil, suffering, and death. Religious explanations legitimize these confusing events,
or to use John Milton's words, give a "justification of the ways of God to
man." By giving the chaos a higher meaning, religion brings life events under
a "sacred canopy" of understanding.[21] This means that claims to historicity
are constantly up against a newly established tradition in which claims to the
miraculous are suspiciously untenable, potentially exaggeration to justify
a religious position. The Bartholomew exorcism story illustrates that one
must discern whether the ancients were constructing religious myth through
fantastic stories to impose supernatural power on the apostles. Sometimes
the writings are so fantastical that they are simply absurd.

Studying religion in an age of a *distrust of sources* is both an asset and a
liability, making a fourth challenge. The current period after the modern era
is characterized by scrutiny and suspicion of sources. German theologian
Walter Schmithals denied that the twelve apostles ever existed, viewing them
as the fabrication of the author Luke to discredit the apostle Paul as part of
a larger explanation of the development of doctrine.[22] Research on the ancient
world as a whole, particularly on subjects of religion with claims to the supernatural, poses these same types of challenges. Michael Licona says: "It is
especially true that historians interested in antiquity are never epistemically
justified in having absolute certainty that an event occurred."[23] It is trendy in

20. Schnabel, *Early Christian Mission*, 1:531.
21. Berger, *Sacred Canopy*, 53–80.
22. Schmithals, *Office of the Apostle in the Early Church*, 266, cited in Ruffin, *The Twelve*, 172.
23. Licona, *Resurrection of Jesus*, 69.

scholarship to deconstruct and dismiss sources by deeming them unworthy, but it is a worthy challenge to identify and defend components of a source that might stem from historical truth.

Finally, studying religion in an age of *religious diversity* makes theological truth claims problematic. This is a fifth challenge. Explorations into the justification of one exclusive faith in an age of diversity are considered narrow-minded. The insight of Collingwood that early Christian historiography represents a universalism beyond Greco-Roman or Jewish historiographies feels ironic. Yet from its inception, Christianity represented a diversification in which "all men are equal in the sight of God: there is no chosen people, no privileged race or class, no one community whose fortunes are more important than those of another. All persons and all peoples are involved in the working out of God's purpose."[24] Such an image of Christianity is lost to the critical historian who views it as merely a religion of Western imperialism rather than recognizing the human need that universally welcomes the gospel. Religious sociologist Philip Jenkins predicts the global potential of the message of the apostles: "Christianity should enjoy a worldwide boom in the next century, but the vast majority of believers will be neither white nor European, nor Euro-American."[25]

Methodology

These challenges bring us to the analytical methodology to be applied with histories and legends in written records. The greatest challenge to a study of the apostles is discerning the quality of a source or part of a source as historical, questionably historical, or ahistorical. There will be numerous occasions for expressions of uncertainty. Early church historical or homiletic voices that make truth claims about the apostles provide the best source for accuracy. Next, passing comments or hesitant conjectures by an ancient author about a detail of the apostles' lives will be weighed tentatively. Apostolic journeys come chronicled in legendary form, moving in and out of our reconstructed maps of the ancient world to challenge our quest. Unfortunately, these apocryphal Acts are considered comprehensively suspicious on theological grounds, sometimes so contrary to orthodoxy that they reveal a likely intention to be religious myth or so bizarre that historical elements are suspect. Even more historically dubious are the apocryphal revelations. However, an apocryphal work can include historically accurate material, just as legends frequently have a historical basis to their myths. As a general rule, the more unorthodox or the more fanciful the work, the less its facts are trusted here. We gravitate toward

24. Collingwood, *Idea of History*, 49.
25. Jenkins, *Next Christendom*, 2.

historical anchors in these works in our effort to reconstruct the path of the apostles. In the end, this methodology brings us in line with Calvin Roetzel's comment on his own exploration of the life of Paul: "All such reconstructions are acts of historical imagination, and the reader will have to decide if the reconstruction presented here is credible."[26]

Dates and Maps

A quest for the apostles requires a foundational understanding of the chronological and geographical settings of their ministries. While all the apostles are thought to have continued the kingdom work inaugurated by Christ, their paths became as divergent as the legends of their experiences.

The apostolic era ranged from Pentecost of 30 CE to the death of the apostle John by the year 98. Even within this window of time we encounter the need for clarifying tentativeness. The year of the crucifixion, resurrection, and subsequent Pentecost has been speculatively based on the landing of Passover (14 Nisan) on Friday during the years 30 and 33 to match the calendar of Christ's experiences in the Gospels. Either year is plausible, but this book will use the former in accord with D. A. Carson, Douglas J. Moo, and Leon Morris.[27] The passing of John typically marks the end of the apostolic era; he appears to have been the youngest among the disciples, and his legends record his old age during the reign of Emperor Domitian (r. 81–96) or Trajan (r. 98–117).

The maps of the apostolic era range eastward to India with the possible ministries of Thomas, Bartholomew, and Matthew; westward to Spain with the possible ministries of Paul and James the Greater; and northward to Britain for the possible ministry of Simon the Zealot. Each chapter contains a map to represent the geographic ministry of that apostle. The ancient terms for regional areas are used in this work, with identifying correlations to modern countries. Achaea is assigned for southern Greece, Anatolia for Asia Minor or modern Turkey across Syria, Phrygia for the landlocked center of Asia Minor, Parthia for the southern Caspian Sea region from Arabia across Iran to India, and Scythia for the northern Caspian Sea region from the Ukraine across Kazakhstan. Both Parthia and Scythia guided the ancients to the border of India.

Movement toward Image

Along with reconstructing biographical details from the lives of the apostles, each chapter inspects the religious images, symbols, and other legends that shape

26. Roetzel, *Paul*, 1.
27. Carson, Moo, and Morris, *Introduction to the New Testament*, 55–56.

Regions Mentioned in This Book

the history of an apostle. These reconstructions are based largely on early church histories and geographical references from apocryphal material. Yet the historical apostle is sometimes linked to a certain image or perception, a picture or a legend, so that apostle's image is shaped by symbols, art, oral traditions, and cultic sites. Caravaggio's painting of the crucifixion of Peter, the rooster atop the church where Peter denied Christ, and the Roman church statues of Peter holding the keys to the kingdom are just some of the images that perpetuate his legend. Relics, tombs, or sites of an apostle's life also complement the art that preserves and promotes their legends, as tourists and pilgrims view the sacred spots with curiosity. All these elements have led to cultural images foundational for how generations prior and contemporary view the apostles.

This realm of consideration in the quest for the apostles is particularly rooted in the life of the medieval church. For example, François Bovon mentions how the ninth-century Byzantine period was highly curious about the lives of the apostles "for hagiographic, liturgical, homiletic, historiographic, and artistic purposes."[28] Viewed by the church as media to enhance the faith, concepts from apocryphal material filled in gaps about the lives of the apostles. Across the eras these activities shaped the image of the apostles. While much of their lives and the accuracy of these works are still uncertain, some components of apostolic images need pruning, and some need nurturing. The more important elements will be mentioned to close out each chapter.

28. Bovon, "Byzantine Witness," 87.

The Launch of a Quest

The quest for the historic apostles takes us along a path with various historic features that warrant definition and explanation in order to proceed with perception and meaning in a background unfamiliar to us. Chapter 1 will lay out the path of this quest. The subjects we call the apostles lived in the world of antiquity, with its complex worldview, landscape, and lifestyles that no longer are part of our natural perception. Greek philosophy had shaped thinking along dualistic lines, enabling ancient citizens to take for granted the familiarity of a story that disdained the earthly while affirming the heavenly. Jewish religion had positioned itself as passionately monotheistic, rejecting the notion that a new religion like Christianity could be a legitimately modified Judaism. International cultures meant that disciples might bear two names, while sometimes employing both for clarity. The natural environment of the lands around the Mediterranean Sea meant that the term "living water" immediately brought to mind a refreshing oasis effect, and a lion might be encountered by a wandering Paul.

This next chapter, titled "The Path," provides background to the sources and illustrates the filtering of their contents necessary for tracking the quest of the historical apostles. The analysis of each apostle will build on the background and assumptions treated in this chapter. The thirteen apostles are then the subject of our study in the chapters that follow, completing the story of how fledgling believers become pillars of the faith. Here is the heart of the book. The apostles began as disciples, serving to reveal further, to accentuate, and to emulate the person and work of Jesus. Richard Taylor remarks, "In a literary sense, the disciple as a group acts as a chorus in the Gospels, asking the questions that elicit vital answers from Jesus, or standing dazed and baffled by Jesus' message or miracles."[29] This principle continues in the gnostic gospels and apocalypses. After the ascension and Pentecost, these twelve acted like traditional apostles. Although the Gospels make the disciples secondary to the overall and primary ministry of Jesus, in Acts these apostles perpetuate this same ministry at a higher level of discipleship.

With the provision of this background, we embark on a quest for the historical apostles. The quest starts not with the first apostle but with preparation for the expedition, which includes familiarization with the identities, sources, and geography that we will encounter on the path to uncover the apostolic legacies. Then, with the lists of their names, the quest for each begins.

---

29. Taylor, *How to Read a Church*, 103–4.

The Path

But be on your guard; for they will deliver you to *the* courts, and you will be flogged in *the* synagogues, and you will stand before governors and kings for My sake, as a testimony to them.

Mark 13:9

For this purpose we have collected the materials that have been scattered by our predecessors and culled, as from some intellectual meadows, the appropriate extracts from ancient authors. In the execution of this work, we shall be happy to rescue from oblivion the successions . . . of the most noted apostles of our Lord.

Eusebius, *Ecclesiastical History*[1]
mid-fourth century, Palestine

The metaphor of a "path" partners nicely with the metaphor of a "quest." While the quest for the apostles naturally reaches for the lives of these men, the path to that legacy encompasses several factors of which the student of the apostles must be aware. This chapter examines the lists of apostles, the confusion of identity that has occurred with certain apostles, and the character of the office of apostle and its mission. Additionally,

---

1. Eusebius, *Hist. eccl.* 1.1.4. All quotations of Eusebius's *Ecclesiastical History* are from *Eusebius' Ecclesiastical History: Complete and Unabridged*, trans. C. F. Cruse, new updated version (Peabody, MA: Hendrickson, 2000).

attention is given to the biggest challenge of the apostles during this early era: the relationship between Judaism and the influx of gentile believers. The path requires a basic consideration and understanding of the sources that will be encountered as the basis of this quest, mainly how extrabiblical sources of apocryphal literature should be evaluated and how patristic figures provide historical details. Part of the historian's task is to comprehend the material found in these primary source texts. Finally, the path explains the eventual conception of saint that developed after each apostle, with their symbols and cultic perceptions.

The Identity of the Apostles

Studies of the apostles always begin with the list of the apostles. The New Testament and extrabiblical surveys of these figures naturally record their names in catalog fashion, but there are minor inconsistences in the lists. Different names apply to the same disciple, leading to the conflation and divergences of disciples in the historical records. A lesser obstacle is the theories of the familial relationships between them, which sometimes lead to making almost half of the apostles related to another apostle.

Disciple Lists in the New Testament

Lists of the names of the apostles appear in all three Synoptic Gospels and in Acts. Only John lacks such a list, although several descriptions of the apostles' activities and behavior are found exclusively in John. The lists are provided here for introduction and later reference.

Matthew 10:2–4	Now the names of the twelve apostles are these: The first, Simon, who is called Peter, and Andrew his brother; and James the son of Zebedee, and John his brother; Philip and Bartholomew; Thomas and Matthew the tax collector; James the son of Alphaeus, and Thaddaeus; Simon the Zealot, and Judas Iscariot, the one who betrayed Him.
Mark 3:16–19	And He appointed the twelve: Simon (to whom He gave the name Peter), and James, the *son* of Zebedee, and John the brother of James (to them He gave the name Boanerges, which means, "Sons of Thunder"); and Andrew, and Philip, and Bartholomew, and Matthew, and Thomas, and James the son of Alphaeus, and Thaddaeus, and Simon the Zealot; and Judas Iscariot, who also betrayed Him.
Luke 6:14–16	Simon, whom He also named Peter, and Andrew his brother; and James and John; and Philip and Bartholomew; and Matthew and Thomas; James *the son* of Alphaeus, and Simon who was called the Zealot; Judas *the son* of James, and Judas Iscariot, who became a traitor.

Acts 1:13	When they had entered the city, they went up to the upper room where they were staying; that is, Peter and John and James and Andrew, Philip and Thomas, Bartholomew and Matthew, James *the son* of Alphaeus, and Simon the Zealot, and Judas *the son* of James.

These catalogs provide a basic identification of the disciples by name as well as theories of some of their familial relationships. In the Gospels, Peter is recognized as Simon, renamed at the great event at Caesarea Philippi in which Jesus declares that he will be the rock on which the church is built. Andrew is recognized as the brother of Peter in Matthew and Luke. James and John are recognized as brothers in Matthew and Mark, twice called "sons of Zebedee" and once given by Jesus the name "Boanerges, which means, 'sons of Thunder.'" It is significant that James is named before his brother John in all three Synoptics, suggesting that he is an older brother, which is important in the evaluation of John's legacy. The youngest disciple would have had the potential for the longest ministry. The lists sometimes vary the order of less notable disciples, which is of little consequence. Judas Iscariot is always listed last and always with the disclaimer "the one who betrayed him" in Matthew and Mark and "who became a traitor" in Luke. The disciples list in Acts omits Judas Iscariot because his departure has already led to his death.

As a general rule, the significance or activity level of a disciple in the historical record places him higher or lower in the list. Since the lists create their own groups corresponding to the New Testament activities of those disciples, the term "tier" can be applied to reflect their relative importance. The catalogs reflect three different tiers. This should not suggest inferiority or a lesser kingdom contribution for the third tier but is only a grouping based on the extent of their recorded activity. In the top tier, James, John, Peter, and Andrew are always named first. In the second tier, Philip, Bartholomew, Thomas, and Matthew are listed. For each of these men the Gospels provide at least one significant encounter with Jesus. Finally, in a third tier of the most obscure of the disciples, another James, another Simon, and a Jude or Thaddaeus are named. The mention of Judas Iscariot as last likely places him in a position of dishonor, reinforced by his betrayal. The disciples in the third tier offer the most difficult historical paths to follow.

Converging Identities

While the identity of nine of the disciples is rarely confused, deduction is required to identify three of the disciples. For one, a common experience of calling can link us to the same figure. For two, an element of conjecture is required to connect two names for one figure. Each is briefly presented here, but their identities will be further elaborated in the chapters devoted to them.

MATTHEW

The disciple named Matthew in each list has an encounter with Jesus depicted in all three Synoptic Gospels. In Matthew 9:9 Jesus sees "Matthew, sitting in the tax collector's booth" and says "Follow Me!" Mark 2:14 and Luke 5:27 record the same event and employ exactly the same language but use the name Levi instead. A simple understanding of the transitive property reveals that the two names represent the same person. As Levi is a Hebrew name and Matthew a Greek one, it seems that the tax collector bore two names, a common occurrence because of the cultural assimilation and diversity of the ancient world.

BARTHOLOMEW

The disciple named Bartholomew in each list is believed by scholars to be the same one who has an encounter with Jesus in John 1:45–51, where he is called Nathanael. The Gospel of John, which records the largest number of events for second- and third-tier disciples by name, fails to reference Bartholomew. This alone does not make Bartholomew converge with Nathanael. There is an abbreviated disciple list in John 21:2: "Simon Peter, and Thomas called Didymus, and Nathanael of Cana in Galilee, and the *sons* of Zebedee, and two others of His disciples." Since the singular term "disciple" is used only for the Twelve in the Gospels, it is clear that both Bartholomew and Nathanael are among the twelve disciples. Given that surnames and polynomics are used for most other second- and third-tier disciples, the immediate conclusion is that Nathanael is a Hebrew name and Bartholomew is a Greek form of another Aramaic name. Such polynomics are biblically or extrabiblically evident for the disciples Levi Matthew, Simon Peter, and Judas Thomas.

JUDE

This leaves only one disciple whose names diverge among the lists without clear deduction through other New Testament historical accounts. A third-tier member is named "Thaddaeus" in Matthew and Mark, while a third-tier member is called "Judas the son of James" in Luke and Acts, often shortened to "Jude" to distinguish him from Judas Iscariot. Scholars deduce that this is also likely a dual name of one disciple. The manuscript tradition behind the

King James Version provides for the translation "Lebbaeus, whose surname was Thaddaeus" (Matt. 10:3). Furthermore, Ronald Brownrigg suggests that Thaddaeus was a miscopying or variation of the name Theudas, the equivalent of Judas.[2] Sometimes early church historians support the theory of one identity when they converge these two list entries. For example, Hippolytus writes of "Jude, who is also called Lebbaeus."[3] Deductively, the only other candidate from the Gospel narratives would be Bartholomew, but his name appears alongside Thaddaeus in the lists of Matthew and Mark. It is highly unlikely that a disciple would have two Jewish names, such as Judas Nathanael. The only remaining question is why the evangelists would refer to one person by two different names. The same question applies to John's calling Bartholomew by the name Nathanael, and it is best answered by the way some persons in first-century Palestine bore both a Jewish and a Greek name.

Although this treatment is a traditional approach to harmonizing the lists along the lines of only twelve disciples, it is worth mentioning that this harmonization is not the only way to treat the list of apostles. According to Daniel Pfeifer, a minority of scholars suggest that the discrepancies are due to a member leaving either for sickness or by dismissal, leading to a group of fourteen different members.[4] Concerning the variation between the members known as Thaddaeus and Jude, John Meier takes this possibility even further:

> The variation may simply reflect the fact that the Twelve as a group quickly lost importance in the early church, and so the church's collective memory of them was not perfectly preserved. Another possible reason for the variation might lie in the fact that Jesus' ministry lasted for two years and some months. Considering Jesus' stringent demands on the Twelve to leave family, home, and possessions to be his permanent entourage on his preaching tours through Galilee and Judea, we should not be astonished that, sometimes during the two years of ministry, at least one member left the group. . . . It may well be that one member of the Twelve departed and was replaced by another disciple.[5]

While the speculation of replacements is interesting, historically the early church recognized the synthesis between variant names in a list of only twelve disciples. That synthesis will continue in this book.

2. Brownrigg, *Twelve Apostles*, 161.
3. Hippolytus, *Twelve* 10 (*ANF* 5:255).
4. Pfeifer, "Which Came First?," 440.
5. Meier, "Circle of the Twelve," 648.

Conflating Identities

While some dual names of apostles can be understood through deduction, in extrabiblical writings church tradition often conflates or blurs (1) the identities of two different apostles, such as James in gnostic writings, or (2) an apostle with an elder or deacon having the same name, such as John. For that matter, family members of the disciples in the Gospels are also conflated, such as James son of Alphaeus being James the brother of Jesus. At times an early church writer seems to be confused by two figures, whom he will blur into one; at other times a writer intentionally and explicitly explains his position that two commonly accepted different persons are the same. For James the Lesser, the conflation is particularly ambiguous. Such conflations will be examined more closely as they apply in subsequent chapters but will be briefly mentioned here.

Philip

In the book of Acts, Peter declares: "It is not desirable for us [the Twelve] to neglect the word of God in order to serve tables. Therefore, brethren, select from among you seven men . . . whom we may put in charge of this task" (6:2–3). The apostles preach the word as a ministry priority; the deacons serve as a ministry priority. Here six other men not bearing disciple names are chosen along with one Philip. This means that there are potentially two Philips: one named as an original disciple (1:13), another named as a deacon (6:5).

One point of potential confusion comes in Acts when one of the two Philips is found preaching independently in Samaria (8:5) and evangelizing in the Gaza desert (8:26). Another occurs when Paul's company stays at the house of "Philip the evangelist" in Caesarea (21:8). Many early church writers conflate the two Philips into one person, while modern scholars tend to separate them. Several issues bear on the determination of which Philip is referenced in these passages. For starters, the term "Philip the evangelist" at Caesarea likely refers to the figure who "preached Christ unto them" in Samaria, as both are associated with evangelism and Caesarea (8:40; 21:8). Likewise, the Samarian Philip is surely the same as the Gaza Philip, as the narrator records how the angel of the Lord "spoke to Philip" (8:26), telling him to go south of Jerusalem to Gaza, maintaining a consistent identity with Philip in the Samarian episode before. This means that the same Philip is on display in the Samaria, Gaza, and Caesarea events.

There are reasons for believing that Philip the apostle is the one active in these passages. First, he is engaging in disciple making in a frontier context, part of the function of an apostle (Acts 8:35). He performs miracles of exorcism and multiple types of healing (8:6–7), which typify the Twelve in the early Gospel commission (Matt. 10:1) and the book of Acts. His supernatural relocation (Acts 8:39–40) reflects a level of the miraculous usually associated with the apostles in Acts. Peter and John follow the ministry leads among the gentiles (8:14) by coming to Samaria and affirming the gentile converts, as they do for Paul when he is to be named apostle (15:2–12).

However, there are reasons for believing that the one acting in these passages is not Philip the apostle but Philip the appointed deacon. Paul does not call him an apostle: "On the next day we left and came to Caesarea; and entering the house of Philip the evangelist, who was one of the seven, we stayed with him. Now this man had four virgin daughters who were prophetesses" (Acts 21:8–9). This displays the evangelism connection and likely harkens back to Acts 6:3, where seven deacons are chosen to serve the body so that the apostles might preach. In the early church John Chrysostom is among those who maintain that the Philip here is the deacon.[6]

JOHN

One Gospel, three epistles, and Revelation are attributed to John. In the early church, all these works were generally viewed as the product of one person, the apostle John, or "the disciple whom He [Jesus] loved," to apply the Gospel designation used five times (John 13:23; 19:26; 20:2; 21:7, 20).

John's biography reveals that this disciple was likely the youngest, with the longest potential for ministry. Therefore the voluminous contribution he makes is not unreasonable. Scholars often interpret the words of the second-century bishop Papias as making allusion to two different Johns, one labeled an apostle and one an elder. Papias is interpreted as saying that he heard the elder rather than the apostle. The church historian Eusebius, who preserves these words for us, is believed to have wanted to discredit Papias by claiming that Papias was never a hearer or eyewitness of the holy apostles. This is because Eusebius rejected chiliasm, or the hope of an early thousand-year reign of Christ on earth, which Papias promoted. Robert Yarbrough points out that the second-century fathers Irenaeus and Dionysius of Alexandria do not distinguish between two Johns, and that Irenaeus's upbringing in Asia Minor would have provided firsthand familiarity. Papias's claims are at worst ambiguous, and he can be interpreted as not distinguishing between two Johns: "The 'presbyter John,' in Papias' parlance, may be taken as a surviving

---

6. John Chrysostom, *Homilies on Acts* 14 (*NPNF*[1] 11:91).

member of the select cadre of presbyters (including 'apostles') whom Papias associated with earlier times."[7]

Critical scholars are quick to name two separate figures at the turn of the second century named John: the apostle and the elder. Some apostle biographers are also comfortable in assigning two figures to the legacy of John: "The conclusion seems to be again that the authority for this Gospel was that of John, son of Zebedee, but that it was either written or edited by an elder, also living at Ephesus and also called John."[8] However, there is no compelling requirement to distinguish between two Johns, as the chapter on John will demonstrate.

JAMES

The name James was common in the first-century church. The disciple lists include a James son of Zebedee and a James son of Alphaeus. The surnames function to distinguish between them in the Gospels, and they are often called James the Greater and James the Lesser, respectively. Additionally, Jesus has a brother named James (Matt. 13:55; Mark 6:3). An epistle is named for James, who calls himself merely "a bond-servant of God and of the Lord Jesus Christ" (James 1:1). Finally, an elder among the apostles is noted in church history as becoming the bishop of Jerusalem, and he is named as authoritative after the death of James the Greater (Acts 15:13; 21:18). Hence there is great potential for confusion and conflation.

The common conclusion that will be followed in this book is that there were three figures named James across these four profiles. The first is James the Greater, son of Zebedee, who was among the original Twelve and martyred under Herod Agrippa (Acts 12:1–2). The second is James the Lesser, son of Alphaeus, who was also a member of the original Twelve. The third is the author of the Epistle of James, who was the bishop of Jerusalem and likely the brother of Jesus. That the author of the epistle does not identify himself as the brother of Jesus is interpreted as a sign of humility, like the humility of Jude in his epistle. In the book attributed to him, Jude calls himself "a bond-servant of Jesus Christ, and brother of James" (Jude 1), tying the half-brothers of Jesus together (Matt. 13:55; Mark 6:3) in rhetoric and authorial humility. This means that Jesus's brothers, who did not initially believe in him, later came to believe (John 7:5). If this historical synthesis is correct, the only remaining challenge is to identify which James is in view (the Lesser

---

7. Yarbrough, "Date of Papias," 184. Another convincing reason for sensing that Eusebius saw Papias as a hearer of John is that he places him among the other apostolic fathers of book 3 in *Hist. eccl.*, where he treats no matters beyond the era of Trajan.

8. Brownrigg, *Twelve Apostles*, 105.

or the brother of Jesus) in the New Testament apocryphal works that do not distinguish between the figures named James.

Jude

With the opening of the letter to Jude (Jude 1), a link of brotherhood is made between the author of James and the author of Jude. According to the Gospels, the names of Jesus's brothers are James, Judas, Simon, and Joseph (Matt. 13:55; Mark 6:3). It is more likely that the authors of the letters are Jesus's brothers and not the two disciples named James son of Alphaeus and Jude (or Thaddeus). Yet, if these disciples were also the brothers of Jesus, it would be odd that the Gospels or Acts fail to make the connection.

In the lists the epithet "son of James" finds a possible reinterpretation below in the section on kindred identities, where the phrase "son of" might mean "brother of," or perhaps "kindred to," such as a brother by association. Regardless of the connection between the disciples Jude and James, the apostles should not be conflated with the brothers of Jesus, whose shared names stand as a coincidence.

Matthew and Matthias

Matthew has already been noted as also being Levi through the common practice of supplementing a Hebrew given name with a Greek name. As we have affirmed, these two names refer to the same disciple and apostle. In the later centuries, however, extrabiblical writings conflate two people who bear similar-sounding names, Matthew and Matthias; in Greek the names are even closer: *Matthaios* and *Matthias*. The Acts of Andrew and Matthias, the Acts and Martyrdom of St. Matthew, and the Martyrdom of Matthew all have the main character, Matthias or Matthew, taking the gospel message to a land of cannibals. In the Coptic Book of Resurrection of Jesus Christ, Matthias is described as a rich man leaving all to follow Jesus, but this is likely a conflation with Matthew's calling (Matt. 9:9). Yet for our purposes, there is no confusion between the two in the New Testament. While Matthew was one of the original Twelve, Matthias was measured as credible enough to be adopted as Judas Iscariot's replacement. The differences between Matthew and Matthias will be highlighted in their respective chapters and will include an assessment of the relevant data from extrabiblical works.

Kindred Identities

Additional family connections sometimes made between the apostles deserve clarification. As mentioned above, that the brothers of Jesus and some of the twelve disciples coincidentally share names leads to conflations. Martin Hengel comments: "Connections with family members played a certain role already within the circle of those who were part of the larger following, who had accompanied the master to Jerusalem. To that group belonged apparently also women from the extended family of Jesus and the disciples."[9] David Criswell more critically summarizes the variety of kindred identities that have been postulated: "A disease among some writers over the centuries has been to attempt to make almost all the apostles related to one another. Conjecture as to the relationship of some of the apostles ranges from possible to absurd."[10] The path to the discovery of the apostles requires a brief introduction to these kinship possibilities.

James, called son of Alphaeus in each list, and Levi, once called son of Alphaeus (Mark 2:14), are sometimes thought to be brothers. There is also overreaching effort in gnostic works to make Thomas the twin be the identical brother of Jesus. While these kindred relationships have limited bearing on the ministry of the disciples, the connections do shape their individual identities and will be addressed in the chapters devoted to each apostle.

From Disciples to Apostles

With the identities of the individual twelve apostles established, the character of the office of apostle deserves attention. The gradation from disciple to apostle for the Twelve appears seamless in the New Testament, but the shift to the development of apostolicity deserves attention in terms of the office, its membership, and the cause of the apostles' larger mission.

The Office of Apostle

The office of apostle has long been recognized as one of leadership and evangelism on a frontier that lacked the message of the gospel. The office is modeled by the twelve disciples, who functioned as leaders in the early church. In the New Testament, Luke identifies the original company of twelve as apostles (Acts 1:26), Barnabas and Paul are named apostles beyond the original Twelve (Acts 14:14), and Paul recognizes an office of apostleship available to believers (Eph. 4:11). The qualification for an "apostle" thus has some variety, leading to some controversy over the use of the label in broad and narrow senses. Broadly speaking, missionaries and church planters pioneer the work

9. Hengel, *Saint Peter*, 133.
10. Criswell, *Apostles after Jesus*, 37.

of ministry like the original Twelve but without having walked with Jesus (Acts 1:21–22). Richard Pervo posits that the essence of the office of apostle in most of the apocryphal works is simply mission.[11] Narrowly speaking, the office belongs only to the generation of the early church just after Jesus. Wayne Grudem proposes that the office is "unique and limited to the first century" and thus that it no longer exists.[12]

WHAT IS AN APOSTLE?

While Jesus had many disciples, twelve of them were called apostles. The term "disciple" has a meaning of "follower," even a novice or undeveloped devotee. The Greek root *mathēteuō* means "I am a pupil."[13] The term "apostle" carries a connotation of authority, like a polished ambassador. In contrast to the follower aspect of "disciple," the Greek root *apostellō* means "I send off or away from."[14] The distinction between the two roles can be seen in 1 Corinthians, where Paul remarks that the church in Corinth is "already filled, you have already become rich, you have become kings without us; and indeed, *I* wish that you had become kings so that we also might reign with you" (4:8). Disciples who are complete are like wealthy kings, spiritually satisfied and royally blessed. In the next verse Paul contrasts this role with that of apostles: "For, I think, God has exhibited us apostles last of all, as men condemned to death; because we have become a spectacle to the world, both to angels and to men" (4:9). As a result, disciples now seem polished, and apostles are ambassadors branded with threats. His contrast continues in the verses that follow as he emphasizes the extensive sacrificial suffering that characterizes apostles. Significant is how Paul distinguishes apostleship from the discipleship of the faithful Corinthians.

Building on this quality of perseverance, Paul describes to the Corinthians how "the signs of a true apostle were performed among you with all perseverance, by signs and wonders and miracles" (2 Cor. 12:12). This miraculous quality finds support in Acts 5:12, where "at the hands of the apostles many signs and wonders were taking place among the people." Such a definition suggests that the "sending forth" would be with an unconventional gifting of miracles to accompany the gospel message. This quality typifies the original Eleven in the book of Acts, where healings, tongues, and other miracles accompany their ministry as evidence of its power. Pfeifer suggests that preaching

---

11. Pervo, "Role of the Apostles," 307.
12. Grudem, *Systematic Theology*, 906.
13. Liddell and Scott, *Greek-English Lexicon*, 1072.
14. Liddell and Scott, *Greek-English Lexicon*, 219.

and exorcising demons may have distinguished them from other followers, perhaps evidenced by Mark 3:14–15: "He appointed twelve, so that they would be with Him and that He *could* send them out to preach, and to have authority to cast out the demons."[15]

Although in Acts being an apostle requires having witnessed the resurrection, this feature implies that apostles were also previously commissioned by Christ as a form of *vocatio*, or calling. Paul makes a case for his mission as an apostle based on the revelation of Christ himself on the road to Damascus (Acts 9:5–6; 26:15–18). In Paul's Epistles, he employs this encounter for authority (1 Cor. 9:1; 15:7–9). Paul's use of "apostle" for himself in 1 Cor. 15:3–9 reinforces that an apostle is one who personally knew Christ. In Paul's case, the vision and call of Christ came after Christ's earthly ministry but were no less legitimate for "one born out of due time" (1 Cor. 15:8 KJV). Paul later calls himself an "apostle of Gentiles" (Rom. 11:13). He describes himself as the "least of the apostles" because he persecuted the church (1 Cor. 15:9). The substitution of Matthias for Judas Iscariot seems to be a replacement for the twelfth disciple in the sense of a call to complete the Twelve (Acts 1:21–22). When Paul speaks of his own encounter with Christ, he speaks of it as not merely a witness to the resurrection but also as an event of *vocatio* for his ministry. We conclude that the difference between an apostle and a disciple is that an apostle received a calling directly from Jesus, displays full perseverance, and shows signs and wonders in ministry. This definition fits the role of the Twelve in the book of Acts.

The twelve disciples are called apostles early in the Synoptic Gospels. John's Gospel does not use the term. The use of the term in these stories likely came after the personal ministry of Jesus, during the time of the writing of the Gospels. As early as Pentecost, the Twelve were transformed from struggling disciples to confident apostles, so that they can be named apostles in the Gospels. The term "apostles" occurs in Matthew 10:2 and Luke 6:13 at the first group commissioning; Luke remarks, "He called his disciples to Him and chose twelve of them, whom He also named as apostles" (6:13). Among Christ's followers, a special cross-section is designated as leaders and representatives. Luke uses the term five more times as a substitute for "disciples," and he also uses "apostles" regularly for the group in the book of Acts. Mark uses the term "apostles" only once (6:30), at the funeral of John the Baptist, interchangeably with "disciples."

Outside the historical narratives of the New Testament, the first chronological use of the term "apostle" comes in Paul's Letter to the Galatians, in

---

15. Pfeifer, "Which Came First?," 444.

a powerful depiction of the office's calling: "Paul, an apostle (not *sent* from men nor through the agency of man, but through Jesus Christ and God the Father, who raised Him from the dead)" (Gal. 1:1). He continues to use the term for himself in the salutations of Romans, 1 Corinthians, 2 Corinthians, Ephesians, Colossians, 1 Timothy, 2 Timothy, and Titus. Peter uses the term for himself in both Petrine Epistles. Paul elaborates on the role of apostle in his letters connected to ministry and evangelism, such as in 1 Corinthians 9:1–2, "Am I not an apostle? . . . You are the seal of my apostleship in the Lord." Likewise, Paul declares that apostleship is a gift given by the Spirit to the church. "God has appointed in the church, first apostles, second prophets, third teachers, then miracles, then gifts of healings, helps, administrations, *various* kinds of tongues" (1 Cor. 12:28).[16]

At the end of the first century, Clement of Rome provides a summary of the function of the apostles: "Having therefore received their orders and being fully assured by the resurrection of our Lord Jesus Christ and full of faith in the word of God, they went forth with the firm assurance that the Holy Spirit gives, preaching the good news that the kingdom of God was about to come."[17] In the contemporary church, Peter Wegner, among others, has made the case that the office of apostle is ubiquitous and experiencing a revival.[18] From the early era to the modern era, the office of apostle has been appealed to more or less widely to refer to evangelistic leadership in a pioneering fashion. Thus, theologically one can recognize the Twelve as apostles with a rationale for mission. With Grudem, we might realize that two definitions are possible: (1) Apostle (with a capital *A*)—one with authority to speak and write the words of God in a special sense because these men were personally with Jesus, and (2) apostle (with a lowercase *a*)—one specially appointed for leadership or pioneering of the gospel message.[19] While many apply the title as an office to be perpetuated, this book focuses on the original disciples as the objects of our quest.

Who Else Is an Apostle?

While this book considers thirteen apostles, some scholars claim that other individuals filled the office. Meier argues that for the Gospel writers, the twelve disciples were an inner circle, that apostles are any individuals

---

16. Additionally, Eph. 4:11, "And He gave some *as* apostles, and some *as* prophets, and some *as* evangelists, and some *as* pastors and teachers."
17. 1 Clement 42.3 (Holmes, 101).
18. Wegner, *Apostles Today*, 6.
19. Grudem, *Systematic Theology*, 911.

sent on mission, and that the Twelve are not the only disciples or the only apostles.[20] Luke 6:13 is a guiding verse: "And when day came, He [Jesus] called His disciples to Him and chose twelve of them, whom He also named as apostles." Meier posits that Luke is consistently using the titles "the Twelve" and "the apostles" interchangeably, so that he is the "main NT catalyst for the later Christian custom of speaking of 'the twelve apostles.'"[21] There is something special about these first twelve, who are disciples and early church apostles. Meier insists that although critical scholars imagine that the Twelve did not exist as an entity in the ministry of Jesus, the opposite is true: they were prominent in his ministry but waned in the development of the early church.[22]

It is no coincidence that Jesus chose twelve disciples as special protégés. The twelve tribes of Israel embodied the notion of the people of God. Daniel Pfeifer explains, "There is general scholarly consensus that Jesus's choice of twelve distinct followers evoked the symbolism of the twelve tribes and thereby the implication of restoration for all Israel."[23] Not only is the number a historical reference, but it also promotes an expectation of a new covenant for Israel. After all, Jesus said that his followers would "sit upon twelve thrones, judging the twelve tribes of Israel" (Matt. 19:28; Luke 22:30). In Revelation, at the restoration of God's people in the great city, the wall "had twelve foundation stones, and on them *were* the twelve names of the twelve apostles of the Lamb" (Rev. 21:14). The Gospel of the Ebionites, an early church work, attributes to Jesus the claim "According to my intention you shall be twelve apostles for a testimony to Israel."[24] A belief in the symbolic value of twelve may be behind Peter's desire to fill the vacancy left by Judas's defection and death (Acts 1:25). Ellsworth Kalas writes of the replacement: "So the absence of one of their number, by the defection of Judas, wasn't simply a reduction by 8.3 percent, it was a violation of a holy symmetry."[25] The number twelve was so powerful in the mind and history of Israel that J. Knox Chamblin can comment that the appointment of twelve original disciples "signaled that Jesus had come to reconstitute the people of God."[26] Their quest was missional.

20. Meier, "Circle of the Twelve," 636–42.
21. Meier, "Circle of the Twelve," 642.
22. Meier, "Circle of the Twelve," 669–72.
23. Pfeifer, "Which Came First?," 447. Note the likely symbolism of twelve baskets of bread at the Gospel feeding (Matt. 14:20) and calling on twelve legions of angels at the betrayal (Matt. 26:53).
24. Epiphanius, *Against Heresies* 30.1, in Ehrman, *New Testament and Other Early Christian Writings*, 137.
25. Kalas, *Thirteen Apostles*, 140.
26. Chamblin, "Matthew," 733.

For about a decade before the death of James the Greater—who, unlike Judas Iscariot, has no recorded replacement—the Twelve dominated the leadership of the early church. The appointment of deacons such as Stephen, the ministry of Philip (if he is a deacon separate from the apostle), and the rise of new apostles such as Barnabas would have diluted the sense of need for twelve as a symbol of Israel's fulfillment. Pfeifer captures the situation: "It is remarkable that the memory of the twelve men was preserved at all, since their collective distinction was obscured by cultural realities, and the duration of their collective activity was rather brief. As time passed after Jesus's resurrection, one by one the members of the Twelve were gone, but their symbolic significance remained."[27]

Paul became an apostle whom we categorize as on the same level as the original twelve disciples. Paul calls himself "one untimely born" (1 Cor. 15:8). With this one apostle an expansion of the apostolic leadership is clearly in view, representative of the great shift that was at work in the church. At first, the lead apostles give the impression that their seal of approval is necessary for this expansion when they affirm the Samaritan Pentecost (Acts 8:14–17). William Baker remarks: "Peter and John verify the genuineness of the Samaritans' faith and, as an official act, place their hands on them, and the Samaritans receive the Holy Spirit." The delay of the reception of the Holy Spirit in Acts 8:16 is "probably in order to reserve this important evidence of genuine conversion for the eyes of the two principal apostles."[28]

However, eventually the presence of the gift of apostleship in the life of the church suggested that the office could be extended beyond the original Twelve (including Matthias). This is seen as others besides Paul are treated as apostles in the New Testament. Barnabas is mentioned by Paul in the context of apostleship (1 Cor. 9:1–6) and called an apostle (Acts 14:14). Andrew Wilson has made a convincing case that Paul is calling Apollos an apostle like himself in 1 Corinthians 3:5–4:1. He argues that the use of the plural "we" references not Paul and the Twelve but Paul and Apollos in the context of the letter.[29] When the apostle speaks of the appearance of the resurrected Lord, "Paul is not saying that either of these things [resurrection appearance or the faith of the Corinthian church] are *necessary* conditions for *all* apostleship. . . . They constitute *sufficient* conditions for *his* apostleship."[30]

27. Pfeifer, "Which Came First?," 448.
28. Baker, "Acts," 895.
29. Wilson, "Apostle Apollos?," 329–32.
30. Wilson, "Apostle Apollos?," 333, italics original.

Commonalities of the Apostolic College

The twelve apostles and Paul were thus a collection of early church leaders who had been commissioned by Jesus to bring the gospel to the uttermost parts of the earth. As individuals, each honored this request as a faith commitment that he would begin a quest, generally independent of the others, to advance the kingdom in the ancient world. As a group, their mission was a shared one, a complementary one, in which they labored as a united front on different frontiers.

A legend arose that the unity of the apostles led them to cast lots to determine their fields of ministry. For example, the Acts of Andrew and Matthias records the event: "About that time all the apostles had come together at the same place, and shared among themselves the countries, casting lots, in order that each might go away into the part that had fallen to him."[31] Eusebius explains that portions or mission fields were "allotted" and "received" by certain apostles, but he does not explicitly mention the casting of lots to determine mission fields.[32] There was already precedent for using lots among the apostles, evidenced by the use of lot casting to identify Matthias as the new twelfth apostle (Acts 1:16). Paul expresses this idea of avoiding overlap of ministry: "And thus I aspired to preach the gospel, not where Christ was *already* named, that I would not build on another man's foundation" (Rom. 15:20). Yet this motive might be unique to Paul, whose ministry to the gentiles was always in contrast to the other disciples, and casting lots as a geographical strategy does not stand on strong historical evidence. Regardless, the commissioning of Jesus to take the gospel to the uttermost parts of the world (Matt. 28:19–20; Acts 1:8) drove them there, whether by the leading of the Spirit, opportunities afforded by historical circumstances, or some decision-making technique. Underlying their mission were commonalities that are foundational to understanding their mission as a united one.

COMMON EXPERIENCE

The depth of experience shared between the disciples by the end of the ministry of Jesus is incomprehensible. Skilled laborers who often repeated their tasks day after day without change or variety began to journey with a Messiah figure for three and a half years of unpredictable itinerant ministry. Their attention to Christ's teaching and their witness to his impressive miracles

---

31. Acts of Andrew and Matthias (*ANF* 8:517).
32. Eusebius, *Hist. eccl.* 3.1.

would have been astounding. This common experience surely fostered a bond of common purpose among the Twelve.

The common experience of *witnessing the resurrection* strengthened their call, although it seemingly was not a requirement for general apostleship. When a replacement for Judas Iscariot is sought among the remaining disciples, the calling of Matthias greatly emphasizes this common experience (Acts 1:21–22). Yet this event was not merely a qualifier for apostolic ministry; the resurrection provided the impetus for their ministry. N. T. Wright captures the profound and empowering significance of the event:

> The truly extraordinary thing is that this belief was held by a tiny group who, for the first two or three generations at least, could hardly have mounted a riot in a village, let alone a revolution in an empire. And yet they persisted against all the odds, attracting the unwelcome notice of the authorities because of the power of the message and the worldview and lifestyle it generated. And whenever we go back to the key texts for evidence of why they persisted in such an improbable and dangerous belief they answer: it is because Jesus of Nazareth was raised from the dead.[33]

Witnessing to the resurrection supplied the credibility and the reason for apostolic ministry. Sean McDowell comments, "The resurrection was central to Christian proclamation from the inception of the church to at least the generation after the death of the apostles. . . . Thus, their preaching only makes sense if they truly believed Jesus had risen from the dead, and if the evidence was there to confirm it."[34] The *kerygma* or preaching of the gospel found its center in the resurrection, shaping both the apostles' common experience and their common purpose.

The teachings of Jesus also guided their ministries, recorded in the historical narratives of their lives. Irenaeus describes how the apostles "departed to the ends of the earth, preaching the global tidings of the good things [sent] from God to us."[35] These teachings along with the resurrection combined to form a powerful message in the ancient world. Among the Lord's teachings, the coming kingdom offered the disciples an impetus for evangelism. First Corinthians 16:22 records the apostle Paul expressing the hope "O Lord, Come!" The apostles' message was also the same, uniting their ministry. Acts 16:4 describes how Paul and Barnabas delivered the decrees set forth by the apostles in Jerusalem.

---

33. Wright, *Resurrection of the Son of God*, 570.
34. McDowell, *Fate of the Apostles*, 23–24.
35. Irenaeus, *Haer.* 3.1.1 (ANF 1:414).

An additional important common experience was the *growth and develop-ment* that the apostles experienced both individually and collectively during their discipleship under Jesus. The writers of the Gospels and Acts do not demur at showing the disciples' weaknesses and ignorance. For example, Peter recognizes Jesus as the Son of God at Caesarea Philippi (Matt. 16:16) but then refuses to allow him to suffer in Jerusalem (Matt. 16:23). The same Peter initially refuses to allow Jesus to wash his feet at the Last Supper (John 13:8). James and John request to sit on either side of Christ in his kingdom, which leads to an explanation of the absurdity of their request (Mark 10:37–38). After the Lord's resurrection, when they fish on the Sea of Galilee in John 21, "the disciples did not know that it was Jesus" (v. 4). The tracks of the apostles' journey show a maturation from bumbling novices in the Gospels to empowered leaders in Acts. That growth was both individual and missional. The high priest and others in Acts "observed the confidence of Peter and John . . . and *began* to recognize them as having been with Jesus" (4:13).

COMMON PURPOSE

Acts consistently depicts the unity of the disciples in the years following their experience with Jesus. This quality became an ideal for the church to follow, as Paul exhorts every generation, "Make my joy complete by being of the same mind, maintaining the same love, united in spirit, intent on one purpose" (Phil. 2:2). While many studies of the apostolic thrust include the opposition between Jews and gentiles in the New Testament, this analysis can be overplayed in contrast to the regular affirmation of the apostles' unity of purpose and endeavors. This unity of purpose came from three aspects important for understanding the history of the apostles in their dispersion stories from the second and third centuries: their status as in one accord, their belief in the resurrection, and their formation by the teaching of Jesus.

On five occasions Acts describes how the disciples were in "one accord" or "one mind" (1:14; 2:46; 4:24; 5:12; 15:25). For example: "Day by day continu-ing with one mind in the temple, and breaking bread from house to house, they were taking their meals together with gladness and sincerity of heart" (Acts 2:46). As mentioned above, in his churches Paul promoted this apostolic priority of unity (Phil. 2:2).

The common experience of *vocatio* or calling was part of the office of apostle. In his introduction to Romans and to 1 Corinthians, Paul emphasizes his call to be an apostle (Rom. 1:1; 1 Cor. 1:1). He also describes the founda-tion of his ministry as being called by Christ himself (1 Cor. 15:3–8). This *vocatio* was shared among the disciples, some of whom abandoned fishing nets and one of whom left his tax booth. The Epistle of the Apostles, a second-century work, describes an encounter between the Twelve and Christ before his ascension. As Jesus describes his mission and the impending judgment of the wicked, the disciples express corporate empathy for the lost, the object of their mission. Two remarks represent the development of their calling: "O Lord, truly we are sad about them," and "We were distressed and sad and wept for those who were shut out."[36] These sentiments precede five chapters that elaborate on Jesus's summons to embark on preaching and teaching in the face of opposition.[37] Such dedication represents the *vocatio* of the disciples more than a hundred years after Jesus first uttered this mandate, when this work was written.

Once again, *the resurrection* was significant for the apostles' shared purpose. Hans Bayer believes that Christ's resurrection was fundamental for his original kingship intentions, writing, "Jesus views his resurrection to immortality as a crucial event of foundational significance in the coming of the everlasting Kingdom of God."[38] The resurrection drove the apostles to live the narratives we will encounter in this historical study and to suffer the deaths that followed as a result of this dedication. McDowell remarks, "The willingness of the apostles to suffer and die for their faith provides a critical step in establishing their sincerity and reliability as the first witnesses to the resurrected Jesus."[39]

COMMON AUTHORITY

Social or intellectual authority would not have come easily for these Jews from Galilee in the ancient world. Ancient philosopher Cicero provides a case study in social norms that illustrates the lack of civic respect for the disciples' occupations. The fisherman status of several disciples and even the carpentry of the Messiah would not have naturally given them credibility or prestige for their purpose: "In regards to trades and commerce, which ones are to be respected and which ones are base, these are generally established. First, those that incur hatred of men are the tax-collectors and usurers. . . . All mechanics are engaged in base trades; for no workshop can have anything refined about it. Least respectable of all are those trades which cater to sensual pleasures: fish sellers, butchers, cooks and poulterers, and fishermen."[40]

36. Ep. Apos. 40, 43 (Hills, 68, 72).
37. Ep. Apos. 46–50 (Hills, 76–80).
38. Bayer, *Jesus' Predictions of Vindication and Resurrection*, 253.
39. McDowell, *Fate of the Apostles*, 262.
40. Cicero, *De officiis* 1.150, in Dyck, *Commentary on Cicero*, 333–36 (AT).

Irony is evident in the early story of Christianity, as a carpenter showed evidence of being the Messiah, while fishermen, a tax collector, and those in other, unnamed professions gained credibility and prestige. Thus the high priest and his associates marvel that Peter and his associates are "uneducated and untrained men" (Acts 4:13).

Several passages taken together establish a theology of the office of apostle as related to the authority the Twelve carried with them. First, *the empowering of the Twelve* is a prelude to the stories of the apostles as they later dispersed into the world for the sake of the gospel: "Jesus summoned His twelve disciples and gave them authority over unclean spirits, to cast them out, and to heal every kind of disease and every kind of sickness. . . . Heal *the* sick, raise *the* dead, cleanse *the* lepers, cast out demons. Freely you received, freely give" (Matt. 10:1, 7–8).

R. T. France clarifies how "the authority displayed was that of Jesus himself. . . . That authority he now vests also in his disciples, whose healing mission is described in the same words used for his mission."[41] They show success, surprising even themselves: "Lord, even the demons are subject to us in Your name" (Luke 10:17). This supernatural ability characterized their ministry, and its proliferation to absurd acts even becomes a stumbling block in our evaluation of the New Testament Apocrypha.

Second, *a pneumatological impetus and fortitude* characterized the authority of the apostles. "He [Jesus] breathed on them and said to them, 'Receive the Holy Spirit'" (John 20:22). This action was an emblematic forerunner of Pentecost, also anticipated in Acts just before Jesus's ascension: "You will receive power when the Holy Spirit has come upon you; and you shall be My witnesses both in Jerusalem, and in all Judea and Samaria, and even to the remotest part of the earth" (Acts 1:8). When signs and wonders accompany the great event of the upper room, the foundation for lifetime ministry is completed, and the apostles are ready to begin their quest. A certain humility characterizes the apostles, who promote the gospel through miracles not of their own power, an ability that could not be purchased by Simon Magus. Paul declares, "But we have this treasure in earthen vessels, that the surpassing greatness of the power will be of God and not from ourselves" (2 Cor. 4:7).

Third, the apostles are *symbolic authorities* for the church in Acts. Church members lay their offerings at the feet of the apostles (4:35), including Ananias and Sapphira (5:2). Stephen and the other deacons are placed before the apostles, who lay hands on them (6:6). The apostles send Peter and John to

---

41. France, *Matthew*, 176. See Matt. 4:23 and 9:35 for comparison with the language for his own mission.

confirm the salvation of the Samaritans and to pray for the filling of the Spirit (8:14–15). Likewise, Barnabas brings the infamous Paul to the apostles for affirmation (9:27). When Barnabas and Paul need wisdom concerning the role of the Jewish law among the new gentile converts, they "go up to Jerusalem to the apostles and elders concerning this issue" (15:2). Paul's ministry finds support by "delivering the decrees which had been decided upon by the apostles and elders who were in Jerusalem, for them to observe" (16:4).

Finally, the *commissioning of Jesus* functioned to buttress the authority of the apostles in a formal fashion. The charge to perpetuate his teaching as lifelong disciples is best found in their commissioning: "Go therefore and make disciples of all the nations, baptizing them in the name of the Father and the Son and the Holy Spirit, teaching them to observe all that I commanded you; and lo, I am with you always, even to the end of the age" (Matt. 28:19–20). An unexplained authority came with the confidence, signs and wonders, and preaching of the disciples. The commissioning of the Twelve extended to their shared ability to replicate the work of Christ.[42] Eusebius summarizes the effect: "The annunciation of the Savior's gospel was daily advancing by divine providence."[43] This authority in turn extended into generations to follow, including a "rule of faith" in which the apostolic teaching remained authoritative.

Rule of Faith

The common experience, purpose, and authority of the apostles had an unintentional impact in the eras subsequent to them, when these qualities combined into a legacy that became an essential standard for the church. Looking beyond the apostles' lives, their unified work was continued through both their message and the eternal image that they display. The commonality of the apostolic college was collected in a phenomenon known as the "rule of faith" in the early church. As the apostles died out, the natural question of the perpetuation of authority arose in the church. The church wondered what would be the source of authority without apostles in their midst. The writings that became the New Testament were already promoting a perpetuation of the authoritative message of Jesus's disciples (Acts 16:4; 2 Pet. 3:1, 15, 20–21). Jude provides an example of how the apostolic testimony was already valued for keeping Jesus's message alive: "But you, beloved, ought to remember the words that were spoken beforehand by the apostles of our Lord Jesus Christ" (Jude 17).

42. Most explicitly in Matt. 10:1; 19:28; Luke 9:1; 22:30.
43. Eusebius, *Hist. eccl.* 1.2.13.

The result was the development of a standard for evaluating the compatibility of a doctrine with the legacy of the church. That legacy was founded on Christ's teaching, perpetuated by the apostles, inherited by church fathers, and later called "catholic," or universal. Perhaps the best description of this rule was penned in the fifth century by Vincent of Lérins: what is "believed everywhere, always, by all" (*quod ubique, quod semper, quod ab omnibus creditum est*).[44] The teachings of the apostles—the Scriptures that were seen as coming from the Lord through the apostles—and the beliefs that all churches agreed on combined to develop into a basic determination of what is theologically true and what is not. This principle is especially employed by Irenaeus against the gnostic thinkers: one cannot arrive with new or secret teaching, claiming to be directly from heaven, if it is contrary to what the church already believes to be from heaven.

Clement of Rome applies this principle in his letter to the Corinthian church: "The apostles received the gospel for us from the Lord Jesus Christ; Jesus the Christ was sent forth from God. So then Christ is from God, and the apostles are from Christ. Both, therefore, came of the will of God in good order."[45] The apostles' work was not only for their time but also provided a legacy, as Clement continues: "They appointed the leaders mentioned earlier and afterwards they gave the offices a permanent character; that is, if they should die, other approved men should succeed to their ministry."[46]

The experiences, purpose, and authority shared among the apostles were foundational to their mission. Comprehending this aspect of their mission is essential for our quest. These commonalities were important in perhaps the biggest two areas of conflict they encountered: the persecution of their faith by competing religious and secular authorities, and the internal struggles of identity between Jewish and gentile Christians. Both of these conflicts require elaboration.

The Pagan Conflict

While the office of apostle was being defined in the church, the task of confronting the complex social scene of the Greco-Roman world had already begun. Any study on the emergence of Christianity through the leadership of the individual apostles requires an examination of how this effort was understood by the world in which the apostles took up their quest.

44. Vincent of Lérins, *Commonitory* 2.6 (*NPNF*[2] 11:132).
45. 1 Clement 42.1–2 (Holmes, 101).
46. 1 Clement 44.2 (Holmes, 103).

The new faith called Christianity arose from within Judaism. Just as Jesus and his followers understood his life, death, and resurrection to be a fulfillment of the Jewish cause, the long-held traditions of Judaism found both continuity and discontinuity in the message of Jesus. While Judaism was synthesizing or rejecting the new faith in its relationship to the Law, the Prophets, and the Writings, Christianity was also engaging the larger Roman Empire with its Greek philosophy, Roman social ideals, and other pagan values.

Theater of Confrontation

The metaphorical path taken by the apostles was possible because of a physical path, the Roman road system. The apostles' diaspora from Jerusalem in 49 was met with the first-century reality that the Roman world offered the easiest road travel for its citizens that history had known. Rome's native lands and conquered lands saw trade and travel benefit from the system of highways running across the empire.

This accessibility naturally led the apostles down roads both to major cities and into extended regions. The diversity of new cultures and the apathetic permission of Roman leadership to allow established religions to perpetuate meant that the monotheistic and antimaterialistic Christianity encountered opposition when its representatives forged new frontiers in the name of their religion. Among Paul's most notable encounters was his engagement with philosophers on Mars Hill in Athens, where he synthesized their "unknown God" with the Judeo-Christian Creator and Redeemer (Acts 17:22–32). When Paul and Barnabas preached in Lystra, the people thought them to be members of the Greek pantheon and sought to worship them (Acts 14:11–15). The Athenians were willing to perpetuate dialogue, while the actions of the Lycaonians caused Paul and Barnabas to rend their clothes in frustration. One sees the range of responses that individuals in ancient cultures had to the gospel message.

Like Old Testament prophets coming among the people with a message of repentance, the apostles were not always well received. Amid these religious conflicts, disciples were gained and individuals were converted to the faith and led to affirm the ministry of the apostles. The theaters of conflict for the apostles' ministry can be grouped into Roman conflict, other pagan conflicts, and Jewish conflict.

Roman Conflict

While Christianity was maturing as a formal movement, the Greco-Roman worldview was well established in terms of its own religious philosophy. Greek thought provided the framework for Roman thinking, but the plurality allowed to ancient Greece's religious philosophers was not extended by ancient Rome's emperors to citizens viewed as religious zealots seeking independence under a supposed Pax Romana. Yet certainly Christianity was wedded to Greek thought from its inception. F. F. Bruce remarks, "Too facile a distinction between Palestinian and Hellenistic phases in primitive Christianity is unwarranted."[47] The Jewish basis for the Christian faith further provided an umbrella of protection, as Judaism was established and permitted in the Roman Empire. However, imperially appointed magistrates had unlimited authority *extra ordinem* (outside the law) with regard to religion, so that "externally, the danger with which the church had to reckon was the hostility of the imperial power."[48] The apostles experienced the unofficial arm of the empire when their message found even regional opposition.

During this early phase of the spreading of the Christian message, the Roman Empire was celebrating the imperial worship of the Julio-Claudian emperors. In this first century, while the apostles propagated the gospel message, an equally strong imperial cultic movement prospered and permeated all sectors of society. Businesses, guild members, and religious establishments had the opportunity to express their allegiance to the comprehensive force of imperial worship. For example, Bruce Winter writes: "There occurred a significant link between imperial cultic activity and daily commerce because the buying and selling of commodities could only be legally undertaken in the official market of the city. . . . Politics, commerce, and cultic activity function comfortably side by side not only in the same public space but also with all three located in the same agora or forum."[49]

As a general rule, Roman cultic allegiance could be a minimal commitment. This commitment was nascent in the first century compared to the imperial cultic initiatives that Christians saw in the generations that followed.[50] Spreading across the European and Eurasian continents, the empire sought unification in terms of respect and honor to the emperor in Rome. At a base level, only a small offering was needed to solidify this honor. The empire did not deny the gods of its various conquered societies; its polytheistic approach sought merely to add allegiance to the imperial cult. The monotheism of Jews and Christians, however, clashed with the imperial demand for cultic participation.

47. Bruce, *New Testament History*, 55.
48. Bruce, *New Testament History*, 421–22.
49. Winter, *Divine Honours for the Caesars*, 7.
50. For a summary of how the persecution of the church by Roman authorities in the first three centuries developed from the pattern of the apostles, see Frend, *Martyrdom and Persecution*, 197–239.

The expulsion of Jews from Rome by Claudius in 49 may have been partially based on the missionary efforts of Christians in the local synagogues being thought of as causing tumult.[51]

Besides Nero, Domitian is the only emperor who shows evidence of having been unfriendly to Christianity during the era of the original apostles. Domitian was committed to the traditional religion of Rome and sought to strengthen the supernatural claim of the Julian dynasty.[52] Brian Jones has noted that at the end of the first century, Domitian does not seem to have systematically persecuted the Christian movement,[53] but there is still evidence that the apostle John was seen as hostile to the *Dominus et Deus* (Master and God) activities of Domitian. John also would have been an icon for a surging religious movement in the empire, and such activities tended to be received with legal resistance. Since it is likely that John was the only apostle remaining by this time, the impact on the apostles themselves was no longer an issue. However, this same tone of opposition because of conflict between religions was present during the ministry of the apostles.

Documented struggles by the various apostles with the Greco-Roman pantheon or imperial worship are rare. Most scholars think that the persecution of Christianity in the centuries that followed consisted of provincial governors and local magistrates acting as idiosyncratic persecutors rather than participants in imperially sponsored persecution. So the apostles were probably not executed for failure to worship Zeus or the emperor. The commands of the Roman throne, however, set the tone for a wider spirit of freedom to persecute Christianity throughout the empire. Peter and Paul came closest to defying the demands of this milieu, but even their martyrdoms did not come directly from a failure to worship the emperor. Instead, their deaths were due to either Nero blaming Christians for the fire in Rome as a political scapegoat, around 64, or his acting generally as an unsystematic megalomaniac who enjoyed the pleasure and social returns of executing his civilians for sport.

In our quest for the historical apostles, we should be careful not to impose the image of Roman persecution of Christians that occurred under emperors between the late second through the early fourth century, before Constantine's favor toward Christianity prevailed. Except for the brief mention of Nero's capricious maltreatment of some Roman Christians and Domitian's policy against them, the apostles moved freely about the empire, and the opposition

---

51. Schnabel, *Early Christian Mission*, 1:3.
52. Jones, *Emperor Domitian*, 99.
53. Jones, *Emperor Domitian*, 114–17. He claims that the evidence for Domitian's persecution of Christians comes "from a frail, almost non-existent basis," and he also dismissively references the testimonies of Clement, Irenaeus, Melito, Tertullian, and Eusebius that suggest otherwise.

they experienced came from local governors for whom the message of the faith was seen as competing with local cults or as critical of aspects of their personal lives. Many of these persecutors were religious pagans of a non-Roman variety.

Additional Pagan Conflict

As the apostles went beyond the borders of the empire, new encounters with various religions and political establishments presented new challenges. Philip's message competed with the magical arts that Simon Magus displayed (Acts 8:9–11). When Paul survived a snakebite on the island of Malta, the natives immediately concluded that he was a god (Acts 28:1–6). If Bartholomew ever commanded the Mesopotamian deity Astaroth to show itself before the people for spiritual battle, as one work relates, such an episode would epitomize a confrontation with a pagan religion. There is a legend that Brahman priests of Mylapore seemed to perceive Thomas and the gospel message as a threat to Hinduism.

Yet even encounters with non-Roman paganism did not automatically result in the persecution of the apostles. Their conflicts with local authorities on new frontiers seem to have been more personal and superstitious in nature rather than a direct threat to the local god. When Andrew encouraged the wife of the proconsul Aegeates to be celibate, the objection of the proconsul was obviously motivated by personal hostility. In view of such accounts, we cannot be sure what mix of political, religious, or personal reasons led to persecution. Of course, in some cases we cannot be sure that the record of such activities is even accurate.

The overall effect of the pagan conflict with the apostolic mission was twofold. First, it shaped the worldview and context in which the Twelve went forth. If the training of the fisherman and skilled laborers among the disciples was not at the formal level of the Jewish religious leaders (Acts 4:13), then one can imagine that their understanding of world religions was equally limited. Since the extrabiblical sources provide little about the intercultural strategies of the apostles, we can only assume that the new cultural encounters must have been stressful. Given that in its earliest phase Christianity was mostly composed of Jews, Andrew Walls declares: "It remains one of the marvels of the ages that Christianity entered a second phase at all."[54]

Second, paganism provided resistance to the monotheistic message of the Twelve. Judaism was familiar with a religious responsibility to be separate

---

54. Walls, *Missionary Movement*, 16.

from other nations and their practices. The law instructed them to avoid acts of immorality and religious polytheism that came with exposure to foreign nations (Lev. 18:24–28). Just as Paul encountered hostility from the Greek cities threatened by the gospel, the other disciples arrived in new cultures with established religions that regarded the Christian message as a threat. At the core was the need to gain the respect of the audience while allowing the gospel to challenge some of the indigenous values of the audience. The message of the apostles caused inevitable conflict by its call to repentance, forsaking of idols, and moral lifestyle. Cross-cultural expert Andrew Walls remarks: "Church history has always been a battleground for two opposing tendencies; and the reason is that each of the tendencies has its origin in the Gospel itself."[55]

The Jew and Gentile Conflict

Since Christianity arose from Judaism, it is natural that a baseline of continuity would be foundational to the new religion. A Jewish carpenter from a Jewish province of the Roman Empire remarked to a Jewish audience, "Do not think that I came to abolish the Law or the Prophets; I did not come to abolish but to fulfill" (Matt. 5:17). All evidence we have leads us to surmise that the twelve apostles had Jewish roots, even if their milieu intersected much with Greek and Roman cultures. The Jewish Paul became the great apostle to the gentiles when the Twelve were at first focusing the message on Jewish synagogues. In one letter he remarks that the gospel is "the power of God for salvation to everyone who believes, to the Jew first and also to the Greek" (Rom. 1:16). In the same letter, he declares that "they [the Jews] were entrusted with the oracles of God" (Rom. 3:2) that pointed to Jesus. The Pharisees' conflicts with the early church were spurred by a vengeance against Jesus after his resurrection but also by a sense of incompatibility between the church's proclamation of Jesus as the Messiah and the Pharisees' own beliefs and practices. Gamaliel stood before the Jewish Sanhedrin to navigate this conflict, insisting that "if it [this movement] is of God, you will not be able to overthrow them; or else you may even be found fighting against God" (Acts 5:39).

Cultural separation from the surrounding nations was a hallmark of Judaism (Lev. 11:44). When Christianity emerged, Jewish leaders were threatened by its claim to be the fulfillment of their oracles. Then, when gentiles responded positively to the gospel, even the Jewish-Christian leaders paused to process the meaning of this new integration. Stories began to be recorded

55. Walls, *Missionary Movement*, 7.

and disseminated, such as the centurion's belief (Matt. 8:8–13) and the Samaritan woman at the well (John 4:4–26), while Peter received a vision to eat unclean foods (Acts 10:9–17) just before Cornelius's household evidenced the filling of the Spirit (Acts 10:44–48). The climactic moment of this developing conflict was the Jerusalem Council, where the apostles recognized the universal opportunity for gentiles to become Christians (Acts 15:22–30).

Paul's own calling to take the message of the gospel to the gentiles was furthering a cause that was not yet fully affirmed in the minds and hearts of Jewish Christians. The Jewish-gentile divide characterizes the quest for the historical Peter and Paul the most. Yet the divide should not dominate a study of the mission of the Twelve, even if it does inform generations of the obstacles to the apostolic mission. This is particularly true of the attempt of critical scholars in the tradition of German Protestant theological liberalism to diminish the message of the gospel through emphasis on the maturing understanding of the apostles. Fred Lapham remarks: "It may be the case that the nineteenth-century Tübingen School of Theology laid rather too much stress on the historical and theological consequences of the antipathy between the two Apostles."[56]

This early church conflict cannot be denied. Yet throughout the first century, it seems that the apostles did overcome this paradigm shift as they all moved into realms of gentiles whom they witnessed believing in the gospel. Regions such as Greece, Macedonia, Scythia, Parthia, Africa, and India, and perhaps Gaul and Britain, saw the apostles move away from adherence to the Jewish law. As we follow their paths, this understanding will help us realize the universality of their message.

The Gnostic Record

The path of the quest for the historic apostles includes a brief consideration of the sources called "gnostic." Gnosticism was a movement of thought whose apostolic-related writings peaked in the second and third centuries CE. Members of this group claimed Jesus and identified themselves with the church, although they were viewed with strong suspicion by the catholic church that claimed an apostolic heritage. Theologically its proponents viewed revelation as centered on a saving knowledge, or gnosis (*gnōsis*), of God; a cosmic worldview with a multilevel divine system that the supreme God transcended; an anthropology that sought spiritual release from the human

---

56. Lapham, *Introduction to the New Testament Apocrypha*, 45.

body, which they viewed negatively; and a larger dualistic myth system to accompany these principles. Gnosticism is difficult to harmonize within a system of thought, in part because of its mysterious nature and in part because any construction must come from ancient writings that did not themselves seek its synthesis. While Matthew's Gospel draws from the Hebrew Scriptures as foundational, and Paul's Letters seek coherence with the work of other contemporary apostles, gnostic writers did not prioritize such theological consistency. Fred Lapham remarks: "There were (it has been said) as many Gnostic systems as there were Gnostics; and the different groupings seem to have been no more accommodating to each other than the mainstream Church was to them."[57]

Contemporary scholarship about gnostic writings is as complicated as the gnostic writings themselves, ranging from scrutiny of the conflicted relationship between catholic and gnostic thinkers to debate on the very use of the term "gnosticism." Its complex cosmic worldview, use of religious myth, and lack of systematic coherence have led to confusion and misinterpretation. The title of an important work by Michael Williams captures this dilemma: *Rethinking "Gnosticism": An Argument for Dismantling a Dubious Category*.[58] Early church author Irenaeus depicts the nature of this theological system in his title *On the Detection and Overthrow of the So-Called Gnosis*, a work commonly called *Against Heresies*. Some gnostic sources must be examined for their historical contribution to our understanding of the ministry and lives of the apostles. In this confusing fray of interpretations of gnosticism, this book recognizes what Carl Smith calls "the misleading generalizations and unwarranted stereotypes that so frequently accompany the terms."[59]

The quest for the historic apostles found an important provision with the mid-twentieth-century discovery of the Nag Hammadi manuscripts in Upper Egypt.[60] Prior to this discovery, Christian scholarship only knew about gnostic writings through the early church heresiologists and historians, who condemned the writings for their theological errors based on what became the canonical works of the Christian faith. Readers should know that some modern scholars have accused the early catholic writers of rejecting the gnostic thinkers not only for theological reasons but also for political reasons. Elaine Pagels remarks, "This campaign against heresy involved an involuntary admission of its persuasive power, yet the bishops prevailed."[61] Our efforts here

57. Lapham, *Introduction to the New Testament Apocrypha*, 186.
58. Williams, *Rethinking "Gnosticism."*
59. Smith, *No Longer Jews*, 8.
60. For a summary of this fascinating tale, see Pagels, *Gnostic Gospels*, xiii–xiv.
61. Pagels, *Gnostic Gospels*, xviii.

will consider the historical locations and themes in these works as possible informants in the quest for the historical apostles.

Early Christian Works and Presuppositions

A history of the early church includes the primary sources that come to us, whether they are treated as Scripture, scripturally compatible, or neither. Since primary sources are such an important part of historical inquiry, some definitions of early church writings will provide a primer here for the less informed and a benchmark for the advanced historian to comprehend the perspective of the work.

Some functional definitions among primary sources are in order. "Canon" refers to the collection of writings recognized by the historic orthodox church as authoritative and to be treated as Scripture. "Apocrypha" (singular "apocryphon") are writings categorized as nonauthoritative for the church but recognized as potentially useful. Its meaning of "things hidden" represents the uncertainty of the books compared to canonical sources. Among these are the "Pseudepigrapha" (singular "pseudepigraphon," meaning "falsely attributed"), which are writings that make historically unsupportable claims to having been written by a notable biblical character such as Moses or one of Israel's patriarchs. "Gnostic" refers to writings from the movement described above, from a worldview clashing with orthodoxy. The meaning of *gnōsis*, "knowledge," represents the mysterious and esoteric spiritual salvation it promotes. "Orthodox" refers to writings of a movement represented by the greater church, prioritizing the values of apostolicity (the authority of the apostles), catholicity (the broad recognition of validity throughout the early church), and theology (congruence with what was known as the teaching of Christ and the apostles). Finally, the term "catholic," meaning "universal," refers to writings of the same movement, emphasizing the common belief among churches with bishops teaching in the apostolic tradition.

In spite of the important scholarly struggles around historians' ability to use labels for trends and periods, these categories are quite effective and standard human constructs for organizing the writings of the early church during and after the establishment of a canon of Scripture. As such, we inherit a corpus of works called the Bible (canon) or called unbiblical (noncanonical), with the latter to be treated somewhere between faith and criticism of their historical or theological validity. Both canonical and noncanonical texts can be treated as historically reliable or as judiciously unreliable. This tension between faith and scientific history will remain throughout this work.

Particularly noteworthy is the definition and regular use of "apocryphal." Generally speaking, at times "canonical" can be viewed as the opposite of "apocryphal." More narrowly, apocryphal works stem from the meaning "secret" or "hidden" and commonly display a special genre of mystery and confidentiality to the hearers or readers. Not all noncanonical works possess this specific apocryphal quality, and some display it only briefly. For example, while the gospels of the disciples in this category communicate secret teachings of Jesus that are categorically and densely gnostic, the Acts of the disciples in this category usually limit their apocryphal elements to the teaching discourses. Christopher Tuckett can thus declare, "Not all non-canonical texts are apocrypha, but all apocryphal texts are non-canonical."[62] For this work, the term "apocryphal" will be used broadly, in line with the publication of primary source works that commonly collect and label them all as "New Testament Apocrypha."

Management of Gnostic Sources

To a high degree, gnostic thought sought to maintain the rich "separation" doctrine that characterized the Jewish people in its practice of personal holiness, reconciling it with the teaching of Jesus for living in the world. The Greek milieu of antiquity offered Platonic dualism as a spiritual solution. Paul's writings strongly distinguish "spirit" and "flesh," the former being the ideal of the faith and the latter a competitor of it. Robert Grant was the first to propose that Judaism had its own early gnostic advocates,[63] which both reinforced and complicated the theological system.

A sample of gnostic writing from the gospel of Thomas can help illustrate the style and emphasis of the work: "Jesus said, 'If those who lead you say to you, "See, the kingdom is in the sky," then the birds of the sky will precede you. If they say to you, "It is in the sea," then the fish will precede you. Rather, the kingdom is inside of you, and it is outside of you. When you come to know yourselves, then you will become known, and you will realize that it is you who are the sons of the living father. But if you will not know yourselves, you will dwell in poverty and it is you who are that poverty.'"[64] This vague instruction can supposedly be understood when gnosis is applied to the words of Jesus.

Gnosticism's belief system is founded on a sapiential tradition, in which wisdom from revelation finds meaning when empowered by saving knowledge. Claudio Moreschini notes: "The *Gospel of Thomas* presents a conception of

---

62. Introduction to Gregory and Tuckett, *Oxford Handbook on Early Christian Apocrypha*, 5.
63. Grant, *Gnosticism and Early Christianity*.
64. Gos. Thom. 3 (Robinson, 126).

the kingdom that differs greatly from that of the Synoptic tradition; in Thomas
the kingdom is a present, not a future reality, and it is heavily spiritualized."[65]
That spiritualization is based on a dualism in which salvation is a casting
off of the earthly through gnostic knowledge. In the same work, "Jesus said,
'Blessed is the lion which becomes man when consumed by man; and cursed is
the man whom the lion consumes, and the lion becomes a man.'"[66] Exegesis of
this passage is difficult because it expects a lens of gnosis for understanding.

Gnostic sources range in type from purported teachings and revelations
of Jesus, Acts of the apostles, and works of wisdom. For our quest, the Acts
will be the most useful of these gnostic works for providing historical data on
the apostles, their ministries, their encounters, and their geographical locations. In the end, even these works will require quality control. As Christine
Thomas notes, the historical difficulty of these works means they are best
viewed as historical fiction.[67]

One element is particularly important for understanding the portrayal of
the apostles in these gnostic Acts. "Encratism" refers to an ascetic denial of
types of eating, marriage, sexual activities, and other lifestyle characteristics.
These rejections were regarded as essential for salvation. Formally, the Encratites were a second-century sect of Christians who promoted celibacy and
abstinence from meat. Several church fathers condemn them and their ascetic
practices by name.[68] Hippolytus describes Encratites: "They suppose that by
meats they magnify themselves, while abstaining from animal food, (and)
being water-drinkers, and forbidding to marry, and devoting themselves during the remains of life to habits of asceticism. But persons of this description
are estimated Cynics rather than Christians."[69] This suggests that some saw
these beliefs as compatible with orthodox Christianity's theological tenets;
thus Hippolytus says they "acknowledge some things concerning God and
Christ in like manner with the Church."[70] While rejecting gnostic salvation—
the soul's transcending the bonds of the body—early catholic writers still
reinforced models of virginity, poverty, and other lifestyle characteristics of
practiced asceticism. These emphases were different from the encratic emphases, as orthodox leaders *invited* sectors of believers to holy lifestyles rather
than *requiring* them as essential components of salvation. Eusebius remarks

---

65. Moreschini and Norelli, *Early Christian Greek and Latin Literature*, 1:70.
66. Gos. Thom. 7 (Robinson, 127).
67. Thomas, "'Prehistory' of the Acts of Peter," 88–89. A special thanks to Sean McDowell
for introducing the story component in Thomas's work.
68. Irenaeus, *Haer.* 1.28 (ANF 1:352–53); Clement of Alexandria, *Instructor* 2.2 (ANF 2:246);
Strom. 1.15; 7.17 (ANF 2:316, 555); Eusebius, *Hist. eccl.* 4.28–29.
69. Hippolytus, *Refutation of All Heresies* 8.13 (ANF 5:124).
70. Hippolytus, *Refutation of All Heresies* 8.13 (ANF 5:124).

about noncanonical gospels and acts: "The character of the style itself is very different from that of the apostles, and the sentiment and the purport of those things that are advanced in them, deviating as far as possible from sound orthodoxy, evidently proves they are the fictions of heretical men. Therefore, they are to be ranked not only among the spurious writings but are to be rejected as altogether absurd and impious."[71] Such movements were part of the tug-of-war that took place between orthodox and gnostic writers.

While this theology was condemned by the catholic stream of thought in the early church, the writings offer a historical contribution to the quest for the apostles. Their miraculous stories or historical narratives may contain absurdities, but they also might reflect a historical reality captured in tradition. Sean McDowell declares, "While it is uncritical to simply accept tradition, it is overly critical to glibly dismiss it. The key is to separate fact from fiction, remembering that the myths and legends do not arise in a vacuum."[72] With this open mind, we allow some features to evidence a historical core. Bryan Litfin agrees: "Though Christian memories and traditions from the first century were expanded by later legends, a historical core often remains. Therefore these texts cannot be considered pure fiction. . . . When we find independent confirmation of their details elsewhere, these texts help us reconstruct the Christian past."[73] Finally, François Bovon states: "Even if the final version of those texts is the editorial result of authors, I suppose that those authors, not separated from communities of faith, were eager to convey or rearrange traditional material."[74]

On a lighter note, Tom Bissell describes the experience of reading these texts, which can serve as a conclusion to our approach to gnostic sources:

> To read any apocryphal work is to vacate a series of expectations. The first vacation is spiritual: However edifying these works purport or attempt to be, their noncanonical standing renders their message curiously distant from the expediencies of faith. . . . The second vacation is formal: The gospels . . . are commendable in many ways. They have structure, contrapuntal detail, rhythm, and style. This helps them remain grippingly relevant to millions of people, most of whom know nothing about life in first-century Palestine or the complicated manner in which Jewish and Greek thought enriched each other in the Roman world. . . . One can certainly become sick of reading the gospels, but one never really tires of them. The optimal reading of an apocryphal work, on the other

71. Eusebius, *Hist. eccl.* 3.25.7.
72. McDowell, *Fate of the Apostles*, 160.
73. Litfin, *Early Christian Martyr Stories*, 30.
74. Bovon, "Canonical and Apocryphal Acts of Apostles," 166.

hand, typically requires a morning cleared of any pressing commitments and a soundproofed room.[75]

Critical Criteria

The gnostic texts among the apocryphal works will most frequently be sifted, filtered, and triaged on our quest for the historical apostles. However, other extrabiblical accounts will receive the same effort in terms of quality evaluation, including the attempt to either harmonize or prioritize orthodox historical writers on the apostles. Therefore, this section offers a broader explanation of criteria used to determine the value of historical sources or their components. While there is not an exact science to be applied consistently, generally these criteria will be employed.[76]

> *Criterion of coherence.* Material that is committed to the larger orthodox tradition is more likely to be true.
>
> *Criterion of historical plausibility.* Material that is compatible with influences on early Christianity is more likely to be true.
>
> *Criterion of attestation.* Material reinforced by another source is more likely to be true.
>
> *Criterion of freedom from opposition.* Material without a competing theory is more likely to be true.
>
> *Criterion of embarrassment.* Material that is genuinely demurring is more likely to be true.

These critical criteria will be at work throughout this book. In the end, the gnostic sources are not valued as highly as the historical writings of the New Testament and the patristic writers. This is not an overly simplistic process, as G. Marcille Frederick recognizes: "Sometimes the shape of the accepted periodization forces you to choose the experiences of one group over another."[77]

These sources can provide a historical core of facts or a factual detail to be weighed in the quest for the historical apostles. This book shares the perspective of Sean McDowell when he says: "Even though they [apocryphal

---

75. Bissell, *Apostle*, 206–7.

76. Adapted from the New Testament criteria of authenticity in Sanders and Davies, *Studying the Synoptic Gospels*, 304–15.

77. Frederick, "Doing Justice in History," 228. While the context of this statement seeks to do justice to the voices of history without the ancient apocryphal works in view, Frederick's instruction about method is relevant.

Acts] contain clear embellishment, external evidence indicates that they reliably convey the travels, preaching, and fate of each apostle. If there were no external corroboration for the post-Jerusalem lives of these apostles, many scholars would likely reject them as entirely fictional. And yet external evidence indicates they retain a historical nucleus."[78] While the historical nucleus is not easy to identify or to claim, the geographical association particularly will be an integral part of the search for a historical core. Ultimately, we cannot know exactly the path of each disciple, because we cannot always confirm the veracity of each historical element. Yet the message of the work will be a measurement of its veracity, since we know the gnostic agenda that characterizes several extrabiblical leads to an apostle's journey. Glen Thompson says it well: "The apostles cannot be separated from their message but they can be separated from their legends."[79]

The Patristic Record

Alongside the gnostic testimony of the apostles, the church fathers recorded and referenced elements of the lives of the apostles and their influence, which will be revisited throughout this book. These extrabiblical works contain historical data in the form of homilies, commentaries, treatises, and historical records of the early church, including the apostles. In order to gain some familiarity with the church fathers, let us begin with a brief list of the most important contributors to understanding the apostolic ministries and journeys. Readers can revisit this list as needed as a reminder.

> *Irenaeus* (fl. 170)—an elder in Lyon, Gaul, who authored the significant *Against Heresies*, which provides insight into the catholic rejection of apocryphal works
>
> *Clement of Alexandria* (d. 215)—the head of a catechetical school in Alexandria, Egypt, who mentions the apostles and apocryphal works
>
> *Hippolytus* (d. 235)—a presbyter in Rome to whom is attributed the brief apostle biographies in *On the Twelve Apostles* and the catalog of false teachings in *Refutation of All Heresies*
>
> *Origen* (d. 254)—heir to the catechetical school in Alexandria after Clement, whose commentaries on Scripture and antiheretical works provide occasional comments on the apostles' lives

78. McDowell, *Fate of the Apostles*, 167.
79. Thompson, review of *After Acts*, by Litfin, 153.

Eusebius (d. 339)—bishop of Caesarea for twenty-five years, whose work *Ecclesiastical History* is the most thorough church history from the early church era, based on libraries at Caesarea and Jerusalem

Jerome (d. 420)—a monk in Rome and Bethlehem whose work *On the Lives of Illustrious Men* provides brief biographies of the apostles

Management of Patristic Sources

In the chapters that follow, the quest for the apostles will rely heavily on the contribution of patristic writers. Several figures provide complete chronologies like modern historians; Eusebius and Julius Africanus are particularly noted for writing comprehensive church histories. Others, such as Origen and Hippolytus, are pastors, homileticians, and theologians, but their works are sometimes historically focused, while other times a homily or theological treatise will allude to the experience of an apostle to gain a past fact.

These sources are treated as significantly more credible than the gnostic sources in our quest. Immediately some contemporary critical historians will accuse this method of favoring the great church of catholic and orthodox predispositions, identifying a circular argument for credibility because these are favored. However, gnostic acts and gospels are considered less credible not just because they are not canonical but because they deviate so much from the apostolic tradition and present a peculiar system of salvation. Gnostic thought was a radical departure from the foundation and mainstream of early Christianity. Those called church fathers drew from what they considered Scripture and the apostolic tradition, anchoring their belief system in this tradition. Concerning the difference between canonical and apocryphal sources, Bruce Metzger says, "It is here that there appears most sharply the difference between such documents and those of the New Testament. The apocryphal writings are, almost without exception, marked by a lush growth of legend to satisfy a craving for the spectacular and the marvelous. In the New Testament, on the contrary, the narratives involving the miraculous are characterized by a remarkable sobriety and chaste restraint."[80] The church fathers believed and reported this system of miracles, while discarding the superfluously miraculous acts and the esoteric teachings of apocryphal works.

Nevertheless, the credibility of catholic patristic figures is not taken for granted here. The church has traditionally considered the theological contribution of certain fathers to not be authoritative on some points, and their

---

80. Metzger, "St. Paul and the Baptized Lion," 17–18.

reports of the history of the apostles reveal conflicting traditions. Irenaeus has been canonized and finds the utmost respect in both Eastern and Western traditions, while Origen has not been canonized, and elements of his theology were condemned at early church councils. Yet their writings draw from the orthodox tradition, and their historical claims are often convincing. The contributions of the church fathers will undergo evaluation by critical criteria similar to what we apply to gnostic sources.

Critical Criteria

There are two obstacles to establishing the reliability of the fathers' accounts of the lives of the historical apostles. First, the *geographical data* on the apostles' ministries from the early church are sometimes in conflict, making this the greatest challenge in reconstructing their historical paths. The diverse mission of the Twelve that leads to our quest did not occur immediately: "And on that day a great persecution began against the church in Jerusalem, and they were all scattered throughout the regions of Judea and Samaria, except the apostles" (Acts 8:1). In a matter of time, mission from Jerusalem came to exemplify the long-term separation of the apostles, who went to the uttermost parts of the earth (Matt. 28:18–20).

Some apostles had diverse experiences in multiple locations. As a general rule, a high concentration of encounters in a single geographical setting increases the likelihood that an apostle actually ministered in that location. Diverse geographical traditions require either a synthesis of multiple traditions or the possibility of extended travel. For apostles such as James son of Zebedee, his short life reduces the likelihood of his travel, despite his posthumous influence in Spain. For Andrew, ministry in both Achaea and Scythia can be viewed as likely by virtue of the locations' proximity, while the tradition of his travel to Scotland is less likely when one accepts that he was occupied with extensive ministry around the Black Sea.

For any conflicting geography, contemporary readers can neither easily dismiss nor readily embrace a diverse or complex travel itinerary in an apostle's legacy. The sense of adventure characterizing these pioneers of the faith need not be limited by the map of antiquity. The apostles were driven far and wide by a hope and belief in the gospel message, by the commission of Jesus to go to the uttermost ends of the earth, by witnessing the coming of the gentiles into the fold, and by a boldness in the Spirit to reach into new cultures in new locations without fear of the travel that their mission entailed. We speak with a notion of "possibility," which can be very different from the category of "likelihood," and each apostle's travels will be weighed independently.

Second, any modern reader of the apocryphal Acts will inevitably have moments of skepticism when reading the miracle stories. For example, the Acts of Paul tells of Paul's encounter with a lion, which does not attack the apostle as a feral beast would but speaks, listens to the gospel, and receives baptism. As if the account were not already hard enough to believe, later, in the arena at Ephesus, the same lion is released to bloody the victims in the stadium before the crowds. When the believing creatures recognize each other, they exchange greetings of grace, like an early church congregation. Humor even follows when Paul asks, "How were you captured?" The lion responds, "Even as you were, O Paul." A hailstorm tops off the miracle, which allows them both to escape.

The miraculous extrabiblical accounts of the apostles seem to replicate almost every kind of biblical miracle, from the raising of the dead to the persuasion of an astounded crowd of thousands. In fact, the episodes with animals seem to be a reminder of remote biblical accounts, from the miraculous speaking of Balaam's donkey (Num. 22:28–31) to Paul's surviving a poisonous snakebite (Acts 28:3–6). Like the signs and wonders of the New Testament that reinforced the claims of the preacher, writings beyond the biblical record perpetuate this miraculous element. Thomas Schmidt recognizes certain patterns of encounter: "healing, successful preaching (often involving an influential individual), and local reprisals" for conversions. He compares this to the early chapters of Acts: "It formed a model for the spread of Christianity for almost a thousand years."[81]

On the one hand, patterns that show continuity between the New Testament and the extrabiblical works of the apostles favor the latter's authenticity, but only if the miraculous is to be believed at all in ancient stories. Reading the apocryphal Acts raises the age-old question of the veracity of miracle accounts. Graham Twelftree's analysis of the difficulty of believing the miracles in the ministry of the historical Jesus applies to the ministry of the historical apostles: these stories are stumbling blocks that raise anew the question of the possibility of miracles.[82]

On the other hand, the pseudepigraphical writings can also be viewed as a mere mimic of the Scriptures. Second-century authors claimed that their writings should be attributed to an apostle, and there are often connections to the New Testament that influenced their credibility. Bruce Metzger points out how the author of the Acts of Paul seems to have taken Paul's claim in

81. Schmidt, *Apostles after Acts*, 150.

82. Twelftree, *In the Name of Jesus*, 38. For a brief analysis of the possibility of miracles in the study of Christian texts, see 38–53.

1 Corinthians 15:32, "I fought with wild beasts at Ephesus," as the basis of his narrative.[83] The author then attributes to the fleeing crowd, "Save us, O God, save (us), thou God of the man who fought with wild beasts!" and to the observer Hieronymus, "O God, who has helped the man who fought with wild beasts."[84] Metzger says that the author may have learned about story traditions at Ephesus, but more likely he was "amplifying and embroidering the statement of Paul with a multitude of details drawn from his own imagination," and thus "the unknown presbyter of Asia incorporated into this religious romance a thrilling account."[85] The more extreme the miracle, the more difficult it is to believe, and the more the credibility of the source diminishes.

While the example of Paul and the baptized lion is an extreme case from a categorically gnostic apocryphal Acts, it can still illustrate the challenge of measuring the miraculous stories in the quest for the historical apostles. The earlier disclaimer about the distrust of sources applies here. Christians do not have to believe a given miracle story simply because they hold a worldview that allows for the possibility of miracles or simply because there is New Testament precedent for miracles. In his discussion of the place of worldview commitments in identifying miracles, C. John Collins remarks: "Christian belief is not simply an acceptance of certain things as factual: it goes beyond that to personal commitment."[86]

Equally, the presence of a miracle story, like the presence of teaching episodes, need not rule out the veracity of the story's historical components, such as the geographical location of an apostle's ministry. The principle of seeking a historical core can be applied in understanding the apostolic legacies. Since recorded miracles can have natural causes or partial natural contributions, the reader is left with the choice to embrace, reject, or suspend belief in a miracle account. Suspending belief can allow us to focus on the historical life of an apostle without being distracted by the question of the veracity of the miracles included in the account.

From Apostles to Saints

Alongside the gnostic and patristic testimonies of the apostles come pictures, symbols, relics, inscriptions, graffiti, and iconography of the apostles that

83. Acts of Paul, in Metzger, "St. Paul and the Baptized Lion," 12.
84. Acts of Paul, in Metzger, "St. Paul and the Baptized Lion," 16–17.
85. Metzger, "St. Paul and the Baptized Lion," 12.
86. Collins, *God of Miracles*, 145.

historically or religiously shape our image of them. Stained-glass window memorials, pulpit and choir relief carvings, marble statues, and ornate illustrations from medieval codices all reflect and in turn promote the historical image of the apostles, which shapes our contemporary perspective. In all of these, faith can be found. Shirley Mullen comments, "Whether we confess our faith in terms of the Apostles' Creed, or in terms of personal experience—our confession of faith is linked to the affirmation that certain things have actually happened in the past and have significance and determine meaning for our lives today."[87] Whether symbols and actions or heroic postures, the visuals of history are powerful forces for image construction.

The collective image of the apostles was boosted early on when Constantine sought to build a cathedral in their honor. Eusebius records: "All these edifices the emperor consecrated with the desire of perpetuating the memory of the apostles of our Saviour."[88] The names of the apostles, bequeathed to newborn males and emergent cities and churches, echo respect and admiration for these figures of the faith. The names of the apostles are ubiquitous and resilient, as millions of men and women bear them. Popes have adopted them, including twenty-three Johns, six Pauls, and two John Pauls. Hospitals bear their names, as well as czars and kings. Cities echo their names, such as St. Petersburg and Jamestown.

The image of each apostle comes from various sources. William McBirnie describes how for early Christians, "it took some time for their spiritual descendants to see them as the fathers of the whole church movement."[89] Through a gradual process, the church actively or passively adopted canonical and noncanonical features of the apostles, connected places and artifacts with them, and employed artists to illustrate them. Part of this developmental process was the acquisition of their bones for memorial purposes and for veneration. A number of modern churches claim a tradition that an apostle experienced an event on its site, that the apostle's tomb rests at a certain place there, or that their reliquaries contain apostles' bones. Bryan Litfin opens his work on the apostles by focusing on the commonly cited phrase "according to tradition," posing the valuable question "Where do these ancient traditions come from?"[90] The authenticity of the many sites and artifacts related to the apostles is impossible to secure. The church, from the early fourth century under Constantine through the Middle Ages, made attempts to procure and keep the bones of the apostles. Potential credibility comes from the realization

87. Mullen, "Between 'Romance' and 'True History,'" 25.
88. Eusebius, *The Life of Constantine* 4.60 (NPNF[2] 1:555).
89. McBirnie, *Search for the Twelve Apostles*, xvi.
90. Litfin, *After Acts*, 13.

that early Christians could very well have kept the artifacts of the apostles as valued mementos. Besides Constantine's basilica effort, his mother's procuring of religious keepsakes from Palestine strengthens a historical connection. The collection of such artifacts by churches gave rise to the veneration of relics in worship. Relics function as symbols of the apostles based on claims of their authenticity and through the power that some Catholic and Orthodox believers attribute to them.

An adopted "regulative principle" for evaluating such data involves placing them in categories of (1) relics with strong archaeological evidence and noncompeting church belief; (2) relics with weaker archaeological evidence, with perhaps competing church belief, arresting a decision; and (3) relics with no archaeological evidence and strongly competing church beliefs. By this principle, relics with greater archaeological support and less competition in tradition are more likely to be deemed authentic.

The Catholic Church is particularly generous in affirming the historicity of some relics and sites that go back for unrecorded generations and serve as religious shrines for pilgrims. For example, the Mamertine Prison in Rome is a popular destination for tourists on the trail of Peter and Paul. There is no historical evidence that Peter and Paul were here; it is only that it is a historical prison from ancient times. Yet its proximity to the Palatine Hill and the Neronian house makes it a reasonable place for celebrity prisoners to have been held. Certainly the image of Peter and Paul chained together to its one stone in the lower recesses of the prison is unlikely. Yet their imprisonment there remains possible.

How one evaluates historical possibility ranges along scholarly standards of judgment. For example, Litfin provides a report card with grades A–F for some of the main traditions surrounding each apostle. The likelihood of Paul having been in Mamertine Prison receives a D grade, also influenced by its reputation as a "gaudy tourist attraction" from an era "when apostolic and martyrological mythmaking was in full swing."[91] On the other hand, a Catholic pilgrimage site guide asserts, "Certainly the most celebrated inmates of the Mamertine were the apostles Peter and Paul in AD 66."[92] Strongly divergent views on such an important site are typical of the apostolic legends. The main attempt of this work is to communicate the traditions of the apostles, using a regulative principle that eliminates weak tradition while withholding judgment against uncertain traditions that have limited support, since there is also not enough evidence for automatic elimination. In this way we will

91. Litfin, *After Acts*, 168–69, 182.
92. Korn, *Catholic's Guide to Rome*, 161.

identify sites that are important to apostolic images even if their historicity cannot be definitively proved.

Peter can provide an example of how art shapes the image of the apostles. When we consider the famous Leonardo da Vinci painting *The Last Supper*, we may discover that the picture of bearded disciples in colored robes shapes our understanding more than we realize. Here Peter is noteworthy for the discourse he is giving to a patient John, his look of consternation, and his bearing a knife in anticipation of the arrest of Jesus. Michelangelo's *Last Judgment* presents Peter by Christ's throne, equally stout as any of the painting's figures, holding two massive keys. In much Christian art, Peter symbolically possesses the keys of his appointment as guardian of heaven, based on Matthew 16:19. Rembrandt's *The Denial of St. Peter* places the apostle in the center of a dimly lit room with a woman sharing words that draw his attention. Nancy Pearcey underscores how Jesus, barely visible in the background, "looks back at Peter with an expression that is both anguished and gentle," highlighting "Peter's darkest moment of temptation and betrayal."[93] Finally, Caravaggio's *Crucifixion of St. Peter* presents a helpless, aged Peter inverted on a cross. His is the only face showing in the painting as inhumane soldiers stoop to lift the heavy burden. In all of these popular portrayals, the famous Peter is presented as suffering and serving, recording the most important events in his apostleship and shaping our image of this follower of Christ.

What must not be done is to study the apostolic figures and imagine that we have the ability to construct personality profiles to edify the church. While contemporary popular literature attempts to make such claims, it is rare that a personality truly emerges from the texts of the early church. The classic endeavor for this is Charles Brown's 1926 work *These Twelve: A Study in Temperament*. He presents the book as "a study of temperament" that addresses "twelve types from the ranks of the original Apostles."[94] His chapters portray his efforts to display the apostles by virtue of their personalities, such as "James: The Man of Silence," "John: The Man of Temper," "Andrew: The Matter-of-Fact Man," and "Thomas: The Man of Moods." While there is legitimate room to attribute a moniker to each apostle based on a specific story, it is illegitimate to offer full character contours from ancient texts. Writers of antiquity rarely dwelled even momentarily on the personality of figures, focusing instead on contributions or causes. Brown certainly overreaches when he claims, "There is something fresh and almost racy in the accounts we have of their action."[95]

93. Pearcey, *Saving Leonardo*, 86.
94. Brown, *These Twelve*, v.
95. Brown, *These Twelve*, viii.

Conclusion

With the provision of this background for our path, we embark on a quest for the historical apostles. Knowing the apostles requires an understanding of their names and identities from the biblical lists, the nature of the office of apostle, the pagan and Jewish conflicts they encountered, the gnostic and patristic records that contain their stories, and the movement toward an image of each apostle. All these combine to give shape to our quest. The path is cleared, and we are ready to embark in pursuit of each apostle.

* 2 *

Peter

The Rooster

"Simon, Simon, behold, Satan has demanded *permission* to sift you like wheat; but I have prayed for you, that your faith may not fail; and you, when once you have turned again, strengthen your brothers." But he said to Him, "Lord, with You I am ready to go both to prison and to death!" And He said, "I say to you, Peter, the rooster will not crow today until you have denied three times that you know Me."

Luke 22:31–34

I have spoken this unto thee, Peter, and declared it unto thee. Go forth therefore and go unto the city of the west and enter into the vineyard which I shall tell thee of, in order that by the sickness of the Son who is without sin the deeds of corruption may be sanctified. As for thee, thou art chosen according to the promise which I have given thee. Spread thou therefore my gospel throughout all the world in peace. Verily men shall rejoice: my words shall be the source of hope and of life, and suddenly shall the world be ravished.

Apocalypse of Peter[1]
third century, Syria

No other apostle embodies apostleship like Peter. No other apostle is habitually mentioned first in lists. No other apostle offers such a matchless personality for lessons of faith. These qualities combine

1. James, 518.

to make a figure who is foundational for the church and for the development of Christianity. Martin Hengel remarks, "The numerous times the Galilean fisherman and disciple of Jesus is mentioned is without parallel in early Christianity."[2] Despite the immense attention to him in the early church, the path of the historical Peter is not fully certain.

An initial personal profile of an apostle can serve as background in the quest. An inauguration of apostolicity can be seen when Jesus renames Simon as "Peter," referring to his function as the rock on which the kingdom is built. *Cephas* is the Aramaic of the Greek word *Petros*, and both are used to refer to Peter. The Gospels interchangeably use his retronym, "Simon who was called Peter" (Matt. 4:18), and his combined name, "Simon Peter" (Luke 5:8). His prominent leadership is recognized by Paul on the latter's reception into the fellowship of the apostles. There Peter is called a "pillar," along with John and James the brother of Jesus (Gal. 2:9).

Biblical and extrabiblical historical records of Peter testify to his marriage and at least one daughter. In the year 53 Paul mentions Peter's marriage (1 Cor. 9:5). According to popular culture his wife's name was Perpetua, but this finds no early church substantiation. She could have played an active role in the apostle's ministry, given the invaluable practical support that a woman in the ancient world could have offered in a traditional role. Hengel hypothesizes about her: "An advantage for a married couple who were active in mission work was that the wife would have had better chances to connect with the women of the family among the more important households in society, who were women of luxury and thus hard to approach."[3]

Peter's wife's martyrdom is supposedly recorded in legend. Clement of Alexandria says that Peter saw his wife taken away to her death in Rome, immediately before his own death. Clement's account captures the sentiment of the moment: "The blessed Peter, on seeing his wife led to death, rejoiced on account of her call and conveyance home, and called very encouragingly and comfortingly, addressing her by name, 'Remember the Lord.' Such was the marriage of the blessed, and their perfect disposition towards those dearest to them."[4]

During Jesus's ministry, Peter and his wife had a home in Capernaum. On one occasion, Jesus goes to Peter's house, where Peter's mother-in-law lies sick, and Jesus heals her (Matt. 8:14; Mark 1:30; Luke 4:38). The Acts of

2. Hengel, *Saint Peter*, 29.
3. Hengel, *Saint Peter*, 123.
4. Clement of Alexandria, *Strom.* 7.11 (*ANF* 2:541).

Peter profiles a daughter named Petronilla; Clement of Alexandria mentions simply that Peter had children.[5] These are the only early biographical details we have about the disciple Peter.

The New Testament provides a detailed record of the many influences Peter had on the early church as well as his substantial lessons of faith from his encounters with Jesus and multiple individuals in first-century Palestine. Material in apocryphal Acts and Revelations provides some limited insight into his ministry beyond the New Testament, including details surrounding his martyrdom.

Palestine Discipleship

The story of Peter begins in the early ministry of Jesus, without great detail. In comparison to Peter's other encounters with Jesus throughout the Gospels, it is somewhat surprising that his calling does not receive greater elaboration.

Discipleship Calling

Simon Peter was originally from the town of Bethsaida, also the home of Philip (John 1:44), from a fishing family on the Sea of Galilee. Jewish historian Josephus describes Galileans in a way that reflects the Peter we see in Scripture, even if the profile is a stereotype: "always able to make a strong resistance on all occasions of war," not "ever destitute of men of courage," and "universally rich and fruitful."[6] Fishing culture in Galilee was made up of stout, courageous, and industrious individuals. Josephus seems moved by their collective hospitality, that they "had that great kindness for me, and fidelity to me, that when their cities were taken by force, and their wives and children carried into slavery, they did not so deeply lament for their own calamities, as they were solicitous for my preservation."[7]

Peter's father's name is given as John or Jonah (Matt. 16:17; John 21:15–17). When Jesus's ministry is still nascent in Galilee, Peter's brother Andrew encounters him. Afterward, Andrew finds Simon, says to him "We have found the Messiah" (John 1:41), and brings him to Jesus. On what is otherwise a regular day of work, Jesus calls the brothers while they are casting their nets into the sea (Matt. 4:18).

5. Clement of Alexandria, *Strom.* 3.6 (*ANF* 2:390).
6. Josephus, *J.W.* 3.3.2.41–42.
7. Josephus, *Life* 16.

Discipleship Episodes

Peter's discipleship formation is a constant theme whenever the future apostle engages Jesus. From his confession of Jesus as the Christ to his desire to prevent Jesus from being surrendered to the authorities intent on harming him in Jerusalem (Matt. 16:13–28), Peter shows dedication, a regular posture of misunderstanding, and human imperfection.

Peter is among the top tier of disciples, along with James and John, who are recognized as privileged enough to see some of Jesus's most significant miracles. He is present at the healing of Jairus's daughter (Mark 5:37; Luke 8:51) and at the Garden of Gethsemane (Matt. 26:37; Mark 14:33). It is to Peter that Jesus speaks about the disciples' succumbing to sleep: "So, you *men* could not keep watch with Me for one hour?" (Matt. 26:40). It is Peter who impulsively cuts off a man's ear at Jesus's arrest (Matt. 26:51; Mark 14:47; Luke 22:50).

The story of the transfiguration provides particular insight into Peter's personality and commitment. When Jesus reveals himself in glory alongside the representatives of the Law and the Prophets, Moses and Elijah, Peter blunders, volunteering to build shelters for the notable guests (Matt. 17:4; Mark 9:5, Luke 9:32). Here his master seems simply to ignore the comment, perhaps because it is made in good faith or perhaps to highlight how misplaced it is. R. T. France says his offering to build tabernacles "may be no more than a spontaneous and rather inept attempt to rise to the occasion with proper hospitality. Or perhaps he wants to 'institutionalize' the fleeting vision; if so he has misunderstood Jesus' mission, which is not to stay on the holy mountain but to go down to the cross."[8] Peter's confusion about Jesus's earthly undertaking abounds.

Yet Peter's unpretentious and optimistic faith, displayed in the Gospels, was a hallmark of the man. The depth of his naive optimism is an inspiration to believers and makes him a favorite among Christians. In one instance, Jesus has commanded the disciples to proceed without him by boat across the Sea of Galilee. There is a strong wind, which batters the boat far out on the sea. In the night, they see Jesus walking on the water amid the storm.

> And when the disciples saw Him walking on the sea, they were terrified, saying, "It is a ghost!" And they cried out in fear. But immediately Jesus spoke to them, saying, "Take courage, it is I; do not be afraid." Peter said to Him, "Lord, if it is You, command me to come to You on the water." And He said, "Come!" And Peter got out of the boat, and walked on the water and came toward Jesus.

8. France, *Matthew*, 263.

But seeing the wind, he became frightened, and beginning to sink, he cried out, saying, "Lord, save me!" Immediately Jesus stretched out His hand and took hold of him, and said to him, "You of little faith, why did you doubt?" When they got into the boat, the wind stopped. (Matt. 14:26–32)

Many sermons have arisen from Peter's sinking, an illustration of unnecessarily faltering faith during tribulation. Craig Keener points out: "While Jesus is disappointed with Peter's inadequate faith, Peter has acted in greater faith than the other disciples—he is *learning*. Faith . . . grows through various tests as we continue to trust our Lord and he continues to teach us."[9]

An event at Caesarea Philippi displays a seemingly impulsive but faith-filled moment for Peter in his discipleship. Jesus inquires about the people's opinions concerning his identity before asking for the disciples' own opinion, and Peter boldly declares that Jesus is "the Christ, the Son of the living God" (Matt. 16:16; Mark 8:29; Luke 9:20). What makes this comment so brave is that nothing in the immediate context invites such a declaration. Jesus honors Peter with one of the most important distinctions of Peter's legacy: "And Jesus said to him, 'Blessed are you, Simon Barjona, because flesh and blood did not reveal *this* to you, but My Father who is in heaven. I also say to you that you are Peter, and upon this rock I will build My church; and the gates of Hades will not overpower it. I will give you the keys of the kingdom of heaven; and whatever you shall bind on earth shall have been bound in heaven, and whatever you shall loose on earth shall have been loosed in heaven'" (Matt. 16:17–19).

The success is short-lived for Peter in the plot of the Gospels. From Caesarea Philippi, Jesus begins explaining about his inevitable suffering and death at the hands of the religious leaders in Jerusalem, followed by his resurrection. As if Peter is only hearing one half of the forecast, he rebukes Jesus, saying, "God forbid it, Lord! This shall never happen to You" (Matt. 16:22). In another grand declaration to Peter, Jesus turns and says, "Get behind Me, Satan! You are a stumbling block to Me; for you are not setting your mind on God's interests, but man's" (Matt. 16:23; Mark 8:33; Luke 4:8). The contrast between the confident Peter and the terrified Peter is stark. France writes, "If his confession in v. 16 was inspired by God, his subsequent words reveal an interpretation of that confession in terms of natural human considerations."[10]

On the night of Jesus's betrayal, Peter insists that although others may fall away, he will not. Jesus responds to his claim by declaring that before the cock crows, Peter will deny him three times. "Peter said to Him, 'Even if I have to die with You, I will not deny You.' All the disciples said the same thing

9. Keener, *Matthew*, 257.
10. France, *Matthew*, 260.

too" (Matt. 26:35). As the evening advances, Peter's denial occurs on three occasions. Here the bold and impulsive confidence characterizing his former episodes wanes into complete timidity and renunciation. Ellsworth Kalas says of his behavior at this crucial climax, "So well-meaning, so consumed by good intentions, but so terribly, terribly human."[11]

On another occasion, Easter morning, Peter is noted for either impulsiveness or courage, both more subtle. On hearing from the women about the resurrection, he runs to the tomb of Jesus. Upon arriving, he goes into the tomb first and believes (John 20:4–8). The text's effort to note John's hesitation in entering the tomb highlights Peter's own boldness or lays a foundation for his apostolic priority. F. F. Bruce remarks: "With characteristic impetuosity Peter went right into the tomb."[12]

Another occasion chronicles how, with a mixture of anxiety and courage, Peter dialogues with the resurrected Jesus concerning his own loyalty and destiny. When a group of disciples encounters Jesus on the shores of the Sea of Galilee, the master revisits Peter's three-part denial and invites him to answer the question, "Simon, *son* of John, do you love Me?" When the disciple insists on his faithfulness, Jesus instructs him, "Tend My lambs." Jesus provides a final prophetic word that foreshadows the course of Peter's eventual death: "'When you were younger, you used to gird yourself and walk wherever you wished; but when you grow old, you will stretch out your hands and someone else will gird you, and bring you where you do not wish to go.' Now this He said, signifying by what kind of death he would glorify God" (John 21:15, 18–19). The Lord's inquiries of Peter seem to revisit and overturn the disciple's betrayal, taking care of unfinished business. The interrogation was important for the discipleship formation of the one who had been unfaithful. Bruce recognizes how the fisherman called to catch people in spiritual fashion (Mark 1:17; Luke 5:10) now is being called to shepherd people in spiritual fashion: "Now to the evangelist's hook there is added the pastor's crook, so that as had often been said, Peter proceeded to fulfil his double commission 'by hook and by crook.'"[13]

The comments in this passage about Peter growing old and being taken against his will are harder to assess. Most scholars believe that by the time the Gospel of John was written, Peter had been martyred. The words spoken in Galilee could have anticipated this event, and thus the Gospel writer drew them from the conversation with renewed awareness. "You will stretch out

---

11. Kalas, *Thirteen Apostles*, 19.
12. Bruce, *Gospel and Epistles of John*, 385.
13. Bruce, *Gospel and Epistles of John*, 405.

your hands" sounds like crucifixion, which is historically evidenced as Peter's means of death in Rome and is comparable to Jesus's own death. This is the first of many indicators of a journey that ended with martyrdom for the sake of the gospel.

For reasons of which we cannot be certain, Peter needs to compare his own destiny to that of John as the narrative continues. In reference to John, Peter asks Jesus, "What about this man?" As a corrective Jesus responds, "If I want him to remain until I come, what *is that* to you? You follow Me!" (John 21:22). Certainly Jesus mitigates Peter's desire to know John's future by directing Peter to remain faithful even unto death, an important discipleship exhortation.

Palestine Ministry

The development of Peter in the Gospels is so complex that one can separate that period of struggling discipleship from the starkly different level of mature ministry leadership seen in Acts. The New Testament analysis of his ministry takes up here, after the ascension of Jesus.

Ministry in Acts

As the book of Acts advances the message and intent of Jesus into the early church era, Peter is prominent from the start. About 60 percent of Acts focuses on him, and of the Twelve he is the only member whose words are recorded. The blind-faith element of Peter's personality matures after Pentecost, when Peter seems boldly and self-assuredly to minister without fear. The first three chapters of Acts outline a church with Peter at the helm. He is portrayed as instrumental in the need to elect a replacement for Judas to rebuild the group of twelve (Acts 1:15–26). Peter arises among the larger group of believers to offer perspective on the Pentecost tongues and explains the significance of their witness, leading to the conversion of three thousand that day (2:14–41). When Peter and John climb to the temple, Peter's significance is evident. The blind man who sits at the entrance to the temple has an encounter that morning like one from a day in the ministry of Jesus. The formula from Jesus's own ministry is at work as Peter commands the attention of the sick one, provides a declaration by the authority of Jesus, heals the man, views the celebration of one made whole, and hears the amazement of the people (3:1–11).

Peter's first confrontation continues the theme of development into becoming more like Christ, as the same religious leaders who oversaw the execution of the Lord are offended by the preaching of Jesus's resurrection. The Sadducees, priests, and temple guards arrest John and Peter. Evangelizing

without discrimination, Peter preaches the next day to his captors, conclud-
ing, "Whether it is right in the sight of God to give heed to you rather than
to God, you be the judge; for we cannot stop speaking about what we have
seen and heard" (Acts 4:19–20). This dedication speaks to the lifelong mission of the twelve apostles.

The Acts narrative continues to highlight the prominence of the fisherman
from Galilee as Ananias and Sapphira withhold a portion of an offering,
seeming to display selfishness in a misleading performance. Through Peter
the judgment of death falls on them both (Acts 5:1–10). This arouses fear in
the people who have witnessed the perpetuation of Christ's earthly ministry
through the ones worthy of a quest in this book: "And at the hands of the
apostles many signs and wonders were taking place among the people; and
they were all with one accord in Solomon's portico" (5:12).

Peter's sway over both the early church and its spectators cannot be overstated from the book of Acts. The texts extraordinarily report how the Lord
added to the numbers of the faithful by the apostolic mission in Jerusalem
that first year (Acts 2:41; 5:14; 6:1). People bring the sick to access these men,
and in desperation they even lay them on pallets along the street in the hopes
that the mere passing of Peter's shadow over them will provide healing (5:15).
When the apostles are arrested and then freed by an angel in a span of two
verses (5:19–20), an invincibility seems to arise around them. Peter represents
the apostles to the council: "We must obey God rather than men" (5:29). After
an internal debate, followed by flogging the evangelists, the council frees them,
and they "went on their way from the presence of the Council, rejoicing that
they had been considered worthy to suffer shame for *His* name" (5:41). In yet
another verse that typifies the pathos of the apostolic mission, these Christians rejoice in their suffering for the sake of the gospel.

In the last episode of persecution that Peter survives, Herod arrests him
after the people's positive response to James's execution. The night before
Peter is to be brought forth publicly, likely to share the same fate as James,
an angel shines forth and awakens Peter to send him away quickly. Passing
through the gate, he begins to realize the mercy of God in his situation. On
arrival at Mark's house, he relates the miracle and instructs the people to tell
the other disciples of his experience (Acts 12:3–17).

These events of persecution are accompanied by other victorious events.
In Lydda, Peter heals the paralytic Aeneas (Acts 9:32–35). In Joppa, he resurrects the charitable Tabitha (9:36–41). Peter's travels in those early days were
itinerant only insofar as they anchored his prominence and activities around
the church in Jerusalem. By Acts 9, the church is expanding in the areas
"throughout all Judea and Galilee and Samaria" (9:31). Yet this expansion still

focuses on the apostolic ministry to the Jews. The preaching of Pentecost did bring diversity to the followers of Jesus: "Parthians and Medes and Elamites, and residents of Mesopotamia, Judea and Cappadocia, Pontus and Asia, Phrygia and Pamphylia, Egypt and the districts of Libya around Cyrene, and visitors from Rome, both Jews and proselytes, Cretans and Arabs" (2:9–11). Yet the earliest ministry initiatives are not to gentiles. Then the time comes in which Peter emerges as a leader once again in foreseeing gentile conversion to the faith.

Peter at first has theological reservations about the presence of gentiles among the people of God. It takes a vision from the Lord telling him to eat food not permitted for Jews before Peter understands the developing principle of Christian inclusivism. In Joppa, Peter receives a vision from heaven with food set before him and the instruction to take and eat animals unclean according to the law (Lev. 11:1–47). Peter protests, and the voice provides instruction that will soon apply to the gentiles: "What God has cleansed, no *longer* consider unholy" (Acts 10:15). Meanwhile, a God-fearing centurion, Cornelius, has received a vision in which an angel instructs him to send for Peter. When Peter arrives at the house, which contains many, he refers to the law: "You yourselves know how unlawful it is for a man who is a Jew to associate with a foreigner or to visit him; and *yet* God has shown me that I should not call any man unholy or unclean" (10:28). As Peter pieces together the mutual leading of the Spirit between Cornelius and himself, he boldly provides his understanding of the broadening of the gospel: "I most certainly understand now that God is not one to show partiality, but in every nation the man who fears Him and does what is right is welcome to Him. . . . Of Him all the prophets bear witness that through His name everyone who believes in Him receives forgiveness of sins" (10:34–35, 43). The Holy Spirit falls on the house, and its members speak in tongues as an outward sign of their acceptance into the fold. On Peter's return to Jerusalem, some Jewish Christians object to his eating with gentiles, but Peter explains, which leads to the declaration "Well then, God has granted to the Gentiles also the repentance that leads to life" (11:18).

Although Paul became recognized historically as the apostle to the gentiles, Peter played an important role in early Christianity as it broadened from a Jewish foundation to gentile inclusion. The incident of the sheet with unclean food is symbolic of this transition. The Jerusalem Council (Acts 15) displays the prominence of Peter in welcoming the work of the gospel among gentiles. He is promoted in the narratives to the lead voice in the early chapters of Acts, and he is again in the lead at the Jerusalem Council, where, unbeknownst to the reader, Peter offers a swan song of his Acts ministry as the gentile cause is recognized. When Paul and Barnabas arrive in Jerusalem around 49/50, they report to the apostles and elders how some Jewish Christians are insisting on circumcision for salvation in fidelity to the covenant. Peter rises for a final recorded time to speak about how grace is sufficient for salvation, independent of circumcision (15:7–11). James the Just comes behind Peter, supporting the position with Scripture and calling for faithful living according to the law as an expression of the gracious salvation that all experience, whether Jew or gentile. That "the apostles and the elders came together to look into this matter" (15:6) evidences the supreme authority of the council, but the prominence of Peter is unmistakable, though the authority of James as well is recognized in Jerusalem. James continued leading in Jerusalem for at least ten years after the apostles had gone forth in evangelism.

Yet the role of Paul waxes in the book of Acts as Peter's prominence in the narrative wanes. This important role of Peter as agent of transition to the gentiles and to Paul as apostle to the gentiles mushroomed into perhaps the greatest issue of scholarly debate in the life of the early church. The divide between Jew and gentile is the basis for an interpretive lens into the mission of the Twelve: the development of the identity of the church. A short passage in Galatians, in which Paul rebukes Peter for his seeming favoritism toward Jews, exemplifies the conflict.

The year is 53 or 54, a few years after the Jerusalem Council, with its formal apostolic recognition of the gentiles as recipients of the gospel. The episode is treated again in the chapter on Paul, from whose perspective it is recorded. Peter had been reasonably eating with gentiles until the arrival of James and a group of Jews. Paul reports that Peter "*began* to withdraw and hold himself aloof, fearing the party of the circumcision" (Gal. 2:12). Paul describes the social influence on the apostle in a letter in which Paul rebukes Judaizing Christians for maintaining excessive Jewish requirements for gentile converts, mainly circumcision as a sign of the covenant. Paul rebukes Peter for his partiality.

The rebuke should not be viewed as merely the impudence of a junior apostle. The actions of Peter seem to warrant the brotherly correction. Peter had promoted including gentiles in the fold, but the Judaizers held enough sway over him that at least socially, if not theologically, the lead apostle was backtracking spiritually. That Peter held himself "aloof" and "fear[ed] the party of the circumcision" does not sound like the apostle portrayed by Luke in Acts. However, cognitive dissonance under social pressure is not unlikely even for a leader in a religious paradigm shift. It is difficult to go as far as Bart Ehrman, who suggests that this Cephas is not Peter, that the distinction between him and another Cephas among the seventy is blurred among early church writings.[14] Yet in this one instance, Peter surely felt the impact of the confrontation as Paul showed the corrective dimension of the early church.

When the Pauline Epistles reference Peter, it is with recognition of his authority and priority among the Twelve. When Paul describes the presentation of the risen Christ to his followers, he prioritizes Peter while lumping the others into a collective group. For example, "He [Jesus] appeared to Cephas, then to the twelve" (1 Cor. 15:5). In the presentation of baptismal celebrants, whom the Corinthians were comparing in a seeming credibility game, Paul describes their voices: "Each one of you is saying, 'I am of Paul,' and 'I of Apollos,' and 'I of Cephas,' and 'I of Christ'" (1 Cor. 1:12). When Paul describes his own discipleship phase, he mentions Peter as an associate worth claiming: "Then three years later I went up to Jerusalem to become acquainted with Cephas, and stayed with him fifteen days" (Gal. 1:18). Finally, this thirteenth apostle lists Peter among the pillars of the church whose acceptance of Paul was a mark of his own credibility: "Recognizing the grace that had been given to me, James and Cephas and John, who were reputed to be pillars, gave to me and Barnabas the right hand of fellowship, so that we *might go* to the Gentiles and they to the circumcised" (Gal. 2:9). Only Galatians 2 speaks negatively of Peter, referring to his siding with the Judaizers concerning meals. This cumulative appreciation of Peter does not proverbially rob Peter to pay Paul but reinforces the recognition of Peter's leadership and reveals Paul's appreciation for the lead apostle.

In perhaps the most mysterious verse in the biography of the great apostle, the New Testament leads him away after his liberation from prison, and he is heard only once more, at the Jerusalem Council: "He left and went to another place" (Acts 12:17). Where Peter went is a mystery, and why the New Testament does not return to his evangelistic endeavors may never be known. Luke does not describe Peter venturing beyond Caesarea and the house of Cornelius. Hengel recognizes that Peter serves Luke's story as "a unique *bridging function* between the activity of Jesus and Paul's mission to the nations."[15] With Paul emerging during these chapters of Acts, Luke shifts the emphasis to the broader application of the gospel as it moves beyond the Twelve and beyond the Jews. Even Peter's arrest at James's death and his dramatic liberation from prison by the angel lead Sean McDowell to say, "The death of James serves more as a backdrop for the protection of Peter and his departure to another place."[16] His speech in Acts 15:7–11 and the conflict in Galatians 2 are the

---

14. Ehrman, "Cephas and Peter."
15. Hengel, *Saint Peter*, 79–80.
16. McDowell, *Fate of the Apostles*, 188.

last New Testament narrative episodes involving Peter, while the references from Paul about him are only echoes of the years after the resurrection. Bruce speculates that the Jerusalem Council likely interrupted Peter's ministry elsewhere, perhaps Syria or Anatolia, which we explore below.[17]

Ministry in Writing

The impact of Peter on the church continued through the writing of the Gospel of Mark and of two epistles attributed to him. Considering each requires evaluating the provenance of the work and then gleaning its theological contribution to better understanding the apostle.

Gospel of Mark

The Gospel of Mark shows evidence of a Roman milieu, both internally and externally, linking Peter to Mark and both of them to the great city. Internally, the audience seems to be gentile and Roman: Jewish customs are explained and Latin expressions are assumed.[18] The centrality of the centurion's declaring Christ as the Son of God seems to be aimed at a Roman audience (15:39). Simon and Peter are the first and last names of a disciple, providing an *inclusio* for the apostle in the Gospel of Mark.[19]

External to the book of Mark but still within the New Testament, there are clear associations between Peter and Mark. The first association between them comes when Peter is freed from prison to proceed to the house of John Mark in Jerusalem (Acts 12:12). A reference in the first epistle attributed to Peter reveals that both are in Rome: "She who is in Babylon, chosen together with you, sends you greetings, and so *does* my son, Mark" (1 Pet. 5:13). The instruction of Paul to bring Mark to him in an epistle traditionally considered to be from a Roman setting invites a possible presence of Mark in Rome (2 Tim. 4:11). Other traditionally Roman epistles include greetings shared by Paul and Mark (Col. 4:10; Philem. 24).

Externally, the patristic sources unite to strongly support Mark's connection with Peter in the writing of the Gospel. Papias reports that Mark was in the company of Peter when he interpreted and wrote down the apostle's account of what was spoken or performed by the Lord.[20] Irenaeus records:

---

17. Bruce, *Book of Acts*, 289, 291n45.
18. Brooks, *Mark*, 28.
19. Hengel, *Saint Peter*, 103; Mark 1:16; 16:7.
20. Eusebius, *Hist. eccl.* 3.39.15–16. Eusebius also attributes to Papias the claim that John the Presbyter was witness to Mark's reliance on Peter for this work.

"After their departure, Mark, the disciple and interpreter of Peter, did also hand down to us in writing what had been preached by Peter."[21] In this passage he also records that Peter preached in Rome as a further reinforcement. A fragment of Clement of Alexandria's *Hypotyposes* describes how the church in Rome under Peter asked Mark to record the components of the Gospel.[22] Jerome calls Mark the "disciple and interpreter of Peter" in the writing of his Gospel, likely relying on Irenaeus and Eusebius but explicitly employing the use of a metaphorical "Babylon" in 1 Peter 5:13 as his evidence.[23] However, John Chrysostom reports that Mark recorded Peter in Egypt as the basis for the Gospel.[24] These patristic accounts along with the biblical evidence lead us to conclude with Hengel: "The gospel of Mark rests upon solid Petrine tradition."[25] They not only indicate Peter's voice in Mark but also contribute to place him squarely in Rome.

Epistles of Peter

The first epistle attributed to Peter addresses Christians of "Pontus, Galatia, Cappadocia, Asia, and Bithynia" (1 Pet. 1:1). The audience suggests that Peter ministered to the churches in these regions and leads to positing the ministry journeys in Syria and Anatolia discussed below. This language of diaspora is more than just a geographical diffusion. Diaspora represents the notion that God's people are exiled from their true home, pilgrims in a world in which they do not belong,[26] typical of Jews immersed in gentile cultures.

The second epistle attributed to Peter addresses a more general Christian community without geographical indicators. This work is considered perhaps the least genuine of any New Testament book regarding its attributed authorship. Eusebius indicates: "But Peter has left one epistle undisputed. Suppose, also, the second was left by him, for on this there is some doubt."[27] Jerome remarks that many think this second epistle was not written by Peter "on account of its difference from the first in style."[28]

An important feature in the farewell address of 2 Peter informs our quest. The author declares "that the laying aside of my earthly dwelling is imminent,

---

21. Irenaeus, *Haer.* 3.1.1 (*ANF* 1:414).

22. Eusebius, *Hist. eccl.* 6.14.6–7. The story here also suggests that Peter was initially unaware of the writing but responded without hindering or, strangely, without encouraging it.

23. Jerome, *Vir. ill.* 8 (*NPNF*² 3:364); see *Vir. ill.* 1.

24. Chrysostom, *Homilies on Matthew* 1.7 (*NPNF*¹ 10:3–4).

25. Hengel, *Saint Peter*, 103.

26. Perkins, *First and Second Peter, James, and Jude*, 12.

27. Eusebius, *Hist. eccl.* 6.25.8; see *Hist. eccl.* 3.3.3.

28. Jerome, *Vir. ill.* 1 (*NPNF*² 3:361).

as also our Lord Jesus Christ has made clear to me" (2 Pet. 1:14). Here he recognizes impending death in a way that seems to allude to the event on the shore of the Sea of Galilee with Jesus: "When you grow old, you will stretch out your hands and someone else will gird you, and bring you where you do not wish to go" (John 21:18). Richard Bauckham suggests that the Roman church community created a hagiographic motif about the legacy of the apostle, but perhaps also the apostle spoke or wrote these words.[29] McDowell captures the weight of this connection: "Peter has been living in the shadow of the prophecy for decades."[30]

From these writings, a Petrine theology emerges that reveals the apostle. Peter provides elements of a Christology (Mark 14:36; 15:39; 1 Pet. 3:22). He calls for baptism in Jesus's name (Acts 2:38) rather than John the Baptist's "for the forgiveness of sins" (Mark 1:4; Luke 3:3). His epistles to Jews in exile condition the righteous to expect unmerited suffering for Christ's sake (1 Pet. 3:17). An awareness of false prophets and the coming of Christ shape Christian eschatology (2 Pet. 1:16–2:22). There is also a theme in Petrine literature of God's people in exile, including Christians in a hostile society. Perhaps most of all, the naming of Peter as the rock of the church has led to a theology of ecclesiastical primogeniture for the bishop of Rome, the Holy See in the West (Matt. 16:18–19).

Apocryphal Works

Several gnostic works should be mentioned that are pseudepigraphal, or written under Peter's name. It is difficult to know whether the author or the community tried to promote the work as Peter's own or whether the gnostic genre intends to employ Peter as a literary prototype. Regardless, their historical value is minimal.

Found in a tomb in Upper Egypt, the Gospel of Peter is written from the perspective of the apostle. While it parallels the basic Gospel narrative, it includes interesting additions and replacements, such as a description of the crucifixion event from a docetic perspective, maintaining that Jesus did not personally suffer on the cross. Eusebius is among those who rejected this document: "For we, brethren, accept Peter and the other apostles as *we would* Christ, but, as experienced men, we repudiate what is falsely written under their name, knowing that we have not had any such things delivered to us."[31] Its pseudepigraphal quality means that no historical insight can be gained about the apostle.

29. Bauckham, "Martyrdom of Peter," 551–53.
30. McDowell, *Fate of the Apostles*, 67.
31. Eusebius, *Hist. eccl.* 6.12.

The Apocalyse of Peter is a vision of judgment that came to the twelve apostles.[32] Dennis Buchholz comments that the work contains trajectories toward orthodoxy, but the emphasis is on a Jesus experienced esoterically rather than a Jesus whose ministry is fulfilled.[33] Like all of the Apocalypses of the apostles, this one provides almost no insight into Peter other than reinforcing his perceived leadership role among the apostles. It does, however, contain perhaps the oldest existing reference to Peter's death in Rome.

From the early second century, the Preaching of Peter is known only through citations. In the Pseudo-Clementine Homilies and Recognitions, Clement meets Peter in the Holy Land, joining him out of curiosity about the faith as the apostle encounters Simon Magus in various towns while preaching and teaching. The Nag Hammadi collection contains the Acts of Peter and the Twelve Apostles, the Letter of Peter to Philip, and another Act of Peter, but their contribution to the historical Peter is no more valuable.

In the early church, writers such as Jerome remarked that the named Acts, Gospel, Preaching, Revelation, and Judgment written under Peter's name should be "rejected as apocryphal."[34] Eusebius also names them as writings not handed down among the catholic writings and not used as testimony by ancient church writers.[35] Tertullian refers to Paul as "the apostle of the heretics," but Lapham remarks, "It might be nearer the truth, in view of Peter's midway position between the legalism of James and the liberalism of Paul, to give to Peter this somewhat dubious title."[36] Likewise, works such as the Gospel of Mary, the Epistle of Peter to James, the Epistle of Clement to James, the Epistle of Peter to Philip, and the Apocryphon of James profile Peter as receiving revelation and engaging Jesus and other apostles. These works are gnostic, docetic, and encratic in nature, providing limited insight into the historical figure.

Syria and Anatolia Ministry

From Peter's departure to an unknown location in Acts 12 through the Jerusalem Council of Acts 15, the apostle ministered on a timeline that cannot be reconstructed with certainty. Since Peter is not mentioned by Paul in his Epistle to the Romans (57 CE), scholars believe Peter had not yet arrived in the

32. Apocalypse of Peter (James, 505–21).
33. Buchholz, *Your Eyes Will Be Opened*, 404–8.
34. Jerome, *Vir. ill.* 1 (NPNF² 3:361).
35. Eusebius, *Hist. eccl.* 3.3.2.
36. Tertullian, *Against Marcion* 3.5.4 (ANF 3:324); Lapham, *Introduction to the New Testament Apocrypha*, 183.

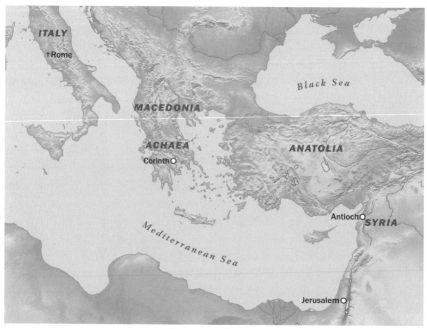

Journey of Peter

capital when the epistle was written. This means that Peter was somewhere between Jerusalem and Rome from 50 to 63. While the New Testament has Peter traveling only around Palestine and the eastern coast of the Mediterranean, the distance from Jerusalem to Antioch, Syria (three hundred miles), makes it not unreasonable that Peter was in Antioch, especially with an easy route to the metropolis of the whole eastern part of the empire.

The most obvious evidence we have of Peter's sojourn in Antioch is the account of Paul's encounter and confrontation with him in the Letter to the Galatians (2:11–14). This is usually considered to be one event in a longer stay there by Peter. Despite this conflict, Peter is frequently viewed as a unifying arbiter between a conservative Jewish element and a pro-gentile Pauline element.[37]

In one part of his *Ecclesiastical History*, Eusebius reports that Ignatius became the second bishop of Antioch, after Evodius.[38] In another part of the same work, he notes that Ignatius was celebrated as the second episcopal officeholder and the successor of Peter there.[39] Reconciling these two

37. Meier, in R. Brown and Meier, *Antioch and Rome*, 36–44.
38. Eusebius, *Hist. eccl.* 3.22.1.
39. Eusebius, *Hist. eccl.* 3.36.2.

entries means that Evodius was the first bishop, Ignatius was the second bishop, and both were in the shadow of Peter in Antioch. Yet Bauckham suggests that the church father is drawing from the name of Peter for historical credibility.[40]

Several other church fathers make undetailed claims about Peter's influence in Antioch. Origen says that Ignatius was the second bishop after Peter.[41] Jerome says that Antioch was Peter's first see.[42] Chrysostom remarks: "This city [Antioch] was of much account to God. . . . At all events the master of the whole world, Peter . . . He bade tarry here for a long period."[43] As in the case of Eusebius, it is easy to sense that these patristic writers intend to depict influence rather than the office. Additional connections have been made from Petrine apocalyptic writings that found popularity in Antioch, such as the Ascension of Isaiah, perhaps the first work to allude to his martyrdom.[44] These voices make a case for the influential ministry and leadership of Peter at Antioch, seemingly years in length.

Peter's presence in any city would have immediately fixed a sense of leadership to the church there. Whether he was a stabilizing force for Jewish Christians against Judaizers or against gentile progressivism, his work was characterized by continuity with the mission of the Messiah and the other apostles. Since his life was constituted by church ministry, he was most likely serving in Syria or Anatolia between his release from Jerusalem prison in 49 and his ministry and martyrdom in Rome in the mid-60s.

While apocryphal works do not provide episodes of ministry for Peter in Asia Minor, patristic writers allude to his ministry there. Hippolytus, Eusebius, and Jerome claim that Peter preached in the dispersion of Jews in Pontus, Galatia, Cappadocia, Asia, and Bithynia.[45] These cities of Anatolia are named in the First Epistle of Peter (1 Pet. 1:1). The Pseudo-Clementine Homilies evidences his efforts to move down to Antioch from northern Turkey.[46] These homilies, attributed to Clement of Rome, are a series of twenty theological discourses supposedly by Peter. Clement's first encounter with Peter introduces the apostle as "being the greatest in the wisdom of God."[47] The incident is depicted as occurring at Caesarea Stratonis, and Peter invites Clement to join

40. Bauckham, "Martyrdom of Peter," 564.
41. Origen, *Homilies on Luke* 6 (Lienhard, 94:24).
42. Jerome, *Commentary on Galatians* 1 (Cain, 121:109).
43. John Chrysostom, *Homily on St. Ignatius* 4 (*NPNF*[1] 9:138).
44. Daniélou and Marrou, *Christian Centuries*, 50.
45. Hippolytus, *Twelve* 1 (*ANF* 5:254); Eusebius, *Hist. eccl.* 3.1.2; Jerome, *Vir. ill.* 1 (*NPNF*[2] 3:361).
46. Clementine Homilies 12.1; 20.23 (*ANF* 8:292, 346).
47. Clementine Homilies 1.15 (*ANF* 8:227).

their travels "as far as Rome itself."[48] In the chapters and homilies that follow, Peter teaches Clement on the matters of faith as they journey together along the Syrian coast of Palestine. The text provides conversations between the two, making a dialogical tool for teaching along the lines of a catholic faith. The cities of their activity included Tyre, Sidon, Berytos (modern Beirut), Byblos, and Tripolis, all in the Phoenicia area of Palestine, with Laodicea and Antioch of Syria named as journey references in the closing sentence of the homilies. Eventually the dialogue shifts from Peter's instructing Clement to a debate between Peter and Simon Magus. Here again, there is a duel of the faith between two theological enemies. Simon eventually "gnashed his teeth for rage, and went away in silence."[49] Theologically, the homilies present spirituality as an ethical and rational lifestyle.

Scholars are unanimous in the opinion that the work is not authentic to the first-century Clement, yet we are left with the reasonable likelihood that Peter ministered in these churches that received his epistle, having encounters and experiences no longer recorded for the church. At the most his sojourn there lasted from 49 to 63, with the possibility of travel to Corinth and Rome before his final tenure in the capital, which ended in his death.

Corinth Ministry

The possibility of a sojourn by Peter in Corinth can be seen in Paul's First Epistle to the Corinthians, when he criticizes them for divisions surrounding the authority of their baptisms: "One of you is saying, 'I am of Paul,' and 'I of Apollos,' and 'I of Cephas,' and 'I of Christ'" (1 Cor. 1:12; see 3:22). While travelers to Judea may have become baptized believers before returning to Corinth, it is less likely that such a contingency based solely on pilgrimage or relocation led to division in the church. It is more probable that Peter ministered in Corinth, either for a time or on an itinerant journey similar to Paul's.

Dionysius of Corinth (fl. 170), in his letter to Roman Christians, remarks, "You have mingled the flourishing seed that had been planted by Peter and Paul at Rome and Corinth," tying together the common reception of their ministries.[50] The comment suggests that Corinthian Christians hosted Peter's ministry as they did Paul's. However, Dionysius might be describing the influence of both apostles without claiming that Peter dwelt in Corinth. John Meier demonstrates the close relationship between Corinth and Rome, evidenced

---

48. Clementine Homilies 1.15–16 (ANF 8:227).
49. Clementine Homilies 19.25 (ANF 8:338).
50. Eusebius, Hist. eccl. 2.25.8.

by Clement of Rome's letter, a shared image of dual founding by the two apostles, and Paul's attention to both cities through his epistles.[51] Ignatius of Antioch uses both Peter and Paul as models for martyrdom, just as Irenaeus in his ties to Rome describes Peter and Paul as church founders there.[52] We cannot be certain whether either of these church fathers is explicitly claiming Corinthian first- or secondhand knowledge of Peter. We are left with no clear indication that the apostle visited this important city.

Britain and Gaul Ministry

In 1961 George Jowett released *The Drama of the Lost Disciples*, which claims that Joseph of Arimathea traveled to Britain, as did Aristobulus, the father-in-law of Peter. Peter's association with these figures accompanies the hypothesis that he himself went to Britain and to Gaul, which Jowett suggests to explain why Paul omits any mention of Peter in his Letter to the Romans. The evidence of Jowett includes the dedication of a church to Peter by King Lucius in Winchester in 156.[53] Yet the claims have little historical support, especially from patristic sources, and they serve as an example of the numerous exaggerated claims about the apostles.

Rome Ministry

The quest to follow Peter into his ministry beyond the New Testament requires entering into the apocryphal works in search of his next phase of ministry. Peter's itinerant ministry north of Palestine typified the Jewish church's assimilation of gentiles, and there he first encountered Simon Magus. Peter's last trip to Rome for a final theater of ministry was inspired by the desire to confront and even silence the ministry of a man of magic harassing the church. Simon Magus plays the literary role of epic antagonist in the life of Peter as presented in apocryphal works. His character "is here virtually a personification of evil, and the contests between him and Peter are in effect a classical battle between God and sin," J. K. Elliott writes.[54]

Jerome says that Peter came to Rome in the second year of Claudius, 43, to overthrow Simon Magus.[55] If this date is accurate, then Peter visited the

---

51. R. Brown, in R. Brown and Meier, *Antioch and Rome*, 166n354.
52. Ignatius, *Letter to the Romans* 4.3; Irenaeus, *Haer.* 3.1–2.
53. Jowett, *Drama of the Lost Disciples*, 174–75.
54. Elliott, 392.
55. Jerome, *Vir. ill.* 1 (NPNF² 3:361).

capital at least twice, potentially engaging Simon there twice, assuming accounts of his death in the mid-60s under Nero are accurate. Eusebius confirms that Peter's purpose in going to the great city was to grapple with the notorious magician.[56]

The most informative extrabiblical legacy of Peter's ministry and geographical experiences comes from a collection of works grouped into the Acts of Peter, written under his name. The Acts of Peter is often split into subwritings under four titles. The Vercelli Acts, so named for the manuscript, centers on Peter's work in Rome, as Paul's preparation to travel to Spain (1–4) leaves a vacuum in the Roman church that Simon Magus seeks to fill. Peter leaves Caesarea for Rome to confront the magician who is infiltrating Paul's disciples and threatening his ministry legacy (5–29). Second, the Martyrdom of Peter centers on his arrest, vision, trial, and crucifixion and seems to have been an original, separate work. Third, a Coptic text often titled Peter's Daughter describes how his own daughter suffers in a state of paralysis as a result of the temptation her beauty caused a rich man named Ptolemy. Another Latin text, often titled The Gardener's Daughter, is also probably an independent work, like the former two, in which Peter offers a prayer for the daughter of a peasant to receive what is spiritually best for her soul before she falls dead. Her father does not understand the blessing, and she is raised by Peter only to be seduced by a man who claims to be a believer. This work is one of the earliest of the Acts, and Eusebius refers to it as doubtfully authentic.[57]

In the book of Acts, as background, Simon Magus believes Philip's preaching and is baptized (8:13), then he envies the power of the disciples (8:18–19) but later repents of his envy (8:24). Eusebius interprets this history, insisting that Simon "artfully assumed and even pretended faith in Christ so far as to be baptized," calling Simon "the lead in all heresy," as he went to Rome and gained notoriety.[58] This effort parallels that of the prebaptized Simon in Acts, where he uses sorcery to astonish Samaritans (8:9–11).

Scholars estimate that thirty thousand or more Jews were living in Rome when Peter and Simon opposed each other there, offering a rationale for Peter to continue a ministry to the Jews among this significant population.[59] The immediate causes for the founding of the church in Rome remain a mystery.

---

56. Eusebius, *Hist. eccl.* 2.13–15.
57. Eusebius, *Hist. eccl.* 3.3.2.
58. Eusebius, *Hist. eccl.* 2.1.11; 2.13.5.
59. Ruffin, *The Twelve*, 52. Schnabel (*Early Christian Mission*, 1:4) estimates 40,000 Christians in the Roman Empire around the year 66, and about 320,000 around the year 100, at the death of the last apostle.

On one hand, patristic figures speak of the influence of Peter and Paul in the church there and even use terms associated with its beginnings. Irenaeus claims that "Peter and Paul were preaching at Rome, and laying the foundations of the Church."[60] Likewise, Gaius the Roman presbyter (ca. 199–217) says Peter and Paul laid the foundations of the church at Rome.[61] Dionysius reports that they planted the seed of the church in both Rome and Corinth.[62] Yet it is not necessary to assume that their foundational contribution meant that their ministry was the evangelistic basis for the city's first converts. Michael Goulder recognizes that the mobility of merchants or soldiers who were Christians could have been responsible, and their efforts could have been followed by Peter's extensive ministry to the Jews there.[63]

Several biblical and extrabiblical references have led scholars across all ages to be comfortable in affirming a Roman ministry for Peter. As evidenced above, the Roman Gospel of Mark is internally compatible with Peter's Epistles. The salutation of the First Epistle of Peter supports Peter being in Rome: "She who is in Babylon, chosen together with you, sends you greetings, and so *does* my son, Mark" (1 Pet. 5:13). The metaphorical use of "Babylon" to identify Rome is commonly accepted, based on the Jewish understanding of Babylon as a city of foreign oppressors ruling God's people.[64] Such a metaphor sheds a negative light on Roman rule, which would not be surprising from a Jewish perspective, given Israel's prior exile in Babylon. Eusebius and Jerome both recognize this metaphor as naming the letter's provenance as Rome.[65] In his *Letter to the Romans*, Ignatius tells the church there, "I am not enjoining you as Peter and Paul did," implying the city's familiarity with the two apostles. Dionysius of Corinth, in his letter to Roman Christians, remarks how "Peter and Paul sowed among Romans and Corinthians."[66] This aggregate of evidence is a significant example of early church voices agreeing on a historical tradition, in this case Peter in Rome.

The most important biography of Peter is found in ministry escapades described in the Acts of Peter. The lengthy narrative about Peter's sojourn in Rome contained in these three apocryphal works warrants a section of its own. While much of the contents cannot be viewed as authentic, the provocative

---

60. Irenaeus, *Haer.* 3.1.1 (*ANF* 1:414). See *Haer.* 3.2.
61. Eusebius, *Hist. eccl.* 2.25.6–7.
62. Eusebius, *Hist. eccl.* 2.25.8.
63. Goulder, "Did Peter Ever Go to Rome?," 392. Noteworthy for Goulder is that these facts led to the later myth of Peter's Roman tenure, not its historical proof.
64. For an assessment of first-century literature evidencing Rome as metaphorical Babylon, see Bauckham, "Martyrdom of Peter," 542–43.
65. Eusebius, *Hist. eccl.* 3.39.15; Jerome, *Vir. ill.* 8 (*NPNF*[2] 3:364).
66. Eusebius, *Hist. eccl.* 2.25.8.

events are important both for the quest and for the image of Peter. The contents of the sources are provided here for interest, with a historical assessment to follow.

In the manuscript tradition titled Peter's Daughter is a story of the complicated healing of Peter's daughter, named Petronilla, who was born after Christ and crippled in her youth.[67] In one of the most bizarre apostolic legends, the story describes Peter healing and then unhealing his daughter. The people inquire why he heals others but neglects his own daughter. Peter explains that when she was younger, a rich man named Ptolemy demanded her hand in marriage and sent for her against the will of her and her parents. As an act of mercy, God protected her from defilement by paralyzing her. Yet to demonstrate the divine power to heal, Peter looks at his daughter and commands her to rise up, and she rises up and walks to him. The crowd rejoices, and he points out the power of God to them. Then he commands his daughter, "Return to your place, sit down there and be helpless again, for it is good for me and you." She obeys and "became as before."[68] The crowd grieves as they beg again for her healing. Meghan Henning describes this story as an ancient rhetorical *chreia*, or "necessity," in which an action or saying justifies some reality.[69] In this case, God has illustrated how his power to heal her is less important than her state of celibacy and preventing the temptation she would cause. The result is that Peter's daughter is an object for spiritual explanation to the recipients of his preaching ministry. Additionally, she also functions as a coevangelist to the power of the gospel, which strengthens the Petrine literary tradition of apostolic authority.[70]

Another story relates Christ providing a vision to Peter in which Simon Magus is perverting the church in Rome by satanic power. The story provides background to the situation that includes Paul's departure for Spain, reinforcement of a legend of the other apostle. From a ship in Caesarea, Peter embarks on a journey to Rome, where he is welcomed by a whole multitude who come out to see the apostle. One victim of Simon's influence is a senator named Marcellus, who was a patron of the poor in Christ's name before yielding his wealth to Caesar under pressure. The senator provided a statue to Simon as "the young god." Peter marches to the senator's house, where Simon Magus has been staying, and he is confronted by a young servant ordered to declare that his master is not home should Peter arrive and inquire. The apostle demonstrates his miraculous power when he unties a nearby dog, ordering it to

67. Acts of Peter 1 (Elliott, 399).
68. Acts of Peter: Peter's Daughter (Elliott, 397–98).
69. Henning, "*Chreia* Elaboration," 151–55.
70. Henning, "*Chreia* Elaboration," 158, 167–68.

go inside and declare to Simon that Peter has come to Rome to overturn his wicked destruction of souls.

Marcellus comes forth and immediately repents. In an interesting lesson in reputation, the senator relates how Simon claimed Peter was an unbeliever because of the disciple's lack of faith on the water (Matt. 14:24–31). Peter's humiliation is now being abused by his enemy. Exorcising the demon from the young servant, Peter watches as the youth goes to the statue of Simon and smashes it in defiant rejection of the false prophet. The repentant Marcellus is instructed to prove his faith by taking water and sprinkling it on the statue, whereupon it is made whole again. Meanwhile, the dog is at work inside the house, debating Simon. The magician keeps repeating the order to tell Peter that he is not at home. The dog rhetorically insults him and curses him to be brought to God's justice. Returning to Peter, the story then describes the dog prophesying that the apostle will have a hard fight against this spiritual enemy, Simon, and then the dog falls at his feet and dies. As the crowd cries for another miracle, Peter takes a smoked fish from a window and drops it into a pool, where it swims actively for hours as the people watch it.

Continuing to provide miracles at the porch of the house from which Simon Magus is not emerging, Peter sends in a nursing mother with her seven-month-old. Taking on a man's voice, the infant rebukes Simon and commands him to be silenced in Jesus's name and to leave Rome immediately. The magician is silenced and leaves until the next Sabbath. The people praise the Lord for showing them these things, reminiscent of Gospel passages in which Jesus has the same effect on the crowds. That night Jesus appears to Peter in a vision, foretelling a contest of faith that will lead the belief of the people away from Simon and toward Jesus.

After much teaching, prayer, fasting, and additional healings of blind women, the day of the contest arrives. Through a series of threats, bets, and resurrections, Peter seems to win the contest, and the faith of the witnesses increases. The contestants seem to allow each other to depart. There is a parallel description of this battle in the Pseudo-Clementine literature.

Several days later, the popular attention shown Peter frustrates Simon, who pledges that he will ascend to God the next day. On a prior occasion, Simon had apparently impressed the crowd with flight. After the crowds gather, he is miraculously lifted to fly over the buildings of Rome. Peter prays to God that Simon will fall and be crippled without dying so that the people might believe. Simon falls, breaking his leg in the predicted three places, and is found and carried to Ariccia, where he dies.

The final episode of Peter's ministry in Rome develops as Xanthippe, the wife of Albinus, a friend of the emperor, refuses to sleep with her husband as an act of spirituality. The preaching of Peter on celibacy in marriage, in encratic fashion, has frustrated unbelieving husbands. When Agrippa the prefect hears the appeal of Albinus, he confesses to be in the same situation as a result of Peter's preaching. Xanthippe and others plead with Peter to leave Rome. He sets out in disguise, setting up one of the most legendary events among the stories of the apostles. "When he went out of the gate he saw the Lord come into Rome. And when he saw him he said, 'Lord, where are you going?' And the Lord said to him, 'I go to Rome to be crucified.' And Peter said to him, 'Lord, are you being crucified again?' and Peter came to himself. . . . Then he returned to Rome, rejoicing and praising the Lord because he had said, 'I am being crucified.' This was to happen to Peter."[71]

The scene is epic. The Latin words between Peter and Jesus are memorable: *Quo vadis, Domine? Venio Roman iterum crucifigi.* Now Peter is confronted with the compelling choice to obey the Lord and suffer persecution unto death. Precedent for escaping is provided by his earlier rescue from prison in Jerusalem (Acts 12:4–11). On his return, Peter is arrested. When the people appeal to Agrippa, Peter insists that they not be angry with him since this is the will of the Lord. "Why do I delay and not go to the cross?" he declares to them.[72] After a career of effective ministry, the path that Peter must follow from prison is a different one this time.

As Peter confronts his fate, a beautiful discourse comes from him in the form of a prayer to God and direct exhortation to the people standing nearby. After saying, "Of you, executioners, I ask to crucify me with head downwards, and not otherwise. And the reason I shall explain to those who listen,"[73] he then clarifies the mystery of creation and of Christ coming from heaven to redeem the first man, whose image is borne by Peter. The crossbeam is the nature of man; the vertical beam is the repentance of man. In this symbolic act, the apostle displays the comprehensive biblical message of the fall and redemption. The work of Adam to invert the natural order of life and obedience has now itself been inverted, as Christ sets life and obedience right-side up. Noteworthy is the popular phrase "I am not worthy to be crucified like my Lord," which does not occur in the Acts of Peter but rather in the Acts of Peter and Paul, thus showing likely reliance on this work.[74]

The final words attributed to Peter from the cross can be inspirational even though they come from an apocryphal work. After quoting a form of 1 Corinthians 2:9, "Things which eye has not seen and ear has not heard,

---

71. Acts of Peter 35 (Elliott, 424).
72. Acts of Peter 36 (Elliott, 424).
73. Acts of Peter 37 (Elliott, 425).
74. Acts of Peter and Paul (*ANF* 8:484).

and *which* have not entered into the heart of man," he prays, the crowd cries "Amen," and Peter surrenders his spirit to the Lord.

The crucifixion episode is worth considering further to segue into an evaluation of Peter's ministry and the apostle's image. Nero's persecution is traditionally associated with Peter's martyrdom. Early second-century Roman historian Tacitus records the persecution of Christians by the emperor: "First Nero had self-acknowledged Christians arrested. Then, on their information, large numbers of others were condemned. . . . Their deaths were made farcical. Dressed in wild animals' skins, they were torn to pieces by dogs, or crucified, or made into torches to be ignited after dark as substitutes for daylight."[75] Yet in the Martyrdom of Peter, Nero is explicitly not involved in Peter's death and is unaware of it until afterward. If scholars want to use the Acts of Peter as a legitimate source for establishing the martyrdom of Peter in Rome, they must address this evidence. Perhaps the emperor should be acquitted of a connection with Peter's crucifixion as a deliberate act associated with Tacitus's claim that he treated Christians as scapegoats after a destructive fire in the city.

Concerning Peter's upside-down crucifixion, Jonathan Smith recognizes that a gnostic approach best explains the theology articulated here.[76] His crucifixion is a symbolic inversion of the cosmic order, creating opportunity for the fall of humanity to be undone through salvation. Thus salvation comes through the gnostic transcendence of human life. "Man is no longer defined by the degree to which he harmonizes himself and his society to the cosmic patterns of order; but rather by the degree to which he can escape the patterns," a typical gnostic liberation element.[77]

Early church fathers did not miss the opportunity to anchor Peter's martyrdom to Vatican Hill. Eusebius writes of these burial sites, called trophies: "A certain ecclesiastical writer, Caius by name, . . . gave the following statement respecting the places where the earthly tabernacles of the aforesaid apostles [Peter and Paul] are laid: 'I can sow the trophies of the apostles. For if you will go to the Vatican, or to the Ostian road, you will find the trophies of those who have laid the foundation of the church.'"[78]

Jerome states that Peter is buried at Rome in the Vatican "near the triumphal way."[79] Peter Lampe believes that since Christians at the time of Constantine and Gaius referenced memorials at the Vatican, "the identity of the

---

75. Tacitus, *Annals of Imperial Rome*, 365.
76. Smith, "Birth Upside Down," 287.
77. Smith, "Birth Upside Down," 296.
78. Eusebius, *Hist. eccl.* 2.25.5–8.
79. Jerome, *Vir. ill.* 1 (NPNF[2] 3:361).

two monuments is as good as certain."[80] Markus Bockmuehl reinforces this position: "There simply are *no competing localities* for Peter's tomb, during this period or indeed after, East or West, orthodox or heretical, Jewish, pagan or Christian."[81]

So ended the life of the greatest of the twelve disciples and the chief of the apostles. The reverberations of his martyrdom were immediate, as Peter supposedly appeared in a vision to Marcellus after the senator had anointed and buried the apostle's body. Peter reminds Marcellus of Jesus's words about expecting the dead to bury their own dead (Matt. 8:22; Luke 9:60) and scolds him for the waste of expenditure on the dead. With other believers, Marcellus finds his faith strengthened until the return of Paul from Spain. Meanwhile, Nero is angry with Agrippa for the execution "without his knowledge,"[82] as the emperor had hoped to extend his punishment more cruelly in vindication for the evangelism of some of his servants. One night Nero awakens to a person striking him and ordering him to punish Christians no longer. Frightened by the vision, the emperor persecutes them no more, the text claims.

Image of Peter

No figure among the apostles stands equally for his leadership and for his humanity as the apostle Peter. Hundreds of millions of Roman Catholics revere him. At the turn of the fifth century, Jerome commented how Peter was "venerated by the whole world."[83] His legacy centers on a tradition of church oversight, with its see in Rome. His unassuming carelessness in the Gospels inspires imperfect Christians to believe that hope is available through discipleship. Peter's character is featured in the 1959 film *The Big Fisherman*, by Lloyd C. Douglas, following his maturation from a fisherman to his reliance on Christ. His authority over Simon Magus in apocalyptic literature is as a hero against magic and heresy, a champion of spiritual warfare. Hengel remarks that the prominence of Peter "cannot be explained simply as the typical portrayal of a disciple, with his strengths and weaknesses, which still survives as a literary topos for the apostolic age, and which is intended to depict an authoritative ideal."[84]

---

80. Lampe, *From Paul to Valentinus*, 104.
81. Bockmuehl, "Peter's Death in Rome?," 22.
82. Martyrdom of Peter 12 (Elliott, 426).
83. Jerome, *Vir. ill.* 1 (NPNF² 3:361).
84. Hengel, *Saint Peter*, 29.

Unlike other apostles, we know of no established communities under Peter. While an untold number of churches bear his name, his ministry in Jerusalem, Antioch, Corinth, and Rome did not result in any one region or church community claiming a legacy of his presence. His legacy is reserved for the Roman Catholic see, a figurehead adopted to represent the apostolic tradition and the primacy of the leadership of the entire church.

Symbolism and Image Construction

The historical episodes associated with Peter connect to the symbols from early Christianity that represent him, including keys, a boat, a fish, a rooster, and an upside-down cross. Additional symbols include a pallium, representing the papal office, and an elderly man holding a scroll, representing his influence on the writing or perhaps the promotion of Scripture. The episode at Caesarea Philippi in which Peter declares Christ to be the Son of God (Matt. 16:17–19) led to the most powerful symbol and source of controversy for the image of Peter, that of the first and primary bishop of Rome, which became the office of pope. In the Roman Catholic interpretation of this passage, it is the basis for a long line of apostolic inheritance and authority of the church on earth. The controversy over the office and Peter's role in Western Christianity is clear: "It is no secret that Protestants and Catholics are more bitterly divided over Peter than any other apostle."[85]

Peter's sojourn in Rome and the patristic testimony to his foundational contribution to the church there certainly support the historicity of his leadership in the Roman church. The Epistle of Clement to James describes how a dying Peter seized Clement's hand before the assembly of the church: "I lay hands upon this Clement as your bishop; and to him I entrust my chair of discourse,"[86] laying a foundation for apostolic succession. After early ecumenical councils recognized the Roman see as a source of authority in ecclesiastical and theological decisions, a notion of ecclesiological primogeniture developed. In the position of bishop of Rome, Innocent (r. 401–417) remarked, "All must preserve that which Peter the prince of the apostles delivered to the church at Rome and which it has watched over until now, and nothing may be added or introduced that lacks this authority or that derives its pattern from somewhere else."[87] The result was the first link in a chain of orthodox succession in Rome through the service of the bishop of Rome. In theological opposition, Timothy Ware remarks: "The Pope viewed infallibility as his own prerogative;

---

85. Criswell, *Apostles after Jesus*, 11.
86. Epistle of Clement to James 2 (*ANF* 8:218).
87. Innocent, *Epistle* 25, in Nichols, *That All May Be One*, 113.

the Greeks held that in matters of the faith the final decision rested not with the Pope alone."[88] The theory perpetuated in the West, however, is that the office held a *depositum fidei* (deposit of faith). A result is the use of keys to represent the one named Peter.

The keys function today as a symbol of papal authority. There are designated spots in Western churches in which the pontiff has declared his mark—the crossed keys representing loosing and binding, the cords showing the uniting of these two powers, and the papal miter representing the supreme authority of pastor, teacher, and priest on earth. Sometimes Peter is dressed with a bishop's robe and a papal crown.[89] The term "the Rock" and images of a rock or a church on a rock perpetuate the idea of Peter as the authority of the church.

Peter's betrayal of Jesus on the night of the trial led to the symbol of a rooster. The dominant male chicken is noted for its vigilance and announcement of the morning dawn. Without providing a source, Tom Bissell describes one conception of the lingering regret experienced by Peter: "One early Christian fabulist had Peter waking up every morning only to burst into tears at the sound of a crowing cock. No wonder, when the gospel he supposedly dictated portrays him as being so inept."[90]

Like other disciples, Peter was a fisherman. As is the case for the other fishermen, it is not rare to find images of Peter in possession of fish. For Galileans who found a career in the catching and selling of fish, the simple animals that teemed in the Sea of Galilee were a source of livelihood. When Jesus declared, "Follow Me, and I will make you fishers of men" (Matt. 4:19; see Mark 1:17), it was not merely a metaphor for these fishermen. It was a powerful and meaningful calling that would prove to be a spiritual artisan's trade through evangelism. The phrase "fishers of men" lent itself to early Christian iconography connected to pictures of fish, and apostles related to the trade have fish in their representations.

The humanity of Peter is one of the most inspiring elements of his image. For readers of the Gospels, the figure of Peter—more than any other disciple—provides a hope for imperfect humanity. Kalas says, "We continue in Peter's style. We are always trying to reroute the way of the cross into a path of comfort, of superficial achievement, of frothy popularity."[91] This element of Peter later offered inspiration to the apostolic mission in the New Testament, as he moves from struggling in the Gospels to capable leadership in Acts.

88. Ware, *Orthodox Church*, 49.
89. Taylor, *How to Read a Church*, 107.
90. Bissell, *Apostle*, 119.
91. Kalas, *Thirteen Apostles*, 18.

Richard Taylor describes Peter's representation in art and monuments: "The depiction of Peter has been consistent down the ages: a square face and curly round or square beard, with either short curly hair or bald/tonsured."[92] He is usually austere and strong, with a sense of authority. Yet his superhuman aura is balanced by a portrayal in the Gospels as perpetually imperfect. He is bold and careless, hotheaded and impulsive. Kalas writes: "We probably like him better as a historical figure than we would as a contemporary coworker."[93] These human expressions are part of the image of the apostle Peter. In the end, we remember him both for his unguarded personality and for his courageous contribution to the seminal efforts of the early church.

The story of Peter's encounter with Jesus before his martyrdom is among the best-known stories from early Christianity and is likely the most familiar of all of the stories related to the martyrdom of the apostles. The classic novel and film by Henryk Sienkiewicz (d. 1916), *Quo Vadis*, has popularized both the encounter and depictions of the persecution of Christians in Rome in the mid-first century. Peter's escaping from Rome only to encounter Jesus provides the archetypal question, *Quo vadis, Domine?* "Where are you going, Lord?" The novel declares Jesus's answer along the Appian Way, "If you desert my people, I am going to Rome to be crucified a second time."[94] This undying tradition of Jesus communicating that the time of Peter's sacrificial death was upon him found popular reinforcement. Regarding the authenticity of the story, J. B. Lightfoot, in his *Ordination Addresses and Counsel to Clergy*, defends its veracity: "Why should we not believe it true? . . . Because it is so subtly true to character and because it is so eminently profound in its significance, we are led to assign to this tradition a weight which the external testimony in its favor would hardly warrant."[95] It is almost alarming that Christians will accept the historicity of this event while not recognizing its source or while inconsistently rejecting the other contents of the source. Together the Acts of Peter and the Acts of Peter and Paul contain episodes of Simon Magus flying, trivial miracles of power, and encratic material related to abstinence.

Meanwhile, Peter's prior imprisonment under Herod Agrippa in Jerusalem is a drama of divine power and an allegory of freedom from sin. Charles Wesley captures this sentiment in his great hymn "And Can It Be?"

> Long my imprisoned spirit lay
> Fast bound in sin and nature's night.

---

92. Taylor, *How to Read a Church*, 106.
93. Kalas, *Thirteen Apostles*, 22.
94. Sienkiewicz, *Quo Vadis*, 476.
95. Lightfoot, *Ordination Addresses*, 145.

Thine eye diffused a quick'ning ray:
I woke—the dungeon flamed with light!
My chains fell off, my heart was free,
I rose, went forth, and followed Thee.

Tomb and Patronage

Perhaps the greatest physical testimony to the legacy of Peter is the very presence of St. Peter's Basilica in Vatican City, just across the Tiber River from central Rome. Here the Holy See of Western Christendom in the tradition of Peter dwells in the papal state, and Mass is celebrated in the basilica of this independent country. A large colonnade of white pillars forms a perimeter to St. Peter's Square, which leads to the steps of the basilica. An Egyptian obelisk stands in the center of the square, the same column that stood in the center of Nero's Circus hosting Peter's crucifixion. A large white dome designed by Michelangelo rises above on the landscape of Rome and looms over the square, announcing the location of the resting place of the apostle Peter. Simply walking through the square to the basilica can conjure up images of the memories of this land. The first-century circus, with chariot racing and crosses hoisting crucifixion victims, took place here. The barbarians of the early medieval period wandered through this square seeking plunder. Medieval pilgrims landed at this spot after weeks of journeying, with fatigue and with undying religious zeal. Mussolini's soldiers and Nazi agents walked beside this square with their military regimes. Crowds of Catholic faithful gather here awaiting the communication of white smoke from the Vatican chimney to announce the election of a new pope. All of these are centered here because of the legacy of the ministry and death of one apostle.

The Acts of Peter provides a testimony about the securing of Peter's bones after his crucifixion. The senator Marcellus took the body and ensured that it could be laid in a worthy tomb on the hillside. The idiosyncratic story of Peter confronting Marcellus in a vision strengthens the veracity of the event because something considered embarrassing to the senator would be less likely to be fabricated. Around the year 200, some Roman citizens began building an edifice over one of the tombs on Vatican Hill. Richard Lampe states that the result was not a pagan edifice but one evidencing a slow process of the expression and solidification of Christian devotion involving both graffiti and marble. By the third century "the revered site on the Vatican was partially clad in marble by the Christians," functioning "like a social-historical *terminus ad quem* for the devotees of the Peter memorial."[96]

---

96. Lampe, *From Paul to Valentinus*, 108; for credible details on the excavation complex at the Vatican, see 104–16.

After centuries of claiming the resting place of Peter, the Vatican hosted excavations of the ancient graveyard. The finds of the 1940s revealed a range of remains, from male to female to animal; a 1968 study of a key skeleton revealed bones of a stocky, muscular man, from sixty-seven to seventy-two years old. Although the 5 foot, 4 inch man was short compared to modern men, C. Bernard Ruffin reminds us that the average height for a Roman was only 5 foot, 2 inches. Julius Caesar was the same height as Peter, and he was considered "tall" for Romans.[97]

The basilica itself contains elements commemorating the apostle. In a left transept of the church is the Altar of the Crucifixion, close to the actual spot of Peter's inverted suffering. The papal chair, a large bronze seat above the Altar of the Chair, is supposedly built around a smaller, wooden chair that functioned as an episcopal chair used by Peter. His bones lie below the papal altar, with a view of the tomb available in an advanced tour of the *scavi* (excavations) below the basilica. Sometimes his jawbone is available on this tour. Across Rome in the Basilica of St. John Lateran, where the papal see functioned until the sixteenth century, the papal altar displays a bust of Peter where supposedly at least part of his skull is contained.[98]

Other sites make claims about the historical presence of the apostle Peter that contribute to the perpetuation of his legacy. Martin Hengel describes an archaeological find in Capernaum from the fourth century constructed on top of a first-century home, seemingly of Jewish Christians in the second or third century. The house may have served as a house church and contains graffiti of the name Peter.[99] In Jerusalem are churches memorializing events in the Gospels, such as the Church of St. Peter in Gallicantu, just outside the old city walls. The epic denial of Peter may have occurred at this spot, where the palace of the high priest Caiaphas was purportedly located. First erected in 457, the church was destroyed under Islamic rule in the eleventh century and rebuilt in 1931. The dual connection of the places offers the suggestion that at least part of Peter's denial occurred while he hoped for Jesus's acquittal outside the palace of the high priest (Matt. 26:3). A golden rooster sits atop the sanctuary roof.

Along the Via Urbana in the old sector of Rome, the Church of Santa Pudenziana sits seven meters below street level. It is the former home of the senator Pudens, whom Paul names in one of the Prison Epistles thought to be written from Rome (2 Tim. 4:21). Pudens is thought to have been Peter's

97. Ruffin, *The Twelve*, 178n1.
98. Thelen, *Saints in Rome and Beyond*, 82.
99. Hengel, *Saint Peter*, 106.

first convert to the faith in Rome. The residence functioned as a titular house church, even considered the ecclesiastical seat of the bishop of Rome until 313, when Constantine identified a church building that would become St. John Lateran. Given the historical accuracy of these details, ordination rites may have taken place here, with Peter laying hands on pastors. The church is named for the later-martyred daughter of Pudens.

The Roman Church of San Pietro in Vincoli (St. Peter in Chains) displays two chains fused together in a glass case over the altar. The chains of Peter from both his Jerusalem and Rome incarcerations supposedly rest here as a reminder that Peter's life was characterized by the suffering of dual impris-onments. F. F. Bruce helps us to imagine the original scene: "The stretching out of hands [John 21:18] could have been for the fitting of handcuffs, and there might be the further picture of his being led off in chains to the place of execution."[100] These fused chains are an emblem and reminder to Christians of the existence and suffering of the lead apostle, and millions of pilgrims and tourists have gazed on the chains over the altar of the church, sometimes with skepticism but more often with optimistic potential of their imagined historicity or with a sense of certainty in faith. Each August 1, this other-wise unassuming church on Oppian Hill recognizes the anniversary of the consecration of the chains in 432.[101]

The Mamertine dungeon in Rome sells itself as the imprisonment site of both Peter and Paul. This prison contained the Tullian or Tullium Keep, a dungeon carved from the rock in the foundation of Capitoline Hill. A column rests in a prison cell, supposedly the pillar where Peter was chained for nine months. As mentioned previously, there is no historical evidence that Peter and Paul were imprisoned here.

The Church of Quo Vadis stands on the Appian Way going out of Rome, commemorating Peter passing through the Capena Gate down the south road. In the ninth century the church was erected to mark the supposed spot not of a vision but an actual encounter. Inside, two walls contain modern murals that capture the encounter. On the right wall, the Appian side of the building, Christ is walking into Rome. On the left wall, the Rome side, Peter is walk-ing down the Appian Way. One Catholic writer reflects on the significance of the spot: "Each time I leave the church, . . . I pause to reflect awhile. For as I pass this way, I might be walking in the very footsteps of the Fisherman *and* the Prince of Peace."[102]

100. Bruce, *Gospel and Epistles of John*, 406.
101. Jöckle, *Encyclopedia of Saints*, 357.
102. Korn, *Catholic's Guide to Rome*, 112.

Peter is the patron saint of the Carolingians, the family of the first Holy Roman emperor. He is also the patron saint of various dioceses in Europe, and veneration sites are numerous. Among tradesmen he is particularly popular: fishermen, sailors, mechanics, bridge builders, blacksmiths, butchers, quarry workers, and watchmakers. Peter is appealed to against fever, thieves, and snakes. The apostle is regarded as having authority over the weather, and his keys are said to protect against rabies and snakebites.[103] His feast day is June 29, together with Paul.

Peter's relics are strewn across Christendom. For example, links from his chain are supposedly contained in both Minden and Aachen, Germany; the knife that cut the ear of Malchus in Venice, Italy; a nail from his cross in Chambéry, France; and a key in both Maastricht, the Netherlands, and Lodi Vecchio, Italy.[104] Yet his greatest site of appreciation, veneration, and image is St. Peter's Basilica in the Vatican City, where the faithful insist that his bones rest.

103. Jöckle, *Encyclopedia of Saints*, 358.
104. Jöckle, *Encyclopedia of Saints*, 358.

✳ 3 ✳

Andrew

The Saltire

[John the Baptist] said, "Behold, the Lamb of God!" The two disciples heard him speak, and they followed Jesus. . . . [Andrew] found first his own brother Simon and said to him, "We have found the Messiah."

John 1:36–37, 41

"But how long delay I, speaking thus, and embrace not the cross, that by the cross I may be made alive, and by the cross win the common death of all and depart out of life?" And the blessed Andrew having thus spoken, standing upon the earth, looked earnestly upon the cross, and bade the brethren that the executioners should come and do that which was commanded them.

Acts of Andrew[1]
third century, Egypt/Syria

The year was 345. Regulus, the bishop of Patras, was asleep and began to dream. His attention was captured by the brilliance of an angel, who instructed him to upset one of the sacred spots of Christendom and remove a most revered treasure of Greece from its shores. Regulus was to

1. James, 360.

take the bones of St. Andrew to "an undisclosed location" to the northwest, "to the ends of the earth." In an effort to honor God, the bishop did so. After being shipwrecked on the shores of Fife in the British Isles, Regulus reached modern St. Andrews, Scotland, where he was told to rest and to build a church to house the relics.[2] Later, while the Picts and the English were preparing for battle in 750, King Hungus of the Picts is said to have received a vision from Andrew with a prediction of victory. When the saltire appeared in the sky during the battle, the Picts advanced with the cry, "St. Andrew, our patron, be our guide!"[3] From this episode arose a great patronage in Scotland of the apostle Andrew. A saltire is a horizontally laid, X-shaped herald that might be seen on any emblem but is also the type of cross on which the apostle was crucified. The symbol has become so recognized on the national flag of Scotland that the flag itself is known as the saltire. This story illustrates how the modern image of an apostle can be shaped by an event beyond the life of the apostle. While Andrew likely never went to Scotland, he has become the patron saint of the country, and the traditional shape of the cross of his martyrdom has flown on Scotland's flag for centuries.

This fisherman from Galilee also bears the association of forever being the brother of Simon Peter (Matt. 4:18). While Andrew was perhaps the first disciple of Jesus, certainly responsible for introducing Peter to Jesus, the prominence of Peter so soared that the personal source of Peter's connection to Jesus was relegated to a common reference of "brother." Ellsworth Kalas describes how the term "brother" can be used "in an emotional or poetic sense, to describe someone of certain qualities of loyalty, compassion, and concern."[4] The name Andrew is derived from the Greek word for "man," so that as a designation it means "masculine," "brave," or simply "manly." The Byzantine tradition depicts him as the *Protoklētos*, the "first called," as he was the first of the Twelve called by Jesus. A disciple of John the Baptist until he introduced Jesus as "the Lamb of God" (John 1:36), Andrew and another disciple followed Jesus (1:40).

New Testament attention to Andrew is scarce. Although he is mentioned at the great feeding episode, at the Olivet discourse, and in a moment of spontaneous coordination for some Greeks to meet Jesus, this apostle is quickly eclipsed in each Gospel incident. Greater renown came to the legacy of Andrew in his travels after the New Testament, during which his life seems to have ended while ministering in Greece. His story begins in Palestine.

2. Taylor, *How to Read a Church*, 116.
3. Brownrigg, *Twelve Apostles*, 56.
4. Kalas, *Thirteen Apostles*, 3.

Ministry in Writing

Scholars believe that Andrew left no legacy in writing. Worth noting, however, is that James Patrick believes that the Johannine Gospel tradition originated not with John but with Andrew. In a series of arguments from the writings of church fathers and deductions from the biblical text, Patrick claims that this Gospel belongs to Andrew because of the logistics of Andrew's presence in the narrative. The Gospel highlights the future coming of the Paraclete in the Last Supper, whose role will be similar to that played by Andrew in the narrative when he mediates between both Peter and Greeks to meet Jesus.[5] While Patrick's analysis is insightful and provocative, the traditions around John as the author and the episode of John 21:23, which suggests that the beloved disciple will live beyond the other disciples, do not support the hypothesis that the Gospel belongs to Andrew.

Palestine Discipleship

The family of the apostle Andrew and his brother Simon Peter hailed from Bethsaida, twenty-five miles east of Nazareth on the Sea of Galilee (John 1:44). Here the Gospel of John makes the point that this was also the city of Philip, suggesting a possible regional affiliation and familial connection with this other apostle. It seems that Andrew's family had relocated to Capernaum, or at least their adult lives were spent there, likely for business. When Jesus comes to that city, he comes to Peter's house (Matt. 8:5, 14); Mark elaborates on the residence by calling it Andrew's house too (1:29).

Discipleship Calling

Andrew shared in the family trade while taking an interest in the teaching of John the Baptist, and when the prophet declared of Jesus "Behold, the Lamb of God!" Andrew immediately shadowed Jesus, perhaps out of curiosity or out of a longing for spiritual leadership, already evidenced by his commitment to discipleship under the ministry of John. He and another disciple follow the referent of John's insightful declaration at a distance until Jesus turns to them, asking, "What do you seek?" (John 1:38), to which they respond by inquiring about Jesus's habitation. They stay the whole day, seemingly to listen to this Messiah figure (John 1:39). In the earliest example of evangelistic activity among the future apostles, Andrew finds his brother Simon and declares to

---

5. Patrick, *Andrew of Bethsaida and the Johannine Circle*, 57–60.

him with confidence, "We have found the Messiah" (John 1:41). This profound statement embodies the mission declaration of this group of men who are the focus of our quest. Their lives were transformed as Andrew recruited a magnificent figure in the history of Christianity. Ellsworth Kalas thoughtfully wonders whether Andrew was ever resentful of Peter's consequential prestige, since Andrew was responsible for introducing Peter to Jesus.[6]

Matthew and Mark provide what seems to be a more abbreviated scene of the brothers' call to ministry. For example: "And as He was going along by the Sea of Galilee, He saw Simon and Andrew, the brother of Simon, casting a net in the sea; for they were fishermen. And Jesus said to them, 'Follow Me, and I will make you become fishers of men'" (Mark 1:16–17). The seeming disparity between the accounts of Andrew's calling is easy to settle. Commentary author R. T. France remarks, "It was not their first meeting, but it was the first time Jesus had demanded their literally leaving home to join in his itinerant ministry."[7] Meanwhile, the pun of calling fishermen to apply their craft to the new ministry of an inaugurating kingdom is notable. Being "fishers of men" involved applying the use of their trade in the powerful evangelism that later characterized the disciples.

Bethsaida and Capernaum were villages on the Sea of Galilee. Fishing was a rugged life, and the chapter on Peter explains that the trade was not highly respected in society yet was deeply meaningful for those who made a livelihood from it.

Discipleship Episodes

Andrew appears in five incidents in the New Testament, accounting for twelve mentions of his name. His initial encounter with Christ and Christ's seaside invitation to follow him are the first two. Soon afterward, they cross the Sea of Galilee, and surrounded by a throng of people, Jesus tests one disciple, Philip, by asking where they can get food for such a crowd (John 6:1–6). Andrew responds by mentioning the seemingly pathetic potential of five barley loaves and two fish, admitting that it will be insufficient for so many (John 6:8–9). Andrew sets up the unimaginable feeding of the five thousand on that day with his realistic response. F. F. Bruce remarks: "Andrew drew attention to it simply to underline its ludicrous inadequacy for so many hungry people. But it was enough for the Lord's purpose."[8] While the expansion of a small food supply was unmistakably amazing, Bernard Ruffin overreaches when

6. Kalas, *Thirteen Apostles*, 7.
7. France, *Matthew*, 104.
8. Bruce, *Gospel and Epistles of John*, 144.

he concludes about the apostle: "This tells us something about Andrew. He had a deep trust in his Lord and an awareness that Jesus was Master."[9] After all, at the time the disciple seems skeptical of the potential of the resources.

On another occasion, deep into the teaching ministry of Jesus about Israel, Peter, James, John, and Andrew are questioning him in a private setting, "Tell us, when will these things be, and what *will be* the sign when all these things are going to be fulfilled?" (Mark 13:4). Jesus elaborates on the signs of the times in the Olivet discourse by providing a series of prophecies that have perplexed scholars trying to determine which apply to that first-century audience and which to subsequent generations.

In another instance of Andrew introducing people to Jesus, John records how Greeks came asking to see Jesus (John 12:20–22). While the passage tells us little about Andrew, it introduces an important dynamic in the lives of the apostles and the early church as one of the first encounters between Jews and gentiles. The request of these Greeks—individuals who longed to talk to Jesus more intimately but did not have access—required a backdoor approach to the Jewish Messiah. Philip apprises Andrew of the dilemma, and together they approach Jesus and trigger a statement from Jesus about what he expects of his own ministry, resulting in a heavenly response that some bystanders mistake as an angel speaking (John 12:29). To this day, we do not know whether those Greeks gained the audience that they sought.

Ronald Brownrigg overextends the personality of the disciple: "Andrew emerges as a sensitive and approachable man who always had time and patience to listen to enquiries, even from children and foreigners. He was a selfless and considerate man, who did not resent the leadership of his brother."[10] Such a conclusion goes beyond what is intended or communicated by the biblical text. Ellsworth Kalas similarly speculates that "Andrew was a person of spiritual hunger. His soul was on the search."[11] Psychological and personality conjecture is unfair to the text, unfair to the apostle, and unfair to contemporary Christian readers. These hypotheses are interesting speculation, but in the end, speculations should not be treated as assertions of truth, even if for the purpose of instruction in the faith, when the biblical text lacks sufficient evidence.

The time in Palestine eventually came to an end for Andrew. David Criswell provides no rationale for his postulation but suggests that Andrew stayed in Jerusalem until at least 42.[12] The fourth-century Pistis Sophia places Andrew

9. Ruffin, *The Twelve*, 64.
10. Brownrigg, *Twelve Apostles*, 47.
11. Kalas, *Thirteen Apostles*, 5.
12. Criswell, *Apostles after Jesus*, 65.

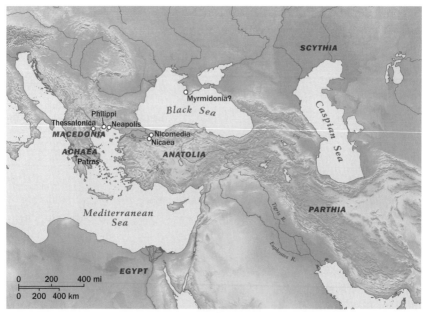

Journey of Andrew

west of Jerusalem compared to the other apostles: "Thomas, Andrew, James and Simon the Canaanite were in the west, with their faces turned east, but Philip and Bartholomew were in the south turned towards the north, but the other disciples and the women disciples stood behind Jesus. But Jesus stood beside the altar."[13] This comment offers historical evidence of the common tradition that Andrew ministered in Greece. But first, there are other fields that claim his apostolic ministry.

Scythia Ministry

In the first segment of the Acts of Andrew, the disciple is allotted Achaea in the tradition of random allotments for ministry among the disciples: "After the ascension the apostles dispersed to preach in various countries. Andrew began in the province of Achaea, but Matthew went to the city of Mermidona [Myrmidonia]. . . . Andrew left Mermidona [likely in Scythia] and came back to his own allotted district," presumably Achaea.[14] Then he moved from city to city in itinerant fashion, with miracles and persecution accompanying his

13. Pistis Sophia (Schneemelcher, 1:258).
14. Acts of Andrew (James, 337–38).

preaching. The communities of the ancient world relied on the stability of the religious economy that structured them, so the visit of an apostle with a message of religious transformation could easily have upset this stability.

Scythia was a region north of the Black Sea, in modern Ukraine and Russia. The ancient image of the people is one of a rough and savage culture, primitive and uncouth. First-century Jewish historian Josephus describes this people group: "As to the Scythians, they take a pleasure in killing men, and differ little from brute beasts."[15] Paul mentions them in a negative fashion, exhorting believers to unity in Christ with even the most surprising characters: "And have put on the new self who is being renewed to a true knowledge according to the image of the One who created him—*a renewal* in which there is no *distinction between* Greek and Jew, circumcised and uncircumcised, barbarian, Scythian, slave and freeman, but Christ is all, and in all" (Col. 3:10–11).

The Acts of Andrew and Matthias relates Andrew's rescue of Matthias from prison and ministry in the city of Myrmidonia.[16] In the casting of lots for ministry assignment, Matthias is sent to Scythia, but the tradition also confusedly substitutes Matthew for Matthias. Myrmidonia is commonly referred to as the "land of man-eaters." A voice from God explains that Matthias will be kept safe from all harm, with a pledge that the apostle Andrew will come to his aid. Meanwhile, Andrew receives a vision in Achaea to come rescue Matthias in Scythia. Instructed to go down to the sea, he encounters the proper boat, captained by a disguised Jesus. When the apostle is initially hesitant about the timing required to rescue Matthias, Jesus confronts Andrew. Across the sea, Jesus dialogues with Andrew to test his faith, continuing the emotional and intellectual sanctification of this disciple who had followed him throughout Palestine. In two dubious episodes, a sphinx comes to life in the temple, and a theophany of Christ in the form of a child is worshiped before he ascends. Matthias is eventually freed, and Andrew moves about freely when seven guards are killed by prayer and other guards have their hands turned to stone. On their departure from prison, Andrew commands a cloud, which lifts Matthias and Andrew's disciples to a mountain where Peter is preaching.

After the rescue of Matthias, the story of the Acts of Andrew and Matthias focuses on the activity of Andrew in the city. Andrew performs miraculous wonders against the cause of the pagan gods. Attributing the chaos of the rulers and the crowds to Satan, Andrew is tied with a rope around his neck and dragged through the city on three consecutive days. God causes a flood

---

15. Josephus, *Against Apion* 2.38, in *Works of Josephus*, trans. Whiston, 810.
16. For the best version of the text, see McDonald, *The Acts of Andrew and the Acts of Andrew and Matthias in the City of Cannibals.*

to soak the city as Michael the archangel encircles the city with a cloud of fire. All the drowned are resurrected by the apostle.

In this episode, Andrew leaves the city freely, without being martyred. This provides a potentially complementary sequel to the Acts of Andrew, if the apostle advanced from Myrmidonia to Achaea. However, another account seems to first follow the Matthias account, found in the Acts of Peter and Andrew, which takes up immediately from his departure to the cloud where Peter, Matthias, and two disciples are sitting.[17] The four set out to an unnamed city, and here some of the most suspect material is found, displaying the tendency toward encratism in these tales. The men of the city place an unchaste woman in their path. With Peter's permission, Andrew prays, and Michael the archangel removes her by her hair for them to pass. After exhorting one Onesiphorus to desert his wife and children, Peter is accosted by him before bringing to reality Jesus's illustration in the Synoptic Gospels that it is easier for a camel to pass through the eye of a needle than for a rich man to enter heaven (Matt. 19:24; Mark 10:25; Luke 18:25). Peter sticks a needle in the ground and commands the camel in Jesus's name; the eye opens, and the camel passes through two times. When Onesiphorus cannot command the same, Peter explains that he lacks baptism. Onesiphorus, his house, and one thousand souls are baptized, the story goes. The unchaste woman repents and founds a monastery of virgins dedicated to the Lord. The work has little historical credibility, starting with the apostles' presence in a heavenly refuge.

The second-century Coptic Abdias tradition reports Andrew's journey to "Sakos, cities of infidels, and of wicked men," "Sakos" being a term for the people of Scythia.[18] When his ministry threatens the local religion, persecutors come blaspheming and intending to burn Andrew on a pyre. Their blasphemy so angers him that he prays for fire from heaven, which comes down and consumes his persecutors. Others come intending to bind him to a cross to stone him, and from prison Andrew again calls for heavenly fire against them. This time the Lord appears and censures his attitude while encouraging him: "Behold, thou hast ended thy conflict, and brought thy ministry to a close, and in this place shall thy martyrdom be accomplished."[19] The apostle praises God throughout the night, facing crucifixion with stoning the next morning. Another Oriental Acts describes how Andrew and Philemon are in this region, including the use of a dove to provide messages between the two.[20]

---

17. Acts of Peter and Andrew (James, 458).
18. Abdias, *Conflicts* 9 (Malan, 113).
19. Abdias, *Conflicts* 9 (Malan, 116).
20. James, 471.

One of the few potentially historical pieces of evidence for a ministry in Scythia is the presence of St. Andrew's Church in Kiev, Ukraine. This spot supposedly marks the northernmost spot of his ministry, where he also placed a cross.[21] Origen claims that Andrew ministered there, which Eusebius seems to affirm by reporting it.[22] In the mid-fifth century, Eucherius of Lyons conceived of Andrew's ministry in Scythia: "Andrew with preaching softened Scythia."[23]

Anatolia Ministry

The Scythian ministry might also have complemented a ministry in Asia Minor, although here scholars operate with limited precision. An ancient Syrian document, the Teaching of the Apostles (ca. 230), reports that the areas of "Nicaea, and Nicomedia, and all the country of Bithynia, and of Inner Galatia, and of the regions around about it, received the apostles' ordination of the priesthood from Andrew, the brother of Simon Cephas."[24] It also mentions labor by Andrew in Phrygia of central Anatolia. Additionally, the Teaching of the Apostles affirms that James wrote in Jerusalem, Peter in Rome, John from Ephesus, and Judas Thomas from India, moving Sean McDowell to write, "Given that the author got these ascriptions correct, it is at least probable that he also got the tradition correct about Andrew."[25]

The Acts of Andrew includes a seemingly separate work on his martyrdom, describing an extensive ministry by the apostle in three geographical locations: Anatolia, northern Greece, and Achaea. This account preserves the primary story of the martyrdom of the apostle in Patras, Achaea. Scholars think that the martyrdom section, called the Acts and Martyrdom of the Holy Apostle Andrew, was written between 80 and the fourth century in Achaea, likely around the city of Patras. The work contains some gnostic emphasis, being dualistic and encratic but lacking a full system of gnostic mythology. It contains a secret teaching of Jesus that does not find easy synthesis with the teachings of Jesus in the canonical Gospels. These mysteries contain no reference to salvation in Christ as the source of human sanctification but emphasize a spiritual conquering by the individual as the process of salvation, based on the covert and sometimes undetectable words of Jesus. Martin

21. Thelen, *Saints in Rome and Beyond*, 177.
22. Eusebius, *Hist. eccl.* 3.1.
23. *Instructions to Salonium*, cited in Peterson, *Andrew, Brother of Simon Peter*, 11.
24. Teaching of the Apostles proem (*ANF* 8:671).
25. McDowell, *Fate of the Apostles*, 179.

Hengel calls the Andrew presented in this work "a radical ascetic who busied himself trying to hinder marriage from taking place."[26]

The apostle journeys to the northern regions of Asia Minor, traveling westward along the Black Sea, ministering to people and villages. In Amasea he heals a blind boy and raises another boy from the dead. As was the case with Paul (Acts 16:26–34), an earthquake occurs when Andrew is imprisoned, and he is released, leading to the conversion and baptism of his captors. At Nicaea, Andrew commands seven devils living among tombs to appear. They manifest as dogs, and Andrew calls for the people's belief as a condition for exorcising the demons. After they cry that Christ is the Son of God, the apostle demands that the spirits go into dry and barren places, and they roar and vanish. He baptizes Callistus, who became the bishop there. At Nicomedia, he resurrects a man whose death he attributes to the same demons. From a boat near Byzantium, he calms the sea by a prayer of intercession. At Perinthus to the west on the shore, an angel directs him to board a ship, where the captain and crew receive his preaching and believe.

Thrace and Macedonia Ministries

As the narrative of the Acts of Andrew continues, Andrew lands at the ancient region of Thrace. When armed men seek to seize him, he makes the sign of the cross in faith, and they are disarmed by an angel. On a journey between Philippi and Neapolis, the apostle, out of encratic beliefs, interrupts the marriage of two brothers to their cousins.

After a stint of miracles in Thessalonica, the proconsul Virinus is angered by Andrew's preaching about their temple's destruction and ceremonial cancellations. When Andrew is arrested, the proconsul threatens him, "I shall throw this man to the beasts and write about you to Caesar, that ye may perish for contemning the laws." The apostle answers, "Write to Caesar that the Macedonians have received the word of God, and forsaking their idols, worship the true God."[27] After being dragged by the hair and beaten with clubs in the stadium, Andrew is left alone as the wild beasts—boar, bull, and leopard—attack the oppressors. One victim is Virinus's own son, whom the apostle resurrects after a long prayer. The proconsul goes away "confounded" as the apostle goes free. Andrew's liberation does not last long, however. First, he encounters a giant serpent, fifty cubits (seventy-five feet) long, which he rebukes and watches vomit poison and blood before it dies. Then he resurrects

26. Hengel, *Saint Peter*, 119.
27. Acts of Andrew (James, 342–43).

a boy whom the snake has victimized. The next night Andrew receives a vision of a great mountain whose light shines across the world, where Peter and John console him. John seems to play the role of Jesus by predicting the death to come. "I am the word of the cross whereon thou shalt hang shortly, for his name's sake whom thou preachest."[28]

In the Peloponnesian islands, Andrew calms a storm from the bow of a ship. In another legendary account, Andrew is in Philippi during the Neronian persecution. He is thrown to lions in the stadium, which do not attack him before he escapes. From Macedonia, the apostle and his followers sail to Patras in Achaea. The fourth-century Gregory of Nazianzus identifies his ministry with Epirus, a region connecting Macedonia to Achaea below it.[29]

Achaea Ministry

The Acts of Andrew commences with the work of Andrew in Achaea. From this initial location, he ventures into Anatolia, Thrace, and Macedonia before moving southward into Greece. The text here is worth treating as an anchor for its chronology, despite the repeated miracles that accompany the journey. His death at the hands of Governor Aegeas seems the best conclusion for a historical study of this apostle. Based on the criterion of freedom from opposition, no other location gains the same comprehensive prestige as Andrew's death by crucifixion on a saltire. Sean McDowell "cannot dismiss the consistent and relatively early account of his fate by crucifixion. . . . There is broad agreement that he died in this manner."[30]

The martyrdom section of the Acts of Andrew provides a foundation for the traditional view that Andrew ministered in Greece and became the patron saint of Patras. From a headquarters in the southern part of Greece, he ministers in cities in Achaea. His renown is described by a witness in the narrative: "He has become renowned not only in this city but throughout Achaea. He performs great miracles and cures which exceed human strength. . . . He proclaims a reverence for the divine and truly shows it to be shining forth into public view."[31] He encounters a corpse on the beach, a representative of a crew of forty who were in pursuit of the apostle's teaching when their ship wrecked. After this man is resurrected and provides an explanation, the other thirty-nine wash onto shore, leading

28. Acts of Andrew (James, 344).
29. Gregory of Nazianzus, *Orations* 33.11 (NPNF² 7:332).
30. McDowell, *Fate of the Apostles*, 185.
31. Acts of Andrew 25 (Elliott, 252).

to their resurrection. From Achaea, Andrew goes to Corinth and Megara, perhaps even down to Sparta.

An important yet abbreviated account of the ministry and life of Andrew in Scythia, Greece, and Achaea was penned by Gregory of Tours, a sixth-century bishop. This historian is recognized for his writing of *The History of the Franks*. In the *Book of the Miracles of the Blessed Apostle Andrew*, Gregory communicates his own purpose in writing the legends surrounding Andrew: "And of this, I thought good to extract and set out the 'virtues' only, omitting all that bred weariness."[32] This statement about the filtering of Andrew's legends can serve as a description of the critical method that is required for scholars. While belief in the feats of the apostle can be suspended because of their miraculous nature, the historical potential must still be considered.

At Patras the apostle heals the fever of Maximilla, the wife of a contemptible proconsul, Aegeates. The proconsul's brother, Strotocles, sees his servant healed of uncontrollable demon possession. Instead of accepting a gift from Aegeates, Andrew exhorts Maximilla to become celibate in encratic fashion, and she pledges herself to do so. Offended by his wife's refusals and the popularity of the new faith, Aegeates reacts officially by arresting Andrew and ordering his crucifixion. He demands that the apostle either renounce Christ or be crucified, likely with the hope that his wife will renege on her vow. But renouncing the faith or worshiping a false god is one demand that an apostle cannot fulfill, along with any prohibition to preach the gospel. Aegeates orders Andrew to be scourged with seven whips before being crucified. The sadistic order comes from Aegeates: "They came and bound his hands and his feet and nailed them not. . . . He wished to afflict him by hanging him up, and that in the night he might be devoured alive by dogs."[33] Then Andrew is crucified.

With his martyrdom in view, as is the case in many other testimonies of the apostles' deaths, Andrew's confidence is sure, and he is certain that his ministry has come to an end. He approaches the cross with a series of greetings: "Hail, O cross, yea be glad indeed! Well know I that thou shalt henceforth be at rest, thou that hast for a long time been wearied, being set up and awaiting me. . . . O cross, device of the salvation of the Most High! O cross, trophy of the victory over the enemies! O cross, planted upon the earth and having thy fruit in the heavens! O name of the cross, filled with all things. Well done, O cross, that hast bound down the mobility of the world."[34] Likewise, the

32. Acts of Andrew (James, 337).
33. Acts of Andrew (James, 360; see 358).
34. Acts of Andrew (James, 359–60).

quote from Andrew found at the start of this chapter is part of the lengthy monologue he offers en route to the cross.[35]

Just as miracles and teaching composed the ministry of Jesus, the apostles were similar gospel agents, and this apostle had one more ministry deed to perform. From the cross, Andrew preaches. Reminiscent of Jesus's powerful and final words on the cross, which exemplified the message of the gospel, Andrew receives the strength to explain the gospel. This strength supposedly sustains him for four days, and he converts more than two thousand hearers at Patras. The changed crowd and the proconsul seek to untie the teacher. Yet Andrew is unwilling to be freed. His final words from the cross are recorded:

> O Master, do not permit Andrew, the one tied to your wood, to be untied again. O Jesus, do not give me to the shameless devil, I who am attached to your mystery. O Father, do not let your opponent untie me, I who am hanging upon your grace. May he who is little no longer humiliate the one who has known your greatness. But you yourself, O Christ, you whom I desired, whom I loved, whom I know, whom I possess, whom I cherish, whose I am, receive me, so that by my departure to you there may be a reunion of my many kindred, those who rest in your majesty.[36]

The perseverance in the story is inspirational, even if it is exaggerated. An effect of the miracle and the message is the changed heart of the governor. The literary role of rulers such as Aegeates in these passages provides insight into the apostles. The figures are often pagan, leading to religious-ideological conflict. The rulers are often portrayed as fickle and heartless, wickedly persecuting Christians. In the apocryphal gospels, the encratic theology includes an exhortation to a lifestyle that conflicts with that of the ruler. Candida Moss remarks:

> A man who could not even order his own household and control his own wives and slaves was hardly a suitable candidate for public office, much less for emperor. By depicting the cause of martyrdom as the infiltration of Christianity even into the household of the emperor, the authors of the apocryphal acts emphasize both the potency of the representatives of Christ and, by implication, the impotency of the Roman emperor and by extension the Empire as a whole.[37]

This assessment helps us evaluate the historical veracity of the story of the apostle by revealing a literary agenda. David Pao describes the agenda:

35. Acts of Andrew (James, 360).
36. Acts of Andrew 63 (Elliott, 264).
37. Moss, "Roman Imperialism," 383–84.

"It becomes apparent that both the healing stories and the contexts in which these stories were placed reflect the careful art of the author in transforming traditional materials to depict the life of the apostle Andrew."[38] While it might be that the events are historical but simply presented from a certain perspective, at the same time the power agenda delegitimizes the authenticity of the work. Couple this with the supernatural feats, and the scholarly consensus builds against the historicity of the apocryphal Acts.

Other Ministry Paths

In the Acts of Andrew and Paul, Andrew finds himself blocked by Jews from an unnamed city where he has disembarked from a ship after "Paul has plunged into the sea to visit the underworld."[39] The text lacks geographical context prior to Andrew and Paul's parting. In this city, called Amente, Andrew encounters Judas Iscariot, who repented of his act of betrayal, returned to Jesus before his trial, and followed Jesus's command to go to the desert in repentance. There Judas encountered Satan and worshiped him in fear. In regret, he hanged himself and resolved to meet Jesus in Amente, which is now functioning as an underworld of souls. The disciples perform miracles to achieve entrance to the city, including the resurrection of one dissident. The story concludes with the conversion of twenty-seven thousand Jews. There is no historical basis for this account. Particularly the encounter with Judas Iscariot in an afterlife setting confirms the work as a literary account, allegorical in nature.

The Coptic Acts of Andrew and Bartholomew relates how Andrew is called from Syria to Parthia to team with Bartholomew for ministry.[40] When he cannot find a ship, he rests for the night, and a large fish swallows him and delivers him to his connecting city, though Andrew does not realize it. Another form of transportation is a glorious light that finally delivers them to Parthia. Stories of exorcisms, angels, Jesus as a disguised shipmaster, and conversions abound.

Likewise, the tradition that Andrew went to Scotland has little historical basis. In fact, except for the image of Andrew in the country, which has a basis in the transport of his bones to Scotland in the fourth century, there is insufficient historical record for his ministry in the British Isles. While the Acts of Andrew provides evidence of a professional ministry career in Scythia

---

38. Pao, "Physical and Spiritual Resurrection," 277.
39. Acts of Andrew and Paul (James, 472).
40. Abdias, *Conflicts* 76, 81.

and Achaea, there is always the remote possibility of his ministry in another, even more distant location.

In an unpublished work titled *He Raised the Cross on the Ice*, George Alexandrou researches the life of Andrew and lines up all the traditions of him into a life span.[41] "It was like a train, one car after another, until I had only twenty years missing from St. Andrew's return to the Black Sea from Valaamo until he went to Sinope—and from there to Patras in Achaia, to his martyrdom."[42] The gap in Andrew's timeline, according to Alexandrou, was a span of twenty years living in a cave in Romania.

Gregory of Tours himself recognized that some of the recorded legends surrounding Andrew needed to be filtered. His methodological statement implies that his own historical work omits much material as ahistorical. Eusebius names the Acts of Andrew along with the Acts of John as ones to be "rejected as altogether absurd and impious."[43] The Acts of Andrew was condemned by Pope Innocent I but popularized by Gregory of Tours. Such is the difficulty of filtering the extrabiblical testimony of the apostles' martyrdoms, which often forces a contemporary scholar to choose between conflicting traditions and to weigh the gnostic tendencies of ancient works. Kalas remarks about the Andrew figure in this work, "The mass of tradition and legend should be viewed with a skeptical, and yet appreciative eye."[44] Likewise, Sean McDowell says about such works, "While [apocryphal Acts] contain legendary accretion, they preserve the most reliable destination and fate for their respective apostles. . . . Although the writer of the various Apocryphal Acts had creative license, he or she was also bound by known tradition."[45]

It seems best to allow ministries for Andrew in both areas of Scythia and Achaea, with the martyrdom account in Achaea possessing a core of veracity. In his biography of the apostles, Hippolytus synthesizes the two geographical ministries in his one statement: "Andrew preached to the Scythians and Thracians, and was crucified, suspended on an olive tree, at Patrae, a town of Achaea; and there too he was buried."[46]

At the same time, an itinerant ministry in Anatolia is not unlikely, given its centrality in a triangulation between Jerusalem, Scythia, and Greece. The Acts of Andrew claims that he began ministering in Achaea, passing through

41. McDowell, *Fate of the Apostles*, 178.
42. McDowell, *Fate of the Apostles*, 178.
43. Eusebius, *Hist. eccl.* 3.25.6.
44. Kalas, *Thirteen Apostles*, 9–10.
45. McDowell, *Fate of the Apostles*, 182–83.
46. Hippolytus, *Twelve* (ANF 5:255).

Anatolia, with a return to Achaea. Tom Bissell suggests that Andrew began in Bithynia, "on to cities Sinope, Amisus, and Trapezus." From there he went on to Scythia and into the Caucasus region, ending in Ukraine, where he planted a cross and where a church bearing his name now stands. Then he returned to Byzantium, founding its first see, and went to Thrace, Macedonia, and Thessaly before returning to Greece.[47]

Image of Andrew

For the church, Andrew remains an apostle forever noted as the brother of Simon Peter. Six times the New Testament relates him to Peter (Matt. 4:18; 10:2; Mark 1:16; Luke 6:14; John 1:40–41; 6:8). At the same time, the legend of his ministry is unique and extraordinary. His path legitimately shows ministry in several regions, including Scythia, Anatolia, Thrace, and Macedonia, before a significant stint in Achaea in southern Greece. His martyrdom tradition is historically solid. That he traveled to Scotland is unlikely, although his popular image continues to be shaped by the patronage of the country.

Symbolism and Image Construction

By far the most common symbol of Andrew is the saltire, an X-shaped cross. This commemorates his crucifixion by this means, providing more time for him to preach but also an opportunity for harassment by wild animals. Additionally, the fishing net is a symbol of the apostle. The picture is natural since he is numbered among the several fishermen of the original twelve disciples. Andrew is often presented with bushy or disheveled gray hair. The passion of Andrew is depicted in a well-known painting by seventeenth-century Spanish artist Bartolome Esteban Murillo.

Tomb and Patronage

The extrabiblical support for an Achaean ministry is significant. There a tomb, church sites, and the legend of his bones find a host, the traditional site in Patras for the Acts of Andrew. The old church of Andreas there was supposedly built on the crucifixion site, where formerly rested a temple to Demeter.

In the fourth century Andrew's relics were supposedly transferred to Scotland by Regulus, who became the first bishop in Scotland. An angel appeared in a dream to him with the instruction to move the bones to modern

47. Bissell, *Apostle*, 154.

St. Andrews, where he built a church to house the relics.[48] At the turn of the fifth century, Jerome confirms that the relics of Andrew were removed from Patras, but he says that they were taken to Constantinople's Church of the Holy Apostles in 356. In this account, the relics were sent to Amalfi in the early thirteenth century, likely by Crusaders in 1204, under the handling of Cardinal Capuana.[49] In 1461 a Byzantine tyrant sent Andrew's skull to Pope Pius II in Rome, where a painting of his receipt was maintained beside Peter's tomb in the Vatican. The bones were eventually placed atop one of four pillar reliquaries around the high altar of St. Peter. In 1964 the pope returned a small collection of bones to the patriarch of Constantinople, restoring to Patras what it claimed to have anyway.[50] The Basilica of Saint Andrew marks the location of his martyrdom. It claims remnants of his cross, his skull, and other relics, including his finger.[51]

In Rome, the Church of Saint Andrew's at the Quirinal, designed by Bernini and housing the significant seventeenth-century painting by Guillaume Courtois of Andrew's martyrdom, once claimed to have relics. In his journey to find the resting places of the apostles, Tom Bissell found nothing there, although guidebooks are not afraid to claim that an urn under the altar contains Andrew's body.[52]

St. Andrew's Church in Kiev, Ukraine, marks the northernmost spot of Andrew's ministry, where he supposedly placed a cross. The Cathedral of Saint Andrew in Amalfi may contain many relics of the apostle within the crypt below the main altar. The Cathedral of St. Mary of the Flowers in Florence, the Duomo, claims an arm, while the Sankt Andreas in Cologne, Germany, claims another arm. The remaining relics in St. Andrews, Scotland, were destroyed by Scottish reformers in 1559.[53]

The apostle Andrew has associations with Russia, Greece, and Scotland. For his ministry in Scythia, he was named the patron saint of Russia by the Russian Orthodox Church. Likewise, he is the patron saint of Romania and Ukraine for this regional legacy. Bissell claims that Andrew is the patron saint of Luxembourg, but this does not find substantiation.[54] For his ministry in Achaea, Andrew is the patron saint of Greece.

48. Taylor, *How to Read a Church*, 116.

49. Brownrigg, *Twelve Apostles*, 53.

50. Bissell (*Apostle*, 167) attributes the gift to Paul VI, while Brownrigg (*Twelve Apostles*, 54) attributes it to John XXIII.

51. Thelen, *Saints in Rome and Beyond*, 182.

52. Bissell, *Apostle*, 167; Tuzzi, *Sacred Rome*, 156.

53. Thelen, *Saints in Rome and Beyond*, 177, 121, 109, 164, 158, respectively.

54. Bissell, *Apostle*, 150. This honor lies with Willibrord, Northumbrian (Britain) apostle of the early eighth century to the Frisians of the Low Countries.

The association of Andrew with Scotland finds its best anchor in the vision of King Hungus of the Picts. Thus Andrew became patron saint of the Scots and is now the patron saint of Scotland. The saltire is on the flag and is supposedly the basis for the shape on the Union Jack flag of the United Kingdom. Even if the historicity is questionable, the effect of the image of Andrew is tangible. His legacy is the basis of several contemporary organizations, such as the Order of Saint Andrew, an Anglican ecumenical religious order. He is the patron saint of fishermen, water carriers, and weddings, and he is invoked against gout, sore throats, and infertility.[55]

His death and feast date is November 30, on the eve of December 1, which is sometimes the date cited based on the Jewish reckoning of sundown as beginning the day. Martyr historians Criswell, Thieleman van Braght, and John Foxe date the year of Andrew's death as 69–70.[56]

---

55. Jöckle, Encyclopedia of Saints, 32.
56. Criswell, Apostles after Jesus, 53.

❋ 4 ❋

James

The Scallop Shell

Now about that time Herod the king laid hands on some who belonged to the church in order to mistreat them. And he had James the brother of John put to death with a sword.

Acts 12:1–2

The man who led James to the judgment seat, moved by the way James bore testimony to the faith, confessed himself Christian. Both therefore were led away to die. On their way, he entreated James to be forgiven of him, and James, considering a little, replied, "Peace be to thee," and kissed him. Then both were beheaded at the same time.

Clement of Alexandria, *Hypotyposes*[1]
third century, Egypt

Among the legacies of the apostles, none is as uncomplicated for our quest as that of James son of Zebedee. Yet even this legacy leads historians to some uncertainty. While most of the apostles

---

1. In Eusebius, *Hist. eccl.* 2.9.3.

journeyed between Rome and India, James's legacy extends to the farthest corner of Spain.

James and John are called the sons of Zebedee, but Jesus ascribed another name to them: "To them He [Jesus] gave the name Boanerges, which means, 'Sons of Thunder'" (Mark 3:17). We cannot know for sure why Jesus made this attribution or whether the thunder quality applied to their father or to them personally. However, that does not prevent scholars from speculating. C. Bernard Ruffin remarks: "In our imagination we might picture James the Great as a large, corpulent man, huge of hand, piercing of eye, imposing, full-bearded, with a powerful resonant voice and an arresting, commanding, authoritative presence."[2] Ellsworth Kalas exaggerates even further, describing James as "loud, rumbling, sometimes threatening and about to burst. This is the kind of person James was, along with his brother, John."[3] Such comments have little basis. The frequency of the name "James" in first-century Palestine is less than its proportional frequency in Acts, with various meanings of the name explained.[4] It might find a root in the Hebrew for "supplanter," as a synonym for Jacob, who supplanted Esau in his birthright (Gen. 27:36).

Since James is often listed before John in the registers of disciples, scholars suppose that he might have been older than John. This would fit the image of John in the Gospels as younger, running ahead of Peter (John 20:4) and perhaps outliving the other apostles (John 21:23). James was probably a native of Bethsaida in Galilee, like Peter, Andrew, and Philip. The reason for this assumption is the close proximity between Jesus's calling of the Zebedee sons and his calling of the Boanerges sons after "going on a little farther . . ." (Mark 1:19). James seems to have been a fisherman by trade.

This James is called "the Greater" to distinguish him from the other disciple James. Meanwhile, the son of Alphaeus is noted as the Lesser due to his limited attention in Jesus's ministry compared to the sons of Zebedee. These two Jameses are distinguished from James "the Just," the brother of Jesus, significant in the leadership of the church in Jerusalem. James the Just is likely the author of the New Testament Epistle of James, not James the Greater. Yet there is much confusion in extrabiblical and even biblical literature among the three, especially in Western sources. For example, when Paul calls James, Cephas, and John "pillars" in Galatians 2:9, he writes of receiving the right hand of fellowship to go to the gentiles. If this occasion is the Jerusalem Council of Acts 15 in the year 50, then the James in view must be the Just, the

2. Ruffin, *The Twelve*, 76.
3. Kalas, *Thirteen Apostles*, 27.
4. Williams, "Palestinian Jewish Personal Names," 86.

heir-apparent leader of the church in Jerusalem. At the same time, apocryphal literature from the second and third centuries frequently mentions a James among the disciples without identifying the intended James. For example, the Apocryphon of James claims that on the eve of his ascension, Jesus delivered sayings to James. Fred Lapham considers the reference to mean James the Just, with the purpose of conforming Peter to Jewish Christianity,[5] as the topic of tension between Jewish and gentile Christians is a common way to identify the James in view. In assessing these sources, we will prioritize the most obvious references to James the Greater and weigh each episode of an unidentified James on a case-by-case basis, suspending less congruent claims that might apply to another James.

One element of James the Greater's legacy that cannot be confused with the Lesser or the Just is the Camino de Santiago, the pilgrimage site to the supposed bones of the apostle and the Cathedral of St. James of Compostela in Spain. Aside from Peter's tomb in the Vatican, this tomb of James is the most popular and best-known resting place of an apostle in Christendom.

Palestine Discipleship

The end of James's life often serves as the only feature of his apostolic career. A discipleship journey that began with an undefined calling in Galilee by a yet-unknown Messiah figure ended in the dramatic death of the apostle. Yet this journey begins with his calling.

Discipleship Calling

James participates in several events in the Gospels. The call of James comes alongside that of James's brother John: "And going on from there He saw two other brothers, James the son of Zebedee, and John his brother, in the boat with Zebedee their father, mending their nets; and He called them. And they immediately left the ship and their father, and followed him" (Matt. 4:21–22; see Mark 1:19–20; Luke 5:10–11). The sense of immediacy evidences the two disciples' belief in the Messiah figure who calls them. Bethsaida was a great center for the fishing trade, even bearing the name "house of fishing."

Like the other two disciples in the top tier of activities in the Gospels, which includes Peter and John, James is named as present at the healing of Jairus's daughter (Mark 5:37; Luke 8:51), the transfiguration (Mark 9:2; Matt. 17:1; Luke 9:28), and the Garden of Gethsemane (Mark 14:33; Matt. 26:37).

---

5. Lapham, *Introduction to the New Testament Apocrypha*, 50–54.

Discipleship Episodes

In an event in which James and his brother John are specifically named, Jesus is focused on Jerusalem when the disciples make housing arrangements in Samaria. When thwarted, they suggest judgment against the villagers. "But they did not receive Him, because He was traveling toward Jerusalem. When His disciples James and John saw *this*, they said, 'Lord, do You want us to command fire to come down from heaven and consume them?' But He turned and rebuked them, [and said, 'You do not know what kind of spirit you are of; for the Son of Man did not come to destroy men's lives, but to save them.']" (Luke 9:53–56). Here may be the basis of the moniker "Sons of Thunder" for the sons of Zebedee (Mark 3:17). Their readiness to call down fire from heaven conjures up images of resounding lightning.

Alongside John and Peter, James is invited to be a more private witness to several events in the ministry of Jesus. He is named among the top tier in posing an isolated question to Jesus, leading to the discourse on the Mount of Olives (Mark 13:3). Only Peter, James, and John are invited to the house of Jairus, the ruler of the synagogue, when his daughter is raised from the dead (Mark 5:37; Luke 8:51). The same three disciples are taken to a high mountain apart from the others when Jesus is transfigured alongside Moses and Elijah (Matt. 17:1; Mark 9:2; Luke 9:28). The trio again accompanies Jesus deeper into the Garden of Gethsemane, when he tells them alone, "My soul is deeply grieved to the point of death; remain here and keep watch" (Mark 14:33). Finally, James is named along with Peter, Thomas, John, and Nathanael alongside the Sea of Galilee (John 21:2). Here the resurrected Lord appears, guides them to fish, and dialogues with Peter about Peter's betrayal and John's death. Sean McDowell points out how three of these James events relate to the issue of death.[6] The combination of the three highlights the small, interior group favored to see the inner workings of Jesus's mission and identity.

Alongside the narrative components of James's formation for ministry, he participates with his brother John in presenting an exceptional request to Jesus. Their request about the afterlife leads Jesus to remark about their deaths. Their appeal begins with what appears to be a brash claim: "Teacher, we want You to do for us whatever we ask of You." Seeming to humor them, Jesus answers, "What do you want Me to do for you?" (Mark 10:35–36). The dialogue continues:

> They said to Him, "Grant that we may sit, one on Your right and one on *Your* left, in Your glory." But Jesus said to them, "You do not know what you are asking. Are you able to drink the cup that I drink, or to be baptized with the baptism

6. McDowell, *Fate of the Apostles*, 187.

with which I am baptized?" They said to Him, "We are able." And Jesus said to them, "The cup that I drink you shall drink; and you shall be baptized with the baptism with which I am baptized. But to sit on My right or on My left, this is not Mine to give; but it is for those for whom it has been prepared." (10:37–40)

The request shows that the disciples already have an eschatological expectation for the ministry of Jesus. Whether this stems from Jesus's teaching alone or the Jewish tradition of the afterlife, we cannot know. Yet the throne is associated with authority in judgment. In the history of Israel, the cup represents an allotment of judgment. For example, the psalmist writes, "Upon the wicked He will rain snares; Fire and brimstone and burning wind will be the portion of their cup" (11:6). In another psalm David writes that the opposite is the case for the faithful, using the cup metaphor: "The LORD is the portion of my inheritance and my cup; You support my lot" (16:5). Jesus calls on this cup metaphor along with the baptism metaphor to represent his coming death and applies the images to the two who request privilege.[7] From the tradition surrounding John, it seems that for him the passage suggests suffering and not martyrdom.

No rejoinder from James and John is given; perhaps they were humbled; perhaps they were confused. Matthew's version centers the request for honor on the motive of their mother (Matt. 20:20), which reduces any insight into these two brothers during the seminal years of the disciples. At any rate, Jesus responds, "Request denied." However, it leads to an important part of the development of James and John. Just as Jesus will drink from the cup of suffering, so shall they. While they request privilege, the privilege that will come to them is the honor of suffering for the kingdom just like its King. It also leads to valuable expectation-setting for the apostolic mission when the other disciples hear of the request and are indignant, leading Jesus to instruct them on servanthood (Mark 10:37–45). The episode initiated by James and John sets up Mark 10:45, in which Jesus describes his own mission as one of sacrifice. In the face of the numerous trials that the group will encounter, these words embody their lifelong mission and characterize the observations of our quest for the historical apostles.

Palestine Ministry

In the era of the early church, James seems to have continued as a leader, without detailed episodes of activity recorded for him. The death of James

7. Brooks, *Mark*, 168.

Journey of James the Greater

comes to the reader of Acts suddenly and surprisingly. The success of the advancing kingdom through the preaching of the gospel and the merciful survival of the other disciples begins to feel like the normal pattern for the apostles' efforts. Peter and John are arrested by the Sanhedrin, scolded, and freed on the condition that they cease preaching. With boldness, they preach anyway. The healing of the paralytic at the Jerusalem gate, the Spirit baptism of gentiles, and the conversion of individuals such as the Ethiopian eunuch seem to signify a developing invincibility of the apostles' ministry. Then in two quick verses at the beginning of Acts 12, tragedy strikes: "Now about that time Herod the king laid hands on some who belonged to the church in order to mistreat them. And he had James the brother of John put to death with a sword." Peter is immediately arrested and heavily guarded by four squads of soldiers (vv. 3–4). For the first time, the apostles are proved vulnerable. The story of Jesus's twelve disciples will not be one in which they are protected from death as they promote the advancing kingdom. They are all at risk in a new and profound way. They will die. The year is 44.

Theologian Wayne Grudem describes how sanctification, the completion process for salvation, can include suffering that shapes our being: "As we become more sanctified in our bodies, our bodies become more and more useful servants of God, more and more responsive to the will of God and the desires of the Holy Spirit."[8] Love for Christ persuades believers that honoring him in death is more important than preserving one's life. So it was for all the martyred apostles. In the words of Revelation, "They did not love their life even when faced with death" (Rev. 12:11).

Nothing else is said of the apostle James, and the lack of attention to him is surprising. Perhaps Luke knew no additional details to report, being a latecomer to the apostolic company. He apparently prefers to report the collective unity of the group in promoting the faith publicly rather than to chronicle individual achievements (Acts 1:14; 2:46; 5:12; 15:25). David Criswell

8. Grudem, *Systematic Theology*, 757.

suggests that Herod viewed James as a leader and may have considered James more important as a church leader than John and Peter.[9]

According to Clement of Alexandria, as recorded in Eusebius, James's escort at his trial was moved by the testimony that James offered. When the escort asked for forgiveness, seemingly for his part in the trial, James blessed him before both were beheaded.[10] The quote that opened this chapter is from that work. The Latin tradition of Abdias records the same and calls the escort Josias. He was a scribe required to secure a rope around James's neck to drag him before Herod. The work also claims that James healed a paralytic en route to the trial.[11]

The death of James is hinted at when he and John request thrones, for in his reply Jesus mentions James's future suffering. Acts 12 records how the apostle discovered the cup of which his Master had spoken. He is the first apostle on record to encounter death. The dating of James's death is important in establishing a timeline of the work of the apostles in the first century. The recorded famine predicted by Agabus in Acts 11:28 took place under Emperor Claudius, who ascended to the throne in 41. Historians affirm that the famine occurred in the fourth year of Claudius, likely 44. The death of Herod Agrippa I (Acts 12:21) seems to have followed closely after James's death and Peter's imprisonment. Since the year of Herod's death is calculated as 44, then James's execution must have been the same year.

Other Ministry Locations

The Coptic Abdias tradition has James ministering in Antioch, while identifying the result of the casting of lots for his ministry as Lydia, presumably Africa.[12] He and Peter heal a blind man, cause soldiers to be too frightened to perform their torture, heal a crippled boy, cause idols to shatter, and build churches. In the Ethiopic text tradition, James is beheaded without detail. In the Latin versions, James the Greater encounters two magicians, Philetus, who is converted, and Hermogenes, who responds in anger by magically binding his colleague. A handkerchief sent from James to Philetus frees him from his bondage, and the demons unleashed by Hermogenes are sent by James to capture their master. The Jews respond by seizing James when Abiathar the high priest stirs up the crowd, and both believers are beheaded.[13]

9. Criswell, *Apostles after Jesus*, 38.
10. Eusebius, *Hist. eccl.* 2.9.2–3.
11. Ps.-Abd. 4.5 (James, 463–64).
12. Abdias, *Conflicts* 13 (Malan, 172).
13. Ps.-Abd. 4.2–8 (James, 462–63).

Several apocryphal works bearing the name "James" reveal either uncertainty about the subject or an intention to make James the Just and brother of Jesus the focus of attention. The First Apocalypse of James comes closest to offering insight into the person of James son of Zebedee. Found in the Nag Hammadi collection, this revelation from Jesus to the Twelve records the other disciples being corrected for lacking gnostic acumen, while James is made the special recipient of a lengthy dialogue with Jesus.[14] The text reports: "It is the Lord who spoke with me: 'See now the completion of my redemption. I have given you a sign of these things, James, my brother, although you are not my brother materially.'"[15] This latter statement suggests that James the Just is not the focus, although this gnostic work could have another intention. Nonetheless, ambiguity in the identity of the subject still remains. In the Acts of Saint James in India, Christ appears to James and Peter to teach them about heavenly rewards and righteous living.[16]

Spain Ministry

In a tradition founded in the medieval *History of Compostela*, James received a vision of Mary in Spain encouraging him to maintain his ministry there. Ruffin seems correct to call the story "farfetched."[17] Discouraged by his small number of converts, the apostle has a vision of Mary by the Ebro River; she is seated on a pillar of jasper and surrounded by angels. James is instructed to build a chapel on the spot, and the Basilica of Our Lady of the Pillar rests in Saragossa. The Spanish tradition maintains that James was apostle to the region before he returned to Jerusalem. Criswell sees a possible conflict between James serving in Spain and the notion that Paul is the first to be called apostle to the gentiles (1 Tim. 2:7), leading McBirnie to deduce that James's target for ministry was Spanish Jews.[18] Within this legend, we cannot be sure whether James ministered to Jews or gentiles in the host city Zaragoza. For that matter, we cannot be historically certain that the apostle went to Spain at all. The largest obstacle is the logistics of James serving so far west, then returning to Jerusalem by 44. There was no apparent reason for leaving Judea, much less going beyond Asia, Greece, or Italy for Spain, when the disciples had not yet dispersed under the threat of Jewish persecution in Jerusalem.

14. Lapham, *Introduction to the New Testament Apocrypha*, 55.
15. First Apocalypse of James 24 (Robinson, 262).
16. McDowell, *Fate of the Apostles*, 188.
17. Ruffin, *The Twelve*, 76.
18. Criswell, *Apostles after Jesus*, 38; McBirnie, *Search for the Twelve Apostles*, 75–76.

. No early church father mentions the legend, and it is of late date. Scholars do not consider this regional ministry likely.

Image of James the Greater

The image of James is simpler than that of the other apostles because his ministry was shortened by death. While he likely never traveled to Spain, his image is primarily centered there. He had a clear ministry in Jerusalem, and journeys as far as Antioch are not unreasonable.

Symbolism and Image Construction

One symbol of this apostle is a sword, the instrument of his death, which the apostle commonly carries in statuary. The other symbol is a scallop shell, denoting his association with the Way of St. James. The twelfth-century Spanish military Order of Santiago uses a cross whose transept bars end in the fleur-de-lis, known in heraldry as the Cross of St. James.

When Herod Agrippa had James put to death by the sword, it was either in the Roman fashion, by beheading, or in the Jewish fashion of thrusting the sword into the body, since beheading was not permitted among the Jews.[19] Scholars have attempted to find connections to the use of a sword in the execution of James. Sean McDowell references Deuteronomy 13:15, in which unfaithful Jews were to be struck "with the edge of the sword," suggesting that the Jewish Herod honored the desires of the Jewish leadership in Jerusalem.[20] This was the motive behind the death of James. Or the sword may mean that James was a Roman citizen, worthy of speedy execution, like that applied to Paul, who claimed Roman citizenship (Acts 22:27). Regardless, Herod sought the favor of the Jewish leaders by this act (Acts 12:3). F. F. Bruce says that Agrippa was more popular than other recent rulers from the Herod family, and "he set himself sedulously to win and retain their goodwill."[21]

Medieval pilgrims who traveled the Way of St. James would carry a scallop shell to function as a bowl for eating or a cup for drinking water. In the Middle Ages the Way of St. James was the third-most commonly traveled pilgrimage route, next to routes to Rome and Jerusalem. For French pilgrims the road was 484 miles, culminating in the arrival at James's tomb. The shell quickly became symbolic of the route, today marking the way on trees, buildings, and

---

19. Polhill, *Acts*, 278.
20. McDowell, *Fate of the Apostles*, 191.
21. Bruce, *Book of Acts*, 233.

milestones for travelers en route to the cathedral of Santiago. In the archbasilica of St. John Lateran in Rome, the James statue by Camillo Rusconi includes a pilgrim's staff, similar to the recognizable painting by Guido Reni. Sometimes James is depicted with a pilgrim's hat to accompany his pilgrim's staff, his garb often adorned with scallop shells.

James is best known for being the only apostle whose martyrdom is reported in the New Testament. His voice is lost in the book of Acts, a silent sacrifice in the cause of the new faith. Yet the minimal data on James does not stop some from speculating on his contribution and personality beyond the historical data. Kalas remarks, "One thing is sure, James was *willing* to be a leader."[22] At Luke 9:54, when James and John ask Jesus whether fire should be commanded from heaven to consume their enemies, Kalas remarks, "That's our James!" as if a personal profile were available.[23] Kalas's application for the Christian includes the claim, "There's a little of James in most of us."[24] Such analysis should be rejected as displaying no more historical credibility than a gnostic gospel.

Tomb and Patronage

Hippolytus summarizes the ministry, martyrdom, and burial of James accurately: "James, his brother, when preaching in Judea, was cut off with the sword by Herod the tetrarch, and was buried there."[25] The Abdias tradition relates that James was originally buried in Bagte and Marke, but the locations are lost to us.[26] One claim is made by St. James Cathedral in the Armenian Quarter of Jerusalem. Here the Eastern Church says that the head of James the Greater remains under a piece of red marble in a side chapel, supposedly marking the location of James's martyrdom by beheading.[27]

The Cathedral of Santiago of Compostela, in La Coruna, northern Spain, claims James's bones. The cathedral was built in the ninth century in honor of the rediscovery of the artifacts, and it is not impossible that they were transferred there, perhaps even in the tradition of the legendary vision. James's relics rest below the main sanctuary within a small silver reliquary.[28] The Way of St. James brought reputation to Spain in medieval Christendom. As its patron saint, James was invoked to drive Islam from the country. His feast day is July

22. Kalas, *Thirteen Apostles*, 26.
23. Kalas, *Thirteen Apostles*, 28.
24. Kalas, *Thirteen Apostles*, 28–29.
25. Hippolytus, *Twelve* 4 (*ANF* 5:255).
26. Abdias, *Conflicts* 13 (Malan, 181).
27. Thelen, *Saints in Rome and Beyond*, 187.
28. Thelen, *Saints in Rome and Beyond*, 136.

25 in the West and April 30 in the East. Syriac martyrology from the early fifth century commemorates James and John together on the same liturgical day. Meanwhile, the path along the Way of St. James is still used, popular among hikers and pilgrims today. The experience for spiritual or recreational purposes is a draw for the modern world. The range of appeal to James is evidenced by the Church of Jesus Christ of Latter-Day Saints, which claims that James, Peter, and John were sent to visit formative Mormon leaders in 1829, instilling apostolic and priestly authority on them.[29] James the Greater is the patron saint of hospitals, orphans, pilgrims, and the grain crop.[30] He is noted particularly for evangelism in the face of death, stemming from the conversion of his guard, Josias, who was supposedly executed beside him.

29. Smith, *Doctrine and Covenants* 27:12.
30. Jöckle, *Encyclopedia of Saints*, 227.

✳ 5 ✳

John

The Eagle

When Jesus then saw His mother, and the disciple whom He loved standing nearby, . . . He said to the disciple, "Behold, your mother!" From that hour the disciple took her into his own *household*.

John 19:26–27

"In your name every idol, every demon, and every unclean spirit is banished. May the deity of this place, which has deceived so many, now also give way to your name." . . . And with these words of John the altar of Artemis suddenly split into many parts, and the oblations put up in the temple suddenly fell to the ground.

Acts of John 42[1]
second century, Anatolia

There was a moment in Christian history when only one apostle was left. The era of the apostles was coming to a close, and only one was still alive to reflect on that era. From his calling by the Sea of Galilee to witnessing the powerful resurrection of a little girl, there was much to reflect on. His experiences included witnessing the feeding of the five thousand, being

1. Elliott, 323.

at the foot of the cross of the crucified Savior, seeing the resurrected Messiah, being in the tumultuous upper room at Pentecost, viewing a ministry of signs and wonders such as the healing of a lame man, and undergoing grief at the death of a brother. After the dispersion of the twelve disciples from Jerusalem, he was plunged into hot oil and exiled on an island, he received revelation from an angel, and perhaps now sat on a quiet porch in Ephesus feeling his age. Once there were twelve; now there was only one. In that moment, John sat on the threshold of an era.

John's sense of solidarity with the cause may have been enhanced if he had information about the nature of the other apostles' deaths. If the legends reaching him were the same as those we are encountering on our quest, then his destiny would have been conditioned by a pattern of death through suffering. But it appears that John broke the mold and was likely the only nonmartyred apostle.

Apparently the youngest of the apostles, John was the brother of James, and together they were the "Sons of Thunder." He is traditionally recognized as "the disciple whom Jesus loved," a term of endearment and favor that makes this one disciple stand out.[2] This same love characterized the writing of a Gospel and letters under his name. While the name "John" is Greek, the Hebrew Yohanan or Yehochanon means "God has been gracious." Among the more uncommon names in first-century Palestine, it can be translated as "Yah has given."[3] Mark's is the only Gospel to mention the name Boanerges, "Sons of Thunder," while also preserving the family name "sons of Zebedee" (Mark 3:17). Scholars have made the comparison to the Greco-Roman myth of the brothers Castor and Pollux, who exercised control of thunder and lightning along with their father, Zeus. The epithet may be associated with their request to sit on each side of the divine throne in heaven.[4]

John is named by Paul in the mid-first century as a "pillar" of the church (Gal. 2:9). The apostle is among the three disciples who witnessed three special events with Jesus, and he is one of two who were arrested and harassed by the Sanhedrin. Unbeknownst to John, this pillar status provided a powerful influence on the church, and his life into the 90s allowed a whole new generation to hear his teaching. That generation had new leaders who gained credibility by perpetuating a living memory deeper into church history. He was a source link for the later leaders who claimed credible teaching in the apostolic tradition.

2. This designation appears five times in John's Gospel: 13:23; 19:26; 20:2; 21:7, 20.
3. Williams, "Palestinian Jewish Personal Names," 88.
4. Bissell, *Apostle*, 187.

John is listed third in disciple lists in two Gospels (Mark, John), fourth in two Gospels (Matthew, Luke), and second in the book of Acts list. Perhaps he was more prominent by the time of the last of these writings. Yet with all of this possible influence, John disappears in the book of Acts. He is not mentioned at the Council of Jerusalem; in the last biblical narrative reference to him, he is cominister with Peter in Samaria (Acts 8:14). He is not listed among the apostles named in 1 Corinthians 9:5–6, such as Peter and Barnabas. This phenomenon has supported a tradition that John died early, while prompting a theory of two Johns—an apostle authoring the Gospel and one epistle, and a later elder authoring two epistles along with Revelation. Evaluation of the identity of John, both in terms of his authorship and in historical legends, begins with a consideration of the biblical testimony to John.

Palestine Discipleship

In most ways the disciple named John is quiet in the narrative of the New Testament. While he is occasionally spotlighted among other disciples, John does not receive the depth of attention given a figure such as Peter. His uniqueness begins with recognition of his epithet as "the disciple whom Jesus loved," which seems to be a self-identification in his Gospel yet reflects some significant relationship between Jesus and John. The fifth and final time that the attribution is given (John 21:20) comes just before the information that this disciple will have a reputation for not experiencing death (21:23). The passage also links this same disciple with the author of the Gospel (21:24). This particular event is focused on Peter but reflects an early anticipation of John's longevity that contributes to our quest.

Like other disciples, John's apostolic profile begins with his calling by Jesus. With his brother James, John is mending fishing nets in a boat with their father, Zebedee (Matt. 4:21–22; Mark 1:19–20; Luke 5:10–11). Each synoptic writer makes the call and response brief and simple: Jesus calls them, and they leave everything and follow him. Luke's account adds the unique saying by Jesus to these fishing professionals: "Do not fear, from now on you will be catching men" (Luke 5:10). With James and Peter, John is mentioned as present at three events that are among the most impressive works of Jesus. These incidents are the raising of Jairus's daughter (Mark 5:37; Luke 8:51), the transfiguration (Mark 9:2; Matt. 17:1; Luke 9:28), and Jesus's agonizing prayer in the Garden of Gethsemane (Mark 14:33; Matt. 26:37). These events, along with the lists of the disciples, place John among the top tier of the disciples.

On two occasions in which John is named, he is profiled as judging others whom he interprets as hindering the ministry of Jesus. In the first event, seemingly in Capernaum, John remarks about a disciple outside their group who is performing exorcisms: "John said to Him, 'Teacher, we saw someone casting out demons in Your name, and we tried to prevent him because he was not following us.' But Jesus said, 'Do not hinder him, for there is no one who will perform a miracle in My name, and be able soon afterward to speak evil of Me. For he who is not against us is for us. For whoever gives you a cup of water to drink because of your name as *followers* of Christ, truly I say to you, he will not lose his reward'" (Mark 9:38–41).

In a second event, explained in our chapter on James, the brothers inquire whether divine judgment is in order for a Samaritan village that refused Jesus as he journeyed to Jerusalem. "Lord, do You want us to command fire to come down from heaven and consume them?" (Luke 9:54) seems harshly vindictive and prompts Jesus's rebuke.

John's mention in both of these chapters reveals a propensity to judge in the Gospel narratives. This historical character seems to stand in contrast to the tone of the Gospel and letters bearing his name, in which love and forgiveness are key themes. Such discontinuity means that either the profiled disciple is not the author of the other works or that his discipleship period was characterized by a sanctification of the acidity of the fledgling disciple. This latter theory suggests that John matured in his discipleship, as all of the apostles did. This tendency toward judgment is reinforced by the episode in which the brothers inquire about the privilege of sitting in judgment on either side of Jesus (Mark 10:35–45).

The next biographical piece on John comes at the site of the crucifixion. John stands as the only named disciple present in a display of faithfulness. In one of the most stirring events of the life of Christ and as a deep expression of his earthly care, Jesus from the cross assigns to John the care of his mother. The emotion of the passage is threefold: the thoughtfulness of Jesus, the security that comes to Mary, and the honor that John might have felt: "But standing by the cross of Jesus were His mother, and His mother's sister, Mary the *wife* of Clopas, and Mary Magdalene. When Jesus then saw His mother, and the disciple whom He loved standing nearby, He said to His mother, 'Woman, behold, your son!' Then He said to the disciple, 'Behold, your mother!' From that hour the disciple took her into his own *household*" (John 19:25–27). Later this event led to the city of Ephesus being associated with both John and Mary.

After the women discover the empty tomb and encounter the resurrected Lord, they alert the disciples, which results in a unique account of Peter and

John running to the tomb to see it empty. "The two were running together; and the other disciple ran ahead faster than Peter and came to the tomb first; and stooping and looking in, he saw the linen wrappings lying *there;* but he did not go in" (John 20:4–5). Such details reflect the personal interests of the author and can represent John's eyewitness account of his role on Easter morning.

Thus John becomes the first of the twelve disciples to see the empty tomb, the first sign of the resurrection. In seeming humility, he lumps himself into the mixture of confusion and belief experienced by Peter. Beyond the fact that his speed in comparison to his companion fits with his youthful profile, John stands out in this narrative for two reasons. It is odd that John would highlight his own speed and his stopping short of entering the tomb, in contrast to Peter's entering the tomb, and then explicitly mention his entering after Peter. The notable first entrance by Peter prioritizes Peter and sets up his boldness to discover the answer about the missing body of his Lord. Second, John is profiled as believing at this event (John 20:8), unlike Peter, who apparently is still processing the meaning of the event. According to F. F. Bruce, although some commentators postulate that the appearance of the resurrected Christ in the upper room launched the disciples' belief, "The beloved disciple believed in his resurrection before he saw him alive again—not indeed because he saw the empty tomb but because the disposition of the grave-clothes suddenly made the truth clear to him."[5] This explains the import of John's delay in entering the tomb and the reason why John distinguished between his first glimpse inside the tomb and his later entrance.

The final event of John's biography is crucial to understanding the quest of the apostle. After the resurrection, along the Sea of Galilee, the fishermen encounter Jesus and heed his fishing instructions, which results in plenitude. Later on the shore, an episode is recorded that will be revisited in evaluating the legacy of John's life:

> Peter, turning around, saw the disciple whom Jesus loved following *them;* the one who also had leaned back on His bosom at the supper and said, "Lord, who is the one who betrays You?" So Peter seeing him said to Jesus, "Lord, and what about this man?" Jesus said to him, "If I want him to remain until I come, what *is that* to you? You follow Me!" Therefore this saying went out among the brethren that that disciple would not die; yet Jesus did not say to him that he would not die, but only, "If I want him to remain until I come, what *is that* to you?" This is the disciple who is testifying to these things and wrote these things; and we know that his testimony is true. (John 21:20–24)

5. Bruce, *Gospel and Epistles of John*, 386.

So arose the legend that John would not die. If John is indeed the author of the Gospel, and the passage here links "the disciple whom Jesus loved" with John, then he is testifying of the anticipated longevity of his own ministry.

At the same time, John is equally the recipient of Jesus's anticipating the Twelve's collective destiny to suffer and die like Christ: "But Jesus said to them, 'You do not know what you are asking. Are you able to drink the cup that I drink, or to be baptized with the baptism with which I am baptized?' They said to Him, 'We are able.' And Jesus said to them, 'The cup that I drink you shall drink; and you shall be baptized with the baptism with which I am baptized'" (Mark 10:38–39; Matt. 20:22–23). Advocates for an early death for John marshal this expectation of suffering as evidence for John's martyrdom, precluding his longevity and natural death.

John is alongside Peter as a de facto leader in several events early in the apostolic ministry. They go together to the temple to pray when the blind man is healed (Acts 3:1). When they are arraigned together afterward, they together impress their inquisitors: "Now as they observed the confidence of Peter and John and understood that they were uneducated and untrained men, they were amazed, and *began* to recognize them as having been with Jesus" (4:13). The Jerusalem church sends them both to Samaria to investigate the acceptance of gentiles into the fold (8:14). There is a powerful image of these two significant apostles leading together. Julian Hills notes that naming John first in the list appearing in the second-century apocryphal work Epistle of the Apostles means that the apostle was "perceived as the spokesman or amanuensis of the college of the apostles."[6] The writing style of the author of this work is like that in the Gospel of John in a way that evidences influence.[7]

Ministry in Writing

The authorship of one Gospel, three letters, and the book of Revelation is traditionally attributed to John. In the early fifth century, Jerome seems to prefer the legend already circulating in his day that the apostle wrote the Gospel and the First Letter of John, while John the presbyter wrote the Second and Third Letters of John along with the Apocalypse.[8] This conflict represents the greatest historical issue related to the authorship of the Johannine corpus; a summary of the problem was provided above in the section on conflated identities in chapter 2. This survey of his writing ministry assumes

6. Hills, 14.
7. Hills, 14.
8. Jerome, *Vir. ill.* 18 (*NPNF*² 3:367).

the apostle's consistent authorship, although the evidence holds in tension the possibility of a disciple of John, the elder, being an author of some books and conflated with the apostle.

Gospel of John

This first-tier disciple is credited with the Fourth Gospel, although the text does not name him. The epithet "the disciple whom Jesus loved" functions as an autonym that John attributes to himself. In the late second century, Irenaeus remarks that John was the beloved disciple who leaned on Jesus (John 13:23–25) and who published the Gospel while at Ephesus.[9] Jerome claims that the historical impetus for its writing was the request of bishops in Anatolia, especially against Cerinthus and the Ebionites.[10] The content includes a high Christology, clear divinity claims, a concentration of teaching, and a framework of contrast between dark and light, belief and unbelief, believers and the world. Since the language of the Gospel is so theologically focused, the author is sometimes called "St. John the Divine," which is Jacobean English for "John the Theologian."[11]

Epistles 1, 2, and 3 John

The first epistle bearing John's name emphasizes the incarnation, forgiveness of sins, the role of love, and our abiding faith in Christ. The second epistle is addressed "to the chosen lady and her children," while the third epistle is to "the beloved Gaius," both epistles offering application of Christ's commands.

The authorship debate takes shape here. On one hand, there is congruence among the themes of the Johannine Gospel, Epistles, and Revelation. For example, John 13:34 reads, "A new commandment I give to you, that you love one another, even as I have loved you, that you also love one another," while 1 John 4:19 states, "We love, because He first loved us." While the case for different authors has been made, so should be the case for apostolic Johannine authorship of all five works. D. A. Carson, Douglas Moo, and Leon Morris remark: "A superficial reading of the fourth gospel and 1 John reveals many striking similarities in themes, vocabulary, and syntax."[12] The apostolic basis for 2 and 3 John, while more challenging, centers on the author as an eyewitness distinct from his readers and on his writing across church congregations, both

---

9. Irenaeus, *Haer.* 3.1.1 (*ANF* 1:414).
10. Jerome, *Vir. ill.* 9 (*NPNF*[2] 3:364).
11. Ruffin, *The Twelve*, 96.
12. Carson, Moo, and Morris, *Introduction to the New Testament*, 447.

characteristics of an apostle with authority.[13] R. Alan Culpepper summarizes the case well before suggesting authorship by John's followers:

> The internal evidence, including self-designation and considerations of thought, language, and style, point to the conclusion that the evangelist, the elder, and the seer were three different persons. Many would also distinguish the Beloved Disciple from the evangelist. On the other hand, distinct similarities in style and thought, especially between the Gospel and the Epistles, point to a close relationship between these writings. The most likely explanation seems to be that they originated in the same community, from a school of early Christian writers who had access to the same traditions and who provided guidance for a loosely related group of churches within the same general geographic area.[14]

Papias, Eusebius, and Jerome describe a theory of distinction between two Johns; yet Carson, Moo, and Morris point out that another interpretation of Papias is his intention to list two generations of testimony: the apostles and the elders. Thus, when John is listed in each, there is a dual role depicted rather than a distinction between two individuals. Furthermore, Carson, Moo, and Morris point out that Eusebius's opposition to Papias's earthly millennial hope justifies the possibility that Eusebius was happy to separate the Revelation from an apostle.[15] Robert Yarbrough notes how second-century fathers Irenaeus and Dionysius of Alexandria do not distinguish between two Johns; Irenaeus's upbringing in Asia Minor provides firsthand familiarity with the details of John's life. Papias's claims are at worst ambiguous, and he can be interpreted as not distinguishing between two Johns: "The 'presbyter John,' in Papias' parlance, may be taken as a surviving member of the select cadre of presbyters (including 'apostles') whom Papias associated with earlier times."[16]

Revelation

The apocalyptic style of the book of Revelation makes it unlike any other book in the New Testament. Its eschatological and mysterious style seems to have made it controversial already in the early church. Dionysius, a pupil of Origen, rejected the claim that Revelation was written by the apostle John.[17] Cyril, John Chrysostom, and Gregory of Nazianzus all thought that the same

13. Carson, Moo, and Morris, *Introduction to the New Testament*, 449–50.
14. Culpepper, *John, the Son of Zebedee*, 102.
15. Carson, Moo, and Morris, *Introduction to the New Testament*, 142.
16. Yarbrough, "Date of Papias," 184.
17. Eusebius, *Hist. eccl.* 7.25.

nondisciple authored Revelation; Justin, Irenaeus, Clement of Alexandria, and Tertullian believed it was authored by the apostle.

The book claims to be authored by John (Rev. 1:1, 4, 9; 22:8), and it lauds the apostles in heaven in two passages (Rev. 18:20; 21:14). Yet the style of Greek is different from the other Johannine works and actually contains solecisms, or improper grammar. Early church apocalyptic works were often pseudepigraphal. Those who seek to connect the work to the apostle explain the differences by saying that John was intending to use solecisms, that an amanuensis or dictation assistant to the elderly John was responsible for the errors, and that the theological differences require a different vocabulary.[18]

Apocryphal Works

Several apocryphal works name John as a participant in their story lines. As a member of the trio composing the first tier of disciples, the respect due him prompted authorship claims for additional works. As the longest-living apostle, his opportunity for decades of additional ministry made the potential for legends even greater. More than other apostles, his figure attracts attributions of received revelation because of his authorship of the canonical Apocalypse.

In the pattern of gnostic literature, the postresurrection Christ lays out secret teaching to John in the second-century Syrian Apocryphon of John. References to a demiurge, aeons, and dualism characterize the Cainite sayings contained in this ancient work. The apostle is the pivotal dialogue figure who sets up Christ to provide the secret teaching contained in the work. Wilhelm Schneemelcher summarizes the dynamic well: "John persists in questioning Christ, who on each occasion briefly furnishes the explanation sought, at the same time congratulating him on the relevance and depth of his questions. So gradually it is revealed: that salvation and access to perfection are assured to men of 'the unshakable race' through the descent of the Spirit of life and his presence among them."[19]

In this source, the role of John is valued in a way that reinforces the leadership and honor of the apostle in the early church. Like other gnostic works, however, the agenda is different from the canonical Gospels, and any peculiar insights into John are not valid. The same applies to another work in which John is the narrator, the Book of John concerning the Falling Asleep of Mary. The apostles are either transported by a cloud from across the globe or are

18. Carson, Moo, and Morris, *Introduction to the New Testament*, 470–72.
19. Schneemelcher, 1:325.

resurrected from the dead to gather at the deathbed of Mary before she is assumed into heaven.[20] Similar gnostic or fantastic qualities characterize Fragments of a Dialogue between John and Jesus, the Book of John the Evangelist, and the Revelation of John on Mount Tabor.

Palestine Ministry

One tradition maintains that John was martyred, likely in Jerusalem, before the Jerusalem Council in the year 50. This theory of his death essentially anchors his ministry to a short stint in Palestine and necessarily conflicts with the tradition of Ephesus discussed below. The legends are so numerous, in fact, that this story lacks a criterion of freedom from opposition and should be doubted.

Extrabiblically, a ninth-century Constantinople monk, Georgius Hamartolus, posits that Papias in the second century claimed John's death at the hands of Jews as a fulfillment of Christ's prophecy (Mark 10:39; Matt. 20:23) of their suffering. The fifth-century Philip of Side, the Pamphylian historian, claims the same death by Jews. Yet neither claim a time period for such a martyrdom. Biblically, Paul's comments about his own persecution of the followers of the Way in Acts 22:4 and 26:10 can perhaps allow for his execution of members of the twelve disciples. Ben Witherington remarks: "Acts 26:10 may be the smoking gun: Saul/Paul voted for the execution of the apostles when he was a member of the Sanhedrin. If we put all these pieces together, it appears likely that Saul had been the instigator of the demise of several apostles in the 30s before his own conversion. One of these may well have been John, son of Zebedee."[21]

The lack of any extensive story about John's early martyrdom suggests that the theory is an argument from silence. In fact, with the immense testimony of extrabiblical sources, particularly reputable patristic historians, the data shifts impressively to support the late death of John. The Sea of Galilee passage (John 21) further suggests that a long life was the path for John.

Possible support for John's martyrdom can be found in the fourth-century author Aphrahat. After listing a large number of martyrs before Jesus, he writes the following and includes John: "Great and excellent is the martyrdom of Jesus. He surpassed in affliction and in confession all who were before or after. And after Him was the faithful martyr Stephen whom the Jews stoned.

---

20. Book of John concerning the Falling Asleep of Mary (ANF 8:587–91).
21. Witherington, "Martyrdom of the Zebedee Brothers," 26.

Journey of John

Simon (Peter) also and Paul were perfect martyrs. And James and John walked in the footsteps of their Master Christ. Also (others) of the apostles thereafter in divers places confessed and proved true martyrs."[22]

However, Aphrahat may simply be writing about the suffering of the apostles, attributing martyrdom to John in terms of his exile to Patmos, which surely entailed suffering. Origen felt that the exile of John not long before his death qualifies him as a martyr.[23] Sometimes the episode of James and John asking for thrones in judgment alongside Jesus is employed to buttress a Johannine martyrdom: "Jesus said to them, 'The cup that I drink you shall drink, and you shall be baptized with the baptism with which I am baptized'" (Mark 10:39; see Matt. 20:23). Yet this need not require crucifixion or even the experience of martyrdom; it likely posits that James and John will suffer severely and sacrificially for the sake of the kingdom, as Jesus did. The conclusion here is that the testimony of John's martyrdom in Jerusalem is not strong enough, unless it is coupled with a view that the apostle and the elder were separate persons, the latter of whom would be the subject of the experiences discussed below.

22. Aphrahat, *Select Demonstrations* 21.23 (NPNF[2] 13:401).
23. Origen, *Commentary on Matthew* 16.6.

Ephesus Ministry

Ephesus is the center for the tradition of John's ministry. In the chronology of early church history, John is usually viewed as coming to the city around 48, founding the church there between 50 and 54. In his missionary journeys the apostle Paul thus followed John at Ephesus.[24] Logistically, Paul's being prevented from going to Asia may have corresponded to John's ministry in Asia, although Acts attributes the strategic change to a vision (Acts 16:6–10). Then the end of John's long life saw a return to Ephesus in 95–100.

The richest but least trustworthy of all the extrabiblical works on John is the Acts of John. The supposed miracles are too many to account for. This volume seems to give the greatest cause for Eusebius to list it among those he describes as "altogether absurd and impious."[25] Tom Bissell describes the source well: "Of all the apocryphal works, none is quite so wearying as *The Acts of John.*"[26] Nonetheless, we will consider it for its testimony of John's ministry in the area without necessarily believing its miraculous details. To open the story, the apostle travels to Ephesus through Miletus in western Asia Minor. He raises multiple dead people, destroys a pagan temple, commands bedbugs to depart, and preaches the gospel. The story closes with John taking a final Eucharist before he requests a grave, closes his career with an address, and lies in the grave to die.[27] The supposed final words of John before he lays himself in the grave come to us: "And grant me to accomplish the journey unto thee without suffering insolence or provocation, and to receive that which thou hast promised unto them that live purely and have loved thee only."[28] After climbing into the grave and before granting peace to his audience, he says simply, "Thou art with me, O Lord Jesu Christ."[29]

The second-century teachings of the Acts are gnostic and show marks of docetism, the belief that Jesus was not fully human.[30] Scholars consider the Acts of John perhaps the oldest surviving apocryphal book.

Among the legends in Acts of John is the story that the high priest at Ephesus gave John poison at the Temple of Diana. John drank it yet was unharmed, but two prisoners who drank the same poison died.[31] This is intended to be the same temple in which Paul finds himself in conflict on his

---

24. Eusebius, *Hist. eccl.* 3.23.4.
25. Eusebius, *Hist. eccl.* 3.25.6.
26. Bissell, *Apostle*, 207.
27. Acts of John (Elliott, 303–49).
28. Acts of John 115 (James, 270).
29. Acts of John 115 (James, 270).
30. Lapham, *Introduction to the New Testament Apocrypha*, 136.
31. Acts of John (James, 262).

missionary journey (Acts 19:24–20:1). In the end, John orders his disciples to dig a trench, makes a final declaration about God, and climbs into the trench that becomes his grave.[32]

Such miracles reveal the apostolic mission as a perpetuation of the miracles of Jesus seen in the canonical Gospels, yet they also seem to go beyond Jesus's mighty works. Graham Twelftree has noted how the second-century works "bring into sharper relief what was seen in New Testament texts."[33] Yet even for a miracles advocate, the idea of commanding bedbugs feels beyond the reach of miraculous necessity. The same disciples who proved to be immune to the physical suffering of martyrdom might find miracles of convenience unnecessary. Yet here principled reconciliation with the canon of Scripture leads to the theological realization that God is already recognized as providing simple necessities for his disciples. With so many episodes of various types of miracles available in Scripture, one should beware of simply dismissing similar miracles in apocryphal works out of theological expediency. The greatest help from this work for our quest is simply support of the claim that John sustained a ministry in Ephesus.

John's life continued to include documented references to Mary, the mother of Jesus, which helped to shape her own legacy in the early church. Always tied to Ephesus, the two might have seen Jesus's crucifixion assignment of John as caretaker of Mary (John 19:26–27) continue for decades. If Mary was a teenager when she bore Jesus, she would have been about seventy when John founded the church in Ephesus around 50. In the second century Irenaeus tells of how John fled the baths in Ephesus when the gnostic Cerinthus arrived, "Lest the bath-house fall down, because Cerinthus, the enemy of the truth, is within."[34]

The unique longevity of this apostle finds its roots in the scene in John's Gospel where Jesus is with select disciples on the shores of the Sea of Galilee. Peter asks Jesus, "What about this man?" in reference to John. Jesus responds with a corrective, "If I want him to remain until I come, what *is that* to you? You follow Me!" (John 21:22). The Gospel writer offers a valuable explanation of the event that reached into the legends of church history: "Therefore this saying went out among the brethren that that disciple would not die; yet Jesus did not say to him that he would not die, but *only*, 'If I want him to remain until I come, what *is that* to you?'" (John 21:23).

A valuable work of late second-century Asia Minor or Egypt, the Epistle to the Apostles prioritizes John as a recipient of the revelation provided by

32. Acts of John 111, 115 (James, 268, 270).
33. Twelftree, *In the Name of Jesus*, 33.
34. Irenaeus, *Haer.* 3.3.4 (ANF 1:416).

Jesus: "We—John and Peter and Thomas and Andrew and James and Philip and Bartholomew and Matthew and Nathanael and Judas the Zealot and Cephas—we write to the churches . . ."[35] While several other apostles are named, John is listed first, and it is rare for Peter to be displaced to the second position. In turn, John's preeminence in Anatolia lends itself to an Asia Minor provenance for the work. Interestingly, the writing style of the Epistle of the Apostles author is like that of the Gospel of John, in a way that evidences influence.[36] These factors combine for a Johannine tradition surrounding the work. However, the insights of the Epistle are less about any uniqueness of John than they are about the explanation that Jesus offers the corporate disciples.

In the Acts of Philip, John arrives on the scene at Philip's crucifixion to rescue Bartholomew from martyrdom in Hierapolis.[37] In the Ethiopic Abdias tradition, lots fall to John to minister in Anatolia. He is indentured to a woman of Ephesus in charge of a bathhouse, who regularly beats John. When a young man is killed by demons and the woman laments her responsibility in the incident, the apostle resurrects him, and she believes. In turn, the boy's family believes. On another occasion, when escorted to the temple of Artemis under the threat of arrest, he performs a successful exorcism of the temple. Later, all temples but one in Ephesus fall down as a sign of God's power. John builds churches and sets over them leaders, and believers increase. While Peter and Paul are named as dead, John continues to preach to an old age, beyond Domitian's reign. The episode of his ordering the digging of his own grave follows.[38]

Eventually the day came when John rested. This was the climactic death day for the last of the original twelve disciples. Second-century Ephesian bishop Polycrates offers a eulogy to the apostle: "John, that rested on the bosom of our Lord, who was a priest that bore the sacerdotal plate, and martyr and teacher, he, also rests at Ephesus."[39] Jerome records: "The blessed John the Evangelist lived in Ephesus until extreme old age. His disciples could barely carry him to church, and he could not muster the voice to speak many words." He kept reciting "Little children, love one another," and when his disciples asked why, he insisted it was the Lord's command and if kept is sufficient.[40] Irenaeus remarks how the one who leaned on Jesus's breast wrote his Gospel

---

35. Ep. Apos. 2 (Hills, 22).
36. Hills, 14.
37. Acts of Philip 9 (James, 449).
38. Abdias, *Conflicts* 10 (Malan, 117–45).
39. Eusebius, *Hist. eccl.* 5.24.3–4.
40. Jerome, *Commentary on Galatians* 6.10 (Cain, 260).

from Ephesus.[41] The Acts of the Holy Apostle and Evangelist John the Theologian sees John raptured into heaven from Ephesus. The next day, his disciples find only his sandals and a fountain flowing out of the ground.[42]

Rome Ministry

"Roman ministry" is a misnomer for John's possible involuntary sojourn there. Two emperors are important in the history of John's legacy: Nero (r. 54–68) and Domitian (r. 81–96). In classical history both figures are noteworthy for multiple reasons, but their personalities and concern with their own cultic worship are particularly striking. Henry Chadwick states: "Except for Caligula and Nero, the emperors had traditionally discouraged over-enthusiastic subjects from offering them divine honors. Domitian took the opposite view, styling himself 'Master and God,' and inclined to suspect of treachery those who had looked askance at his cult. The customary oath 'by the genius of the emperor' became officially obligatory."[43] It might be no coincidence that this legendary apostle found himself a target of both of these emperors.

In his study of six different early opinions regarding the dating of Revelation, Francis Gumerlock cites several less familiar sources claiming a strong Neronian link to John's biography. An ancient Syrian document called the History of John the Son of Zebedee and the Syriac translation of the New Testament by the chorepiscopus Polycarp (507/8) posit that John was exiled by Nero (r. 54–68). Theophylact of Ochrida (d. 1109), a Byzantine bishop in what is now Bulgaria, says in his preface to a commentary on the Fourth Gospel that John was "banished on the island of Patmos thirty-two years after the ascension of Christ into heaven." Additional medieval commentators followed the tradition of a Neronian martyrdom.[44]

Legend relates how Jews, objecting to John's message, influenced Domitian to bring John to Rome for trial. After engaging the emperor in dialogue on the merits of the gospel and miracles surrounding him, John asks for poison to demonstrate the power of God. While a criminal drinks from it and dies, John drinks and is protected. The apostle then raises the man from the dead. Eventually Domitian sends him to the island of Patmos until John's return to Ephesus at an old age.[45] Tertullian narrates that John was lowered into

---

41. Irenaeus, *Haer.* 3.1.1 (*ANF* 1:414).
42. Acts of the Holy Apostle and Evangelist John the Theologian (*ANF* 8:564).
43. Chadwick, *Early Church*, 26.
44. Gumerlock, *Revelation and the First Century*, 37–44.
45. Acts of the Holy Apostle and Evangelist John the Theologian (*ANF* 8:560–62).

hot oil in Rome but was unharmed, leading to his exile.[46] The oratory of San Giovanni in Oleo, southern Rome, rests on the spot where the apostle was supposedly submerged.

The authority's inability to execute John easily supposedly resulted in John's exile to Patmos. Eusebius places his life and final persecution in the reign of Domitian: "In this persecution [of Domitian], it is handed down by tradition that the apostle and evangelist John, who was yet living, in consequence of his testimony to the divine word, was condemned to dwell on the island of Patmos."[47] Legend favors the explanation that John survived the exile and the harsh conditions of Patmos. Clement of Alexandria tells that, after his release from the island, the old man traveled extensively through his territories, organizing new churches, appointing bishops, and ordaining men as the Spirit led.[48] One might expect that Papias and Polycarp heard the apostle or even studied under John's tutelage.

Patmos Ministry

Jerome records that fourteen years after Nero, in 82, Domitian's second persecution sent John into exile on Patmos, a small island just off the coast of Ephesus. It was during this exile, Irenaeus says, that the apostle's vision led to the writing of Revelation, toward the end of Domitian's reign.[49] Hippolytus likewise records, "John, again, in Asia, was banished by Domitian the king to the isle of Patmos, in which also he wrote his Gospel and saw the apocalyptic vision."[50]

The biographical report leading to this banishment is found in an apocryphal work. The reputation of the apostle leads to the attention of an emperor characterized by a passion for the Roman cult: "It came to the ears of Domitian that there was a certain Hebrew in Ephesus, John by name, who spread a report about the seat of the empire of the Romans, saying that it would quickly be rooted out, and that the kingdom of the Romans would be given to another."[51] It is also in this account that John drinks poison unharmed (reminiscent of Mark 16:18), cannot be executed, and is sent to Patmos, where he writes Revelation, then returns to Ephesus under Trajan and ascends into heaven without dying.

46. Tertullian, *Prescription against Heretics* 36 (ANF 3:260).
47. Eusebius, *Hist. eccl.* 3.18.1.
48. Eusebius, *Hist. eccl.* 3.23.6.
49. Irenaeus, *Haer.* 5.30.3 (ANF 1:559–60).
50. Hippolytus, *Twelve* 3 (ANF 5:255).
51. Acts of the Holy Apostle and Evangelist John the Theologian (ANF 8:560).

After the Emperor Domitian's death and the senatorial renunciation of his cruelty, John returned to Ephesus under Nerva and survived until the reign of Trajan. Several church fathers relate how the Patmos exile was followed by his return to Anatolia, where he strengthened the churches until he died there under Trajan, whose reign began in 98.[52] Clement describes John's return to Ephesus: "Being invited, to the contiguous territories of the nations, here to appoint bishops, there to set in order whole Churches, there to ordain such as were marked out by the Spirit."[53] Hippolytus records how, after writing Revelation on Patmos, "In Trajan's time he fell asleep at Ephesus, where his remains were sought for, but could not be found."[54] Jerome reports that he died of old age after founding a church in Asia, sixty-eight years after Christ's passion, a specificity that suggests precise knowledge.[55]

Image of John

The ubiquitous forms of John's name perpetuate his legacy: Juan, Ian, Jan, Johann, Jean, Ivan, Janet, Jeanne, and Johanna, as well as the generic John and Jane Doe.[56] In pictures throughout church history, John is often depicted as youthful, without facial hair among bearded apostles. At other times he is presented as old, perhaps because of his longevity, with white hair and a white beard. These two opposites are unique among apostolic depictions. There is an additional, elusive legend that John stood as the groom in the wedding at Cana in John 2, where Jesus turned water into wine, with Mary Magdalene as the bride. After the miracle of wine, they devoted themselves to the great Vinedresser as virgins.[57]

Symbolism and Image Construction

The symbol of the eagle represents John and his Gospel. The emblem captures the inspiring and uplifting nature of the Gospel. Like the other four evangelists, John is often presented as holding a scroll or a book. On rare occasions, John is shown with a chalice alongside a serpent or dragon,

---

52. Irenaeus, *Haer.* 2.22.5 (*ANF* 1:392); Eusebius, *Hist. eccl.* 3.23.2; 3.1.1; Jerome, *Vir. ill.* 9 (*NPNF*[2] 3:364–65).

53. Clement of Alexandria, *Who Is the Rich Man?* (*ANF* 2:603–4).

54. Hippolytus, *Twelve* 3 (*ANF* 5:255).

55. Jerome, *Vir. ill.* 9. See Acts of the Holy Apostle and Evangelist John the Theologian (*ANF* 8:562).

56. Litfin, *After Acts*, 69.

57. Bissell, *Apostle*, 206.

likely for his association with drinking poison unharmed or the depiction of Satan in Revelation. Both hold symbolism of his power over his spiritual enemy.

John is the link among some critical scholars who are sympathetic to gnostic movements in the early church. In this way of thinking, John's Gospel was a transition to allow the gnostic gospels to be partnered alongside the canonical Gospels.[58] Against the gnostic movement, several church fathers seek to establish the apostolic tradition through John. Irenaeus remarks: "When I was still a boy I saw you [Florinus] in Lower Asia with Polycarp. . . . He reported his discussion with John and others who had seen the Lord. He recalled their words."[59] In this case, Irenaeus establishes his own authority as protégé of Polycarp, protégé of John. This authority is essential for his case against the heresies, since the catholic teachings inherited from the apostles stand in opposition to the esoteric authority of the gnostic writers. Appealing to the power of apostolic tradition, Tertullian provides an inherited continuity among catholic churches that is lacking among the heresies. Calling the heretics to show records of their bishops passing down authority, he mentions "the church in Smyrna, that which records that Polycarp was placed therein by John; as also the church of Rome, which makes Clement to have been ordained in like manner by Peter. In exactly the same way the other churches likewise exhibit (their several worthies)."[60] Finally, Irenaeus says, "Then, again, the Church in Ephesus, founded by Paul, and having John remaining among them permanently until the times of Trajan, is a true witness of the tradition of the apostles."[61]

Tomb and Patronage

Bissell mentions an unfinished sixth-century work by Procopius of Caesarea (ca. 500–565), who visited structures under Emperor Justinian to document panegyrics. Concerning Saint John's Basilica, he remarks:

> On that site the natives had set up a church in early times to the Apostle John; this Apostle had been "the Theologian," because the nature of God was described by him in a manner beyond the unaided power of man. This church, which was small and in a ruined condition because of its great age, the Emperor Justinian tore down to the ground and replaced by a church so large and beautiful that, to

58. Funk, *Five Gospels*.
59. Eusebius, *Hist. eccl.* 5.20.5.
60. Tertullian, *Prescription against Heretics* 32 (*ANF* 3:258).
61. Eusebius, *Hist. eccl.* 3.23.4.

speak briefly, it resembles very closely in all respects, and is rival to, the shrine which he dedicated to all the Apostles in the imperial city.[62]

Here in Selçuk, Turkey, near ancient Ephesus on the Ayasoluk Hill, the Latin cross-shaped church has been replaced by a mosque. A fourteenth-century German priest noted that the tomb was empty.[63] In the early fifth century, Augustine seemed to believe a miracle story that the ground around John's body lives and breathes on his corpse. Sleeping is not a euphemism for death here but a "gift of protracted sleep in the body," in contrast to Peter and Paul. For the church father, it seems to fulfill Jesus's prediction "Thus I wish him to remain till I come."[64] The Middle Ages saw the perpetuation of myths surrounding his tomb, whose dust held healing properties.

The feast day of John is December 27 in the West and September 26 in the East. He is the patron saint of sculptors, bookbinders, printers, booksellers, candlemakers, painters, authors, writers, and speculative theologians. He is invoked against epilepsy, burns, poisoning, and hailstorms, while invoked for friendships and a good harvest.[65]

---

62. Bissell, *Apostle*, 200.
63. Bissell, *Apostle*, 200–202.
64. Augustine, *Homilies on the Gospel of John* 124.3 (NPNF[1] 7:448).
65. Jöckle, *Encyclopedia of Saints*, 238.

✳ 6 ✳

Philip

The Bread

Therefore Jesus, lifting up His eyes and seeing that a large crowd was coming to Him, said to Philip, "Where are we to buy bread, so that these may eat?" This He was saying to test him, for He Himself knew what He was intending to do. Philip answered Him, "Two hundred denarii worth of bread is not sufficient for them, for everyone to receive a little."

John 6:5–7

He ordered Philip to be hanged, and his ankles to be pierced, and to bring also iron hooks, and his heels also to be driven through, and to be hanged head downwards, opposite the temple on a certain tree; and stretch out Bartholomew opposite Philip, having nailed his hands on the wall of the gate of the temple.

Acts of Philip[1]
fourth century, perhaps Anatolia

While a New Testament reader can become bewildered by the identity or identities of the apostle and the deacon both named Philip, the tales of Philip that follow the book of Acts are even

1. *ANF* 8:499.

more bewildering. The disciplemaker is independently in Samaria and Gaza, but scholars are legitimately split on whether the apostle or the deacon is in view in these passages. After Acts, his travels were extensive, and perhaps the legends of two figures were merged into one, but the lack of distinction among early church sources robs us of the solution to the dilemma.

Philip means "lover of horses," and Margaret Williams writes that the name was "a well-established, even if not especially popular, name among first century Palestinian Jews."[2] This apostle was from the town of Bethsaida, the same city of origin of Andrew and Peter (John 1:44). This fishing village was by Lake Gennesaret (Sea of Galilee), twenty-five miles east of Nazareth. This means that Philip was possibly a fisherman, like other disciples. A guild might have been the foundation for the introduction of these disciples to Jesus. Significant is that Philip is named with the only other disciple to bear an original Greek name, Andrew. Ellsworth Kalas wonders whether Philip was named for Philip the tetrarch of Iturea, who named Bethsaida the capital of the province, which led to its prosperity and transformation from a small fishing village.[3]

Palestine Discipleship

The discipleship of Philip receives little attention in the Gospels. However, there are episodes in which he finds challenges to his faith that provide slight insight.

Discipleship Calling

The biblical text relates this apostle's calling as a simple event. Somewhere in Galilee, Jesus calls Philip: "The next day He purposed to go forth into Galilee, and He found Philip. And Jesus said to him, 'Follow Me'" (John 1:43). Nothing else besides his hometown of Bethsaida is provided about the call or background of Philip in the Gospels.

Philip is also believed to have been the other disciple of John the Baptist who accompanied Andrew in following Jesus, after the Baptist declared Jesus to be the Lamb of God (John 1:35–42). The reason for this association is the chronology of Philip's call, which precedes the calling of Nathanael. However, John does not mention the other disciple's name and Philip is introduced in the verses immediately thereafter, which suggests that he may not be that unnamed disciple.

2. Williams, "Palestinian Jewish Personal Names in Acts," 98.
3. Kalas, *Thirteen Apostles*, 36.

Philip is straightaway presented in the Gospel of John as engaging in a form of evangelism that might make him the first to have spread the word of Jesus to another person. While the episode goes on to describe Bartholomew's calling, Philip is instrumental in bridging the relationship between the Messiah and another future apostle: "Philip found Nathanael and said to him, 'We have found Him of whom Moses in the Law and *also* the Prophets wrote, Jesus of Nazareth, the son of Joseph.' And Nathanael said to him, 'Can any good thing come out of Nazareth?' Philip said to him, 'Come and see'" (John 1:45–46).

Philip perseveres in inviting Bartholomew to come and see for himself. While any Jew would have anticipated the coming of the Messiah, Bartholomew's dismissive remark about Jesus's upbringing requires Philip to persist.

Discipleship Episodes

Beyond the lists, Philip appears in four episodes in the Gospels, and all are exclusively in John. Three of these scenes involve encountering Jesus, twice by the instrumentality of Philip and once by the economic plan of the Son of God. The first episode is the introduction of Bartholomew to Jesus, described above.

The second episode involves not an individual encounter but rather one of the greatest miracles of Christ: the feeding of the five thousand (John 6:1–15). At times Jesus seems to employ a Socratic method of engaging disciples by posing questions that require thought, reflection, and realization. This story is one example, even explicitly saying that Jesus's question is an intellectual and spiritual examination, and Philip is the disciple of choice. "Where are we to buy bread?" Jesus asks Philip in the opening quotation of the chapter. The testing of Philip is an unusual event, one of many characteristic of the ministry of Christ in training his disciples. F. F. Bruce says: "He put the question to Philip to see what he would say, since he already had a plan of his own."[4] This miracle of feeding the crowds is in all four Gospels, but only in John is Philip named in the preceding dialogue. The number of people fed is stated as including about five thousand men (John 6:10).

The third episode is unique to John (12:20–36), who consistently provides passages on the disciples not found in any of the other Gospels. Some Greeks are in Jerusalem for a feast, probably the feast of Passover. They come to Philip, "Who was from Bethsaida of Galilee" (John 12:21), although the reason for the connection to his place of origin is indiscernible. They declare their desire to see Jesus, Philip tells Andrew, and together they tell Jesus. It may

---

4. Bruce, *Gospel and Epistles of John*, 143.

be that these Greeks come intentionally to the only two disciples with Greek names. Here we see Philip again in the position of dialoguing with Jesus on behalf of others.

The fourth episode comes in the lengthy Last Supper discourse (John 14:8–21). While various disciples ask questions that lead Jesus to explain his own plans in Jerusalem and subsequent ministry from heaven, Philip asks a question that yet again fits the theme of access to Jesus: "Philip said to Him, 'Lord, show us the Father, and it is enough for us.' Jesus said to him, 'Have I been so long with you, and *yet* you have not come to know Me, Philip? He who has seen Me has seen the Father; how *can* you say, "Show us the Father"? Do you not believe that I am in the Father, and the Father is in Me? The words that I say to you I do not speak on My own initiative, but the Father abiding in Me does His works'" (14:8–10).

Even the feeding episode, where Philip says "Two hundred denarii worth of bread is not sufficient for them" (John 6:7), and Philip's here saying "Show us the Father, and it is enough for us" (14:8) depict Philip's nascent recognition of Jesus's power. This passage continues to describe how Jesus will be accessed through the work of the Spirit in the economy of the Trinity: belief in Jesus means augmenting the very works that he performed (v. 12), there is power in asking in Jesus's name (vv. 13–14), the Holy Spirit will be provided (vv. 16–17) and abide among them (v. 17–18), and Jesus will depart from the world although the disciples will still be "in" him (vv. 19–21). "I will not leave you as orphans" (John 14:18) embodies the continual access that the disciples will have to Jesus. While Philip provides a forum for insight into Jesus's work, the apostle himself seems to display an underestimating faith.

Ministry in Writing

The theological treatises attributed to Philip as part of the New Testament Aprocrypha are not original to Philip. A gospel and two letter-styled works from the early church show characteristics of gnostic influence in their writing although they attribute the works to the apostle's name.

The Gospel and Letter of Philip

An early third-century work likely from the Antioch region, the Gospel of Philip is known by modern scholars only from the Nag Hammadi collection. It opens: "Hear, Philip, thou blessed one, that I may speak with thee, for you and Thomas and Matthew are they to whom the charge is given by the first mystery, to write down all the things which I shall say and do, and all the things which ye shall see."[5] The work focuses on the ascent of the soul and is replete with gnostic rhetoric. Its late date, discontinuity with the canonical Gospels, and gnostic nature make it untrustworthy for our quest. In the fourth century Epiphanius remarked against gnostics: "They produce a Gospel forged in the name of Philip the holy disciple."[6] Likewise, the mid-fourth-century Coptic Gospel of Philip and the third-century Letter of Philip reveal little about the apostle and are gnostic in nature. A Nag Hammadi codex, the Epistle of Peter to Philip, provides supposed instructions from Christ to preach and teach. A prior but otherwise unspecified separation prompts the letter: "But as for you, you were separate from us, and you did not desire us to come together to know how we should organize ourselves in order that we might tell the good news."[7] While the story evidences a strong gnostic milieu, justifying the need to stay assembled in the face of persecution, the work may provide an interesting reference to Philip as an apostle independently on mission, as in Acts. In contrast to the argument that Philip the deacon rather than the apostle is the independent figure in the wilderness (Acts 8:5–40), this text suggests that the apostle is the one in the desert.[8] Except for this postulation of Philip's independent mission, it offers no reliable insights on the apostle.

Palestine Ministry

After the Gospels, there are two episodes of a person named Philip beyond the Acts listing of disciples. The problem of the identity of the Philip in Acts 8 and 21 immediately arises, relating to whether this Philip is the disciple or the deacon, or whether they are the same person.

Ministry in Acts

With much attention given to Peter in Acts, Philip is unique among the other apostles for the attention he receives. When a diaspora has begun to take place (Acts 8:4), Philip goes to Samaria to preach and perform miracles of mercy. A sorcerer named Simon has the attention of the people, who attribute his power to God. He is among those who believe Philip's preaching and is baptized but is enamored with the display of power (8:5–13). Philip is eclipsed in the narrative as Peter arrives to pray that the Samaritans receive

5. Gospel of Philip (Schneemelcher, 1:272).

6. Epiphanius, *Against Heresies* 26.13.2 (Williams, 102).

7. Letter of Peter to Philip 133 (Robinson, 434).

8. Lapham, *Introduction to the New Testament Apocrypha*, 67. See Coptic Apocalypse of Peter 81.

Journey of Philip

the Holy Spirit. When Simon sees the laying on of hands, he offers money for power. Peter rebukes him, and by now Philip is gone from the story (8:14–24).

The passage relating Philip's encounter with the Ethiopian eunuch in the desert (Acts 8:26–40) is the basis for the confusion between the apostle and the deacon, as the ambiguity of the person arises in the first verse of the passage: "But an angel of the Lord spoke to Philip saying, 'Get up and go south to the road that descends from Jerusalem to Gaza'" (8:26). While the conversion of the Ethiopian eunuch is a magnificent feat of evangelism, the identity of the evangelist is not given. The debate is summarized above in chapter 2 under "Conflicting Identities."

Distilling the factors surrounding the identity of Philip in Acts 8 does not lead to a clear conclusion about whether the apostle or the deacon/evangelist is in view. There is no sure reason to ascribe the discipleship of the eunuch to the deacon, since the Acts author, Luke, profiles the work of the apostles and does not identify this Philip as the deacon in the text. On the other hand, the figure is called an evangelist and a member of the seven and is found in Caesarea. While many New Testament scholars easily let the deacon eclipse the apostle, this is a rare case where the two perspectives should be held in tension. Martin Hengel summarizes it well: "An identity as both apostle and evangelist is thus not to be rejected as impossible."[9]

Greece Ministry

The Acts of the apostle show miraculous works in a historical context and require discernment when examined. Tom Bissell argues that the apocryphal

---

9. Hengel, *Saint Peter*, 118.

Acts can be viewed as "a group of writings that seem based on vague historical traditions enriched by forceful portrayals of the apostles as unparalleled thaumaturges. Acts such as Philip's owe as much to Christian doctrine, which they try to endorse, as they do to the raw material of Eastern and Mediterranean mythology, which they shamelessly exploit."[10] Along with historical works, they combine to contribute only a few details to the quest for this apostle.

The Acts of Philip is likely of early fifth-century origin in Asia Minor around Hierapolis, where the tradition of Philip is the strongest. Its flavor is encratic, emphasizing chastity and physical self-denial. The narrative begins with Philip going from Galilee to Athens, before going on to Parthia and then to Anatolia. His first encounter after leaving Galilee captures the nature of the work as encratic and not in harmony with the Gospels or Acts, and thus not of the apostle's authorship. A widow en route to her son's funeral laments her unsuccessful efforts to call on the Greek pantheon and a diviner for help. Philip offers to raise her son in Jesus's name, attributing her solutions to the devil's deceit. "It seems better for me not to marry, and to eat nothing but bread and water," she says. Philip responds, "You are right. Chastity is especially dear to God."[11] All are baptized, and the boy follows Philip.

In Athens, three hundred philosophers gather for dialogue and debate with the apostle. As he explains Christ, performs miracles, and makes converts, they complain to Ananias the high priest in Jerusalem, who comes promptly. When he comes to smite Philip, his hand is withered and his eyes are blinded, as well as the hands and eyes of the five hundred who came with him. The priest remains obstinate during further debate about Jesus, and the apostle commands the earth, which opens and partially swallows him into Hades. The priest reports how one foot is ice-cold and the other disturbingly hot before the earth swallows him further in his unbelief. Philip heals all five hundred enemies and raises a youth from the dead, leading to five hundred baptisms. The text says that Philip lived in Athens two years, founding a church. The apostle then goes on to Parthia.

The Acts of Philip explains how Jesus divided the apostles by lots for extended ministries. Having ministered with opposition in Greece, when that region falls to Philip, he regrets it and weeps. The Lord offers encouragement by declaring that he will send Bartholomew and John "to suffer hardships in

---

10. Bissell, *Apostle*, 96.
11. Acts of Philip 1.3 (James, 439). The most recent translation of the most complete set of narrative texts is by Bovon, one of the 1974 codiscoverers of the manuscript, in Bovon and Matthews, eds., *Acts of Philip*. While the M. R. James version is now dated, it is maintained here for ease, and the contents are comparable for our study.

the same city,"[12] offering a foreshadowing of the Anatolia martyrdom narrative, where both apostles appear. As they set out for the land of the Ophiani, Philip encounters a leopard in the wilderness, who speaks in a human voice. After worshiping Philip, the leopard narrates apologetically how it seized a kid goat the night before but was moved by its childlike weeping and speech, which called for peace and prophesied about the coming of Philip. The apostle prays for the sanctification of the leopard, to put aside his beastly nature, and includes a similar prayer for the kid, leading them to lift their forefeet and worship the apostles. These creatures remain with Philip throughout the narrative, seeking the Eucharist and remaining at the church built for their protection after his death.

In the same wilderness five days later, the group finds itself in a mist before encountering a dragon and a congregation of snakes following it. As the disciples pray to the Lord of power, lightning strikes the dragon and its followers, withering them and piercing their eggs. The apostles remain unscathed. Additional stories relate how Philip's teaching in Nicatera, Greece, results in both faithful followers and Jewish opposition. His encounters include the resurrection of a lad named Theophilus as a dare from unbelievers.

Parthia and Scythia Ministry

The Acts of Philip then describes how Philip comes to Parthia, where he finds Peter and other disciples. John tells Philip that Andrew, Thomas, and Matthew have gone abroad into various dangers and that Philip should not be fearful because Jesus's presence is with him. After Philip boards a ship, a storm comes, and the crew panics. Philip consoles them, calms the storm in the name of Jesus, preaches that they should forsake the worries of this life, and baptizes them upon landing.

The regions of Parthia and Scythia also include another important story about Philip. Twenty years after the ascension, Philip encounters a cult of the god Mars, centered on an idol hosting a dragon that emerges to slay the son of a priest. Philip banishes the dragon, breaks the image, raises dead people while healing the sick, and supposedly sees thousands baptized. He ordains a bishop in the city before returning to Anatolia.

The Coptic tradition of Abdias relates the apostles casting lots for ministry, and the lot falls to Philip to go to Assakia, sometimes connected to modern Afghanistan, which in the ancient world is southeastern Scythia or eastern

---

12. Acts of Philip 8 (James, 446).

Parthia around Bactria.[13] In this account, Peter is with Philip, and he commands a demoniac to climb a pillar and testify against the city on behalf of God. A church follows, as well as the consecration of its leaders. Here the regions and characters of the Acts and Abdias traditions overlap.

Anatolia Ministry

The Acts of Philip relates how in the days of Trajan (r. 98–117) Philip is ministering throughout Asia Minor when he comes to the city of Ophioryme, or Hierapolis. Bartholomew is with him, identified here as one of the seventy, as well as his sister Mariamne. The people of the region worship a dragon represented as a snake, which Philip preaches against. Among the converts is Nicanora, the wife of the proconsul. Angered by his wife's intention to be celibate, the proconsul threatens to kill her while arresting the apostles and Mariamne: "They stripped and searched the apostles for charms, and pierced Philip's ankles and things and hung him head downward, and Bartholomew they hung naked by the hair. And they smiled on each other, as not being tormented. But Mariamne on being stripped became like an ark of glass full of light and fire, and every one ran away."[14]

As Philip asks Bartholomew whether they should call down fire from heaven on their tormentors, John arrives on the scene. When the people realize John's association with the apostles, they threaten him, only to find their hands paralyzed as they try to seize him. John then reminds Philip not to return evil for evil, yet Philip replies, "I will endure it no longer."[15] The next moment what seems to be an incantation comes from Philip, leading the earth to open and swallow seven thousand men. Jesus appears to rebuke Philip, declaring his death in glory and barring him from paradise for forty days. Meanwhile, prophecy reveals that Bartholomew is to advance to Lycaonia to be crucified, and Mariamne's body is to be laid in the Jordan River. Jesus then resurrects those whom the earth swallowed. Recognizing his imminent death, Philip orders a church to be built on his death spot, for the leopard and the kid to find care before they should be buried at the church gate, and for his own body to be buried in papyrus rather than linen like the Lord. Then Philip dies. Forty days later, Jesus appears in the form of Philip to Bartholomew and Mariamne, assuring them that Philip entered paradise.

13. Abdias, *Conflicts* 8 (Malan, 66–67).
14. Acts of Philip 9 (James, 449).
15. Acts of Philip 9 (James, 449).

The story of Philip's crucifixion upside down deserves commentary. Like Peter's tradition, the interpretation of inversion has either a positive value, through a reversal of the cosmic order by the descent of Jesus, or a negative value, through a reversal by the "first man" that now must be overcome in salvation. "In either case, man is called upon to imitate the upside-down posture if he has gnosis. . . . In either case, to be upside down is to be upright, to be converted."[16]

Though there are reasons to affirm the credibility of the Acts of Philip—such as the historical anchors of Trajan, Ananias, Hierapolis, and the traditional report of other apostles—the stories are incredible. The vengeful act of an apostle, the encounters with dragons, and the careless generality of so many healings and resurrections make the historical details untenable. Among the apocryphal Acts, this one did not receive the same ancient circulation and reception that others did.

The crucifixion of Philip in Anatolia is the most commonly accepted account of his death. The Breviary of the Apostles captures this but supplements his martyrdom: "He was crucified in Hierapolis in the province of Phrygia and he died lapidated [stoned]. And there he rests with his daughters."[17]

Other Ministry Trials

Isidore of Seville (560–636) and the Breviary of the Apostles report that Philip made missionary trips to Gaul, the land of modern France. Els Rose points out that there is no cult to Philip in the region.[18] C. Bernard Ruffin supposes the original author confused Gallia (France) with Galatia.[19] However, it is not impossible that Philip went to Gaul, though the numerous other places he is said to have visited compete with the possibility that he visited Gaul.

In the Syriac work Acts of the Apostles and the History of Philip, he charts a ship to Carthage, where he encounters a Jewish man who says that the Jesus whom Philip preaches is dust in Jerusalem. The man repents in a storm, and this draws the ire of many Jews in the city. The Roman governor threatens them for disturbing the peace before an angel smites forty priests.[20] The Coptic Abdias tradition also provides a short account in which Philip "came to the city of Afrika" without naming a specific location.[21] In general fashion, Philip

16. Smith, "Birth Upside Down," 301.
17. Rose, *Ritual Memory*, 136.
18. Rose, *Ritual Memory*, 128, 136–39.
19. Ruffin, *The Twelve*, 109.
20. Acts of Philip (James, 450–52).
21. Abdias, *Conflicts* 8 (Malan, 72).

preaches, encounters opposition to his message, performs miracles, and sees people renounce their gods before the pagan faithful cast him into prison. He is crucified upside down, similar to the Anatolian tradition.

Image of Philip

The image of Philip is not as distinctive as many of the other apostles. Yet he potentially traveled broadly, with record of his visiting Greece, Anatolia, Palestine, Africa, and Bactria, with a remote possibility of Gaul. The experiences of his life are captured in the symbols associated with him.

Symbolism and Image Construction

The symbols of Philip reflect his participation in the Gospel narratives and his mode of martyrdom. Because he was uniquely involved in the dialogue leading to the feeding of the masses by Jesus, he is often represented by loaves of bread, either two or five in number. In formal heraldry, the loaves can be represented in simple circles.[22]

The martyrdom of Philip by crucifixion in Hierapolis became the basis of another symbol. The statue in St. John Lateran of Rome by Giuseppe Mazzuoli depicts him stepping over a serpent while bearing a cross. In one tradition, Philip is crucified on a saltire cross like Andrew, and their colors distinguish them: blue for Andrew's saltire cross, and red for Philip's.[23]

Rose reports how the Breviary of the Apostles captures the image of Philip as a lamp, a light for those to whom he preached: "Philip, whose name is interpreted as 'the mouth of a lamp . . .'" She also reports how the liturgical *Benedictio de sancto Philippo apostolo* comments similarly: "He who shines brightly through the interpretation of his name as the mouth of a lamp may liberate you through his prayer from all temptation."[24] Similar is an Irish legend that pagans cut out Philip's tongue in order to silence his preaching.[25] One tradition considers Philip the man who wanted to bury his father in an encounter with Jesus (Matt. 8:21; Luke 9:59).[26] One scholar has posited that Philip was the author of Mark 1–13, some Lukan material, the Samaritan tradition in John, and the book of Hebrews.[27]

---

22. Taylor, *How to Read a Church*, 112.
23. Taylor, *How to Read a Church*, 115.
24. Rose, *Ritual Memory*, 150.
25. Rose, *Ritual Memory*, 137.
26. Clement of Alexandria, *Strom.* 3.4.25; 4.9.73.
27. Spencer, *Portrait of Philip in Acts*, 15–16.

Predictably, the personality of Philip has been described beyond the details the texts provide. Kalas claims that "he was the deliberate one: matter-of-fact, retiring, perhaps a little shy."[28] Taylor posits that he was shy, for first asking Andrew about the Greeks accessing Jesus (John 12:22–23); enthusiastic, for telling Bartholomew about Jesus (John 1:43–50); and sincere, for asking Jesus to "show us the Father" at the Last Supper (John 14:8).[29] Kalas offers an explicitly exaggerated contrast between Philip and Andrew: Andrew is the "all ablaze" evangelist, while Philip is the "soft sell."[30]

The legacy of Philip includes conflict with a particular heresy. The Latin manuscripts of Pseudo-Abdias describe how in Hierapolis Philip "extinguished the wicked heresy of the Ebionites," a movement claiming that Jesus was adopted to become the Son of God, rather than being born so of Mary.[31] Perhaps the metaphor of Philip as a light is at work here, as the light of the spiritual enemy was extinguished.

The reputation of Philip's daughters remains as a theme throughout the Philip literature. The Latin Apostolic History of Pseudo-Abdias reports that his two daughters "converted many." At his death the apostle exhorts his daughters, and later they are buried on each side of him.[32] Unknown to many women named "Phyllis," they bear the feminine version of "Philip."

Tomb and Patronage

The Coptic Abdias tradition records that at his death Philip's body was taken by an angel before the people could cast him into a fire. When the faithful fast and pray for the body to be returned, the angel provides, and it is laid in a beautiful tomb.[33] This episode is an example of the development of immediate attention to the bodies of the apostles that shaped the cult of these martyrs.

A church in Hieropolis, near Denizli in modern Turkey and dated to about 400, stands on the supposed site of Philip's martyrdom. However, Francesco D'Andria claims to have found his original tomb in 2011 at a recently excavated church about forty yards away. The sepulcher was empty.[34] The Cathedral of Florence claims to have acquired the arm of the apostle in 1205.[35]

28. Kalas, *Thirteen Apostles*, 38.
29. Taylor, *How to Read a Church*, 114.
30. Kalas, *Thirteen Apostles*, 39.
31. Rose, *Ritual Memory*, 131–32.
32. Ps.-Abd. 10 (James, 469).
33. Abdias, *Conflicts* 8 (Malan, 75–76).
34. D'Andria, "Philip's Tomb Discovered," 18.
35. Thelen, *Saints in Rome and Beyond*, 109.

The primary claim to Philip relics is recognized as belonging to the Church of the Holy Apostles in Rome. It is recorded that in the sixth century Pope Pelagius dedicated a church to Philip and James the Lesser in celebration of the expulsion of the Goths from Rome. The bones of Philip were transferred from Constantinople to Rome. An archaeological unearthing of the altar in 1873 confirmed bones in the sarcophagus. In memory of the apostles, eighteenth-century artist Domenico Maria Muratori painted a work depicting them, which is forty-five feet high and twenty-one feet wide, reputedly the largest painting in Rome. Tom Bissell describes the painting:

> In the upper left of the painting, a kneeling, youthful James, wearing blue and pink robes, looks to the heavens while a savage, shirtless Hebrew prepares to brain him with a club. In the painting's lower right, an old, loincloth-wearing Philip is being pulley lifted into position while a rabble jeers him from the base of his cross. From above, an angel rushes down to place the crown of martyrdom on Philip's head. Adrift around both doomed apostles is the usual swarm of portly cherubs, while behind them looms an opened porthole into Heaven itself—a swirling maw of pink light.[36]

Philip is the patron saint of bakers for his participation in the feeding of the crowds. Likewise, he is recognized by hatters, grocers, tanners, and fullers, while also being invoked as a guardian angel in battle.[37] His Western feast day is May 3, moved from May 1 in the sixteenth century, and shared with James the Lesser. In the Greek rite, the day is November 14.

36. Bissell, *Apostle*, 94.
37. Jöckle, *Encyclopedia of Saints*, 367.

✳ 7 ✳

Bartholomew

The Knife

Philip found Nathanael and said to him, "We have found Him of whom Moses in the Law and *also* the Prophets wrote—Jesus of Nazareth, the son of Joseph." And Nathanael said to him, "Can any good thing come out of Nazareth?"

John 1:45–46

For the blessed apostle Bartholomew was cruelly cudgeled by the savage king Astriges, and his skin was pulled off as if to make a bag on his command. But he remained steadfastly alive and joyful before Christ, and he went up to heaven as a victor when at the end his head was cut off.

Ivrea Antiphonal[1]
eleventh century, Italy

I n the Renaissance, biblical and ecclesiastical ideals found expression with new realism in painting and sculpture. In one of the most famous paintings of the historic era, *The Last Judgment*, Michelangelo painted a bearded man holding his skin. The skin hangs like the shell of a snake, scaly

1. In Rose, *Ritual Memory*, 103, 115.

and epidermal. Sitting atop a heavenly cloud, the man seems attentive, facing backward and upward toward the muscular figure of Jesus. The Renaissance painter knew well the tradition that Bartholomew suffered martyrdom with scourging. Michelangelo painted him next to the throne of God in the tradition that martyrs receive a special place in heaven, and in this case he is portrayed at the foot of Jesus in judgment. This work graphically depicts the severity of final judgment as it sits above the altar of the Sistine Chapel in the Vatican. The history of Bartholomew is as interesting as this painting.

Bartholomew has another name in some New Testament lists of the disciples: Nathanael. The oldest reference linking the two names is Elias of Damascus in the late ninth century.[2] The two are thought of as having convergent identities for two reasons. First, Bartholomew is always named along with Philip in the disciple lists in the Synoptic Gospels (Matt. 10:3; Mark 3:18; Luke 6:14), but Nathanael is introduced alongside Philip in the narrative of John. He might be paired with Philip in lists because of traditions in which they later ministered together. Second, John's Gospel records that Philip introduced Nathanael to Jesus, linking them in the only narrative uniquely featuring Nathanael.

There is precedence for having a second name, such as Simon Peter and Judas Thomas. Bartholomew could be a patronymic, "Son [Bar] of Tolmai." Margaret Williams claims that apart from the apostles, no other certain Jewish instances of double names exist.[3] Some scholars have suggested that Maacah, wife of King David, was daughter of King Talmai of Geshur (2 Sam. 3:3). This connection would make Bartholomew of Davidic royal descent. The Hebrew name Nathanael, meaning "God has given," could be a first, given name. Yet Nathanael Bartholomew is nowhere used as a full name for the apostle.

The New Testament introduces Bartholomew as a friend of Philip and fellow disciple of John the Baptist. He hails from Cana in Galilee (John 21:2), about twelve miles from the Sea of Galilee and twenty miles from Bethsaida, the home of Philip. In this geographical region we encounter one of the best stories of the disciples in the New Testament.

Palestine Discipleship

Bartholomew has a low profile in comparison to the other disciples during the ministry of Jesus. However, his first encounter with Jesus is as interesting as any discipleship calling.

2. Ruffin, *The Twelve*, 112.
3. Williams, "Palestinian Jewish Personal Names in Acts," 94.

Discipleship Calling

In the Gospels, Philip encounters Jesus seemingly only a short time before he reports to Nathanael (Bartholomew), "We have found Him of whom Moses in the Law and *also* the Prophets wrote—Jesus of Nazareth, the son of Joseph" (John 1:45). The statement would have been profound for a Jew. The fulfillment of the lawgiver Moses's writing and the expectation of the prophets actualizes the heart of the Old Testament instruction and anticipation. It is a claim that the long-anticipated Messiah has come. The response of Nathanael is classic: "Can any good thing come out of Nazareth?" (John 1:46). Cynical, sarcastic, and dismissive, the comment disdains Philip's claim to the discovery of the Messiah. Here is the first potential rejection of Jesus, even if the accusation is brief and comes from one who is about to be recognized as guileless. Such a response contrasts with the silence of Peter, who dropped his nets, and Matthew, who left his tax booth. In fact, it is more like Thomas's remark after the resurrection, signaling his unbelief. Yet Philip's discovery likely bore on Nathanael with confidence as Philip responds, "Come and see." F. F. Bruce recognizes the bantering here between a believer and his skeptic friend: "Honest inquiry is a sovereign cure for prejudice. Nazareth might be all that Nathanael thought, but there is an exception to prove every rule; and what an exception these young men had found!"[4]

John's Gospel records the first encounter between the future disciple and his Master:

> Jesus saw Nathanael coming to Him, and said of him, "Behold, an Israelite indeed, in whom is no deceit!" Nathanael said to Him, "How do You know me?" Jesus answered and said to him, "Before Philip called you, when you were under the fig tree, I saw you." Nathanael answered Him, "Rabbi, You are the Son of God; You are the King of Israel." Jesus answered and said to him, "Because I said to you that I saw you under the fig tree, do you believe? You shall see greater things than these." And He said to him, "Truly, truly, I say to you, you shall see the heavens opened and the angels of God ascending and descending on the Son of Man." (John 1:47–51)

The comments of each dialogue participant are important. First, Jesus calls Nathanael "an Israelite indeed, in whom is no guile." His comment is a compliment to the Jewish recipient and echoes Psalm 32:2, "How blessed is the man to whom the Lord does not impute iniquity, And in whose spirit there is no deceit!" Saying Nathanael is an honest son of Israel is ironic

---

4. Bruce, *Gospel and Epistles of John*, 60.

because the patriarch's other name, Jacob, means "supplanter" and would have suggested deceit.[5]

Second, Jesus makes a claim whose full significance is lost to us: "Before Philip called you, when you were under the fig tree, I saw you." Apparently this reveals Jesus's miraculous powers of perception and impresses Nathanael enough that he calls Jesus "Rabbi," "Son of God," and "King of Israel." Nathanael's skeptical tone has changed. Reminiscent of Thomas's "My Lord and my God" (John 20:28), Nathanael declares a high Christology at the moment that evidence for messiahship is provided (John 1:49).

Third, the rhetorical a priori question comes to Nathanael from Jesus: "Because I said to you that I saw you under the fig tree, do you believe? You will see greater things than these." Then comes a prophetic statement evocative of Jacob's experience of witnessing the opening of the heavens with angels moving up and down (Gen. 28:12). Jesus calls himself the "Son of Man" for the first time as a self-indicator of his identity.

More important for our quest for this disciple, it is no coincidence that the disclosure of a Messiah figure came to one sitting under a fig tree, as Nathanael was. The fig tree was highly symbolic of Israel as a nation. Jeremiah's judgment against Israel depicts "no figs on the fig tree" when its people lack the fruit of righteousness (8:13). On his final entrance into Jerusalem, characterized by his being rejected by the religious establishment and his uttering the prophecy of a destroyed temple, Jesus curses a fig tree (Matt. 21:19–21). In the Olivet discourse, he uses that fig tree as a sign of the times of destruction to come (Matt. 24:32), which came to Jerusalem about forty years later. In contrast to the evergreens of Palestine, a deciduous plant like a fig tree would have signified the seasons with its cycle of leaves. It is no coincidence that the barren fig tree resonates as an indictment against the religious establishment. Nathanael's association with the fig tree suggests a principle of the twelve disciples: their mission will be related to the work of God among his people Israel.

This revelation comes to a mere man of Cana (John 21:2), likely a fisherman. Cana and Nazareth were neighboring cities, perhaps communicating that a network of friendship or business was already in place for these early disciples.

Discipleship Episodes

Like an inclusio bracketing an event, the only other mention of Nathanael besides the disciple lists comes at the end of John's Gospel, after

5. Bruce, *Gospel and Epistles of John*, 60–61.

the resurrection, on the Sea of Tiberias (John 21). Here Bartholomew is named in the company of Peter, Thomas, James, John, and "two other of his disciples." While the other two might have been from among the original Twelve, the mention of the relatively obscure Nathanael implies that James the Lesser or Jude would have been named if either was part of the two. The group proceeds to fish through the night to no avail. In the morning, Jesus is on the shore and instructs them to fish on the right side of the boat, leading to a heavy catch of fish. Jesus welcomes his weary disciples on the shore with a fire and the great christological episode of the resurrected Jesus eating fish and breaking bread (John 21:12–13). The encounter shifts to focus on Peter and his expectations about his future and John's. Bartholomew's role is eclipsed.

The quest for the path and influence of Bartholomew might be the most complex and difficult of all the apostles. While his trail may have moved from east to west, with a recorded presence in three locations as he passed through, these three locations with independent traditions also compete with one another. Ministry episodes across a geographical span can be linked together for an itinerant ministry, as long as the historical markers, such as reigning kings, coincide with historical records. However, when the tradition of Bartholomew's martyrdom is considered, the only conclusion is that the veracity of part or all of a tradition is in jeopardy. Each tradition will be weighed on its own merits and its compatibility with the tradition of Bartholomew in other locations. The geographical range of itinerant ministry for Bartholomew is wide, from Anatolia to Parthia, Egypt, and India. Three of these locations have a martyrdom tradition varying from the others, so the quest for this apostle will be among the most complicated.

Ministry in Writing

The Gospel (Questions) of Bartholomew includes a series of dialogical teachings of Jesus with Bartholomew after the crucifixion. Questions arise concerning Christ's suffering in the underworld, the dynamics of souls after death, Mary's role in revelation, and details of angels. A text set called Coptic Texts of Bartholomew is sometimes included in the Book of the Resurrection of Jesus Christ by Bartholomew the Disciple, which contains a series of brief encounters between Jesus and individuals around the days of Jesus's passion. The narrative describes Bartholomew's reactions to glorious events, such as seeing Jesus on the chariot of the cherubim and a glorious Adam ascending to heaven and receiving nourishment from his visions to displace his need for

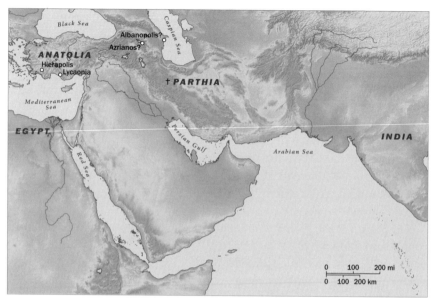

Journey of Bartholomew

food.[6] Jerome rejects this gospel, along with those of Matthias and Thomas, as literary monuments that are the beginning of various heresies.[7]

Anatolia Ministry

An early ministry in Asia Minor may have launched a serial ministry for Bartholomew in a region commonly accessible to Jerusalem on the way to farther regions of the empire. The Acts of Philip relates a story of the mutual imprisonment and cocrucifixion of Philip and Bartholomew at Hierapolis in the region of Phrygia, in Greek Anatolia. One challenge is immediate: the text centering on Philip identifies Bartholomew as one of the Seventy, although Hippolytus does not identify one by that name in his list.[8] The area includes Derbe, where Paul and Barnabas served around 46–48. Going through the cities and regions of Lydia and Asia, Philip and Bartholomew come to Hierapolis. There they preach against idolatry and satanic affiliations, and Nicanora, the wife of the proconsul, communicates her intent to become celibate. In rage, the proconsul orders "Philip and Bartholomew and Mariamne to be

6. Book of the Resurrection of Christ by Bartholomew the Apostle (James, 184).
7. Jerome, *Commentary on Matthew* proem, trans. Scheck, 51.
8. Acts of Philip (*ANF* 8:497); Hippolytus, *On the Seventy Apostles* (*ANF* 5:255–56).

beaten, and after they have been scourged with the thongs, he ordered their feet to be tied, and them to be dragged through the streets of the city."[9] After this, the proconsul orders: "Stretch out Bartholomew opposite Philip, having nailed his hands on the wall of the gate of the temple." Supposedly Philip prays for his colleague's release, which soon comes. Philip is martyred there but first appeals to the multitude to release Bartholomew. His freedom comes with a prophecy by Jesus to Philip of Bartholomew's upcoming crucifixion in Lycaonia.[10] John the apostle is also present to persuade the crowd of its wrongdoing in punishing the other two apostles. Els Rose reports that the Lycaonian tradition of Bartholomew's crucifixion there entered into liturgical traditions of the apostle.[11] Patristic writers confirm a Phrygian ministry in central Anatolia for Bartholomew. Chrysostom and Ephraim say he preached for a time in Lycaonia of central Asia Minor before ministering in Armenia, four hundred miles northeast.[12]

Parthia Ministry

The modern state of Armenia was part of the Parthian region of the first century, along the border of Scythia and the Caspian Sea, a region with regularly changing borders and representing the general area east of Roman jurisdiction.[13] The Coptic Acts of Andrew and Bartholomew relates Bartholomew's call to the city of Azrianos to team with Andrew for ministry.[14] There he feels pulled to minister to the demon-possessed wife of a judge in Macedonia who had a significant ministry to the poor of the city when Satan came upon her, but he finds the Lord commanding him to Parthia. A miraculous rise in the sea facilitates a quick detour, taking him to northern Greece. Bartholomew spreads out his hands and commands from afar that the demon leave the judge's wife. Michael the archangel descends to the rescue and brings her to the apostles, who are on a ship where Jesus himself is disguised as the captain. The exorcism is successful. In Parthia the apostle also confronts idolatry, partnering with Andrew to destroy idols and build a church. Both apostles depart gloriously to other fields of ministry.

In the Coptic Abdias narrative, Bartholomew moves to what seems to be Africa at Naidas on the seashore, although we cannot be sure this is not a

9. Acts of Philip (*ANF* 8:498–99).
10. Acts of Philip (*ANF* 8:501).
11. Rose, *Ritual Memory*, 86.
12. Starowieyski, "Bartholomew."
13. Schmidt, *Apostles after Acts*, 149n13.
14. Abdias, *Conflicts* 76, 81.

Parthian milieu. The people's hearts are opened, and they forsake idols, forgive debts, and believe in God. Yet the king connects the apostle's fame to the message of celibacy in marriage. On trial before King Acarpus, the apostle testifies that it is God and not himself who troubles the city or commands wives to separate from their husbands in line with encratic theology. The monarch orders that he be cast into the sea in a sack of sand, which results in his death.

The Breviary of the Apostles is a Latin text that contains biographies of the apostles, written in Gaul by the beginning of the seventh century. It reports on Bartholomew's ministry in Anatolia and his death in southern Parthia: "The apostle Bartholomew . . . preached in Lycaonia. In the end he was skinned alive by the barbarians of Albanopolis, Great-Armenia, and at the command of king Astargis, beheaded and buried on 24 August."[15] David Criswell describes the effects: "The whips used in scourging had tiny bits of metal and bone tied to them, thereby tearing the flesh from a person's body."[16] Isidore of Seville's *Birth and Death of the Fathers* and Hrabanus Maurus's ninth-century martyrology relate the same details of his martyrdom.[17]

These traditions concretize the strong patronage of Bartholomew in Armenia. The tradition of martyrdom by flaying is late in origin, a seventh-century tradition, and is sometimes set in Persia, which was also part of ancient Parthia. One might conceive of a ministry from Phrygia to Armenia, on a journey that advanced on to India, although no records remain for experiences in the vast Persia between them. However, the traditions of Bartholomew's death in Parthia, or in modern Armenia and Azerbaijan, conflict with the legacy of his death in India.

Egypt Ministry

The Ethiopic accounts related to Abdias describe lots falling to Bartholomew to preach in Elwa, rendered "the land of the Oases" in the Arabic versions. Peter and Bartholomew travel together, pretending that Bartholomew is a servant, whom a traveler pays Peter to procure, seeming to indenture Bartholomew as a vinedresser: "Then Bartholomew went to his lord's vineyard, and worked in it all the days of vinedressing."[18] Through various encounters, some of which have encratic themes, Bartholomew preaches and performs miracles. On one occasion, a man falls dead after a snakebite. The apostle's prayer leads the serpent to come out; it inquires why it must obey the apostle, then proceeds to

---

15. Rose, *Ritual Memory*, 86.
16. Criswell, *Apostles after Jesus*, 89.
17. Rose, *Ritual Memory*, 87–89.
18. Abdias, *Conflicts* 5 (Malan, 35).

suck the venom from the man so he is resurrected. The effect of Bartholomew's work is to see the building of a church and its workers baptized.

India Ministry

The Martyrdom of the Holy and Glorious Apostle Bartholomew relates how Bartholomew goes to the lower section of India as a pilgrim among the poor. As he dwells at the temple of Astaruth, his presence prevents demons from performing supernatural works for their worshipers. An unusual passage provides Bartholomew's physical description and his temperament as a neighboring demon reveals Bartholomew's identity to an inquirer:

> He has black hair, a shaggy head, a fair skin, large eyes, beautiful nostrils, his ears hidden by the hair of his head, with a yellow beard, a few grey hairs, of middle height, and neither tall nor stunted, but middling, clothed with a white undercloak bordered with purple, and upon his shoulders a very white cloak; and his clothes have been worn twenty-six years, but neither are they dirty, nor have they waxed old. Seven times a day he bends the knee to the Lord, and seven times a night does he pray to God. His voice is like the sound of an angry trumpet; there go along with him angels of God, who allow him neither to be weary, nor to hunger, nor to thirst; his face, and his soul, and his heart are always glad and rejoicing; he foresees everything, he knows and speaks every tongue of every nation.[19]

When King Polymius hears of one exorcism by Bartholomew, he brings his demon-possessed daughter to him. With a simple command, the girl is freed. When the king seeks to reward the healer with precious goods, Bartholomew cannot be found to receive them. Instead he appears at the king's bedside and provides an explanation of the gospel story, centered on the virgin birth but tracing the narrative of sin and salvation back to Adam. In one moment, Bartholomew presents the mission of the apostles that is the basis for our quest:

> When the Lord had conquered the tyrant [in the wilderness], He sent His apostles into all the world, that He might redeem His people from the deception of the devil; and one of these I am, an apostle of Christ. On this account we seek not after gold and silver, but rather despise them, because we labour to be rich in that place where the kingdom of Him alone endureth for ever, where neither trouble, nor grief, nor groaning, nor death, has place; where there is eternal blessedness, and ineffable joy, and everlasting exultation, and perpetual repose.[20]

19. Martyrdom of the Holy and Glorious Apostle Bartholomew (*ANF* 8:553).
20. Martyrdom of the Holy and Glorious Apostle Bartholomew (*ANF* 8:555).

After Bartholomew exorcises a demon seeming to be Astaruth from the temple, the king and people from surrounding cities all believe and are baptized. However, when nearby Greeks relate the events, Astreges, the elder brother to Polymius, angrily seizes Bartholomew, declaring, "As thou hast made my brother deny his gods, and believe in thy God, so I also will make you reject thy God and believe in my gods."[21] After learning that his threats have caused his own idol god, Baldad, to be broken to pieces, Astreges orders the apostle beaten and beheaded. Here Greek manuscripts add "flayed" in the Latin Abdias heritage to reflect the later tradition.[22] Supposedly twelve thousand believers secure the body, carrying Bartholomew's remains to Lipari. On account of the apostle, the demons overpower King Astreges, strangling him and his priests. King Polymius then becomes a bishop for twenty years. Adolf von Harnack writes that for early Christians "exorcism formed one very powerful method of their mission and propaganda."[23]

A possible synthesis of the Armenia and India martyrdom accounts comes from Hippolytus: "Bartholomew, again, preached to the Indians, to whom he also gave the Gospel according to Matthew, and was crucified with his head downward, and was buried in Allanum, a town of the great Armenia."[24] Eusebius describes how Pantaenus, a philosopher in the late second century, came to India, where he encountered the Gospel of Matthew. The historian reports that Bartholomew preached and left the Gospel in Hebrew.[25] Jerome affirms the tradition of Bartholomew.[26] Around 850 the monk Ado of Vienne wrote a martyrology and recorded that Bartholomew ministered in India and died by decapitation, but one should be careful of his claim that the decapitation was in India.[27] David Criswell is convinced that Bartholomew spent about ten years in Armenia before going to India, if he really went at all.[28]

Image of Bartholomew

The quest for the historical Bartholomew is difficult, shrouded in various competing traditions that shape his image, especially involving the Armenians and his opposition to idols. Ronald Brownrigg imagines compatibility between

21. Martyrdom of the Holy and Glorious Apostle Bartholomew (ANF 8:557).
22. Ps.-Abd. 8 (James, 498).
23. Twelftree, In the Name of Jesus, 26.
24. Hippolytus, Twelve 6 (ANF 5:255).
25. Eusebius, Hist. eccl. 5.10.3.
26. Jerome, Vir. ill. 36 (NPNF² 3:370).
27. Rose, Ritual Memory, 88.
28. Criswell, Apostles after Jesus, 85.

all of these various traditions: first, a ministry in Phrygia; second, work in India; and third, efforts in Armenia that resulted in martyrdom.[29]

The sixteenth-century scholar Richard Adelbert Lipsius sums up the variety of martyrdom accounts: "The gnostic legend of Bartholomew has him crucified, the Coptic narrative has him put in a sack full of sand then sunk in the sea, the local Armenian saga has him beaten with clubs, a fourth tradition (probably originating in Persia) has him flayed, and finally a fifth tradition has him beheaded."[30] Sean McDowell considers the various executions all valid options.[31]

Criswell achieves a strong synthesis between the Armenian and Indian traditions by suggesting that Bartholomew went to India about 60 for a short-lived ministry and returned to Armenia no later than 64. Although Criswell allows for the possibility of Bartholomew's death in India about 62, he considers it equally possible that the apostle died in 70, after his return to Armenia.[32] This summary seems like the best path to adopt for the apostle Bartholomew.

Regardless of the path, the image of Bartholomew is centered on the late tradition of his martyrdom by flaying. His primary symbol is skin, representative of the peeling of his own epidermal tissue in one tradition of his martyrdom.

Symbolism and Other Imagery

The legend of Bartholomew's martyrdom by flaying was adopted by medieval artists to shape the most popular image of his death in contrast to the legends of beheading and crucifixion. As in the Michelangelo painting above the altar of the Sistine Chapel, he is often portrayed holding a knife and his skin in separate hands or arms. A flaying knife is likewise a symbol for the apostle. His statue in St. John Lateran Basilica by Le Gros has a human skin resting on an open cloak.

The tradition of the removal of his skin is promoted in a liturgical response given in the Ivrea Antiphonal of northwestern Italy. It embellishes the tradition of the Martyrdom of Bartholomew: "For the blessed apostle Bartholomew was cruelly cudgeled by the savage King Astriges, and his skin was pulled off as if to make a bag on his command. But he remained steadfastly alive and joyful before Christ, and he went up to heaven as a victor when at the end his head was cut off."[33]

29. Brownrigg, *Twelve Apostles*, 136.
30. Klauck, *Apocryphal Acts of the Apostles*, 244.
31. McDowell, *Fate of the Apostles*, 220.
32. Criswell, *Apostles after Jesus*, 86.
33. Rose, *Ritual Memory*, 103, 115.

Ellsworth Kalas says concerning the Gospel account of Nathanael encountering Jesus, "The apostle Nathanael was the childlike one."[34] Claims based on one passage and one encounter in the man's life lack sufficient foundation, even if done to promote a childlike faith.

Tomb and Patronage

The Frankfurt Cathedral in Germany claims that Bartholomew's skull rests in a Gothic reliquary in a transept.[35] German kings were anointed at the central altar in the late Middle Ages.

In the tradition of Bartholomew's ministry and death in India, legend claims that Indian pagans witnessed how his remains were honored due to miracles he had performed. They placed his bones in a lead coffin, which they cast into the sea. By the divine will, the coffin floated to Lipari, off the coast of Sicily. When the Muslims invaded Sicily in 831, they laid waste to the island of Lipari, where the body reposed, breaking the tomb open and scattering the bones. Supposedly Bartholomew appeared to a monk, instructing him to gather the bones, which he collected and sent to Benevento. By the thirteenth century, Jacobus de Voragine reports how the bones had even then been claimed by Rome, perhaps after the sacking campaign of Emperor Frederick II in Benevento. A supposed vision of Bartholomew protecting his bones during this campaign may have fueled the legend around their final resting place.[36]

This claim to the body of Bartholomew in Rome comes from the small Tiber Island, at the Basilica of St. Bartholomew on the island. The tomb is a porphyry basin on the main altar supported by marble, with a plaque reading *Corpus San Barthomai Apostoli,* "The body of Saint Bartholomew the Apostle." The church dedicates its space to martyrs from various parts of the world: Asia, Oceania, and the Middle East, with a Bible, chalice, and miter from sacrificial witnesses there.

Yet the city of Benevento contests the legend of the interred Bartholomew's transfer to Rome.[37] Now the Basilica of St. Bartholomew in Benevento, Italy, claims to have the apostle's relics in a porphyry urn below the main altar, with an additional bone fragment in a bust of the saint. The Cathedral of St. Bartholomew in Lipari claims to have his thumb in a silver arm reliquary.[38]

34. Kalas, *Thirteen Apostles*, 69.
35. Thelen, *Saints in Rome and Beyond*, 165.
36. De Voragine, *Golden Legend*, 483–84.
37. Thelen, *Saints in Rome and Beyond*, 57.
38. Thelen, *Saints in Rome and Beyond*, 122, 128. Ado, the monk of Vienne, relates the transfer of the relics from Lipari to Benevento in his mid-ninth-century martyrology; Rose, *Ritual Memory*, 88.

Regardless of the location or locations of the bones of Bartholomew, these legends offer credibility to the story of his original burial in Armenia.

In the eleventh century, an arm of Bartholomew was supposedly sold to Edward the Confessor of England, who turned it over to Canterbury Cathedral. This helps to explain the strong veneration of Bartholomew in England, with churches and hospitals devoted to his name and legacy.[39]

Bartholomew is the patron saint of tanners and leatherworkers, as well as bakers, miners, bookbinders, shepherds, butchers, millers, winegrowers, and various food merchants.[40] He is also the patron saint of Armenia, joining Jude in being called the "First Illuminators of Armenia."[41] A number of British churches are named after him, with his popularity rising after one of his arms was donated to Canterbury in the eleventh century. A developing image of Bartholomew as a prototype of martyrs might be seen in the basilica on the Tiber Island. In Jubilee year 2000, John Paul II declared that the church would commemorate all Christian martyrs, leading to having art and artifacts in the church dedicated to all Christian martyrs. As one example, Tom Bissell reports the stole of a Salvadoran priest on display, including a photograph of his dead body slumped over a book after being executed by communists.[42] Bartholomew's feast day is celebrated on August 24 in the West and June 11 in the East.

39. Rose, *Ritual Memory*, 80–81.
40. Jöckle, *Encyclopedia of Saints*, 53.
41. McDowell, *Fate of the Apostles*, 241.
42. Bissell, *Apostle*, 52.

✳ 8 ✳

Thomas

The Builder

"Unless I see in His hands the imprint of the nails, and put my finger into the place of the nails, and put my hand into His side, I will not believe." . . . Thomas answered and said to Him, "My Lord and my God!"

John 20:25, 28

Then the Apostle spread forth his hands, and made supplication unto God, and said, "O my God, my Lord, and my hope and my Saviour, who hast strengthened me, and has made me prepared for this judgment." . . . Then the four men came near and pierced him with spears, and he fell upon the earth, and gave up the ghost.

Abdias, *Conflicts of the Holy Apostles*[1]
second century, Parthia

With the exception of Judas Iscariot, no apostolic legacy has a singular defining blemish like Thomas's. Iscariot is synonymous with betrayal in the same way that Thomas is synonymous with

1. Abdias, *Conflicts* 15 (Malan, 218).

doubt. For that matter, Thomas is the one disciple ascribed a negative descriptor: "doubting Thomas." The name stands symbolically for the individual in a group who is the last to embrace a rational hypothesis without substantial proof. When philosopher Mike Hockney introduces the concept of sufficient reason in his work *Causation and the Principle of Sufficient Reason*, there appears the illustration of "doubting Thomas" as a metaphor for empiricism and sensory reason.[2]

Reservation and disbelief in the legacy of Thomas expand from one biblical account into a confusing geographical legacy. It has proved difficult for scholars to secure an exact journey for the apostle. Among the sure legends of the apostles, the expansion of ministry to India is unparalleled in distance and in terms of a given apostle's influence in an area. In an apocryphal work Thomas poses as a builder in order to build the church on the eastern border of the empire, and he is the only disciple with a denomination named after him.[3] In order to alleviate the perpetual image of Thomas as doubter, in this chapter he is called a builder.

The nomenclature surrounding Thomas is important for the shaping of his identity. John's Gospel alone records the surname Didymus for Thomas (11:16). "Thomas" is an Anglicization of the Hebrew word for "twin," which is *didymus* in Greek. Margaret Williams writes that it is best seen as a second name, with no evidence that first-century Palestinian Jews used it as a given name.[4] While the New Testament tells us nothing of his twin, second-century gnostic legends surrounding Thomas embellished this fact to make him the twin brother of Jesus. The relationship was so important, in fact, that Fred Lapham observes: "Thomas is portrayed as being so closely bound up with Jesus that at times he appears to *become* him."[5]

While the Western tradition tends to call the disciple Thomas or Thomas Didymus, the Eastern tradition prefers Judas Thomas.[6] Eusebius reports his name as Judah.[7] Thus he shares the Hebrew name Judah and the Greek name Judas with two other apostles. The Syriac tradition, such as in the Acts of Thomas, calls him Judas and Judas Thomas. The Teaching of the Apostles (ca. 230) uses this name as it introduces us to his sphere of influence: "India, and all the countries belonging to it and round about it, even to the farthest sea, received the apostles' ordination to the priesthood from Judas Thomas,

2. Hockney, *Causation*, n.p.
3. Kalas, *Thirteen Apostles*, 102.
4. Williams, "Palestinian Jewish Personal Names in Acts," 103.
5. Lapham, *Introduction to the New Testament Apocrypha*, 114.
6. Schneemelcher, 1:286.
7. Eusebius, *Hist. eccl.* 1.13.

who was guide and ruler in the church which he had built there, in which he also ministered there."[8]

Palestine Discipleship

The Synoptic Gospels mention Thomas only in the disciple lists. The Johannine Gospel highlights him in four brief episodes, attributing profound and moving quotations to him. However, his doubt after Jesus's resurrection stands out as the most significant. In fact, Thomas's words to the other apostles are the most quoted of any apostle's and are indelibly linked to Thomas: "Unless I see in His hands the imprint of the nails, and put my finger into the place of the nails, and put my hand into His side, I will not believe" (John 20:25). His engagement with Jesus is one of the few that provides understanding of the personality of a disciple.

The first attention to Thomas occurs when Martha and Mary send word that their brother, Lazarus, is sick (John 11:3–15). Jesus seems intentionally to delay coming to help, instead launching a dialogue with the disciples on the nature of death. Thomas remarks, "Let us also go, that we may die with Him" (John 11:16). While the NASB capitalizes "Him" to refer to Jesus, the KJV does not, providing two interpretations in translation. The first communicates a willingness to die with Lazarus; perhaps the heaviness of the conversation and the hopelessness of death have led Thomas to despair. The second communicates a willingness to die with Jesus; F. F. Bruce says, "If his Master is to die, he [Thomas] has no wish to survive him."[9] Certainly this death event anticipates the hope to come with Jesus's resurrection.

Second, at the Last Supper discourse in the upper room, several disciples ask questions that enable Jesus to give an insightful explanation of his mission. When Thomas asks, "Lord, we do not know where You are going, how do we know the way?" it prompts one of Christ's greatest quotes: "I am the way, and the truth, and the life; no one comes to the Father but through Me" (John 14:5–6).

The most significant event involving Thomas comes because Thomas is absent when the resurrected Lord first appears in the disciples' midst (John 20:19–23). "But Thomas, one of the twelve, called Didymus, was not with them when Jesus came. So the other disciples were saying to him, 'We have seen the Lord!' But he said to them, 'Unless I see in His hands the imprint of the nails, and put my finger into the place of the nails, and put my hand into His side, I will not believe'" (John 20:24–25).

8. Teaching of the Apostles 3 (*ANF* 8:671).
9. Bruce, *Gospel and Epistles of John*, 242.

Eight days later, with the door shut, Jesus again appears among them. The author makes sure to emphasize that Thomas is there. "Then He [Jesus] said to Thomas, 'Reach here with your finger, and see My hands; and reach here your hand and put it into My side; and do not be unbelieving, but believing.' Thomas answered and said to Him, 'My Lord and my God!'" (John 20:27–28). With this declaration, the matter of Thomas's doubt is satisfied, and we inherit a christological confession of hope.

Thomas is mentioned one other time in John's Gospel, in the episode at the Sea of Galilee, listed with some of the Twelve on the seashore (John 21:2). Here Peter is highlighted and John is mentioned, but the other disciples are in the background.

Ministry in Writing

The apostle Thomas is a popular figure among the gnostic texts. Several works are highlighted here to reveal Thomas as a gnostic prototype, a model disciple who provides esoteric insights from Christ. While the gnostic features cannot be systematically organized, characteristics such as dualism concerning this world and the next can be recognized. One unique feature of Thomas in these works is his presentation as the twin brother of Jesus, enhancing his spiritual proximity to Jesus in his role as apostle of an esoteric message. In works of sayings, the Book of Thomas the Contender records Jesus calling Thomas his "brother," or "twin."[10] In works of narrative, the king of Andrapolis sees Jesus appear in the form of Thomas as the Lord calls himself the brother of Thomas.[11] A serpent calls Thomas the twin of Jesus as the serpent calls himself the offspring of the oppressor in the Garden of Eden.[12]

The Infancy Gospel of Thomas contains miraculous legends clearly incongruent with our understanding of Jesus based on the canonical Gospels.[13] For example, a careless bump by another boy leads an exasperated Jesus to slay him on command and to blind the boy's parents after they express their objections to Joseph. The father grabs his son by the ear, but Jesus commands the father not to irritate him. There is no reason to believe this work comes from the apostle; it is pseudepigraphal.

Found in the second-century Nag Hammadi collection, the Book of Thomas the Contender provides the following role for this apostle: "The

---

10. The Book of Thomas the Contender (Robinson, 201).
11. Acts of Thomas 11 (James, 369).
12. Abdias, *Conflicts* 15 (Malan, 207).
13. Infancy Gospel of Thomas (Elliott, 68–83).

secret words that the savior spoke to Judas Thomas. . . . The savior said, 'Brother Thomas, while you have time in the world, listen to me, and I will reveal to you the things you have pondered in your mind.'"[14] Lapham says that this dialogue between Thomas and Jesus was written "for the admonition and encouragement of Christian souls and their leaders who are struggling to uphold an ascetic or encratite tradition within an ethos of moral turpitude and sexual laxity."[15]

The Gospel of Thomas in the Nag Hammadi codices is a collection of 114 logia, or sayings attributed to Jesus (singular "logion"), about half of which parallel those in canonical Gospels.[16] Written about 150, the work has received an immense amount of attention compared to other gnostic texts.[17] Thomas is affirmed in the text as the writer: "These are the secret sayings which the living Jesus spoke and which Didymos Judas Thomas wrote down."[18] In one logion, Jesus pulls Thomas aside and speaks privately. When the other apostles inquire about the words, Thomas remarks, "If I tell you one of the things which he told me, you will pick up stones and throw them at me; a fire will come out the stones and burn you up."[19] The most unusual sections show a gnostic influence. This sample illustrates the ambiguous spiritual exhortation of the Jesus who teaches in these works: "Jesus said, 'When you make the two one, and when you make the inside like the outside, and the outside like the inside, and the above like the below, and when you make the male and the female into one and the same, so that the male not be male nor the female female; and when you fashion eyes in place of an eye, and a hand in place of a hand, and a foot in place of a foot, a likeness in place of a likeness, then you shall enter the kingdom.'"[20]

In a different logion that seems to stand alone, Jesus says: "Become passers-by."[21] Such commands reflect the desirability of transcendence in gnostic thought, the desire to evade the undesirable human element of this earthly life. Like many apocryphal gnostic works, the theology does not cohere with the apostolic tradition, which in turn excludes the possibility of any contribution to better understanding the ministry of Thomas. Lapham insists: "We find no evidence of an orthodox belief in the salvatory or redemptive role

14. The Book of Thomas the Contender (Robinson, 201).

15. Lapham, *Introduction to New Testament Apocrypha*, 128.

16. Lapham, *Introduction to New Testament Apocrypha*, 115.

17. For a treatment of the history of the manuscript of the Gospel of Thomas, see Moreschini and Norelli, *Early Christian Greek and Latin Literature*, 1:68–71.

18. Gos. Thom. proem (Robinson, 126).

19. Gos. Thom. 13 (Robinson, 128).

20. Gos. Thom. 22 (Robinson, 129).

21. Gos. Thom. 42 (Robinson, 131).

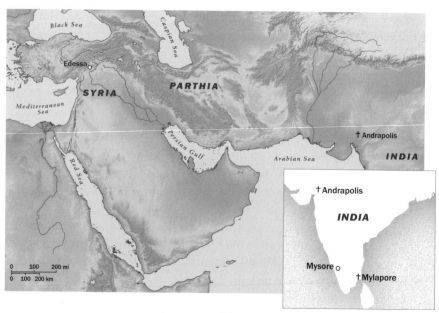

Journey of Thomas

of Christ. . . . There is no place for the cross; and the concept of vicarious sacrifice is completely foreign to this Gospel."[22]

The sixth-century Apocalypse of Thomas is a revelation from Christ that anticipates the signs of the times typical of apocalyptic language, with days unfolding various tribulations from heaven and an antichrist.[23] The Hymn of Jude Thomas the Apostle in the Country of the Indians is an allegorical poem of the soul entering into the body and eventually finding liberation from it.[24] Both works are strongly gnostic and dualistic. The strong gnostic tradition about Thomas provides us almost no insight into his journey, except to recognize an anchor to his travels in Syria to help these expressions of the gnostic myth take form.

Parthia Ministry

The journey of Thomas seems to have begun with a land voyage to Parthia that passed through Syria. The region of Parthia extended from southeast

22. Lapham, *Introduction to New Testament Apocrypha*, 119.
23. Apocalypse of Thomas (James, 555–63).
24. Sometimes cited as a separate work, it is an interlude in the Acts of Thomas 109–13 (James, 411–15).

Anatolia, south of the Caspian Sea, over into modern India. The legends of Thomas's ministry in northeast India discussed below could overlap with his Parthia experiences. Mesopotamia was where Thomas tradition literature developed, and it tends more strongly toward encratite practices—such as abstinence from marriage and eating meat—than other apostolic apocryphal Acts.

Thomas's calling to Parthia begins with the story of the apostles' division of the known world into ministry regions, with Parthia falling to Thomas.[25] The Ethiopian Abdias story records Thomas, along with Peter and Matthias, launching out on a trip by land to India. After forty locations, Matthias breaks off to his appointed country, Syria or Scythia. The Lord appears in the story and indentures Thomas to a guardsman of the Indian King Cantacoros as the apostle describes his skills: "I am a builder and an architect, and I am a physician."[26] At this point Thomas is taken to India.

The Syriac preference for Thomas in its literary traditions supports a genuine historical connection. The Abgar tradition related below in the chapter on Jude reports how Thomas sent Jude to Edessa when the king petitioned Jesus.[27] A hymn by Ephraim suggests Thomas's burial in Edessa, which implies a historical connection there.[28] By the fifth century, Gregory Nazianzus, Ambrose, Jerome, and Paulinus of Nola all spoke of Thomas's travels to Parthia or India without clear distinction.[29] The sixth-century Syriac Acts of Mār Mārī the Apostle centers on the ministry of one Mārī at the turn of the second century in the Mesopotamian region. As Mārī travels to its lower parts, he is said to have "detected the traces of Saint Thomas the Apostle."[30] In the late 300s a pilgrim named Sylvia is said to have visited Thomas's tomb in Edessa, and her record still exists.[31] The proximity of Syria to Parthia makes a joint heritage possible and even provides a possible path for Thomas from the Middle East to India, not along the common sea route but along the equally common land route through Syria, Parthia, and then into modern India. With this evidence, the legitimacy of the northwest Indian tradition is strengthened, especially when considering that this section of India was part of ancient Parthia.

---

25. Eusebius, *Hist. eccl.* 3.1.1.
26. Abdias, *Conflicts* 15 (Malan, 190).
27. Eusebius, *Hist. eccl.* 1.13.4.
28. Ephraim, *Nisibene Hymns* 42.1 (NPNF² 13:205).
29. Gregory of Nazianzus, *Orations* 33.11 (NPNF² 7:332); Ambrose, *Works*; Jerome, *Epistle 40 to Marcellus; Paulinus of Nola*, all cited in Medlycott, *India and the Apostle Thomas*, 44–46.
30. Acts of Mār Mārī 32, in Harrak, *Acts of Mār Mārī the Apostle*, 75.
31. Brownrigg, *Twelve Apostles*, 182.

India Ministry

The early third-century Acts of Thomas is the earliest known account of Thomas's missionary activity in India and was likely written around Edessa. The story begins in Jerusalem with the apostles' division of evangelism by geography. Thomas refuses India, but at the docks Jesus sells him into slavery to a merchant of King Gundaphorus, charged to find carpenters for a building campaign. Trade was common between the Jews of the Near East and India.

En route the travelers land at the wedding of a king's daughter in Andrapolis, where the apostle proclaims to the bride his ascetic gospel of celibacy. The king becomes angry when his daughter chooses a spiritual marriage to Jesus rather than a temporal marriage to her fiancé. He accuses Thomas of sorcery for his miracles and message and orders his arrest, but the apostle has already set sail.

A second encounter comes when Thomas lands in the realm of King Gundaphorus. As a carpenter, Thomas receives a commission and funding to build the palace of the king. However, the apostle goes about the villages and gives away the resources as alms. Even the advisers to the king report on the apostle's kindness. When called to account, Thomas presents no effort toward the king's earthy palace but claims that he is building a palace in heaven. When the king's brother, Gad, dies, he envisions the heavenly palace, is resurrected, and reports to the king about the apostle's work in a heavenly palace, and the king acquiesces. A harvest of ministry in the king's realm ensues.

A third encounter, mentioned above, is with a serpent who bit a boy, leading to the boy's death. The serpent explains his actions to Thomas. The snake calls the apostle the twin of Jesus and himself the offspring of the oppressor in the Garden of Eden. In service to Thomas, the snake sucks the venom from the dead boy until the boy resurrects and the snake bursts. In another encounter, a donkey speaks to reveal himself as a descendent of Balaam, whereby the apostle mounts him and rides to the city gates, where the donkey dies. Later a different donkey is commanded by Thomas to enter a city and order an exorcism of the general population, which is effective. A woman who dies from the sword of an infatuated youth is resurrected and reports her experience in hell: her experiences remind us of Dante's *Inferno*.

So the encounters continue in the Acts of Thomas, accompanied by long dialogues and theological explanations. Thomas advances through India with miracles and sermons as his ministry activities lead to local conflicts. His evangelism comes into conflict with the religious establishment, and his encratic message of celibacy angers leading husbands when their wives dedicate themselves to God. Thomas's final imprisonment follows a lengthy story in which he dialogues with the wives of King Mazdai and sees the conversion of the king's son and his captain, Vazan and Siphor, who become a deacon and presbyter, respectively. At trial, the king asks Thomas, "Are you a slave or a free man?" The apostle answers, "I am the bondsman of one only, over whom thou hast no authority."[32] Judas Thomas is ordered to be taken to a mountain and slain by four spearmen. His final prayer was supposedly recorded; a piece of that speech is quoted to open this chapter.

After some time, the same king brings his demon-possessed son to the tomb of Thomas, planning to open it and touch a bone to his son in hopes of healing him. Thomas appears to him, declaring: "Thou didst not believe in me when alive; how wilt thou believe in me when I am dead? Fear not. Jesus Christ is kindly disposed to thee, through His great clemency."[33] The son is healed, and the king expresses his wish to believe and asks Christians in his realm to pray for him.

In these stories Thomas works powerful miracles and is such a close twin of Jesus that he seems to be Jesus himself. When commissioned to build by King Gundaphorus, Thomas remarks: "For to this end am I come, to build and to do the work of a carpenter."[34] He appears in visions, such as when the king brings his son to the tomb. The number of resurrections he performs is considerable.

The Ethiopian Abdias tradition relates many of the same episodes.[35] In addition, Thomas prays in a city so that their idols collapse, he converts aristocrats' wives, and he draws the ire of local leadership, which leads to his flaying. The city of Quantaria is once named, where a priest and worshipers of Apollo seek to stone him, but their hands wither. At the prayer of Thomas, the priest is suspended in the air, turned head downward, and carried around above the crowd until he professes faith in God. In this account, Thomas finally leaves India for Actabodi and Macedonia. He is imprisoned as an enchanter, and the king orders his delivery to a high mountain for execution, as in the Acts of Thomas.

The historical details of these events in India anchor the path of Thomas in three traditional locations. They can be viewed in thirteen separate acts presented in the Montague Rhodes James version of the text, cited in this chapter. The first tradition is described in act 2 of the James version, while the second tradition is described in acts 7 and 9–12. The other acts are presented as itinerant in their setting, with act 1 including the calling and indenturing

32. Acts of Thomas 163 (James, 435).
33. Acts of the Holy Apostle Thomas (*ANF* 8:552).
34. Acts of Thomas 17 (James, 371).
35. Abdias, *Conflicts* 15 (Malan, 187–220).

of Thomas as well as the Andrapolis wedding episode. Fred Lapham suggests that the opposing internal traditions between north and south may represent two traditions merged in one work.[36]

In the first historical tradition, King Gundaphorus IV is associated with the Punjab people in the northwestern part of India, even into modern Pakistan and Afghanistan, all composing the ancient region of Parthia. This matches the testimony of Eusebius and others that Thomas was given the assignment of Parthia for ministry.[37] The weight of this location is that it ties Thomas to Syria by land travel, connecting his work in India with the similar tradition of the Syriac Thomas heritage.

In the second historical tradition, King Mazdai is associated with Mylapore in the suburbs of Madras in southeast India, now known as Chennai. Thomas's ministry in this area would likely have stemmed from his journey by boat across the Indian Ocean and centered on the east coast before his burial in this location. There stands a huge Gothic cathedral along with oral traditions and recorded songs about Thomas. "Thomas Christians" is a name claimed by the surrounding Christian community, and Marco Polo is said to have visited the nearby tomb of Thomas in a province of the Malabar region. The Acts of Thomas sees King Mazdai execute the apostle; writers who assign Thomas's death and burial to a rocky hilltop in Calamina would link his legacy here. A 1523 excavation of the tomb revealed bones.

In the third historical tradition, a king of Gona is associated with Mysore in the southwest part of India along the Malabar Coast. The close ties between Rome and Mysore lead scholars such as Ronald Brownrigg to speculate that a rajah named Kutnappar, etymologically close to the name Gundaphorus, sent for him from the West.[38] The tradition here finds minor support in the Ethiopic version of the Acts of Thomas.

The early historical attestation of Thomas in India seems accurate, in part because it generalizes the region, supporting the theory that "India" was used for the lands beyond Parthia. The record in Hippolytus provides the needed combination of both Syriac and Indian ministries, logically moving from Jerusalem east through Syria to India. He records the apostle's ministry in India and Iran: "Thomas preached to the Parthians, Medes, Persians, Hyrcanians, Bactrians, and Magi, and was thrust through in the four members of his body with pine spears at Calamene, the city of India, and was buried there."[39] This supports the Mazdai tradition above. An early-fourth-century

---

36. Lapham, *Introduction to New Testament Apocrypha*, 122–23.
37. Eusebius, *Hist. eccl.* 3.1.1.
38. Brownrigg, *Twelve Apostles*, 192.
39. Hippolytus, *Twelve* 8 (*ANF* 5:255).

missionary, Theophilos the Indian, was sent by Emperor Constantius III to set up churches for local regions and Roman travelers. Somewhere along the way, he encountered Indians holding regular church services, with Syriac Gospel readings.[40] In the fourth century, Ephraim writes in a hymn of the evil one wailing concerning the power of Thomas, tying together his India ministry and his eventual Syrian burial site: "I stirred up Death to slay the Apostles, that I might be safe from their blows. By their deaths now more exceedingly am I cruelly beaten. The Apostle whom I slew in India is before me in Edessa; he is here wholly and also there. I went there, there was he: here and there I have found him and been grieved. Blessed is the might that dwells in the hallowed bones."[41]

This geographical synthesis is yet again reinforced below in the legend of Thomas's bones traveling from India to Edessa. The range of locations for the physical remains of Thomas either is due to a diversity of claims without historical foundation or it represents the range of Thomas's ministry, speaking to the presence and influence of the apostle in various regions.

Image of Thomas

The image of Thomas is forever associated with his ministry to India. "India" in the ancient world meant generally the far reaches of Parthia and beyond, so we cannot determine the exact influence that disciple had there. However, Thomas is valued highly by Indian churches. There is a strong oral and phenomenological tradition, including legends, poems, and themes among churches. There are also unparalleled miraculous feats in the Acts of Thomas in the India tradition. The Syriac Thomas tradition is more certain, especially around Edessa and in the culture of churches in modern Syria and Armenia. Thomas's long and profound discourses have led to his reputation as the "Israelite Philosopher." His symbols match the character of his experiences and martyrdom.

Symbolism and Image Construction

A carpenter's square is often in the hands of Thomas statues because of the legend that he was sold as a carpenter to enter India and for his building of a palace for the Indian king. Both the T- and L-shaped squares are his symbols. Likewise, the symbol of a spear, for his martyrdom, represents the apostle.

40. Medlycott, *India and the Apostle Thomas*, 197–201.
41. Ephraim, *Nisibene Hymns* 42.1 (*NPNF*[2] 13:205).

Thomas's name metaphorically refers to doubt or incredulity. "Doubting Thomas" is a common expression, and the apostle is the patron saint of poor eyesight for his lack of faith, referring to spiritual blindness. Ellsworth Kalas overreaches concerning the personality of the apostle when he explains this doubting quality: "Thomas had an essentially scientific turn of mind."[42] At the same time, it is unfair to take the one episode of Thomas's doubt and extend it into a perpetual quality, as the church has done.

Thomas embodies the geographical reach of the apostles, taking the gospel to the uttermost when he went to India, the farthest boundaries of the Roman Empire and the lands of Alexander the Great's conquest. Scholars speak of the phenomenon of "Thomas Christians" to refer to India's believers, and there is a rich pride about Thomas among Indian Christians. Tom Bissell describes the pride: "Indian Christians want something more than the bragging rights of having encountered the Christian faith six hundred years before Russia, nine hundred years before Sweden, or a thousand years before Lithuania."[43]

In an interesting development, Thomas's legacy is being used in a new way in critical biblical scholarship. The pseudepigraphal gnostic gospel bearing his name is sometimes compared to the Gospel of John, which contains a developed Christology and a more advanced system of soteriology. This comparison functions as a foundation for the Gospel of Thomas to serve as a transitional gospel account to gnostic literature. The Jesus Seminar was a collection of scholars in the late twentieth century who critically evaluated the sayings of Jesus recorded in the Gospels for authenticity, notably casting votes of opinion by colored beads for items that Jesus (1) did say, (2) probably did say, (3) probably did not say, and (4) did not say. The boundaries chosen reflect the scholars' openness to the idea of the gnostic tradition containing authentic sayings of Jesus, and analysis of the Gospel of Thomas was included in their first publication, *The Five Gospels*.[44]

Tomb and Patronage

The tomb of Thomas in India may be under the St. Thomas Basilica in Mylapore, Chennai, India. This is the supposed location of the mountain on which he was executed by spears. The tomb is empty, and a few minor relics can be found there.[45] Bissell describes how "My Lord and my God" is

---

42. Kalas, *Thirteen Apostles*, 94.
43. Bissell, *Apostle*, 233.
44. Funk, *Five Gospels*.
45. Thelen, *Saints in Rome and Beyond*, 194.

displayed across the hem of the cloth draping the tomb.[46] Bryan Litfin entirely discredits the tomb: "The tradition that Thomas himself went to southern India is based on flimsy evidence passed down by word of mouth."[47]

A fourth-century legend says that Syrian Christians moved Thomas's bones from India to Edessa on July 3, leading to this date as Thomas's feast day. Legend continues that, to avoid Muslim destruction, in 1258 the remains were sent to Ortona, Italy, by way of the Greek island of Chios. The Cathedral of St. Thomas the Apostle in Ortona houses relics in a golden casket within a white marble altar in the crypt.[48] Meanwhile the Basilica of the Holy Cross in Jerusalem in Rome holds a silver reliquary reputed to contain the finger that Thomas used to examine the wounds of Jesus, which it displays four times a year.[49] The Church of St. Thomas in Parione in Rome is the national church of Ethiopia, dedicated to the apostle, who is depicted over the altar.[50]

Thomas's feast day is July 3 in the West and October 6 in the East. He is the patron saint of Portugal, the East Indies, and the pontifical state. Additionally, his patronage covers engaged people, architects, builders, surveyors, carpenters, and theologians.[51]

46. Bissell, *Apostle*, 259.
47. Litfin, *After Acts*, 107.
48. Thelen, *Saints in Rome and Beyond*, 132.
49. Thelen, *Saints in Rome and Beyond*, 18, 86, 251.
50. Thelen, *Saints in Rome and Beyond*, 251.
51. Jöckle, *Encyclopedia of Saints*, 433.

❋ 9 ❋

Matthew

The Publican

As Jesus went on from there, He saw a man called Matthew, sitting in the tax collector's booth; and He said to him, "Follow Me!" And he got up and followed Him.

Matthew 9:9

Therefore the wicked and unclean devil said to him, "O king, why art thou thus put to the worse by this stranger and sorcerer [Matthew]? Knowest thou not that he was a publican, but now he has been called an apostle by Jesus, who was crucified by the Jews?"

Acts of Matthew[1]
sixth century, Persia

The expansion of the Roman Empire saw a higher demand for taxes and increased attention to the organization of collection. In first-century Palestine, the occupying Romans used three main types of taxes to gain imperial revenue from their subjects: a tax on the ground of one-tenth of harvested grain and one-fifth of harvested fruit, a poll tax that was a set amount for each adult, and an income tax of 1 percent of total business

---

1. Acts and Martyrdom of St. Matthew the Apostle (*ANF* 8:530, adapted).

income. There were a number of other taxes on goods, travel crossings, and business locations.[2] A massive endeavor was needed to enforce all this. Many imperial initiatives, such as Augustus's census, which led Joseph and the expectant Mary to Bethlehem, functioned primarily for measuring and securing taxes: "Now in those days a decree went out from Caesar Augustus, that a census be taken of all the inhabited earth. . . . And everyone was on his way to register for the census, each to his own city" (Luke 2:1, 3).

Meanwhile, the occupied Jews were a highly nationalistic and passionately monotheistic people, not easily amenable to an occupying foreign nation imposing taxes on them. The most committed citizens regarded homeland, religious law, and self-governance as covenantal rights for God's chosen people. When the Roman tax enterprise needed workers, it fell to the governors of the province. The governors in turn hired publicans, or "tax farmers," to collect taxes at the local level. Such individuals were usually locals who knew the social landscape, individuals of means, and general economic dynamics. For financially minded Jews, this business opportunity was a necessity under Roman occupation. The potential publican would bid for the collection privileges. Imperial loans were sometimes the basis of cash flow, and the process was replete with corruption. Cicero remarks, "In regards to trades and commerce, which ones are to be respected and which ones are base, these are generally established. First, those that incur hatred of men are the tax-collectors and usurers."[3] When some Jewish individuals served as publicans, they clashed ideologically with fellow Jews who were often religious leaders or political zealots. These enthusiasts despised their publican peers for both the ingrained corruption and the principled cooperation with an occupying gentile force.

And so, when the Jewish Messiah calls Levi, the tax collector for the Romans, while in his booth, the context is loaded with irony and consequence. The disciple was likely an individual of personal means, skilled in finance. Tax collectors or publicans were notoriously dishonest, and his bearing the Jewish name Levi could exacerbate how he is a sellout to Rome against Israel. The best word to describe kindness to a first-century tax collector is simply "grace." Levi was perhaps more accustomed to contempt, and such a Jewish man receiving an invitation to join an effort of Jewish fulfillment is astounding. This grace typifies the mercy that Jesus shows socially despised individuals who are willing to honor God. Such responses to Jesus even become programmatic: he rejects those perceived as religious while accepting tax collectors and sinners (Mark 2:15–17).

2. Kalas, *Thirteen Apostles*, 84.
3. Cicero, *De officiis* 1.150, in Dyck, trans., *Commentary on Cicero*, 333–36 (AT).

The tax office at Capernaum would have had interest in materials entering the territory of Herod Antipas through roadways and through the waters of the Sea of Galilee and the Jordan River. Thus Matthew would have been attentive to Jewish activities for Antipas rather than directly for Roman taxes.[4] The fish of Galilean fishermen, including the disciples of Jesus, could have been taxed. Although the Gospel writers record little conflict between disciples, the ideology and interpersonal dynamics between a Galilean tax collector and Galileans of any skilled trade surely made for potential disagreement between them. Perhaps the grace that Jesus displayed spread to the disciples interpersonally.

Matthew means "gift of Yah," *mattanyâ*, and as a name it had a high frequency at the time of the apostles.[5] Its Greek meaning is "disciple." It has already been established above that the names Matthew and Levi in the Gospels apply to the same apostle: "Matthew" is called from his tax booth (Matt. 9:9) in the same fashion as "Levi" (Mark 2:14; Luke 5:27). At the turn of the second century, Clement of Alexandria describes the contribution of several apostles as united in confessing their faith. Yet when he does so, he introduces a complication by naming a Matthew and a Levi separately: "There is a confession by faith and conduct, and one with the voice. The confession that is made with the voice, and before the authorities, is what the most reckon the only confession. Not soundly: and hypocrites also can confess with this confession. But neither will this utterance be found to be spoken universally; for all the saved have confessed with the confession made by the voice, and departed. Of whom are Matthew, Philip, Thomas, Levi, and many others."[6]

Two challenges face this distinction between Matthew and Levi. First, the source for Clement is the gnostic Heracleon, and his full endorsement of the details might not be intended as much as the overarching quality of their common purpose. Second, the reference to "many others" invites the possibility that beginning with Levi, Clement is moving beyond the original Twelve to name others with the common purpose profiled here. There is insufficient evidence from Clement to conclude that Matthew and Levi of the Gospels are different people. Clement of Alexandria, based on Matthew's being a tax collector and thus likely a wealthy person, says that Matthias is in fact Zacchaeus, found in Luke's Gospel, described as rich and noted for his climbing a tree to see Jesus (Luke 19:1–6).[7] Yet for every voice that names Levi and Matthew as separate disciples, there are numerous voices, such as Jerome,

---

4. France, *Matthew*, 167.
5. Williams, "Palestinian Jewish Personal Names in Acts," 91.
6. Clement of Alexandria, *Strom.* 4.9 (ANF 2:422).
7. Clement of Alexandria, *Strom.* 4.6 (ANF 2:415).

that make them interchangeable: "Matthew, also called Levi, apostle and aforetimes publican."[8] Interestingly, Clement claims, "The apostle Matthew partook of seeds, and nuts, and vegetables, without flesh."[9] Mention of this type of unique personal attribute of an apostle is rare in early church writings.

Palestine Discipleship

The attention to Matthew in the New Testament is brief. Yet included in this brief treatment is one of the greatest episodes of response and sacrifice to the call of Jesus. To this day the image of Matthew is one of a tax collector who seems to follow without pause, deserting his post in response to the invitation of the Messiah. The drastic departure from collecting the taxes of fellow Jews to following the Messiah figure of those Jews is so radical that Bryan Litfin compares it to the career change of John Newton, the slave trader turned hymn writer.[10]

Discipleship Calling

In Matthew 9:9 Jesus sees "Matthew, sitting in the tax collector's booth" when he instructs him simply, "Follow Me." Mark 2:14 and Luke 5:27 chronicle the same event and employ the same language, but these accounts use the name Levi instead. With Levi being a Hebrew name and Matthew a Greek name, it is simple to deduce that the tax collector bore two names, common in cultural assimilation and the diversity of the ancient world.

The powerful response of a tax collector immediately leaving his booth in commitment to Jesus has been inspirational to the church. Imagine a tax booth, a living symbol of Roman oppression, staffed by a Jew commissioned to collect from his own people. Ellsworth Kalas depicts the situation well: "It's possible to become so absorbed in the paraphernalia of success that we drown out the voice of God. It could have happened to Matthew. The flow of human traffic, the sounds of the marketplace, the struggle to keep a step ahead of other people, the exhilaration of winning, the excitement of accumulating still more—all of these could have captured Matthew's attention so that he might have missed Jesus' call."[11]

Yet the would-be disciple did not miss the call. He responded with a sense of spontaneity and immediacy. First-century Palestinian Jews must have reacted

8. Jerome, *Vir. ill.* 3 (NPNF[2] 3:362).
9. Clement of Alexandria, *Instructor* 2.1 (*ANF* 2:241).
10. Litfin, *After Acts*, 39.
11. Kalas, *Thirteen Apostles*, 90.

with astonishment to the conversion of a tax collector. Speaking to those influenced by John the Baptist, Jesus insists that the least in the kingdom are greater than John (Luke 7:28). The covenantal faithful among the people seemed moved by the paradigm shift, as recorded in the next verse: "And when all the people and the tax collectors heard *this*, they acknowledged God's justice, having been baptized with the baptism of John" (7:29). The humility of a tax collector and the significance of his acceptance, which led to the people's praise, are contrasted with the unbelief of the religious leaders immediately afterward: "But the Pharisees and the lawyers rejected God's purpose for themselves, not having been baptized by John" (7:30).

Discipleship Episodes

The New Testament mentions almost nothing of the role of Matthew among the twelve disciples during the ministry of Christ or in the book of Acts. We have only one glimpse of Matthew's individual actions, just after his calling. Luke mentions that Matthew provided a feast at his home in 5:29, perhaps in appreciation of his newfound mission. The real insight comes with the omission of the name of the feast sponsor in Matthew's Gospel. At Matthew 9:10, the same feast is taking place, yet without any attention to Matthew himself. This can be viewed as a criterion of humility that supports Matthew's own authorship of the work and gives us a glimpse into the possible personal humility of the disciple himself.

Ministry in Writing

Scholars have suggested that a tax collector would have been skilled in note taking as part of his responsibilities.[12] Matthew's financially oriented, scribal lifestyle makes sense of the Gospel's parables on money and the frequent rabbinical appreciation of the Old Testament. This profile functions as credibility for Matthew's authorship of the Gospel, with a criterion of dissimilarity because this person was not otherwise a prominent member of the disciples.[13]

The Gospel of Matthew

Among the four Gospels, the one attributed to Matthew is regarded as distinctive mostly for its Jewish-Christian nature. R. T. France summarizes the

12. Gundry, *Use of the Old Testament in St. Matthew's Gospel*, 182–85.
13. France, *Matthew*, 33.

qualities: "In its constant reference to the Old Testament, the strong Jewish flavoring, its explicit discussions of the conflict between Jesus and the Jewish authorities, it forms a fitting bridge between Old and New Testaments, a constant reminder to Christians of the 'rock from which they are hewn.'"[14] Its Semitic qualities extend to style, focus, language, and themes. A Jewish reader would have recognized these features, including the use of a Jewish put-down such as *raka* (Matt. 5:22) and the quoting of a verse such as Isaiah 7:14 that a virgin will conceive a child to be called Emmanuel (Matt. 1:23). The structure of certain chapters illustrates Matthew's intent to show Jesus as parallel to Moses when he teaches from the law (chaps. 5–7) and performs miracles (chaps. 8–9), offering fulfillment to the promise that God would raise up a prophet like Moses among the brethren (Deut. 18:18). These themes would have resonated with a Jewish heart.

The Gospel represents the greatest contribution to the apostle's legacy. Yet twentieth-century voices such as form critics George Kilpatrick and Krister Stendahl are noted for attributing its authorship to a Matthean school after the apostle rather than the apostle himself.[15] The earliest centuries of Christianity did not entertain this notion, whether because they lacked knowledge of form criticism or because they had firmer reason to believe in Matthew's pen. Examination of the church fathers on the Gospel authorship is important in the question of the contribution of Matthew the apostle.

In one of the most curious and ambiguous citations in all the church fathers, Eusebius reports a remark of Papias, bishop of Hierapolis, at the turn of the second century: "Matthew composed his history in the Hebrew dialect."[16] The comment helps to discover the provenance of the Gospel of Matthew. Interpretations of "in the Hebrew dialect" range from the idea that the Gospel was an Aramaic work to its being a Greek writing with Jewish themes. While there is a range of scholarly opinion on the authorship of Matthew, many scholars concede that at least the core of the Gospel should be associated with the apostle, if it was not authored entirely by him. This puts its writing in the latter half of the first century. R. T. France provides two important factors in support of this date. First, if Matthew relied on Mark's Gospel material, which can be dated to 65 for its reliance on Peter in Rome, then Matthew must have been alive and writing in the decade to follow. Second, the destruction of Jerusalem in 70 is likely evidenced by Matthew 22:7; 23:38; and chapter 24, placing the

---

14. France, *Matthew*, 16.
15. Carson, Moo, and Morris, *Introduction to the New Testament*, 75.
16. Eusebius, *Hist. eccl.* 3.39.

Gospel's earliest possible date after this event, if it comes from the personal observation of the author.[17]

Irenaeus writes in the late second century: "Matthew also issued a written Gospel among the Hebrews in their own dialect, while Peter and Paul were preaching at Rome, and laying the foundations of the Church. After their departure, Mark, the disciple and interpreter of Peter, did also hand down to us in writing what had been preached by Peter."[18] About 392, Jerome claimed that Matthew "composed a gospel of Christ at first published in Judea in Hebrew for the sake of those of the circumcision who believed." Jerome provides several marks of credibility for a Hebrew version of the Gospel: written in Palestine, preserved at Caesarea, diligently gathered by Pamphilus, and equally reported by the Nazarenes of Berea in Syria.[19] Eusebius reports how Pantanaeus, missionary to India, found a copy of Matthew's Gospel in Hebrew there about 180.[20] Interestingly, scholar George Howard reports on the finding of a Hebrew document dated to the fourteenth century, the Gospel of Matthew. This is evidence that a Hebrew Gospel of Matthew was at least in existence in the late medieval manuscript tradition, though it does not prove that the Gospel was originally written in Hebrew.[21] Both the patristic testimony and the Howard implication allow for a *terminus post quem* for the dating of Matthew's Gospel earlier than the temple destruction, as early as 50.

An additional dimension of apostleship is worth noting in relation to this apostle as a Gospel writer. Matthew sets out a model for discipleship by using the commands of Jesus. This theme was important for the formative mission and image of the apostles themselves. As Jeannine Brown describes, "The characterization of the disciples primarily functions as part of Matthew's broader configuration of discipleship."[22] The apostle reveals a prototype that embodied the mission of the disciples, a type that they themselves shaped. Their own experience of being with Jesus shaped their apostleship and shaped future generations through the recording of those experiences. After examining the gravity of several discipleship instructions in the Gospel of Matthew, Brown concludes: "A disciple of Jesus should fear God and stand in awe of his miraculous activity. This is a proper kind of fear. What Matthew warns against, however, is a fear of human response

---

17. France, *Matthew*, 28.
18. Irenaeus, *Haer.* 3.1.1 (*ANF* 1:414).
19. Jerome, *Vir. ill.* 3 (*NPNF*[2] 3:362).
20. Eusebius, *Hist. eccl.* 5.10.3.
21. Howard, "Textual Nature," 49–63.
22. Brown, *Disciples in Narrative Perspective*, 138.

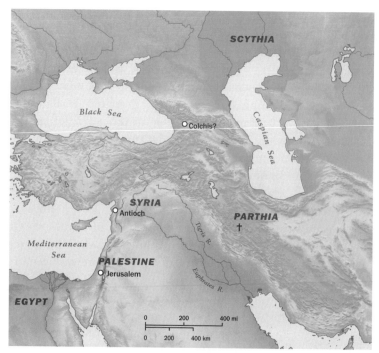

Journey of Matthew

and approval."[23] This insight into one apostle exemplifies the ministry activities that guide our quest.

A plausible conclusion is that Matthew wrote the Gospel we know for Jewish Christians during the decades of 50–70. The biography of his life could offer support to this possibility, if the legends surrounding him provide a window for the crafting of a significant work such as the Gospel of Matthew.

Gospel of Pseudo-Matthew

An infancy gospel from the ninth century has been associated with Matthew, perhaps because it reports the journey to Bethlehem, the presence of the star, and the slaughter of children under Herod, although it contains as many of the infancy topics from Luke's Gospel.[24] It also contains fantastic material, such as the peaceful presence of lions and wolves at the nativity, the provision of fruit when a tree bends over to provide for Mary, and Jesus's slaying of a boy who harassed him on his way home. The work shows reliance on the

23. Brown, *Disciples in Narrative Perspective*, 144.
24. Gospel of Pseudo-Matthew (Elliott, 84–99).

Protevangelium of James and the Infancy Gospel of Thomas while offering no insight into Matthew himself since it is a pseudepigraphal work. In defense of the apostle Matthew, Clement of Alexandria criticizes the convention of attributing works such as this to the apostle: "Of the heresies, some receive their appellation from a [person's] name . . . although they boast of adducing the opinion of Matthew [without truth]."[25] Eusebius also comments on how some gospel works attributed to Matthew were viewed as heretical.[26]

Palestine Ministry

We cannot be sure how long Matthew ministered in Palestine and Syria. Most scholars maintain that the Gospel was written from there, likely reflecting years of residence and apostolic service before he departed to other parts of the empire. In the northern part of Antioch during the early second century, Ignatius wrote his epistles with a clear influence from the Matthean tradition. Eusebius describes how Matthew eventually went beyond the Jews in his ministry: "Matthew also having first proclaimed the gospel in Hebrew, when on the point of going also to other nations, committed it to writing in his native tongue and thus supplied the want of his presence to them by his writings."[27] Irenaeus remarks that Matthew wrote while Peter and Paul were in Rome, making his Palestine sojourn last until around the mid-60s.[28] The second-century Coptic version of Abdias has Matthew encounter Peter and Andrew coming from Syria while also ministering in Jerusalem and Judea.[29]

Ethiopia Ministry

The first of these other nations where Matthew sojourned seems to be the region called Ethiopia, described in the Latin Apostolic History of Pseudo-Abdias.[30] The apostle is in the city of Nadaver when he encounters two magicians, Zaroes and Arphaxat. When the sorcerers first paralyze and then free the people, the people worship the two magicians as deities. While making the sign of the cross, Matthew engages in spiritual warfare against the two that draws the attention of the eunuch whom Philip had baptized, here named

25. Clement of Alexandria, *Strom.* 7.17 (*ANF* 2:555).
26. Eusebius, *Hist. eccl.* 3.25.6.
27. Eusebius, *Hist. eccl.* 3.24.6.
28. Irenaeus, *Haer.* 3.1 (*ANF* 1:414).
29. Abdias, *Conflicts* 7 (Malan, 44, 56).
30. James, 466.

Candacis. The eunuch insists that Matthew stay in his home. On the way to that house, conversions ensue before the magicians arrive with two dragons. Again using the sign of the cross, Matthew chases away the profane dragons, and the magicians temporarily disappear from the story. The narrative includes an important amount of theological teaching on Christ, the incarnation, and the resurrection, mostly orthodox but without clear congruence with Matthew's Gospel.

Then word arrives about the death of the king's son. While the magicians recommend treating the boy as a god by building a statue of him, the eunuch convinces the queen to call on Matthew. The apostle raises the boy, named Eufranor, in the name of Christ. When the king calls the people to worship the apostle, Matthew refuses and points to Christ, leading the people to desert their paganism. The Church of the Resurrection is built on the basis of twenty-three years of ministry service by Matthew in Ethiopia.

Although King Aeglippus is converted, his family is baptized, and his daughter takes a vow of chastity, his successor and brother, Hyrtacus, is not so amenable to the teachings of the apostles. While Matthew encourages a princess to marry Christ through an encratic lifestyle, the new king is hoping she will marry him. After the apostle consecrated her along with several other virgins, he stood at the altar praying as "a soldier sent by Hyrtacus pierced him in the back and he died."[31] While the people respond angrily and seek to punish the king, Matthew's disciples discourage revenge on a theological basis, leading the people instead to celebrate the martyrdom of the apostle. The legacy of Matthew is profiled as the king finds his own efforts to kill the princess and the other virgins futile, so he takes his life before the princess's brother succeeds him as king. King Beor reigned for sixty-three years in peace, and the church expanded in the kingdom of Ethiopia.

There is historical support for an Ethiopian ministry and martyrdom for Matthew. Early in the fifth century, the church historian Socrates names Ethiopia as the region assigned to Matthew, although he could be drawing from the conflated tradition with Matthias.[32] Hrabanus the archbishop of Mainz and Florus of Lyon both claim that Matthew died in Ethiopia, the former writing that he was slain by a spy of Hirtacus in Ethiopia.[33]

One challenge to the story of Matthew's martyrdom is that it initially seems to compete with another account of his death in Parthia, complete with encounters with the royal family of the region. The competition is immediately

31. James, 467.
32. Socrates, *Ecclesiastical History* 1.19 (NPNF[2] 2:23).
33. Rose, *Ritual Memory*, 176.

mitigated by understanding that Ethiopia is the name of a region of Parthia and does not necessarily have to be in East Africa. The Greek historian Herodotus describes how the Egyptian pharaoh Semostris established a colony of Ethiopians in the region of Colchis, south of the Caspian Sea. Jerome and Sophronius called the city "second Ethiopia." The ancient references that speak of Matthew's sojourn in Ethiopia could easily be referring to the Parthian region, where other legends place him. Although the two accounts still differ on the names of the kings he encountered and the mode of Matthew's death, it is possible that they agree about Matthew's regions of service and the fact that he was martyred. The same geographical insight applies to Matthias, often confused with Matthew in stories.

On the other hand, the Abdias tradition from the second century employs the name "Abyssinia" for Ethiopia, which is the name for the kingdom of Aksum in East Africa. Malan speculates that the claim that Matthew ministered in "the country of Kahanat" is a reference to the Abyssinian word for "priests."[34] In the text, in dialogue with a priest of the god Apollon, Matthew's prayer leads to a bright light, an earthquake, and the smashing of the idol. A miraculous feast appears before the believing priest, strengthening his testimony to the king when he is called to account for Apollon. When the king's son dies, Matthew challenges him to have the false god raise the son before the apostle resurrects him in Jesus's name. The temple where the idol rested is razed, and a church is built in its place.

Parthia Ministry

The Greek Acts of Matthew describes a mission to the cannibals of Myrna, called the city of man-eaters and seemingly in Persia.[35] By way of a vision, Jesus instructs Matthew to plant his staff at the gate where he had served with Andrew so that it may become a tree and purify the cannibals.[36] One bishop, named Plato, is already there, which means that the gospel arrived before the apostle. Matthew delivers the queen, son, and daughter-in-law from demon possession before the demon dominates King Phulbanos. The king tricks Matthew into coming to the palace, where he nails him to the ground—perhaps in crucifixion imagery—covers him in fuel, and tries to burn him. This attempt

34. Abdias, *Conflicts* 7 (Malan, 43–44n2).

35. The most accessible version is Acts and Martyrdom of St. Matthew the Apostle (*ANF* 8:528–34).

36. This reference assists Elliott (520) to maintain that this sixth-century document likely relies on the Acts of Andrew and Matthias.

fails when Matthew prays for deliverance, and the fire burns up nearby idols, kills soldiers, and takes the form of a dragon, chasing the king to the palace before the apostle rebukes the fire. The apostle eventually dies as the palace and its idols burn. At the funeral people who touch the burial materials are healed, and two visions follow. One is of Matthew ascending to receive the crown of martyrdom; the other leads to the conversion of the king.

Historical support surrounds a Parthian martyrdom. Hippolytus remarks: "Matthew wrote the Gospel in the Hebrew tongue, and published it in Jerusalem, and fell asleep in Hierees, a town of Parthia."[37] The Breviary of the Apostles from the turn of the seventh century declares: "He first preached the gospel in Judea, and after that in Macedonia, and he suffered martyrdom in Persia. He has his resting place in the mountains of the land of the Parthians."[38] Isidore of Seville's On the Birth and Death of the Fathers records that Matthew "preached the gospel first in Judea, and after that in Macedonia. He has his resting place in the mountains of the land of the Parthians."[39] Ambrose claims that his labor was in Persia.[40] Although we have no apocryphal or patristic narrative of Matthew's ministry to northern Greece, it need not be immediately rejected. However, the reasonableness of significant ministries in Palestine, Ethiopia, and Parthia reduces the likelihood of another significant field of ministry in Macedonia.

The fifth-century Acts of Andrew and Matthias chronicles how Matthias goes to Myrmidonia in Scythia, a city of cannibals, where he is blinded and imprisoned.[41] The Acts tradition has other manuscript copies with Matthew in place of Matthias, cooperating in the conflation of elements between these stories. However, the interdependence of these texts and the nature of their elements make the legend suspect. At the same time, it places Matthew in Parthia.

Abdias reports that after Matthew's East African ministry, he comes to Jerusalem and Judea, where he writes the Gospel. Afterward he advances to the city of Apayanno in the country of Parthia, where he preaches and heals the sick.[42] While ministering in the prison, the apostle encounters a man incarcerated for losing the king's goods at sea during a storm. Matthew says that God will miraculously restore the goods, but the king does not believe the prisoner when he presents them in court. This leads to an order to behead and

37. Hippolytus, Twelve 7 (ANF 5:255).
38. Rose, Ritual Memory, 174.
39. Rose, Ritual Memory, 175.
40. Ambrose, Psalm 40, cited in Abdias, Conflicts 7 (Malan, 43–44n2).
41. Acts of Andrew and Matthias (ANF 8:517–25).
42. Abdias, Conflicts 7 (Malan, 56).

quarter Matthew and then cast the parts on the ground. Despite the strong tradition of Matthew in Ethiopia of Africa, here a primary source for that account sees the apostle's life end in Parthia.

Image of Matthew

Any comprehensive image of Matthew is inseparable from the Gospel episode in which he walks away from his tax booth. Epiphanius records how the Gospel of the Ebionites depicts this single call in its list of disciples: "You also, Matthew, when you were sitting at the receipt of custom, did I call and you followed me."[43] Yet his ministry after this calling to Parthia among the Persians appears just as dramatic. His field of service was certainly there, although visiting Africa is not precluded. His final work and martyrdom should be anchored in central Asia rather than Africa.

Symbolism and Other Imagery

Matthew is usually represented by a man or an angel holding a book or a scroll. Any of the four Gospel writers can be portrayed as possessing a book or a scroll in hagiography, and this is an equally common portrayal of Matthew. An angel with a scroll can also accompany Matthew, showing divine direction for his writing of the Gospel.

Tax-related symbols also represent this publican-turned-apostle. Interestingly, the only two disciples associated with money face mistrust from others. For Judas Iscariot, the Gospels relate two episodes involving money, when he is stealing from the funds (John 12:6) and when he betrays Jesus for silver (Mark 14:11). Matthew's overall identity as a tax collector made him socially questionable, but there is no record of his being greedy or any suspicions about him as a disciple. As a former tax collector, Matthew is sometimes represented with money bags or a money box. Additionally, he can appear as a man wearing spectacles, due to his attention to ledgers and recording.

Finally, the tradition of his execution by spear or sword contributes to his image, just as the other disciples' form of martyrdom shapes how they are represented. The Ethiopian tradition relates that when the agent of the king finds Matthew alone at the altar after discipling the king's wife in encratic fashion, the agent slays him, likely with a spear or sword. Whether scholars adopt a Persian pyre or an Ethiopian slaying for the death of the apostle, the

---

43. Epiphanius, *Against Heresies* 30.1–3 (Williams, 30:13.3).

symbol illustrates how the form of an apostle's death becomes concretized as a part of his image.

Tomb and Patronage

In his work *Apostle: Travels among the Tombs of the Apostles*, Tom Bissell cannot fully explain the historical justification for his choice to visit the Monastery of Armenian Brotherhood, in Kurmanty, Kyrgyzstan, for the tomb of Matthew. Across thirty-four pages of narrative, he finds no tomb there. Bissell concludes about the site: "It has to be the only potential apostolic site in the world to be so ill-tended and forgotten."[44]

Legend records that in 954 the bones of Matthew were transported from Ethiopia to the Salerno Cathedral, Italy, where they rest in a decorated crypt.[45] An annual May 6 festival in Salerno honors the movement of his body there.[46] The Church of St. Louis of the French in Rome is particularly noted for its recognition of Matthew, with paintings of his martyrdom and his inspiration for the Gospel together in the Contarelli Chapel, with the famous Caravaggio painting of his calling.

Matthew's Western feast day is September 21, and his Eastern celebration is November 6 and December 16. Matthew is the patron saint of bankers. He is also the patron saint of the city of Salerno, of tax collectors and financiers of all types, and of alcoholics, hospitals, and ships.[47]

44. Bissell, *Apostle*, 340. While no legend offers a connection to the path of Matthew, Bissell (356) mentions a legend that a sarcophagus there has his bones.

45. Thelen, *Saints in Rome and Beyond*, 123.

46. Thelen, *Saints in Rome and Beyond*, 123.

47. Jöckle, *Encyclopedia of Saints*, 316.

✳ 10 ✳

James

The Lesser

Simon said, "I see him [the Lord] also among the angels; moreover, an angel has said to me: 'Go out hence and the temple shall fall,' but I said: No, for some here may be converted."

> Apostolic History of Pseudo-Abdias
> second century, Parthia

James was the soul in which the Father was pleased to dwell, which the Only Begotten chose and on which the Holy Spirit came to repose marvelously.

> Eighth Homily of Nicetas David[1]
> tenth century, Anatolia

Little is known from the Bible or other sources about James son of Alphaeus. He likely received the epithet "the Lesser" to distinguish him from James son of Zebedee, whose role in the Gospels is more prominent. The addition to his name seems to match his reduced historical importance. Ellsworth Kalas remarks how James the Lesser is a disciple who does not seem even to qualify for Andy Warhol's axiom "In the future

---

1. Nicetas David, *Oration octava*, quoted in Bovon, "Byzantine Witness," 93.

everyone will be famous for fifteen minutes."[2] The NRSV translates "lesser" as "younger," suggesting an age distinction. While some scholars suppose that the nomenclature of "the Less" refers to size and physical stature,[3] the name most likely serves to distinguish this James from the more significant, top-tier James the son of Zebedee.

James the Lesser may have been part of a family network around the ministry of Jesus, and biographical surveys of the apostle usually fill their pages with kinship connections. The crucifixion witnesses included one Mary the wife of Clopas. Meanwhile, on the road to Emmaus, one of the two conversationalists with Jesus is named Cleopas (Luke 24:18). The names Clopas and Cleopas share a basis in the Hebrew names Chalpai or Halphai; the form Halphai in Hebrew corresponds to the Greek Alphaeus.[4] This synthesis means that the woman at the cross might have been James the Lesser's mother, while the man on the road to Emmaus might have been his father. This is further reinforced when Mark 15:40 (at the crucifixion) and 16:1 (at the resurrection) call Mary "the mother of James the Less and Joses" and "the mother of James," respectively (see Matt. 27:56). If the connection is legitimate, both parents of one disciple were among the witnesses to Christ's crucifixion and resurrection. This would be a tremendous legacy. Such an influence might have reinforced the mission of this apostle, as familial ties buttressed the ministry of the son on the home front. Of additional interest is the possible relationship between Mary the wife of Clopas and Mary the mother of Jesus (John 19:25). This would make James and Jesus first cousins. Yet the New Testament provides no clear familial links for any members of the Twelve except the two sets of brothers: Peter and Andrew, and James and John.

In the early fourth century Jerome made this same postulation about the kinship of Jesus and James the Lesser:

> Do you intend the comparatively unknown James the Less, who is called in Scripture the son of Mary, not however of Mary the mother of our Lord, to be an apostle, or not? If he is an apostle, he must be the son of Alphaeus and a believer in Jesus, "For neither did his brethren believe in him." The only conclusion is that the Mary who is described as the mother of James the Less was the wife of Alphaeus and sister of Mary the Lord's mother, the one who is called by John the Evangelist "Mary of Clopas."[5]

2. Kalas, *Thirteen Apostles*, 45.
3. Ruffin, *The Twelve*, 78; McDowell, *Fate of the Apostles*, 230.
4. Brownrigg, *Twelve Apostles*, 142.
5. Jerome, *On the Perpetual Virginity of the Blessed Mary* 13 (trans. Hritzu, 28–29).

Likewise, Eusebius relates how Hegesippus claimed that Clopas was an uncle to Jesus (John 19:25). The relationship finds reinforcement when Eusebius reports that the disciples sought to replace James son of Zebedee by the election of Simeon son of Cleophas, whom he calls cousin but describes as half-brother.[6] The replacement for this member of the Twelve is reminiscent of Judas Iscariot's replacement by Matthias (Acts 1:22–26) and reinforces a possible kinship between Jesus and James the Lesser.

Meanwhile, the four lists of disciples use the moniker "James son of Alphaeus" each time, but a reference in Mark 2:14 complicates the network by narrating the call of "Levi the son of Alphaeus." If Matthew and James the Lesser were sons of the same Alphaeus, they would have been brothers. If true, it would be surprising for the Gospel writers not to mention this connection since they regularly refer to the other fraternal pairs.

We cannot be certain of the relationship between James the Lesser and Jesus, whether cousins or brothers or unrelated. The similar names among Jesus's brothers have led to conflations of James the Less, Judas Thaddaeus, and now Simon. Apostle scholar David Criswell represents the most generous conflation, as he is convinced that all three are the same person, with "Jesus' brother" meaning "cousin."[7] Perhaps Hegesippus's statement can be viewed as a summary understatement of the situation: "Many indeed are called James."[8] Assumptions need to be questioned, or dialogue about the possibilities simply spirals into analysis of contrasting legends to explain an unsustainable theory. All three were common Hebrew names in the first century. And there were "many women at the cross," according to Matthew 27:55. In the end, Tom Bissell remarks on the difficulty of isolating James the Lesser: "The available evidence is confusing enough to baffle the most dogged New Testament detective."[9] We conclude that James the Lesser is not necessarily the cousin of Jesus and likely not the same as his brother, despite traditions that seem to claim otherwise. Certainly any brother or cousin relationship had no recordable impact on the ministry of these disciples.

The real challenge to the quest for the historical James is the conflation of the two Jameses into one person. Hippolytus merges the Lesser into the Just when he states that the original disciple died like Jesus's brother: "And James the son of Alphaeus, when preaching in Jerusalem, was stoned to death by the Jews, and was buried there beside the temple."[10] This conflation is a

---

6. Eusebius, *Hist. eccl.* 3.11.1.
7. Criswell, *Apostles after Jesus*, 110.
8. Jerome, *Vir. ill.* 2 (NPNF² 3:361).
9. Bissell, *Apostle*, 85.
10. Hippolytus, *Twelve* 9 (ANF 5:255).

perpetual theme in historical and apocryphal writings. The many apocryphal works named for James usually have in view the brother of Jesus or the son of Zebedee, not the Lesser. Kalas describes James the Lesser individually as "a figure lost in the deadening shadows of obscurity."[11]

Palestine Discipleship and Ministry

There is no biblical record of James's calling. Nor is there any record of any event specific to him in the Gospels during the era of discipleship development. This lack of data makes it hard to gain any perspective on the person of James the Lesser. A tenth-century hagiographical sermon on James describes "[his] body, [his] sacred tent" belonging to the Trinity and "the soul in which the Father was pleased to dwell, which the Only Begotten chose and on which the Holy Spirit came to repose marvelously."[12]

The conflation of James the Lesser with James the Just, the brother of Jesus, is constant in both ancient writings and contemporary scholarship when they center on the Palestine ministry and martyrdom. The deaths of both James the Greater and Jesus's brother, not one of the Twelve, occurred in Jerusalem. The fate of the latter is worth mentioning for clarification. Josephus writes that a Sadducee, Ananus ben Ananus, took the high priesthood, being "a bold man in his temper, and very insolent," and saw the political situation in Jerusalem as ready for rigid judgment by Jews. The historian records: "He assembled the Sanhedrin of judges, and brought before them the brother of Jesus, who was called Christ, whose name was James, and some others; and when he had formed an accusation against them as breakers of the law, he delivered them to be stoned."[13] Hegesippus first fostered the amalgamation of the two, as recorded by Eusebius, describing James the Just being thrown from the temple peak. A nearby fuller, armed with the club he used to pound woolen cloth, crushed his head.[14]

The early eighth-century Breviarium Apostolorum reports James's survival after these events, but this is likely another conflation.[15] The Coptic Abdias tradition also likely brings the story of James the Just into its biography of

11. Kalas, *Thirteen Apostles*, 46.
12. Nicetas David, *Oration octava*, quoted in Bovon, "Byzantine Witness," 93.
13. Josephus, *Ant.* 20.9.1. Tom Bissell is an example of an author who conflates the two, appealing to the ambiguity of the New Testament and the patristic writers as allowing the son of Alphaeus to be the brother of Jesus (82–87). Thus he attributes the martyrdom of the brother of Jesus to James the Lesser (98–99).
14. Eusebius, *Hist. eccl.* 2.23.
15. Rose, *Ritual Memory*, 138.

James the Lesser.[16] He ministers to the Jewish community in Jerusalem. There is mention of the temple, the launching point for the Just's martyrdom. The people bring him to Claudius, accuse him of promoting civil disobedience, and stone him to death. Yet these descriptions could also apply to the brother of Jesus and do not assist in the quest for the Lesser if there is to be a distinction between the two Jameses. In a rare description that is not a conflation, tenth-century hagiographer Nicetas David relates a ministry of James in the city of Tyre, just north of Palestine, preceding a sojourn and his martyrdom in Egypt.[17]

In light of all this overlap, it is easy to see that distinguishing James the Lesser is not easy. Thomas Schmidt has written a historical fiction of the apostles, anchored in the best sources available but inventing a theoretical narrative interspersed with historical information. He describes it as "an attempt to use a biblical format to convey what *may* have happened. . . . The fictional element of this volume is not merely a work of imagination; it is a work of reconstruction."[18] In this reconstruction, Schmidt proposes that James and Matthias were accused of blasphemy, brought before the chief priests and council, and stoned.[19] Even in Schmidt's fictitious version, Matthias is given the floor to preach Christ at the trial, while James says not a word. The hypothesis of Ben Witherington takes on new credibility: "Acts 26:10 may be the smoking gun: Saul/Paul voted for the execution of the apostles when he was a member of the Sanhedrin. If we put all these pieces together, it appears likely that Saul had been the instigator of the demise of several apostles in the 30's before his own conversion."[20] The limited data on James might be explained by his early death.

Parthia Ministry

The Armenian tradition accepts James the Lesser as a brother of Jesus. The community in Jerusalem claims to have his relics in the Cathedral of Saint James on Mount Zion, suggesting a ministry in Parthia. The bones may have been moved there after the destruction of the monastery that originally housed his remains.[21] Although the community conflates him with the brother of Jesus, the assertion is that he lived there and that now a cathedral rests where

16. Abdias, *Conflicts* 11 (Malan, 145–46).
17. Bovon, "Byzantine Witness," 96–97.
18. Schmidt, *Apostles after Acts*, 2.
19. Schmidt, *Apostles after Acts*, 115–18.
20. Witherington, "Martyrdom of the Zebedee Brothers," 26.
21. McBirnie, *Search for the Twelve Apostles*, 143.

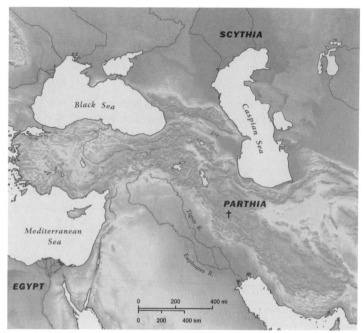

Journey of James the Lesser

his house once stood. The claim to his body made by Jerusalem's Armenian quarter may also be based on the tradition that he ministered in Armenia.

A crucifixion story is linked to a fifth-century source, the Hieronymian Martyrology, which identifies a ministry and crucifixion of James in Persia.[22] The details elude us.

Spain Ministry

The tradition of James the Greater in Spain may in fact be the tradition of James the Lesser gone awry. In the ninth century, the bishop of Iria claimed that a star guided him to James's burial spot. The patron saint of Spain and the Way of St. James have James the Greater in view. Els Rose does cite the presence of James the Lesser in some medieval Spanish liturgy. However, she attempts no historical link to the presence of the apostle there.[23] Thus there is no evidence of a Spanish ministry for the Lesser James, despite some contemporary claims to the contrary.

22. Bovon, "Byzantine Witness," 93–94; Hagner, "James," 3:618.
23. Rose, *Ritual Memory*, 144–48, 159–60.

Egypt Ministry

Nicetas David was a priest in tenth-century Paphlagonia in northeast Anatolia who provides a brief homily on James. His *Oratio octava* on the feast day of James explains in unspecific terms both the spiritual gifting of the saint by the Holy Spirit and his sufferings in ministry. François Bovon summarizes the Latin text: "Nicetas describes the holy man as a genuine child of divine grace, a noble branch of the true grapevine, which was pruned by God, the heavenly farmer, rooted in the Son, and enriched by the Holy Spirit."[24] After identifying various ministry sufferings for James in Eleutheropolis, thirty miles southwest of Jerusalem, as well as mentioning his travel from Gaza to Tyre, Nicetas identifies Ostrakine in lower Egypt as the place where James the Lesser was crucified. Bovon combines the Nicetas David liturgy and an untranslated Passion of James to relate James's crucifixion, describing a sermon from the cross, great agony, and the gesture of a smile as accompanying an exhortation against idolatry and to faith in Christ.[25] Bovon believes that this work, as well as a similar Gaza crucifixion story provided by thirteenth-century Nicephorus Callistus Xanthopulus, drew from a traditional martyrdom narrative of the early Byzantine period.

Image of James the Lesser

The image of James must be formed independently of the brother of the Lord and the son of Zebedee. A theater of apostolic ministry beyond that of James the Just is necessary to secure a criterion of freedom from opposition. However, tradition has merged the two and their martyrdom so that the symbol related to his death is the same as that of the Just's death at the Jerusalem temple. The Parthian and Egyptian theaters offer the only hope for discovering the path of this elusive apostle. While both are limited to one source each, the possibility of ministry in Parthia before dying in Ethiopia or vice versa is legitimate. The testimony of the Armenian tradition favors this location.

Symbolism and Image Construction

The distinction of James the Lesser from the son of Zebedee and the method of the former's martyrdom construct his image. James is often depicted as

24. Bovon, "Byzantine Witness," 93.
25. Bovon, "Byzantine Witness," 94–96.

a short man, probably due to thinking "the Lesser" to be related to height.[26] Such an understanding would be more likely if there were not another James, a first-tier disciple who is worthy of his own epithet, "the Greater." Thus we should conclude that any portrayal based on his height should yield to the symbolism of his lesser prominence when compared to the other James; it is an uncertain symbol if based on his physical height.

The tools that might have led to the martyrdom of James are the saw and the club, and they became symbols associated with the apostle. The conflation with James the Just, bishop of Jerusalem and brother of Jesus, continues even to the Lesser's martyrdom. In one account, the Just is thrown from the temple in Jerusalem, then stoned, and then sawed in two. In another account, he is beaten to death with clubs.[27] Thus the saw or fuller's club became symbolic of the Lesser, and he is often portrayed holding one or the other of these instruments.

Although Kalas strangely remarks, "He must have been the kind of person whose work simply never attracts attention,"[28] Kalas still manages to provide eight pages reiterating that we know nothing of him from Scripture, leading to repeated use of the term "nothing."[29] This author projects thoughts about apostleship and personal feelings onto the disciples, illustrating the exaggerated leeway found in many popular studies. Ronald Brownrigg takes the shared surname "Alphaeus" between Matthew and James to claim that both brothers were customs officers.[30] Such comments are given without consideration of the biblical author's limited space or writing intentions.

In the conflation with James the Just, this apostle is often cited as abstaining from meat and wine, wearing wool garments, and praying on his knees until they hardened like a camel's knees. This description is centered on the martyrdom of the other James, however.[31]

The Apostolic Constitutions is a late fourth-century document containing instructions for clergy. Probably of an Antioch, Syria, provenance, it contains clarifications attributed to various apostles, and James the Lesser is credited with providing two constitutions. The first concerns confessors who remain faithful under persecution and survive, who should be considered worthy of honor unless they claim to have been ordained under false pretenses. The second concerns virgins who voluntarily remain celibate, that there should

---

26. Taylor, *How to Read a Church*, 110.
27. Jerome, *Vir. ill.* 2.
28. Kalas, *Thirteen Apostles*, 50.
29. Kalas, *Thirteen Apostles*, 45–53.
30. Brownrigg, *Twelve Apostles*, 145.
31. Eusebius, *Hist. eccl.* 2.23.

be freedom for this type of piety but that their choice is not a censure of marriage.[32] Although interesting, these constitutions offer limited perspective on the image of James.

Tomb and Patronage

Relics of James the Lesser rest at the Church of Holy Apostles in Rome alongside those of Philip. The best reason for their coburial is their transfer there from Constantinople in the mid-sixth century, when they were placed together and the church was named for them both in celebration of the victory over the Goths. The remnants were last examined in 1873 after excavations under the main altar.[33] The description given by Tom Bissell of the nearby art deserves repeating here for our image of James: "In the upper left of the painting, a kneeling, youthful James, wearing blue and pink robes, looks to the heavens while a savage, shirtless Hebrew prepares to brain him with a club. . . . Adrift around both doomed apostles is the usual swarm of portly cherubs, while behind them looms an opened porthole into Heaven itself—a swirling maw of pink light."[34]

Meanwhile the Armenian Church claims to have his relics in the Cathedral of Saint James in Jerusalem. Although this tradition at times merges his identity with the brother of Jesus, the claim is that he lived there and that now a cathedral rests where his house once stood. A throne or bishop's chair under a *baldacchino* (canopy) that supposedly belonged to him rests on one side of the sanctuary, next to his burial spot.[35]

Since tradition maintains his death by clubbing, he is the patron saint of fullers and pharmacists, both of whom use club-like devices. Likewise, hatmakers and dyers look to James in reverence. The Italian cities of Frascati and Monterotondo have adopted him as their civic patron saint, along with the Catholic Church of Uruguay, which again partners him with Philip in patronage. He is also the patron saint of grocers and pie makers.[36] His feast day is May 11, formerly May 1 and 3.

---

32. Constitutions of the Holy Apostles 23–24 (*ANF* 8:493).

33. Thelen, *Saints in Rome and Beyond*, 40, 83, 239.

34. Bissell, *Apostle*, 94.

35. Thelen, *Saints in Rome and Beyond*, 187. Such a throne would have been symbolic of the episcopate in Jerusalem, and the see is mentioned by Eusebius in *Hist. eccl.* 7.19. However, this is a reference to James the Just, the brother of Jesus, evidencing either an intentional conflation with James the Just or at least an imprecision about James the Lesser.

36. Jöckle, *Encyclopedia of Saints*, 228.

❋ 11 ❋

Jude

The Exorcist

Judas (not Iscariot) said to Him, "Lord, what then has happened
that You are going to disclose Yourself to us and not to the world?"
Jesus answered and said to him, "If anyone loves Me, he will keep
My word; and My Father will love him, and We will come to him,
and make Our abode with him."

John 14:22–23

For, according as my Lord commanded me . . . I preach and publish the Gospel, . . . and the seed of His word do I sow in the ears
of all men; and such as are willing to receive it, theirs is the good
recompense of the confession of Christ.

The Teaching of Addaeus the Apostle[1]
third century, Syria

An obscure disciple named Jude bears the common Hebrew name
of Judah. Judas likely has a root meaning of "God be praised,"
and the name was immensely popular in first-century Palestine.[2] It
was so common, in fact, that three of the twelve disciples share the name in

1. *ANF* 8:658.
2. Williams, "Palestinian Jewish Personal Names in Acts," 89.

biblical and extrabiblical literature: Jude, Judas Iscariot, and Judas Thomas. It is logical that a name adjustment would come to the lesser-known "Judas" disciple, with Judas Iscariot receiving more attention.

A third-tier disciple is named "Thaddaeus" in the Matthew and Mark lists, while a third-tier member is named "Judas the son of James" in the Luke and Acts lists. According to philologists, Thaddaeus and Labbaeus are Greek diminutives for the Hebrew name Theudas—"heart," "breast," meaning "beloved" or "courageous."[3] Most scholars associate Jude with Labbaeus and Thaddeus. The name Labbaeus is given only in Matthew 10:3 in the manuscript tradition behind the King James Version, "Lebbaeus, whose surname was Thaddaeus." Meanwhile, the problem of relating Jude the disciple (Luke 6:16; Acts 1:13) to Thaddaeus the disciple (Matt. 10:3; Mark 3:18) has already been established above. The result is a disciple of Jesus likely bearing two names, one Hebrew and one Greek, Judas Thaddaeus, as was the case for some other apostles. Hippolytus equates Jude and Lebbaeus and places them in Edessa with influence throughout Mesopotamia; the evidence for this decision is provided below.[4]

Yet the historical obscurity of the apostle does not prevent theories of possible remote connections with other New Testament figures. From the surname "son of James" ascribed to Jude (Luke 6:14–16; Acts 1:13), William McBirnie deduces that his father was another disciple, James son of Zebedee.[5] The genitive "Jude of James" in Lukan literature can mean "relation of" without specifying the exact relationship. It could just as easily mean "brother of" as "son of." Some Bible versions render the name in the Luke and Acts lists as "Jude, brother of James" because of the influence of the New Testament Epistle of Jude, where the author calls himself James's brother (Jude 1).

Barnabas Lindars believes that Jude is Levi the tax collector (Luke 5:27), because of a combination of manuscript evaluation and the shared root of the names Levi and Lebbaeus.[6] The Epistle of the Apostles calls Jude "the Zealot" while substituting the name "Cephas" in place of Simon the Zealot.[7] Ronald Brownrigg believes they were both Zealots.[8] In this chapter Jude is depicted as "the exorcist," because while other apostles are recorded as engaging in a ministry of exorcism, Jude's final encounter in Persia with two

3. Ruffin, *The Twelve*, 149. The Breviary of the Apostles says the name also means "confessor." Rose, *Ritual Memory*, 222.
4. Hippolytus, *Twelve* 10 (ANF 5:255).
5. McBirnie, *Search for the Twelve Apostles*, 150–51.
6. Lindars, "Matthew, Levi, Lebbaeus," 220–22.
7. Ep. Apos. 2 (Hills, 22).
8. Brownrigg, *Twelve Apostles*, 163–70.

demons is more climactic than other apostle narratives. Bartholomew could just as easily be awarded this title.

Finally, the early church at times confused Jude with Judas, the brother of Jesus (Matt. 13:5; Mark 6:3). The Synoptic references to Jesus's brothers (Matt. 13:55; Mark 6:3) have led to conflation with James the Less, Judas Thaddaeus, and even Simon the Zealot. In his list of apostles, Jerome describes Jude as the brother of James, and possibly of Jesus.[9] This raises the question whether the association describes brotherhood to Jesus or merely a name shared between these brother disciples and the brothers of Jesus. If Jude and James are brothers to Jesus, then Judas shows humility by not identifying himself as Jesus's brother. Yet assumptions should not be made, and discussions of the possibility simply spiral into analysis of contrasting legends to explain an unsustainable theory. All three are common names in the ancient world, and the possible brotherhood of two should not extend to the speculation that these disciples were Jesus's brothers.

Eusebius says that Jude was one of the Seventy whom Jesus commissioned for ministry (Luke 10:1).[10] In his list of the Seventy, Hippolytus names the fourth as "Thaddeus, who conveyed the epistle to Augarus."[11] This appears to be a reference to the Syrian legend related below that Jude, known as Addai, delivered a return letter from Jesus to Abgar, the king of Edessa. This preliminarily makes the Syria legend about a Thaddeus who was one of the Seventy rather than one of the Twelve. However, as David Criswell points out, the legend of the apostle in the Parthian lands of Syria and Mesopotamia proves extant across multiple ancient sources, including the foundation of the story itself.[12] Jude shares a tradition of ministry experiences with Simon, and they are always named adjacent to each other in the apostle lists.

Palestine Discipleship

The New Testament tells us almost nothing about the disciple Jude. We have no report of his background, his calling, or his contribution to the apostolic college. John's Gospel ascribes one single sentence to this apostle, a question posed to Jesus during the intimate Last Supper discourse.

In Jesus's dialogue with the disciples, their curiosity is met with messianic explanation by Jesus. At one point he says to his disciples, "After a little while

---

9. Jerome, *Vir. ill.* 4.
10. Eusebius, *Hist. eccl.* 1.13.4.
11. Hippolytus, *On the Seventy Apostles* 4 (ANF 5:255).
12. Criswell, *Apostles after Jesus*, 121–22.

the world will no longer behold Me; but you *will* see Me; because I live, you shall live also" (John 14:19). In response, we encounter the irreplaceable voice of Jude: "Judas (not Iscariot) said to Him, 'Lord, what then has happened that You are going to disclose Yourself to us and not to the world?'" This profound question prompts Jesus to explain the Father's love, the abiding of the Son, and the coming of the Spirit, assurances needed by the disoriented disciples this last night together in Jerusalem. Here we see Jude seeking to formulate an expectation of the messianic mission. Sean McDowell remarks: "The writer of John makes it clear that Judas does not yet grasp the true identity of Jesus or the full purpose of his mission."[13]

We know nothing else biographical about Jude from the Bible. He is listed among the disciples in Acts, so we know that he maintained a presence with the Twelve into the early church period. However, one epistle might come from him.

Ministry in Writing

Some view the disciple Jude as the author of the Epistle of Jude. However, the reference to the apostles in Jude 17 has led many to believe that the author was not an apostle and thus was not the Jude of the Twelve: "You, beloved, ought to remember the words that were spoken beforehand by the apostles of Lord Jesus Christ." The reference to the apostles is to those who founded the churches to which Jude writes. The importance of this verse is captured by Richard Bauckham: "The full expression is not paralleled elsewhere in the New Testament, but it stresses the authority of the apostles as derived from the Lord, in a way which is quite natural from a contemporary of the apostles."[14]

A more likely candidate for epistolary authorship is Judas the brother of Jesus. The basis of this theory begins with the list of brothers of Jesus naming both a Judas and a James (Matt. 13:55; Mark 6:3). Meanwhile, Jude opens his letter by claiming an association with James: "Jude, a bond-servant of Jesus Christ, and brother of James" (Jude 1). This theory makes it likely that the two authors were the half-brothers of Jesus, however this is defined.[15]

---

13. McDowell, *Fate of the Apostles*, 237.
14. Bauckham, *Jude, 2 Peter*, 104.
15. Those who believe in the perpetual virginity of Mary hold that Joseph had children from a previous marriage. According to this view, James and Jude are Jesus's half-brothers because they had a different mother. Those who believe that Mary gave birth to other children after Jesus may still refer to James and Jude as Jesus's half-brothers if they also believe in Jesus's virgin birth. According to this view, James and Jude are Jesus's half-brothers because they had a different father.

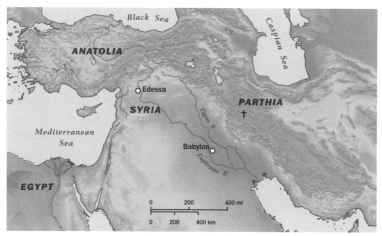

Journey of Jude

John Calvin and Matthew Henry believed that Jude was related to James, and the King James Version even supplies "brother" for Judas of James (Luke 6:16; Acts 1:13). However, Jude could also be James's brother without being related to Jesus.

Syria Ministry

The Acts of Holy Apostle Thaddeus from the third century represents the Syriac tradition when it records the story of Jude.[16] Although the present book customarily extends Syria into Parthia because of overlapping regional ministries, the tradition regarding this one region warrants a narrower designation for Jude. The story begins with Lebbaeus or Thaddeus in Edessa, the capital of the Osroene Empire in upper Mesopotamia and an important center for ancient Syriac Christianity. He came down to Jerusalem to worship when he heard the preaching of John the Baptist, who seems to have baptized him. The story relates how, at the end of his Palestine discipleship under Jesus, King Abgar V the Black sent a letter to Jesus inviting him to come to Edessa and avoid the plot of the Jews against him. The written letter and Jesus's written response are reported in Eusebius's *Ecclesiastical History*.[17] While it is easy to discount the legend, Fred Lapham suggests that the story may be "not entirely without historical foundation."[18]

---

16. Acts of the Holy Apostle Thaddaeus (*ANF* 8:558–59).
17. Eusebius, *Hist. eccl.* 1.13.
18. Lapham, *Introduction to the New Testament Apocrypha*, 37.

Interestingly, the narrative stops just short of physically describing Jesus when Abgar directs his ambassador Ananias to "take accurate account of Christ, of what appearance He was, and His stature, and His hair, and in a word everything."[19] Jesus cannot come to Edessa but offers to send his disciple Thaddaeus to guide the king and his city. Soon afterward, the apostle arrives and instructs multitudes of people about Christ, imparting the Holy Spirit to them. The apostle and the king see the destruction of idols and the construction of churches. Church leaders are appointed, and worship resources are provided to the city before the apostle departs.

In the city of Amis along the Euphrates River, Thaddaeus and his disciples explain Christ to the Jews and heal the people. There he remains for five years, according to the text, baptizing people and building a church. He begins an itinerant ministry in Syria, then in Berytus of Phoenicia, before "falling asleep on the twenty-first of the month of August."[20] This is a rare reference to an apostle's death that does not mention martyrdom.

The Coptic Abdias tradition describes how lots fall to Jude to minister in Syria.[21] His attention first comes to the city when a full green field of corn is produced for a farmer during planting season. Fearing that Jude and his companion Peter are enchanters, and knowing of their encratic gospel message, the people strip a prostitute and place her at the gate of the city. The apostles pray that Michael the archangel will suspend her by the hair out of their path, and she is suspended there while exhorting to the city to believe their message. As they minister, Michael himself drives out unclean spirits from the city and its citizens. When the apostles encounter a rich young man who asks how to work miracles like they do, Jude quotes Jesus concerning how it is easier for a camel to pass through the eye of a needle than for a rich man to enter heaven (Matt. 19:24; Mark 10:25; Luke 18:25), leading the young man to attempt to choke Jude. In a story reminiscent of the Acts of Peter and Andrew, a camel passes by, a needle is gained, and Peter commands the camel to pass through twice, leading the amazed people to quote Jesus, "With God all things are possible" (Matt. 19:26). Churches are built, bishops consecrated, and priests are ordained to serve in the city. Here the narrative mentions only that Jude died without event.

In the third-century Syriac work the Teaching of Addaeus the Apostle, either the apostle Jude or his protégé Addaeus is in view. With some uncertainty because of a gap at the top of the manuscript, it seems that Addai's

19. Acts of the Holy Apostle Thaddaeus (*ANF* 8:558).
20. Acts of the Holy Apostle Thaddaeus (*ANF* 8:559).
21. Abdias, *Conflicts* 15 (Malan, 221).

laying hands on King Abgar leads to his healing and conversion. The apostle refuses a monetary gift, explaining that at the time of Jesus's ascension he received the same power that the Lord had used for his miraculous works. Addai declares: "For, according as my Lord commanded me, lo! I preach and publish the Gospel, and lo! His money do I cast upon the table before you, and the seed of His word do I sow in the ears of all men; and such as are willing to receive it, theirs is the good recompense of the confession of Christ."[22] A long discourse calling for response to Jesus's work follows, to great success. An important disclaimer about conversion is included: "But neither King Abgar nor yet the Apostle Addaeus compel any man by force to believe in Christ, because without the force of man the force of the signs compelled many to believe in Him. And with affection did they receive his doctrine—all this country of Mesopotamia, and all the regions round about it."[23] His death is stated as due to an illness.[24] Although the month of death differs between the Acts of Thaddeus and the Teaching of Addaeus, there is the common claim of his death without martyrdom. Criswell maintains, "It seems that a later Christian king may have altered or added to the old archives in hopes of 'restoring' Edessa's Christian heritage or affirming one of their patron saints' visit."[25]

The Teachings of the Apostles uses the term "guide" for the disciples of Jude's ministry, as if there were an office of oversight related to his leadership that does not occur in the New Testament. Certainly the work evidences a ministry in Syria: "Edessa, and all the countries round about it which were on all sides of it, and Zoba, and Arabia, and all the north, and the regions round about it, and the south, and all the regions on the borders of Mesopotamia, received the apostles' ordination to the priesthood from Addaeus the apostle, one of the seventy-two apostles, who himself made disciples there, and built a church there, and was priest and ministered there in his office as Guide which he held there."[26]

Here not only is Addai mentioned, either a conflation with Jude or a disciple of Jude, but also his disciple Aggaeus. They equally affect "the whole of Persia, of the Assyrians, and of the Armenians, and of the Medians, and of the countries round about Babylon . . . as far as the borders of the Indians."[27]

---

22. Teaching of Addaeus the Apostle (*ANF* 8:658).
23. Teaching of Addaeus the Apostle (*ANF* 8:661).
24. Teaching of Addaeus the Apostle (*ANF* 8:663–64). This account reports that he died of illness in the month of Iyar, which runs April–June.
25. Criswell, *Apostles after Jesus*, 123.
26. Teaching of the Apostles 9 (*ANF* 8:671).
27. Teaching of the Apostles 10 (*ANF* 8:671).

Other Parthia Ministry

The lands of modern Armenia and Persia were part of the ancient Parthian Empire. A strong tradition of Jude's ministry in these two areas makes them the most likely field of his missionary work. Furthermore, a western Persia ministry is geographically close enough to allow for the common heritage with Syria described above. McDowell estimates that Jude ministered in Armenia from 43 to 66.[28]

The Acts of Simon and Jude in the Latin tradition of Abdias describes how Simon and Jude went to Persia, encountering the two magicians (Zaroes and Arfaxat) whom Matthew had forced to leave Ethiopia.[29] The proximity of Edessa allows for its placement in this geographical tradition. The narrative is summarized below, in the chapter on Simon. An addition to the story summarized there is a contest between the apostles and the magicians of the king, who call in a brood of snakes in their anger with the evangelists. The snakes turn and bite the magicians, who howl like wolves. When the king orders the magicians to die, the apostles refuse to allow it but make the snakes suck out the venom before the apostles heal the magicians in the hospital three days later. Yet the magicians still do not believe and slander the apostles throughout Persia. The apostles' ministry in Persia supposedly leads to sixty thousand converts around Babylon before they move to the city of Suanir.

In this town the people immediately call them "the enemies of our god" and take them to the temple of the sun.[30] Again, the story is related below, in the chapter on Simon, because slightly more attention is given to him. The priests try to force the apostles to sacrifice to the four-horse chariot of the sun in the eastern part of the temple and the four-oxen chariot of the moon in the western part. Jude says to Simon, "I see the Lord calling us."[31] The apostle first exorcises the demon from the chariot of the moon, and likewise Simon exorcises the demon from the chariot of the sun, and two black men flee with a howl. Then the priests and the people slay the apostles, leading these two apostles to be associated with swords or spears. Brownrigg remarks that they came under "a showering of stones and a battering of sticks,"[32] and sticks or clubs are sometimes part of the legend. After lightning strikes the temple and incinerates Zaroes and Arfaxat, King Xerxes builds a basilica supposedly on the spot of the former temple now destroyed by the ministry of the two apostles.

---

28. McDowell, *Fate of the Apostles*, 241.
29. Ps.-Abd. 6 (James, 464–66).
30. Ps.-Abd. 6 (James, 466).
31. Ps.-Abd. 6 (James, 466).
32. Brownrigg, *Twelve Apostles*, 174.

The Acts of Thaddeus relates how a picture of Jesus that possessed healing properties came to Edessa. It seems to match a legend defending icons in which a picture is presented to the people of Edessa when the Persians besiege the city in 544.[33]

The sixth-century Syriac Acts of Mār Mārī the Apostle centers on the ministry of one Mārī at the turn of the second century. This disciple is ordered to Mesopotamia by Addai, who is also known as the apostle Thaddeus from Edessa. Mārī ministers through preaching and miracles, founds churches, and eventually dies at Qunni, to become known as the apostle of Babylonia. Modern scholar Amir Harrak believes the mixed tradition positing Addai as one of the Twelve or one of the Seventy.[34] While the insight into Jude in this work is limited, especially if Jude is the mentor and not the apostle Addai, deep in the narrative the biographer describes the influence of Jude on the tradespeople journeying in the western part of Parthia: he "instructed them in the fear of God."[35] Still, the legacy of Jude includes here his influence on the generation after the apostles. The commissioning of Mārī prepared the region for the gospel of Christ.

About 600, the Breviary of the Apostles affirms the geography, saying that Jude evangelized Mesopotamia and the mainland by Pontus, also citing his burial in Armenia.[36] Isidore's *Birth and Death of the Fathers* affirms this same location, adding that through his teaching "he domesticated untamed and uncivilized people, as if they were wild beasts, and he submitted them to the faith of the Lord."[37] Isidore also calls Jude the brother of James. Ado distinguishes the appointee to the Jerusalem see as a different Simon, who died under Trajan. He explains the founding of the church of Persia as due to both Simon and Jude ministering and being martyred there.[38]

Assorted other material contributes to piece together the life of Jude. A teaching supposedly to the people of Edessa describes his feelings when he realized the tomb of Jesus was empty.[39] A homily about Jude claims: "To Edessa he made his journey, and found in it a great work.[40] A homily about Antioch states: "Addaeus [was allotted] the country of the Assyrians."[41] Reconciling

33. Klauck, *Apocryphal Acts of the Apostles*, 249.

34. Harrak, "Introduction," in *Acts of Mār Mārī the Apostle*, xi, 9.

35. Acts of Mār Mārī 31, in Harrak, *Acts of Mār Mārī the Apostle*, 75.

36. Rose, *Ritual Memory*, 222.

37. Isidore, *Birth and Death of the Fathers*, quoted in Rose, *Ritual Memory*, 223.

38. Rose, *Ritual Memory*, 223–24; Eusebius, *Hist. eccl.* 3.32.

39. Extracts from Various Books concerning Abgar the King and Addaeus the Apostle 1 (*ANF* 8:655).

40. Extracts concerning Abgar 7 (*ANF* 8:656).

41. Extracts concerning Abgar 8 (*ANF* 8:656).

these two theaters of ministry and death is not impossible when Edessa, Mesopotamia, and Agel Hasna of Armenia occur in the same passage as ministry locations.[42] As Criswell points out, "It is fairly apparent that his entire ministry career focused on the western Parthian empire."[43] Jude likely did minister near Antioch, Syria. The shared boundary between the Syrian and western Parthian Empire makes it reasonable to locate the acts of Jude under the umbrella of these regions.

Image of Thaddaeus

The ministry work of Jude Thaddaeus was centered in what is now Armenia, with other activities across the border into Parthia. Legends involving Persian activities are not ruled out based on the historical core behind the Armenian ministry legends. The exorcism of the Parthian moon-god typifies Jude's image as an exorcist, reinforced by reflections on this topic being attributed to him in the fourth-century Apostolic Constitutions. The geographical range of ministry among his disciples shows the region from Syria to India under their influence.

Symbolism and Image Construction

Jude is represented by a number of symbols associated with his possible martyrdom. These representations include a saw; a club; a short, curved sword called a falchion; and a lance. St. John Lateran in Rome displays a sculpture by Lorenzo Ottoni of Jude with a large partisan spear. A fish or a boat is often associated with Jude. The ship is also a symbol of the church itself, alluding either to Jude's sailing on missionary journeys or to speculation that he was a fisherman.[44] Yet the boat, fish, and writer symbols represent multiple disciples. The universality of Jude's symbols corresponds to the genuine uncertainty surrounding his influence. Since the Epistle of Jude is associated with the apostle, sometimes he is presented with a book or a scroll. Jude, along with Simon, is sometimes portrayed with sticks in his hands to represent their martyrdom legend.

Jude's image is also connected with exorcism. The Apostolic Constitutions of the fourth century attributes to him advice concerning widows and exorcists. On widows, he says a woman who has lost her husband and who has

---

42. Extracts concerning Abgar 4 (*ANF* 8:655). This passage states that the Zophenians slew him at Agel Hasna, both the people and place indicating ancient Armenia.

43. Criswell, *Apostles after Jesus*, 124.

44. Taylor, *How to Read a Church*, 113.

lived honorably should be allowed to hold the nonordained office of celibacy.[45] On exorcists, he says this nonordained role is a voluntary pledge to suffering, empowered by grace in the Spirit. Yet if there is occasion, an exorcist can also be ordained in an office of the church: bishop, presbyter, or deacon.[46]

Jude is always named next to Simon the Canaanite in lists, and they appear together in ministry adventures. In popular culture, if a church is named after Jude and another, it is usually Simon the Zealot. An example is the significant Cathedral of Saints Simon and Jude in Phoenix, Arizona, which was visited by Pope John Paul II and Mother Teresa. Meanwhile, Jude and Bartholomew together are called the "First Illuminators of Armenia."[47] Two additional legends whose sources cannot be located surround Jude. A Greek tradition claims that he was the bridegroom in the wedding at Cana (John 2:1–11).[48] Supposedly another legend exists that he was a shepherd boy who visited at the nativity, where Mary placed the child Jesus in his arms.[49]

Tomb and Patronage

There are relics of Simon and Jude in repositories around the world. The Basilica of St. Peter's in the Vatican City has a transept where the Blessed Sacrament is kept, and there relics of Simon and Jude rest under the altar of St. Joseph.[50] A side chapel in the Church of the Holy Savior in Lauro, Rome, contains a small bone fragment said to be from Jude's arm.[51] Meanwhile, the National Shrine of Jude in Chicago claims two small bone fragments in the altar reliquary and the kneeler of the St. Jude Chapel.[52] When Tom Bissell went in search of the tombs of the apostles, he chose the crypt of St. Sirnan's Basilica in Toulouse, France, as his spot for the resting place of Jude and Simon the Zealot.[53] In the Middle Ages the church served pilgrims as an important stop on the Way of St. James.

The Armenian Church is identified with Bartholomew's ministry in its ancient lands, but Jude's ministry provides additional historical apostolic support. The story goes that in the late nineteenth century, when Pope Leo XIII invited the Armenian Church to unite with the Catholic Church, the Eastern

45. Constitutions of the Holy Apostles 8.3.25 (*ANF* 7:493).
46. Constitutions of the Holy Apostles 8.3.26 (*ANF* 7:493).
47. McDowell, *Fate of the Apostles*, 241.
48. Taylor, *How to Read a Church*, 114.
49. Kalas, *Thirteen Apostles*, 104–5.
50. Thelen, *Saints in Rome and Beyond*, 16, 85.
51. Thelen, *Saints in Rome and Beyond*, 85.
52. Thelen, *Saints in Rome and Beyond*, 201.
53. Bissell, *Apostle*, 293–322.

Bishop Mouriadantz responded with the sufficiency of their apostolic founding: "Why should the Armenians go from Apostle to Apostle? What Peter is, the same also is Thaddaeus."[54]

The feast day of Jude is October 28 in the West and June 19 in the East, shared with Simon the Zealot, as they are found together in their apocryphal Acts in the Pseudo-Abdias tradition. Since an eighteenth-century devotion in France and Germany, Jude has been recognized as the "Saint of Lost Causes."[55] Likewise, he is associated with the desperate and despairing. Ellsworth Kalas calls him the "Saint of Last Resorts."[56] Perhaps this image is shaped by his healing of the prince of Osroene, but at the same time other apostles were champions of lost causes in their encounters with individuals in hopeless situations. Richard Taylor suggests that "Jude's name is so similar to that of the despised Judas Iscariot that he was invoked as a saint only in the most extreme circumstances."[57] Thus Jude is the patron saint of lost causes.

54. Buxton, *Armenian Church*, 5.
55. Ruffin, *The Twelve*, 148.
56. Kalas, *Thirteen Apostles*, 112.
57. Taylor, *How to Read a Church*, 113.

✳ 12 ✳

Simon

The Zealot

Simon said: I see him [Jesus] also among the angels; moreover, an angel has said to me, "Go out hence and the temple shall fall," but I said, "No, for some here may be converted." As they spoke in Hebrew an angel came and said, "Choose either the death of all here or the palm of martyrdom." They chose the palm. . . . The priests and the people attacked the apostles and slew them.

Acts of Simon and Jude[1]
third century, Syria

And I Simon the Canaanite make a constitution to determine by how many a bishop ought to be elected. Let a bishop be ordained by three or two bishops; but if anyone be ordained by one bishop, let him be deprived, both himself and he that ordained him.

Apostolic Constitutions[2]
fourth century, Syria

Simon the Zealot, the Cananaean, and the Canaanite—the apostle with the most complex epithet is one of the two most obscure apostles. The name Kananaios is transliterated from Aramaic *qan'ānayā'*, meaning

---

1. Elliott, 530.
2. Constitutions of the Holy Apostles 8.3.27 (*ANF* 7:493).

"zealot." The KJV renders it as "Simon the Canaanite" (Matt. 10:4; Mark 3:18), confusing the geographical location with the transliteration. Yet Luke 6:15 has the rendering "Zelotes" in the same translation. The name "Simon" finds a root in "Yah has heard," and Margaret Williams calls it "a perennial favourite with Jews, especially those in Greek-speaking areas." She says the name was the "commonest male name by far in first century Palestine."[3]

This disciple of Jesus may have been drawn toward the Zealot movement within Judaism. First-century historian Josephus describes these Zealots: "These men agree in all other things with Pharisaic notions; but they have an inviolable attachment to liberty; and say that God is to be their only Ruler and Lord, . . . nor indeed do they heed the deaths of their relations and friends, nor can any such fear make them call any man Lord."[4] Such tenacity led them to revolt against the Romans; the group included Judas the Galilean, whom the Bible says revolted against the Romans with other Galileans (Acts 5:37). Some viewed them as assassins. At the same time, a zealous nationalistic spirit does not necessitate membership in a party or a movement. Josephus's description in the year 66 is the first formal reference to them as an official faction in the apostolic era.[5] We cannot know with certainty that Simon was a Zealot.

Even given Simon's affinity for revolutionary ideas, he was likely taken aback when he encountered the message of Jesus. The calling of Simon is not recorded, but we might imagine that it was as personal as the calling of Peter and as unconventional as the calling of Matthew. If a Zealot were among the twelve disciples, one can imagine the debates and conflicts in terms of political worldviews that existed among the followers as they processed the implications of Jesus's teaching. A particularly strong disparity would have existed between a Zealot and a tax collector such as Matthew, with the one radically opposing Roman rule while the other was making a career of assimilating into the system of Roman rule. Simon could have initially imported his own ideology into the ministry of Jesus, hoping for revolution or political independence before understanding Jesus's message of peace. Ellsworth Kalas comments how "Simon may well have envisioned a great new movement under the direction of this Jesus of Nazareth."[6] Simultaneously, a Zealot's religious devotion and hope for theocracy could have been compatible with Jesus's message, with some reevaluation if Jesus's message did not display patriotism in the form of revolution.

3. Williams, "Palestinian Jewish Personal Names in Acts," 93.
4. Josephus, *Ant.* 18.1.6.
5. Bruce, *New Testament History*, 94–95.
6. Kalas, *Thirteen Apostles*, 64.

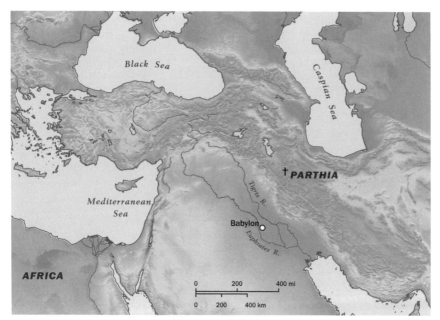

Journey of Simon

The familial ties of Simon are as confusing as they are for other third-tier apostles. From Byzantine to Coptic traditions, the common names of James, Judas, and Simon among Jesus's brothers (Matt. 13:55; Mark 6:3) led to their conflation with Jesus's third tier of disciples—James the Less, Judas Thaddaeus, and now Simon the Zealot. Frequently books on the apostles report on possible conflations, and speculation about kinship ties usually results in blurring the legends to explain an unsustainable theory. No assumptions should be made, as all are common names, providing three distinct disciples.

Palestine Discipleship

There is no strong tradition concerning Simon during the early years of the apostles in Palestine. Hippolytus confuses Simon the Zealot with a Simon who was another son of Alphaeus: "Simon the Zealot, the son of Clopas, who is also called Jude, became bishop of Jerusalem after James the Just, and fell asleep and was buried there at the age of 120 years."[7] Hans-Josef Klauck reports that most Eastern texts associate Simon with ministry in Jerusalem

---

7. Hippolytus, *Twelve* 11 (*ANF* 5:255).

and Samaria, merging the disciple with the brother of Jesus who was named bishop of Jerusalem after James the Just's death.[8]

Parthia Ministry

Persia was part of the ancient Parthian Empire. A strong tradition of Simon's ministry in this area makes it the most likely field of his missionary work. Furthermore, the proximity of western Persia to Syria accommodates the traditions that associate Simon with Jude, if their shared accounts warrant locating them there.

In the Latin Abdias tradition, an Acts of Simon and Jude describes how the two apostles go to Persia.[9] They encounter the two magicians Zaroes and Arphaxat, who fled Ethiopia under Matthew's ministry and preached a Manichaean-toned message centering on light and dark, soul and body, and denying the physical nature of Christ. The work corresponds to the drama of the Martyrdom of Matthew. The apostles find themselves with the commander of the army of King Xerxes, Varardach, whose magicians cannot offer advice from their deities because of the presence of the apostles. On his request, the apostles predict peace, while the king's counselors predict war, and when the Indians offer peace, the apostles are proved accurate. The commander seeks to punish his own counselors, but the apostles intervene in love against vengeance. When the commander seeks to offer gold to them as a reward, they decline it as earthly treasure. Finally, they are presented to the king as gods for their feat.

This conflict leads to a debate before the king between the lawyers of the land and the apostles. At first the apostles make their opponents unable to speak, move, and see. At a second trial, the lawyers hear the words of Simon and believe. Then the magicians are made powerless in their craft. When they do successfully call in snakes, the snakes turn and bite their masters, leading the magicians to slander the apostles for days from the hospital. Converts are made, healings take place, clergy are ordained, and a church is founded as the apostles are honored in Persia.

Soon afterward, two aggressive tigers escape and attack townspeople. The apostles calm the beasts, which peacefully stay with the men for three days. For fifteen more months, the apostles dwell there, seeing sixty thousand baptized and the ordination of Bishop Abdias, important for the legend of the apostles in the historical work noted as Pseudo-Abdias.

8. Klauck, *Apocryphal Acts of the Apostles*, 246.
9. Ps.-Abd. 6 (James, 464–66).

Zaroes and Arphaxat continue to contest the travels of the two apostles in an effort to prevent their message from succeeding. At the city of Suanir in Persia, they rouse seventy priests to confront them, taking the apostles to the temple of the luminaries. The resident demons cry out that they are burning because of the presence of the two men. When the priests call on the apostles to sacrifice to the temple gods, Jude turns to Simon to declare a sense that their time is up (see the quote that opens this chapter). The palm branch was a symbol of victory awarded to athletes and conquering heroes and is associated with Christ's entry into Jerusalem, where the people waved branches and lauded him (John 12:13) before some turned on him and called for his death within a week (18:40; 19:15). Adopted into Christian literature and iconography as a symbol for the martyrs, here the palm branch represents the death that ensues for these two apostles. The temple hosts an idolatrous chariot of the sun and a chariot of the moon, and Simon commands the devil of the sun chariot to leave while Jude does the same to the devil of the moon chariot. Two gruesome black men flee the idols, howling as the people attack the apostles. This legend describes swords or spears as being used in the temple slaying, while others refer to sticks or stones, with Simon also suffering from the saw. King Xerxes himself sees the bodies moved to his city, where he builds a basilica to house them.

Western works tend to partner Simon in ministry with Jude. Ninth-century martyrologist Ado explains the founding of the church of Persia as being a result of their mission and the location of their martyrdom.[10] Fifth-century historian Movses Khorenatsi claims that Simon experienced martyrdom in Persia, naming the city of Veriospore.[11]

Egypt Ministry

Several medieval authors relate a North African ministry of Simon before citing his role as bishop and martyr in Jerusalem. This latter fact seems to be a conflation with Simeon, the brother of Jesus and bishop of Jerusalem after James the Just. In the ninth century Florus mentions Simon's ministry in Egypt and Jerusalem, with his death occurring under Trajan at the age of 120.[12] Likewise, the Breviary of the Apostles reports that Simon ministered in Egypt before serving as bishop in Jerusalem after James the Just, living to the age of 120 into Hadrian's reign, dying by crucifixion, and being buried in a

---

10. Rose, *Ritual Memory*, 223–24.
11. Movses Khorenatsi, *A History of Armenia* 9, cited in McDowell, *Fate of the Apostles*, 247.
12. Rose, *Ritual Memory*, 223–24.

place called Portoforo. It also describes Simon as zealous, "burning with zeal for God," and "equal to Peter in honour." The liturgy called the Antiphonal of Florence also mentions his "reign over Egypt," a claim that he held ecclesiastical leadership in northeast Africa before holding an episcopate in Jerusalem.[13]

Dorotheus, bishop of Tyre in the early fourth century, claims, "Simon Zelotes preached Christ through all Mauritania and Africa."[14] Likewise, the Coptic tradition generally records Simon in Egypt, then deeper into Africa, then in Britain, and finally as martyred in Iran. This ministry on the African continent is an important component of the legacy of Simon and the apostles on the whole. While their collective influence extends most obviously to Africa through Simon, his own influence was instrumental in the development of the church there. David Alexander and Edward Smither remark: "It is significant that vibrant rural Christianity would endure as a shaping influence in the African church perhaps more than in any other region of the empire."[15]

Britain Ministry

In the fourth century Dorotheus reports how Simon, after preaching in North Africa, sailed north to Britain: "At length he was crucified in Britannia, slain and buried."[16] Ninth-century Constantinople Patriarch Nicephorus also confirms travels in Mauretania and Libya before Simon arrived at the "Isles called Britanniae."[17] Twentieth-century scholar George Jowett has articulated what seems to be a thorough case for Simon the Zealot traveling to Britain and ministering there.[18] Jowett's argument includes a lengthy analysis of how Joseph of Arimathea's travels there were a basis for Peter's visit, which in turn could create a precedent for Simon's visit. David Criswell also feels strongly that Simon ministered in Britain. During Nero's reign there was a revolt by Queen Boadicea, which led to Roman withdrawal, and if Simon remained, this theory lends itself to a late crucifixion on the island. Criswell remarks: "I believe the mass of evidence that favors the belief that Simon chose to stay with his new converts and continue his mission field."[19] William McBirnie suggests that Simon arrived in Britain around 60, preceding the departure of Roman influence under violent

---

13. Rose, *Ritual Memory*, 237–39.

14. Dorotheus, *Synopsis of the Apostles* 9, cited in A. Eedle and R. Eedle, *Albion Restored*, 62.

15. Alexander and Smither, "Bauer's Forgotten Region," 171–72.

16. Dorotheus, *Synopsis of the Apostles* 9, cited in A. Eedle and R. Eedle, *Albion Restored*, 62.

17. Nicephorus of Constantinople, *Concise Book of Chronography* 2.40, cited in A. Eedle and R. Eedle, *Albion Restored*, 62.

18. Jowett, *Drama of the Lost Disciples*, 149–60.

19. Criswell, *Apostles after Jesus*, 135.

uprisings there.[20] Thomas Schmidt believes that both the Roman roads and maritime travel make it reasonable to think that Simon ministered in Britain.[21] Perhaps Origen has this tradition of Simon in mind when he writes how the gospel has gone forth: "The power of the Lord and Savior is with those who are in Britain, separated from our world, and with those who are in Mauretania, and with everyone under the sun who has believed in his name."[22]

Yet there is no British historical evidence that Simon the Zealot ministered in its lands. As Sean McDowell points out, the church record there is lacking, Bede's eighth-century history from Britain does not mention his legacy, and modern history books recognize early Christianity but never the presence of apostles. "The fact that British scholars largely ignore his visit is a sign that it may be apocryphal."[23] Yet a surprising number of scholars remain open to this tradition, in which a ship from Africa might have sailed to Britain.

Image of Simon the Zealot

When the apostle Simon is separated historically from Simeon, the brother of Jesus and later bishop of Jerusalem, a distinct figure emerges. His traveling to North Africa is likely, before ministry and martyrdom in Persia. A sojourn in Britain is historically a challenge, but the theory has not been disproved. Meanwhile, Simon and Jude's shared apocryphal legends and relic sites suggest that even their images are conflated.

Symbolism and Image Construction

Simon, along with Jude, is sometimes portrayed with sticks in his hands to represent his martyrdom legend. Other tools used as instruments of his death are often employed as symbols: a saw, a short curved sword called a falchion, and a lance.[24] In a statue crafted by Francesco Moratti in St. John Lateran Basilica in Rome, Simon is pictured examining a book while holding a human-length saw. The apostle is sometimes pictured with fish when his counterpart Jude is pictured with the ship. Richard Taylor reports that Simon is rarely seen with the fishing boat.[25]

20. McBirnie, *Search for the Twelve Apostles*, 145.
21. Schmidt, *Apostles after Acts*, 160–70.
22. Origen, *Homilies on Luke* 6 (Lienhard, 27).
23. McDowell, *Fate of the Apostles*, 248–49. McDowell does not entirely rule out its possibility, however.
24. Taylor, *How to Read a Church*, 114.
25. Taylor, *How to Read a Church*, 114.

Els Rose has shown comprehensively how the apocryphal Acts capture the legacy of six apostles from the second and third tiers in the liturgy from the days of the early medieval West. One example is worth mentioning here for illustration. In an eighth-century Gelasian Mass, so named for its connection with Pope Gelasius I (r. 492–96), a Christian community in southern France remembered the ministry and fidelity of the apostles Simon and Jude each time they recited the liturgy of the mass. Rose remarks:

> In this prayer, the faithful of Gellone (or Angoulême or the monks of Sankt Gallen or the other liturgical centers using this mass) equal themselves to the people of the 1st-century Babylon or Suanir, by claiming that "we have come to the knowledge of God's name through the blessed apostles Simon and Jude." These Christian communities of the 8th century consider the apostles as their founding fathers of their faith. Through the liturgical commemoration of the Acts of the apostles, the past is presented anew, and as procuring salvation.[26]

Additional legends surround Simon the Zealot. Without providing ancient sources, Bernard Ruffin and Taylor mention a legend that Simon was one of the shepherds who came to the nativity scene at the birth of Jesus (Luke 2:8–18).[27] Taylor reports a Greek tradition that Simon was the bridegroom at the Cana wedding at which Jesus turned water into wine (John 2:1–11).[28] It is noteworthy that among the legends of the apostles, Simon and Jude are the only two disciples to die together in any story.

Tomb and Patronage

A summary of Simon's resting places is the same as the summary of Jude's tomb sites in the previous chapter, with repositories of their bone fragments in various places. St. Peter's Basilica in Rome claims Simon's bones in a side transept,[29] while the crypt of St. Sirnan's Basilica in Toulouse, France, also claims his bones.[30]

Simon's feast day is October 28 in the West and June 19 in the East, along with Jude. He is considered the patron saint of tanners, lumberjacks, and woodcutters for the tradition of his martyrdom by saw, as well as masons, weavers, and henpecked husbands.[31]

---

26. Rose, *Ritual Memory*, 227.
27. Ruffin, *The Twelve*, 145; Taylor, *How to Read a Church*, 114.
28. Taylor, *How to Read a Church*, 114.
29. Thelen, *Saints in Rome and Beyond*, 16, 85.
30. Bissell, *Apostle*, 317.
31. Jöckle, *Encyclopedia of Saints*, 409.

13

Matthias

The Elected

Peter stood up in the midst of the brethren . . . and said, " . . . There-fore it is necessary that of the men who have accompanied us all the time that the Lord Jesus went in and out among us—begin-ning with the baptism of John, until the day that He was taken up from us—one of these *must* become a witness with us of His resurrection." . . . And they drew lots for them, and the lot fell to Matthias; and he was added to the eleven apostles.

Acts 1:15, 21–22, 26

He was accused by the high priest of many things, to which he re-plied: "I cannot answer much as to the offense of which you accuse me. It is not an offense to be a Christian, but the highest honour."

The Golden Legend[1]
thirteenth-century hagiography

When Jesus remarks that the last shall be first and the first shall be last (Mark 10:31), he likely does not have in view the permanent status that Matthias has in the legacy of the apostles. Yet for the apostle elected last, the only one elected by lots, and the one mentioned in

---

1. De Voragine, *Golden Legend*, 176.

only one list in the New Testament, the proverb relates when he gets ranked among the primary leaders of the early church. Apostle scholar Bernard Ruffin says he was "a man of little consequence."[2] Ellsworth Kalas even names a complex after him: "a Matthias complex, the feeling of being a blessed afterthought."[3] Meanwhile, New Testament apocalyptic literature and early church works diminish his identity even more by confusing him with Matthew. For example, the Coptic Book of Resurrection of Jesus Christ makes Matthias a rich man who leaves all to follow Jesus, a clear description of the call of Matthew (Matt. 9:9). Yet limited information on an apostle does not necessarily bear on the measure of that apostle's success or contribution. Matthias is a Greek shortened form of Mattathias, originally a Hebrew word meaning "gift of God."

Palestine Discipleship

The earliest discipleship of Matthias is lost to us. In fact, we would not know that he was among the early followers if not for his replacing Judas Iscariot in Acts. There Peter lays out the criterion of early discipleship for qualification to serve as an apostle. This is the only passage with attention to Matthias, but it is an important one in capturing the leadership development of the apostles.

Discipleship Calling

In a story from a gnostic text that can hardly be historically credible, Matthias is described as rich when he forsakes all to follow Jesus.[4] A Coptic manuscript associated with the work tells a story of a woman bringing a dead rooster to the Last Supper, which Matthias places on a dish on the table. After handing Judas the bread and sending him forth, Jesus resurrects the rooster, empowers it with human speech, and instructs it to follow and watch Judas Iscariot. The rooster follows Judas home, overhears the plan to betray Jesus, returns to report it, and weeps before Jesus. Jesus discharges the bird, empowering it to ascend to the sky for a thousand years.[5]

After the ascension but before Pentecost, Peter advances the proposition of replacing Judas Iscariot among the Twelve. He proposes the criteria of electing one who has been a follower from the days of John until the present, is seemingly faithful, and was a witness of the resurrection:

2. Ruffin, *The Twelve*, 170.
3. Kalas, *Thirteen Apostles*, 138.
4. Book of the Resurrection of Christ by Bartholomew the Apostle (James, 382).
5. Book of the Cock (James, 149).

And at this time Peter stood up in the midst of the brethren (a gathering of about one hundred and twenty persons was there together), and said, "Brethren, the Scripture had to be fulfilled, which the Holy Spirit foretold by the mouth of David concerning Judas, who became a guide to those who arrested Jesus. . . . Therefore it is necessary that of the men who have accompanied us all the time that the Lord Jesus went in and out among us—beginning with the baptism of John until the day that He was taken up from us—one of these *must* become a witness with us of His resurrection." So they put forward two men, Joseph called Barsabbas (who was also called Justus), and Matthias. And they prayed and said, "You, Lord, who know the hearts of all men, show which one of these two You have chosen to occupy this ministry and apostleship from which Judas turned aside to go to his own place." And they drew lots for them, and the lot fell to Matthias; and he was added to the eleven apostles. (Acts 1:15–16, 21–26)

One cannot help but wonder whether the apostle Paul was a better candidate to take the place among the Twelve. The significance and influence of Paul's ministry surpass the recorded legacy of all of the other apostles. G. Campbell Morgan maintains that the company of the apostles was wrong to select a replacement for Judas: "We have a revelation of their inefficiency for organization; that the election of Matthias is wrong." Campbell believes that casting lots was outdated, that the appointment of Matthias was misguided, and that Paul "was God's man for the filling of the gap."[6] Yet it is dangerous to question the decision making of the apostles here, including Peter, even if Pentecost has not yet empowered them. The group prays for God's will in a way that seems honorable (Acts 1:25–26). The casting of lots for divine application has precedent in the choosing of Aaron (Lev. 16:8), Joshua (Josh. 18:6), David (1 Chron. 24:31), and Nehemiah (Neh. 11:1). Proverbs 16:33 claims that when lots are cast, the decision made is from the Lord. At the time of this election, Paul does not meet the criterion of being in the company of the apostles on account of his lack of participation in the ministry of Jesus and of witnessing the resurrection.

There is no further mention of Matthias or Justus in the New Testament. Origen explicitly groups Matthias among the "twelve apostles" who saw the resurrected Jesus (1 Cor. 15:5).[7] If Origen is accurate, then he simply views Matthias as an apostle ex post facto. Both Hippolytus and Eusebius also remark how Matthias was among the Seventy, the group commissioned by Jesus for ministry in Luke 10:1–20.[8]

6. Morgan, *Acts of the Apostles*, 21.
7. Origen, *Contra Celsus* 2.65 (*ANF* 4:457).
8. Hippolytus, *Twelve* 12 (*ANF* 5:255); Hippolytus, *On the Seventy Apostles* 3 (*ANF* 5:255); Eusebius, *Hist. eccl.* 1.12.3.

Eric Titus has posited that Matthias could be the beloved disciple of John's Gospel, possibly the unnamed apostle alongside Andrew when John the Baptist points out Jesus (John 1:35–40).[9] Most convincing in this argument is the association with the activity of the beloved disciple at the Last Supper discourse in John 13:21–25, as he attempts to ascertain who will betray Jesus, the one whom he ultimately replaces.[10] Finally, Titus suggests that Judas is a symbol of Judaism passing, while Matthias is a symbol of Christianity and the church unfolding.[11] However, this scholar is up against the unanimous testimony of the early church fathers, as well as the similar themes in both the Gospel and the First Epistle of John. Tradition maintains longevity for John, ascribed to the beloved disciple in John 21, which does not match the traditions surrounding the death of Matthias in the same era as the other ten apostles.

Three separate locations are traditionally connected to the ministry of Matthias: Scythia, Ethiopia, and Jerusalem. Matthias is also thought of as the author of some texts in some traditions. The primary challenge to this identification is the overlap between Matthias and Matthew. For example, the Coptic Book of the Resurrection of Jesus Christ comments that Matthias is the rich man who left all to follow Jesus, but this is likely a conflation with Matthew (Matt. 9:9).[12] Clement of Alexandria comments that some view the chief publican Zacchaeus (Luke 19:2–10) and Matthias as the same person, but this connection may be a mistaken link based on Matthew's wealth and occupation.[13]

Ministry in Writing

A work seeming to originate in second-century Egypt, the Gospel according to Matthias is now lost to us. There were also a Secret Traditions of Jesus and Matthias and the Traditions of Matthias, known only through citations and perhaps the same work as the gospel in his name. In the Book of Thomas the Contender, Matthias is credited with writing the secret words of the resurrected Jesus to his brother Jude Thomas.[14] Small pieces and references come from various church fathers that suggest these words are gnostic and potentially encratic in nature. For example, Clement of Alexandria makes this comment about gnostic teaching: "They say that Matthias also taught

9. Titus, "Identity," 324.
10. Titus, "Identity," 324–25.
11. Titus, "Identity," 325–26.
12. Book of the Resurrection of Christ (James, 185).
13. Clement of Alexandria, *Strom.* 4.6 (*ANF* 2:415).
14. Book of Thomas the Contender (Robinson, 201).

Journey of Matthias

this: fight with the flesh and use it properly, yielding to it nothing immoral for the sake of pleasure, but make the soul grow by faith and knowledge."[15] Hippolytus criticizes the gnostic writers who claim that Matthias gave a secret teaching from the Lord: "Basilides, simultaneously with Isidorus, and the entire band of these (heretics), not only absolutely belies Matthias, but even the Saviour Himself."[16] Origen remarks: "I know of one gospel called *According of Thomas* and another *According to Matthias*. . . . We approve of nothing but what the Church approves of, namely only four gospels."[17]

Scythia Ministry

The fifth-century Acts of Andrew and Matthias reports how via the casting of lots for ministry assignment, Matthias is sent to Scythia, sometimes cited as the city of Myrmidonia. Unfortunately, this city is also lost to us; scholars

15. Clement of Alexandria, *Strom.* 3.4 (*ANF* 2:385 [AT]).
16. Hippolytus, *Refutation of All Heresies* 7.8 (*ANF* 5:103).
17. Origen, *Homilies on Luke* 1 (Lienhard, 94:6).

speculate that it was in either Scythia or Ethiopia. There is an Eastern tradition that places him in Scythia, which would accord with Myrmidonia being located there, while the Ethiopian tradition provides another set of names not associated with this region. The Ethiopic Abdias tradition also reports that Matthias's lots fell to the unknown city of Ba'alatsaby as well as to the city of Damascus, Syria, to the southwest of Scythia.[18]

The Acts of Andrew and Matthias chronicles Matthias going to a city of cannibals, *anthropophagi*, to the "land of man-eaters."[19] Other manuscript copies have Matthew named in place of Matthias. In the early second century, Pliny the Elder seems to substantiate this element of the narrative, saying that Scythians feed on human flesh.[20] This practice included the seizure of visitors and prolonged control over their captives by drugs. In the narrative Matthias is seized, blinded, drugged, and imprisoned on his arrival in the city.

In prison, while praying to the Lord, Matthias's sight is restored. A voice from God explains that he will be kept safe from all harm and that the apostle Andrew will come to his aid before he is scheduled for execution. Meanwhile, Andrew receives a vision in Achaea to go to rescue Matthias. Matthias is freed, and on their departure from prison, Andrew commands a cloud, which lifts Matthias and Andrew's disciples to a mountain where Peter is preaching.[21] After the rescue of Matthias, the story focuses on the activity of Andrew, and eventually the disciples leave rejoicing.

The Ethiopic Abdias narrative reports that when Andrew arrives at the prison, the imprisoned apostle is singing.[22] The depravity of Matthias's captors is exemplified when the presence of the apostles hastens them to gather all of the dead from their cities and eat them. In this account, the Lord commands the apostles to submit to recapture, so that their enemies "dragged the apostles along the road of the city until their blood ran like water."[23] Here Matthias is presented as bold but realistic, drawing on his faith for strength: "Yes, I know it, my brother; but I said, if it should be our Lord Jesus Christ's good pleasure that I should finish [my course] in this city, then I heard a voice that said in the holy Gospel: Behold I send you forth as sheep among wolves."[24]

The apostles make the sign of the cross in prayer while looking to a stone pillar with a statue in their prison, as waters burst forth and flood the city.

18. Abdias, *Conflicts* 12 (James, 147, 163).
19. Acts of Andrew and Matthias (James, 453).
20. Pliny the Elder, *Natural History* 7.2, cited in McDowell, *Fate of the Apostles*, 254.
21. Acts of Andrew and Matthias 21.
22. Abdias, *Conflicts* 12 (Malan, 154).
23. Abdias, *Conflicts* 12 (Malan, 158).
24. Abdias, *Conflicts* 12 (Malan, 154).

After further prayer by Matthias, a cloud of darkness made by Michael the archangel surrounds the citizens, and the apostles escape the waters. Andrew commands the flood to cease as Matthias rebukes the merciless crowd for its irony in now asking for pity. The transporting cloud is part of this version too. Jesus confronts the two apostles on their acts of vengeance: "Why, then, do ye give precepts to men and then send them into the deep?"[25] The apostles return to the city to build a church.

Meanwhile, manuscripts of the Acts and Martyrdom of St. Matthew conflate Matthias and Matthew while telling a similar story. Matthias goes to the land of the man-eaters, where he is sentenced by the king to be nailed to the ground and set on fire.[26] An Eastern tradition maintains that Simon the Zealot and Matthias joined Andrew on a third missionary journey along the border of ancient Scythia and Parthia, in modern Georgia. A general Greek tradition supposes Matthias preached in the region of Colchis, south of the Caucasus Mountains and on the east coast of the Black Sea. In this legend, Matthias dies in the town-fortress of Asparos. There is a tradition that his bones are still there.[27]

Ethiopia Ministry

From Matthias's experiences in Myrmidonia, one tradition relates his experience among the cannibals as occurring in a different region, although it does not discern whether this local reference is to the Ethiopia of the Caspian Sea region or of the East African region. The Latin Pseudo-Abdias tradition has the apostle in Naddaver, Ethiopia, under King Aeglippus in confrontation with two magicians. While this is traditionally recognized as referring to Matthew, scholars are divided about the geographical location of the two apostles, confronting two options for an Ethiopian setting involving cannibals.

Some scholars place the cannibal episode among the East Africans; Ellsworth Kalas, for example, believes that Matthias was first among the Ethiopians before moving to Arabia Felix on the Red Sea coast.[28] Other scholars, such as Thieleman van Braght in the seventeenth century, perpetuate the tradition that Matthias went to Ethiopia before returning to Judea in a way that lends itself to the Caspian Sea region. There he is accused of not sacrificing

25. Abdias, *Conflicts* 12 (Malan, 162).
26. Acts and Martyrdom of St. Matthew (*ANF* 8:528–34).
27. McDowell, *Fate of the Apostles*, 254.
28. Kalas, *Thirteen Apostles*, 145.

to Jupiter and is put to death. In another reported account, van Braght says Matthias was accused of blasphemy against God, Moses, and the law by Jews. When his crucifixion does not succeed, he is stoned and beheaded with an ax.[29] This Ethiopia, however, means a region of Parthia constituting modern Georgia. As in the chapter on Matthew, this episode could be placed not in East Africa but in the Ethiopia around the Caspian Sea. The location is proximal to Scythia, allowing the Acts of Andrew and Matthias above to correspond to this account.

Early in the fifth century the historian Socrates names Ethiopia as the region assigned to Matthew, although he could be drawing from the tradition conflated with Matthias.[30] The sixth-century *Synopsis* by Dorotheus contains the tradition that Matthias preached to barbarians and cannibals in the interior of Ethiopia, at the sea harbor of Hyssus near Cappadocia, before dying and being buried at Sebastopolis near the temple of the sun.[31] These references around the Black Sea confirm his location there and provide the most likely location of his death.

Judea and Syria Ministry

The ministry of Matthias likely began in Palestine, but it is possible that he remained there. He could have preached in Jerusalem in the early phase of the apostles before going to the Caspian Sea area or to East Africa. However, the Palestine tradition includes legends of his death there.

The Ethiopic Abdias account relates Matthias's journey to Damascus, Syria, where at first his message was not well received. In the narrative he is quickly bound and laid on a bed of hot iron, such that the smell of his burning body is evident. Yet the people wonder at how the fire does not consume Matthias for twenty-five days. Reminiscent of the episode of the youths in the fiery furnace in Daniel 3:12–30, the people here declare Jesus unlike any god in heaven. Idols are broken, the temple is razed, and a church is built. In this episode, "He slept a good sleep, and rested [of his labours], in the city of Phalaon, which is of the cities of Judah."[32] This suggests a natural death for Matthias.

Hippolytus claims: "Matthias, who was one of the seventy, was numbered along with the eleven apostles, and preached in Jerusalem, and fell asleep and

29. Van Braght, *Bloody Theater*, 92–93.
30. Socrates, *Ecclesiastical History* 1.19 (NPNF² 1:23).
31. Smith and Cheetham, *Dictionary of Christian Antiquities*, 1159.
32. Abdias, *Conflicts* 12 (Malan, 166).

was buried there."[33] This report does not necessitate a natural death, although it can be inferred. Despite popular understanding, Heracleon does not claim that Matthias died a natural death.[34] Eusebius says that a Matthias was the eighth of fifteen bishops in Jerusalem, making the period too long to include the apostle Matthias, unless the office had a fixed term or the list includes several elders in service simultaneously.[35]

Thirteenth-century writer Jacobus de Voragine reports that Matthias preached and worked wonders in Judea many years and "at last fell asleep in the peace of the Lord." Others, de Voragine recognizes, declare that Matthias was crucified.[36] De Voragine also relates a story that Matthias in Macedonia drank a cup of a poison that blinded the drinker. Not only was he not blinded, but he healed more than 250 others blinded by it. The account describes an imprisonment, spiritual warfare, and conversions.[37]

The evidence surrounding a Palestine ministry and martyrdom for Matthias is historically slender. However, the entire ministry record for Matthias is meager. Despite this, it is not uncommon for scholars tracing the apostles to conclude that Matthias ministered in Palestine and died at the hands of the Jews, typically by stoning.[38] A fifth-century passage from the tractate Sanhedrin of the Babylonian Talmud is often brought up to support his death in Jerusalem. It states how one "Yeshu" (perhaps Jesus) had a disciple named Matthai, and at Matthai's trial a passage from the rabbinical writings was quoted that one by that name should die. Sean McDowell has shown that the allusion is too ambiguous for the historical Matthias, the writing is late, and the details do not necessarily refer to the apostle.[39]

Image of Matthias

The image of Matthias is persistently that of a replacement because he became an apostle as a substitute for the fallen Judas Iscariot. Beyond this New Testament passage, the history of Matthias is unclear. Activities in western Scythia or Parthia seem likely, as well as in Ethiopia, meaning the area that is

33. Hippolytus, *Twelve* 12 (*ANF* 5:255).

34. This claim is often attributed to Clement of Alexandria, *Strom.* 4.9, which is a misreading of apostolic deaths.

35. Eusebius, *Hist. eccl.* 4.5. References to elders alongside the apostles occur in Acts 6:3; 15:2, 22–23; 16:4.

36. De Voragine, *Golden Legend*, 175.

37. De Voragine, *Golden Legend*, 176–77.

38. Criswell, *Apostles after Jesus*, 141; McDowell, *Fate of the Apostles*, 257; Schmidt, *Apostles after Acts*, 118.

39. McDowell, *Fate of the Apostles*, 255–56.

now modern Armenia or Georgia. Perhaps the historical silence about Matthias is because he simply ministered around Jerusalem, where he eventually died. The lack of a martyrdom report in some early church commentaries may be because he was among the few apostles who died naturally. However, his symbolism includes references to his martyrdom traditions.

Symbolism and Image Construction

One symbol of Matthias, like so many other apostles, comes from the instrument involved in his martyrdom story. The tradition of his beheading produces a symbol of an axe or halberd, even though the early church does not record this execution.

Matthias takes on a connotation of self-denial in some minor episodes of early church writings. The above-cited Clement of Alexandria quotation refers to gnostics claiming that Matthias taught to "fight with the flesh and use it properly, yielding to it nothing immoral for the sake of pleasure, but make the soul grow by faith and knowledge."[40] Clement also describes an episode in Matthias's ministry in which a deacon, Nicolaus, the founder of a gnostic heresy, offers up his young, beautiful wife for the sake of his own purity. He declares: "Any one of you who wants her can have her."[41] Afterward, Nicolaus lives a life of celibacy and austerity.[42]

Tombs and Patronage

The remains of Matthias are claimed in four locations in Europe. Helena, the mother of Constantine, is commonly connected to their acquisition and placement in Trier and Rome. The Saint Matthias Benedictine Abbey in Trier, Germany, is said to hold the tomb of Matthias within the nave, and it is claimed that a sarcophagus in its crypt also contains his relics.[43] Ernst Haenchen provides a tradition of the abbey that the remains sent under Constantine to Trier were lost in the Norman assault but later rediscovered.[44]

Meanwhile the Archbasilica of St. Mary Maggiore in Rome claims that some relics of Matthias rest within the porphyry urn on the papal altar.[45] The Abbey of Saint Justina in Padua, Italy, dedicates a transept chapel to his tomb. Daniel Thelen remarks that although the inscription reads *Sors cecidit*

40. Clement of Alexandria, *Strom.* 3.4 (*ANF* 2:385 [AT]).
41. Ruffin, *The Twelve*, 171.
42. Eusebius, *Hist. eccl.* 3.29.
43. Thelen, *Saints in Rome and Beyond*, 174.
44. Haenchen, *Acts of the Apostles*, 162n5.
45. Thelen, *Saints in Rome and Beyond*, 70.

super Mathiam, "The lot fell on Matthias," no other support of the tomb's authenticity is provided by the abbey. The tradition is that when Luke's relics came there in the eighth century, Matthias's relics accompanied them.[46] His are the only primary remains found in Germany.

In an Eastern tradition, the remains of the apostle are buried in the castle at Gonion, Georgia, on the west coast of the Black Sea. Burial in this location would support a Parthian or Scythian ministry and martyrdom for Matthias. His Western feast day is May 14, formerly February 24, and his Eastern feast day is August 9. Matthias is the patron saint of builders, engineers, blacksmiths, tailors, butchers, and boys who are beginning school, and he is invoked against whooping cough, smallpox, and infertility.[47]

46. Thelen, *Saints in Rome and Beyond*, 96.
47. Jöckle, *Encyclopedia of Saints*, 317.

* 14 *

Paul

The Sword

But even if I am being poured out as a drink offering upon the sacrifice and service of your faith, I rejoice and share my joy with you all.

Philippians 2:17

If today I must tell you any of my teachings then listen, O proconsul. The living God . . . has sent me that I may rescue them from corruption and uncleanness and from all pleasure, and from death, that they may sin no more. . . . If then I teach the things revealed to me by God what harm do I do, O proconsul?

Acts of Paul[1]
early second century, Anatolia

No apostle is quite like Paul. His devotion to the covenantal God provides irony, paradox, and surprise, which combine with his unpredictable and resilient personality to describe a passionate devotee of Jesus. An apocryphal work, the Acts of Paul, captures a second-century legend of his appearance when one Onesiphorus sought him at Iconium. Access

---

1. Acts of Paul 3.17 (Elliott, 367).

to a physical description is rare among the apostles but is provided here: "A man little of stature, thin-haired upon the head, crooked in the legs, of good state of body, with eyebrows joining, appeared like a man, and sometimes he had the face of an angel."[2] Another story relates that dissenters, knowing that Paul was bald, seized Paul's bald shipmaster, Dioscorus, mistaking him for Paul, and beheaded him erroneously.[3]

The story of Paul's life is well known. He was trained in and passionate about Jewish law and culture. A persecutor of the church, his life took a dramatic turn after a visionary encounter with Christ on the road to Damascus. After a period of discipling in Christianity, he became equally enthusiastic about the Way (Acts 9:2; 22:4) and became an extraordinary missionary to Jews and gentiles. He famously planted churches, promoted inclusion of believing gentiles into the church, pressed the frontiers of the faith, testified at the highest levels of government, and modeled being persecuted as a standard consequence of evangelism. His life can be broken into three notable geographical periods, each of which receives attention here.

Palestine Discipleship

The discipleship of Paul began before he became a Christian, when he was a devoted follower of Judaism. Like the gospel itself, Paul's roots are in Jewish tradition and its Scriptures, before he broadened his vision to include the gentiles (Rom. 1:16).

Jewish Period

Paul provides credibility for his ministry through a summary of his biography. He was a Jew of Tarsus of Cilicia, a citizen named Saul, educated under the prestigious teacher of Judaism Gamaliel, and zealous for God (Acts 21:39–22:4). He spoke with a Semitic accent that accompanied his arguments, silencing his Jewish audience (22:2). In his Letter to the Philippians, he describes his pedigree and passion: "Circumcised the eighth day, of the nation of Israel, of the tribe of Benjamin, a Hebrew of Hebrews; as to the Law, a Pharisee; as to zeal, a persecutor of the church; as to the righteousness which is in the Law, found blameless" (Phil. 3:5–6). He was born a Roman citizen, so that when he is tried by the local authority of the Roman Empire, he can appeal for the better treatment that citizens enjoyed (Acts 22:25–29). A member

2. Acts of Paul 2.3 (James, 273).
3. Acts of Peter and Paul (ANF 8:477).

of the ruling council of Judaism, the Sanhedrin (5:34–39), he stood among the leadership of the faith that was wary of the rise of Christianity. From this position of prestige, Paul in his zeal persecuted the church (Acts 7:58; 8:1–3; 9:1–2, 13; 22:4–5; 26:10–12; 1 Cor. 15:9; Gal. 1:13, 23; Phil. 3:6). His role is foreshadowed in Acts at the persecution of Stephen, when he stands nearby as the stoners lay their garments at his feet. It is not until he receives a vision of the resurrected Lord that his loyalty shifts (Acts 9:1–19), an event that also makes his apostleship valid (Acts 22:4–21; 26:12–18; 1 Cor. 15:8–11; Gal. 1:11–16).

Discipleship Calling

His endeavor to persecute the church leads Paul along the road to Damascus, where he has a vision of the risen Christ challenging him to true obedience: "Saul, Saul, why are you persecuting Me?" (Acts 22:7). Paul responds: "'What shall I do, Lord?' And the Lord said to me, 'Get up and go on into Damascus; and there you will be told of all that has been appointed for you to do'" (22:10).

The stoning of Stephen by a Jewish synagogue contingent is a shocking first execution of a Christian disciple. The event is somber and glorious as the innocent Stephen is taken out of the city and stoned. In what seems a passing comment to the reader of Acts, "The witnesses laid aside their robes at the feet of a young man named Saul" (Acts 7:58). A later verse builds this drama, "And Saul was in hearty agreement with putting him to death" (8:1). Before his life is over, Paul evaluates his credentials and his zeal for the law, remarking: "But whatever things were gain to me, those things I have counted as loss for the sake of Christ" (Phil. 3:7). The encounter on the road to Damascus redirects his passion from devout rejection of Christ to full embrace. This pinnacle of devotion was preceded by a period of apprenticeship in the faith.

Discipleship Period

Paul's conversion seems to be held with suspicion by the early believers (Acts 9:21, 26–27). Such hesitancy among the church leaders about one who has persecuted the faith is certainly warranted. Barnabas is instrumental in Paul's acceptance, as he brings Paul to the twelve disciples to describe the vision of Christ and his missionary initiatives in Damascus (9:27). Later Barnabas recruits Paul from Tarsus and brings him to Antioch (11:25–26). Paul's own version of this period includes a noteworthy delay in going to Jerusalem to be among the Twelve in the form of a three-year hiatus in Arabia and Damascus (Gal. 1:15–18).

However, the suspicion seems to be short lived. Paul remarks in his Letter to the Galatians that the Twelve received him and that a mission to the gentiles was an early priority: "Recognizing the grace that had been given to me, James and Cephas and John, who were reputed to be pillars, gave to me and Barnabas the right hand of fellowship, so that we *might go* to the Gentiles and they to the circumcised" (2:9). Yet even when he self-identifies as an apostle, there is sometimes a sense that he is not numbered among the Twelve. Jerome says Paul was "an apostle outside the number of the twelve apostles."[4]

Eventually Paul "was with them, moving about freely in Jerusalem, speaking out boldly in the name of the Lord" (Acts 9:28). The apostles' ministry to the two people groups was united; Alan Cole sums up the phenomenon well:

> Paul's apostolate to the Gentiles was recognized as freely as Peter's apostolate to the Jews. . . . They took this course not as a result of a complicated process of reasoning, but from observation of spiritual facts. Just as Peter's apostolic ministry to the Jews was sealed by the work of the Spirit in the hearts of the hearers, so the seal of Paul's apostolic ministry was the harvest of the Gentiles given him by God.[5]

With this acceptance during his early Palestine ministry, Paul is free to be the minister of his vision. He is an apostolic partner with the other apostles for the faith, not a hindrance. Cole describes how Peter's initial vision for the gentile mission meant that his mantle essentially fell on Paul.[6] In a sort of credo statement, Paul proclaims his own ministry strategy:

> For though I am free from all *men*, I have made myself a slave to all, so that I may win more. To the Jews I became as a Jew, so that I might win Jews; to those who are under the Law, as under the Law though not being myself under the Law, so that I might win those who are under the Law; to those who are without law, as without law, though not being without the law of God but under the law of Christ, so that I might win those who are without law. To the weak I became weak, that I might win the weak; I have become all things to all men, so that I may by all means save some. I do all things for the sake of the gospel, so that I may become a fellow partaker of it. (1 Cor. 9:19–23)

Yet Paul's style might not have always been appreciated. Cole remarks, "The way in which he was hurried from place to place in the early church

---

4. Jerome, *Vir. ill.* 5 (NPNF² 3:362).
5. Cole, *Galatians*, 69.
6. Cole, *Galatians*, 70.

(Damascus, Jerusalem, Caesarea, Tarsus), usually as a result of the opposition that his fiery preaching stirred up, suggests that the leaders may have been somewhat embarrassed by the enthusiasm of this young convert."[7] This level of speculation is not always supported by biblical writers, especially in the case of Paul. Likewise, his propensity to encounters with conflict reveals either a ministry character or a personal temperament comfortable with and potentially prone to opposition. We might speculate that sometimes the human Paul was overzealous, excessively confrontational, or not strategically passionate. Such reflection is warranted in the face of the superhuman impression that his heroic initiatives foster. Perhaps like Moses in the wilderness, at times he became impatient with the people of God (Num. 20:11–12). Perhaps the people of Philippi represent a common response to Paul; guided by selfishness and revenge, they rend their clothes in frustration not only at the message but also at the individual himself (Acts 16:22). While Luke does not describe such imperfections in Acts, the humanity of Paul is a legitimate subject of consideration in the otherwise efficacious ministry recorded of him.

Certainly the apostle shows no inclination toward self-pity in the New Testament. He seems to graciously accept conflict and punishment, contextualizing his sufferings in his discipleship to Jesus. For example, Acts 20:23 shows him willing to shoulder whatever persecution awaits him in Jerusalem: "The Holy Spirit solemnly testifies to me in every city, saying that bonds and afflictions await me." Unlike Elijah, Paul reveals no loneliness or depression in his ministry and persecution (1 Kings 19:14, 18). His resilience is astounding, serving as an inspiration to faithful ministry. While he often comes first to the synagogues of the cities he visits, inevitably his great contribution is to the gentiles of those cities. This development enables Paul to later call himself an apostle to the gentiles (Rom. 11:13; 1 Tim. 2:7).

An important episode in the formative period of Paul's faith was an encounter with Peter at Antioch over the inclusion of the gentiles alongside the Jews in the faith. Paul himself describes the strategic difference in their mission just before he recounts the incident: "I had been entrusted with the gospel to the uncircumcised, just as Peter *had been* to the circumcised" (Gal. 2:7). Yet on one occasion, Paul catches Peter partnering with the Judaizers, who demand continued faithfulness to the law even for gentile converts.[8] Paul relates the incident:

7. Cole, *Galatians*, 68.
8. Although this event takes place in Antioch rather than Palestine, we will consider it here.

But when Cephas came to Antioch, I opposed him to his face, because he stood condemned. For prior to the coming of certain men from James, he used to eat with the Gentiles; but when they came, he *began* to withdraw and hold himself aloof, fearing the party of the circumcision. And the rest of the Jews joined him in hypocrisy, with the result that even Barnabas was carried away by their hypocrisy. But when I saw that they were not straightforward about the truth of the gospel, I said to Cephas in the presence of all, "If you, being a Jew, live like the Gentiles and not like the Jews, how *is it that* you compel the Gentiles to live like Jews?" (Gal. 2:11–14)

If the event took place not during a mere meal but during a celebration at the Lord's Table, as Cole suggests, then Paul's concern for division would have been greater.[9] John Chrysostom captures the event's significance: "As Paul had yielded to the apostles at Jerusalem, so in turn they yield to him at Antioch."[10]

There is much to analyze about the division between Peter and Paul, which was not just personal but ideological. Perhaps the division was more permanent than the New Testament reports. For example, Martin Hengel remarks: "It thus remains a rather well-supported suspicion that Peter was the direct missionary opponent of Paul in these tension-filled years that affected both of them after their clash in Antioch."[11] Such analyses about the conflict may be overstated. Perhaps the gospel went forth with this underlying conflict, just as it did for Paul and Barnabas (Acts 15:35–40), who disagreed about the role of John Mark.

A formative event for Paul was the result of the Jerusalem Council, the gathering of apostles and elders (Acts 15:4) to evaluate the place of the gentiles in the new covenant called Christianity. When Paul and Barnabas arrive in Jerusalem about 49/50, there are reports to the apostles and elders about how some Jewish Christians are insisting on circumcision for salvation as fidelity to the covenant. While Peter is prominent and James is recognized as a leader, the theology of gentile inclusion develops as a result of Paul and Barnabas. F. F. Bruce states: "Barnabas and Paul spoke as witnesses, not as consultants or as participants in the debate; and in Jerusalem their words could carry nothing like the weight that Peter's did."[12] The council decides that circumcision is not required for gentiles (Acts 15:19–24) but that morality and faithfulness define the faith.

---

9. Cole, *Galatians*, 74–77.
10. Chrysostom, *Commentary on Galatians* 2 (NPNF[1] 13:19).
11. Hengel, *Saint Peter*, 74.
12. Bruce, *Book of Acts*, 291.

Ministry in Writing

The apostle Paul was a prolific writer, noted for writing several letters to various churches that he had visited to instruct them in godly living and in solving issues in the life of the church. A great benefit of the writings of the apostle Paul for discovering his path of ministry is that the letters coincide directly with his ministry experience. Bruce remarks: "It is, however, not only as a man of letters but perhaps even more as a man of action that Paul has made his mark on world history."[13]

New Testament

Bruce pronounces about the apostle: "Of all the New Testament authors, Paul is the one who has stamped his own personality most unmistakably on his writings."[14] While the image of a sword might represent Paul's martyrdom, it has come equally to symbolize his contribution to the writing of the New Testament. In his Letter to the Ephesians, he exhorts believers to take up "the sword of the Spirit, which is the word of God" (Eph. 6:17). His writings are briefly summarized here as a sample of his contribution to the churches spread through Anatolia, Macedonia, Greece, and Italy.

GALATIANS

As an epistle for circulation among several churches in the Galatia region of Anatolia, Galatians may be Paul's earliest letter, written about 49. Written to the Christians in several cities that he visited, the focus on the letter is the freedom we have in Christ in the face of Judaizers, who insisted on imposing the Jewish law (Gal. 1:6; 3:1). Abraham becomes Paul's case study in grace and insists that the patriarch's belief in God preceded formal covenant: "So then, does He who provides you with the Spirit and works miracles among you, do it by the works of the Law, or by hearing with faith? Even so Abraham BELIEVED GOD, AND IT WAS RECKONED TO HIM AS RIGHTEOUSNESS" (Gal. 3:5–6). Paul builds up the church by exhorting the people to "bear one another's burdens, and thereby fulfill the law of Christ" (Gal. 6:2).

1 AND 2 THESSALONIANS

On his second missionary journey, Paul moves through the Greek city of Thessalonica, where his preaching shows success: "And according to Paul's

13. Bruce, *Paul*, 17.
14. Bruce, *Paul*, 15.

custom, he went to them, and for three Sabbaths reasoned with them from the Scriptures, explaining and giving evidence that the Christ had to suffer and rise again from the dead, and *saying*, 'This Jesus whom I am proclaiming to you is the Christ.' And some of them were persuaded and joined Paul and Silas, along with a great multitude of the God-fearing Greeks and a number of the leading women" (Acts 17:2–4).

As he moves south to Athens and then into Corinth, he writes the First Letter to the Thessalonians in 50–51 and then writes the Second Letter to the Thessalonians in 51, when he receives news from Timothy about the people's strong faith. Since they are converts from idolatry, he encourages them to stand strong in the faith (1 Thess. 1:9–10). He promotes the second coming of Christ to them (1 Thess. 5:1–11) as a source of comfort, while warning them of a lawless one who is to come (2 Thess. 2:1–12).

1 AND 2 CORINTHIANS

From the city of Ephesus during his third missionary journey, in 55 Paul confronts the lifestyle of Christians at Corinth in his first letter to them. Divisions (1 Cor. 1:10–17), sexual immorality (5:1–5), and legal actions (6:1–11) characterize their behavior toward one another. In a second letter from Ephesus, about 57, Paul addresses false teachers (2 Cor. 11:3–4) and establishes his own credibility as a teacher (11:5–12:13). The works combine to provide insight into a church community struggling more than the other recipients of his letters. Perhaps the greatest chapter of the apostle is found in the Corinthian correspondence, where the spiritual gifts that are causing competition among believers are trumped by the gift of love (1 Cor. 13:1–13). Equally important is Paul's treatise on the resurrection, declaring this doctrine absolutely essential for the faith: "If Christ has not been raised, your faith is worthless; you are still in your sins" (15:17).

ROMANS

From the city of Corinth, at the end of his third missionary journey in 57, Paul likely penned the Letter to the Romans. He admits that he has longed to come to Rome but has not yet achieved this goal (Rom. 1:11–15). In a classic treatise on the human condition and the need for salvation, the apostle describes all people as sinners (3:23) before describing how God's promise is received by faith (5:13–25). One victorious chapter about the benefits of salvation begins with the declaration "Therefore there is now no condemnation for those who are in Christ Jesus" (8:1). Paul draws on Old Testament law, figures, and experiences to encourage believers to "present your bodies a living and holy sacrifice, acceptable to God, *which is* your spiritual service of worship. And do not be conformed to this world, but be transformed by the renewing of your mind, so that you may prove what the will of God is, that which is good and acceptable and perfect" (Rom. 12:1–2). The gospel is explained in systematic fashion and with practical application.

1 and 2 Timothy

In the first two of three letters termed the Pastoral Epistles, Paul writes to pastors who are novices in their ministries. It is thought that these letters came after a first liberation from his imprisonment in Rome, about 65 and 67. By 2 Timothy, Paul seems to have been arrested again (4:6–8) and given a preliminary trial (4:16). The letters come specifically to encourage and coach Timothy, with application to churches everywhere. Instructions for selection of overseers and deacons have been timeless for the church (1 Tim. 3:1–16).

Titus

In a third Pastoral Epistle, Paul writes to Titus on the island of Crete, whom Paul left to build up the church there by appointing elders (Titus 1:5). False teachers are clearly in view (1:10–16): "They profess to know God, but by their deeds they deny *Him*, being detestable and disobedient, and worthless for any good deed" (1:16). Believers are to recognize that they are saved to display good works (3:1–11).

Ephesians

One of the Prison Epistles written from Rome in 60–62, this letter comes to a church that Paul has visited on a prior missionary journey. Its lack of personal names, unlike other epistles, has led many to speculate that it was meant to be spread around to the churches in the larger Ephesus area, a reasonable expectation given the significance of the city on the west coast of Anatolia. The letter has great similarity to Colossians, so it is thought to have been written in the same period of Paul's life. One main theme of the work is that salvation comes to Christians by grace through faith (Eph. 2:8–9). The unity of the Trinity in their work (1:3–14) is a model for Christians to live in unity (4:1–7).

Colossians

One of the Prison Epistles, written 61–63, this letter is dedicated to the church at Colossae, a city in Phrygia on mainland Anatolia and along an important trade route to the East. Paul gives attention to a doctrinal problem reported by one Epaphras. The church seems to have legalism intersecting with some early gnostic beliefs. Paul describes Christ as the reason for the people's lifestyle of obedience, cautioning against requirements of the law (Col. 2:16–23; 3:17). He describes Christ as both creator (1:15–16) and sustainer (1:17; 3:11), thus differing from gnostic thinkers who see a different demiurge in Jewish history. Mark is with Paul again (4:10), suggesting reconciliation and a resolution of the earlier question of Mark's suitability for mission work (Acts 15:37–40).

PHILIPPIANS

This one of the Prison Epistles could easily find a dating of 61–63 from Rome, although it might be Paul's last letter and perhaps is from a second imprisonment. Of interest is the lengthy, weary tone about this imprisonment (Phil. 1:12–20), the reference to a palace guard (1:13), and the reference to Caesar's palace (4:22). This supports the theory of Paul's detention at the highest level during his final imprisonment in Rome, which resulted in his martyrdom. "Rejoice in the Lord always; again I will say, rejoice!" (4:4) and "The Lord is near" (4:5) combine to reinforce his attempts to focus on hope in the face of the end. This is one of the epistles in which Paul provides valuable personal biography (3:4–6), only to minimize those credentials for the glory of the Lord: "I count all things to be loss in view of the surpassing value of knowing Christ Jesus my Lord, for whom I have suffered the loss of all things, and count them but rubbish in order that I may gain Christ" (Phil. 3:8).

PHILEMON

Another of the Prison Epistles, the letter is addressed to Philemon, who lived near Colossae, about 62. This Christian had a slave, Onesimus, who fled from his master and was converted by Paul in Rome (Philem. 10). Paul appeals to Philemon to receive his slave back as a fellow believer (Philem. 8–21). The apostle appeals to the common fellowship they all share as encouragement for Philemon to forgive Onesimus, observing what he wrote in Galatians 3:28, "There is neither Jew nor Greek, there is neither slave nor free man, there is neither male nor female; for you are all one in Christ Jesus."

Apocryphal New Testament

Not surprisingly, other works have been attributed to Paul. They either were deemed pseudepigraphical by the early church or possess a gnostic element central to their themes. They are naturally not considered to be genuinely Pauline.

Epistle to the Laodiceans

Paul mentions a letter to Laodicea that should be exchanged with the Letter to the Colossians and in turn read in the churches of the city of Colossae (Col. 4:16). J. K. Elliott describes its second- to fourth-century contents: "As a document it is a harmless theological forgery, being a cento of Pauline phrases taken mainly from Philippians and Galatians. There is no obvious doctrinal motive behind its composition."[15] The Muratorian Fragment explains how an epistle to the Laodiceans and one to the Alexandrians were forged in Paul's name. These works, as well as any association with Marcion, "cannot be received into the Catholic Church, for it is not suitable for gall to be mingled with honey."[16]

3 Corinthians or Lost Letter to the Corinthians

The Syrian tradition represented by Aphrahat and Ephraim gave greater standing to a supposed letter of Paul to the church in Corinth, thought to be a follow-up to his other letters. It is considered pseudepigraphical, and scholars date the work to at least the second century. This letter can be found in the Acts of Paul corpus along with the purported letter from the Corinthians to Paul that prompted Paul's reply.[17] While some topics and language echo Paul himself, Claudio Moreschini and Enrico Norelli comment: "The Pauline elements have lost their unifying center . . . and have been reorganized in the service of a polemic, alien to Paul, against the denial of Christ's human reality and of the value of the material creation."[18]

Correspondence of Paul and Seneca

Fourteen short exchanges between Paul and the Roman Stoic philosopher Seneca comprise this work, which contrasts the merits of Christianity and pagan philosophy.[19] There is no evidence that the two greats ever met or corresponded apart from this work, which was considered pseudepigraphical by the early church.

15. Elliott, 543. He provides the text of the short work, Elliott, 546.
16. Fragments of Caius 3 (*ANF* 5:603).
17. Elliott, 380–82.
18. Moreschini and Norelli, *Early Christian Greek and Latin Literature*, 1:29.
19. Correspondence of Paul and Seneca (James, 480–84).

Journey of Paul

APOCALYPSE OF PAUL

A revelation attributed to Paul when he was caught up in a vision to the third heaven (2 Cor. 12:2), this work has the apostle witnessing souls departing from this life and in the afterlife.[20] Latin, Greek, and Coptic varieties of the story exist. Paul encounters Old Testament saints; he experiences the pain and joy of judgment. While the work is likely third-century Egyptian and not authored by the apostle, its influence is noticeable. Elliott remarks: "The Apocalypse of Paul more than any other of the apocryphal apocalypses was responsible for the spread of many of the popular ideas of Heaven and Hell throughout Christianity and especially in the Western church of the Middle Ages."[21]

Palestine and Syria Ministry

Maintaining our previous pattern of listing the ministry activity of each apostle by region, we will depict the journey of Paul here, which moved back and forth across regions. The information available to readers on the life

20. Apocalypse of Paul (Elliott, 616–51).
21. Elliott, 616.

and ministry of Paul is abundant. This chapter will summarize his works in the book of Acts but will elaborate more on the apocryphal works related to his legacy. While the biblical narratives are viewed as more credible than the stories elaborated on here, more detail comes from other texts on the assumption that the New Testament version of Paul is better known than the apocryphal version.

Paul's ministry begins in partnership with Barnabas as they move from Antioch to Jerusalem at least twice. In the years that follow, Paul serves the Lord as minister and apostle (Col. 1:23–29). Acts relates how, as the two go first in each city to the local synagogue, the Jews generally reject the message, while individual gentiles accept it. Then Paul intentionally extends the gospel beyond the Jews to the gentiles in each city (Rom. 11:13; Gal. 1:16; 2:7), planting new churches in these places in order to avoid building "on another man's foundation" (Rom. 15:20; see 1 Cor. 3:6; 4:15; Gal. 4:19).

Following his discipleship period, Paul begins a ministry in Syria and Cilicia, where he claims he was "*still* unknown by sight to the churches of Judea which were in Christ" (Gal. 1:22). His preaching in Damascus seems to be effective until the Jews plot to kill him there (Acts 9:20–25). He speaks boldly at the church in Jerusalem before Greeks there seek to kill him (9:28–30). He preaches at Antioch (11:26) and delivers the Antioch church's famine relief gift to the elders at Jerusalem (11:30). From there the Holy Spirit guides the setting apart of Barnabas and Saul for a special ministry (13:1–2). Paul's first missionary journey, in 46–48, takes him to Salamis and Paphos in Cyprus (13:4–12) before he moves into Anatolia.

The next significant time for Paul in Palestine comes as he and Barnabas pass through Phoenicia and Samaria, testifying to the conversion of gentiles. These activities confuse some Jewish Christians, which in turn leads to the Jerusalem Council. The two apostles receive the letter from the council encouraging their ministry among the gentiles (Acts 15:22–31).

As his third missionary journey is ending, Paul's disciples warn him through the Spirit to avoid Jerusalem. He responds, "I am ready not only to be bound, but even to die at Jerusalem for the name of the Lord Jesus" (Acts 21:13). While James the Just and the brethren receive him well, the Jews are offended by his teaching and inspire a crowd to seize him. His arrest and sermons in Jerusalem follow, along with Paul's appeals to his Roman citizenship (21:39; 22:25; 25:11). His mission becomes clear when Jesus appears to him in a vision: "Take courage; for as you have solemnly witnessed to My cause at Jerusalem, so you must witness at Rome also" (Acts 23:11). In Caesarea he remains a prisoner, but he preaches the gospel to Governors Felix and Festus as well as to Herod Agrippa II. From there he is sent to Rome, in 59.

Anatolia Ministry

Paul's first three missionary journeys take him through Syria, down to Cyprus, and across Asia Minor. Again, although he programmatically begins by preaching in the local synagogue, the Jewish rejection of his messages leads to his centering on the gentiles. Unlike in the other apostolic Acts among the New Testament Apocrypha, Paul's ministry stories primarily concern preaching and conflict rather than a regular pattern of wonders.

On Paul's first journey, from 46–48, he is accompanied by Barnabas and John Mark (Acts 13:4–14:28). As previously mentioned, a council of the apostles in Jerusalem articulated the decision to welcome the gentiles to the faith in a letter sent with Paul and Barnabas (15:22), which provides both a resource in hand and an affirmation of their ministry. His second journey, from 49–52, begins with separation from Barnabas and John Mark (15:36–39). Silas joins Paul as they return to the churches of Syria and Cilicia before going across the Taurus Mountains to Lystra and Derbe (15:39–16:10; 18:19–23). At Troas, Paul receives a call to go to Macedonia, described below. On the west coast of Asia Minor, Troas and Ephesus are new cities for Paul as he treks to and from Europe. His third missionary journey, in 53–57, includes the apostle's return to many of the cities in Anatolia (19:1–41; 20:6–21:6). The ministry of Paul in Asia Minor includes encounters with key figures in his ministry, such as Timothy, and consistent opposition, such as at Ephesus.

Not to be ignored in the legends of this apostle, the late second-century Acts of Paul is a collection of stories and teaching. Anthologies of New Testament Apocrypha commonly break the collective work into pieces by original manuscripts, including Paul and Thecla and the Martyrdom of Paul.

In the Acts of Paul, the apostle journeys to Iconium with Demas and Hermogenes the coppersmith, who are described as "full of hypocrisy, and [they] flattered Paul as though they loved him."[22] They stay at the house of Onesiphorus, likely the figure referenced in 2 Timothy 1:16 and 4:19. Demas plots betrayal against Paul either (1) in an effort to overcome the obstacle preventing Thamyris from marrying his fiancée, Thecla, who is devoted to Christ and to Paul, or (2) out of some contempt for Paul's ministry and cause. In the home of Onesiphorus, Paul preaches a message of abstinence and the resurrection along encratite lines, for example: "Blessed are they that possess their wives as though they had them not, for they shall inherit God."[23] Thecla hears the message and wants to be counted among the virgins of the

22. Acts of Paul 2.1 (James, 272).
23. Acts of Paul 2.3 (James, 273).

church community. The narrative shifts to the drama between Thamyris and Thecla, with Paul providing theological speeches intermittently. Because of this conflict, Paul is scourged and freed, while his virgin disciple is condemned to be burned. Stripped naked but covering herself with the sign of the cross and encountering God's compassion, Thecla is immune to the flames. Rain and a hailstorm quench the fire, and her life is preserved. Stripped again and thrown to beasts, she survives as a lioness not only lies at her feet but defends her from a bear and a male lion. In a declaration of her baptism, she casts herself into nearby water, survives another round of animal mistreatment, is freed by the governor, and "after she had enlightened many with the word of God, she slept a good sleep."[24] Although Paul is not the center of these activities, Thecla's faith and her fascination with Paul speak to the witness of the apostle.

Elsewhere in the Acts of Paul, as Paul is preaching in Myra, he heals Hermocrates of dropsy; his son Dion through resurrection; and his other son, Hermippus, of a murderous heart. Other characters in these stories bear names mentioned in the biblical texts. Second Timothy 1:15 includes an allusion to Paul's traveling comrade, Hermogenes, whom Paul describes as having "turned away from me." Similarly, in 2 Timothy 4:10, Paul depicts how Demas, "having loved this present world, has deserted me."

A Coptic manuscript records Paul's presence in Ephesus when Hieronymus is governor. The people are angered at Paul's preaching and imprison him to later be killed by beasts. Paul escapes at night in order to baptize his liberators before voluntarily returning to his bonds. In the amphitheater a massive lion is released. To understand the rest of this narrative, we must understand an earlier story concerning Paul and a lion, preserved in three Ethiopic manuscripts. While Paul is walking on a mountain, a huge lion greets Paul and asks to be among the Christians. Bruce Metzger writes, "The meaning of this request is not absolutely certain but doubtless is a periphrasis for baptism."[25] Paul explains the law, and the lion and the apostle bid farewell.

In the amphitheater, Paul recognizes the lion now in the arena as the one who was baptized, and he asks the beast, "And how were you captured?" The lion answers cleverly, "Just as you were, Paul." So the lion lies down before Paul. Likewise, other beasts do not attack him while he is "standing like a statue in prayer."[26] A violent thunderstorm descends on the people, and Hieronymus is wounded, which leads to his conversion and baptism. The lion

24. Acts of Paul 2.43 (James, 281).

25. Metzger, "St. Paul and the Baptized Lion," 16n13. Metzger reinforces this elucidation with Jerome's reference to a *totam baptizati leonis fabulum*.

26. Acts of Paul 8 (James, 292).

escapes to the mountains as Paul advances to Macedonia and Greece, and to Troas and Miletus, before setting out for Jerusalem.

The extrabiblical lion encounter at Ephesus might be connected to Paul's claim in 1 Corinthians 15:32: "I fought with wild beasts at Ephesus." Hippolytus, who is noticeably unkind to apocryphal works, seems to think of the story of Paul's subduing of the lion as authoritative in his *Commentary on Daniel*, the earliest orthodox commentary on a book of Scripture: "If we believe, when Paul was condemned to the beasts, the lion set before him lay down at his feet and licked him, why do we not also believe the events of Daniel?"[27] Such an affirmation by one who is generally critical supports a possible historical core behind even the legends of these Acts. Jerome says the Acts is merely apocryphal, claiming that Luke would have surely cited this event before Paul's Roman arrival: "Therefore the *Acts of Paul and Thecla* and all the fable about the lion baptized by him we reckon among the apocryphal writings, for how is it possible that the inseparable companion of the apostle in his other affairs, alone should have been ignorant of this thing."[28] Concerning the nature of this event, Richard Pervo explains: "On the moral, fictitious level, this creature, famed for sexual potency and prowess, shames human males. Symbolically, the creature represents the Christian victory over feral lust."[29]

Macedonia and Greece Ministry

On Paul's second missionary journey (49–52), across Anatolia, a new geographical region opens up to his ministry. Paul's recorded vision in Acts 16:6–10 redirects his missionary efforts from Asia Minor to Europe. A man of Macedonia calls for his help (16:9), so Paul deserts his Bithynian intentions and goes to the Roman colony across the Aegean Sea. David Criswell postulates that Paul's being prevented from going to Asia corresponds to John's ministry there, so that their efforts were complementary.[30] Paul's journey takes him to Neapolis, Philippi, Apollonia, Amphipolis, Thessalonica, Berea, Athens, and Corinth (Acts 16:11–18:18). His third missionary journey (53–57), into Macedonia and Greece, takes him back to strengthen the churches in these cities (20:1–6). Key figures include Lydia, Priscilla and Aquila, Apollos, Gallio, and the Athenian philosophers. Conflict ensues at several cities; at Philippi, for example, the apostle is imprisoned and converts his jailer. During his stay

---

27. Hippolytus, *Commentary on Daniel* 3.29.4 (AT). See translation by Lefèvre, 161.
28. Jerome, *Vir. ill.* 7 (NPNF² 3:363).
29. Pervo, "Role of the Apostles," 313.
30. Criswell, *Apostles after Jesus*, 44.

in Corinth, Paul is noted as making tents among the people, using his trade skill to participate in the church community (18:3; 20:34).

Rome Ministry

The fourth missionary journey of Paul (59–62) takes him by shipwreck to Malta. After that the book of Acts provides us only with Paul's arrival in Rome. The intent of Acts seems to be to demonstrate that the gospel extended to the capital of the Roman Empire rather than to provide a full biography of the apostle. I. Howard Marshall says, "Whatever be the truth [about his Rome experience], the fate of Paul is secondary to that of the gospel."[31]

In Italy the assembly lands at Puteoli, a city along the famous Appian Way. It seems that Paul had some liberty in his captivity, for he rents out quarters with only a lone guard (Acts 28:16; 30). This allows him to call together Jewish leaders to explain the gospel (28:17), true to his pattern of starting ministry in each city with the Jewish population. He preaches from his rented quarters, and the Acts of Paul summarizes the effects of his ministry: "He became noised abroad and many souls were added unto the Lord, so that there was a rumor throughout all Rome, and much people came unto him from the household of Caesar, believing, and there was great joy."[32] The Acts description of the freedom Paul had during his stay in Rome has led many to surmise that neither the Jews there nor the provincial Romans could maintain a viable case against him. He stayed for two years (Acts 28:30).

While Paul's time in Rome eventually led to his martyrdom, there is a theory that he stayed two separate times in Rome, with a possible journey to Spain in between. Bryan Litfin proposes a possible travel itinerary between Paul's two Roman imprisonments: his release from house arrest in 62; travels to Greece, Asia Minor, or Crete but more likely Spain in 63; a second arrest in the western provinces in 64; and his trial and indictment for treason in 65/66.[33] One fragmented section of the Acts of Paul includes additional references to suffering in Rome; perhaps the broken narrative is from this intermediate period, anticipating a return to the capital city.[34] The evidence for travel to Spain is provided below.

The Acts of Paul describes one preaching episode in Rome, when a cup-bearer of Nero named Patroclus falls from a window to his death. The story seems to parallel the death and resurrection by Paul of the youth Eutychus, who

---

31. Marshall, *Acts*, 427.
32. Acts of Paul 10.1 (James, 293).
33. Litfin, *After Acts*, 174.
34. Acts of Paul 9 (James, 293).

falls from a window while listening to the apostle's preaching (Acts 20:9–12). In the Acts of Paul, Nero is distraught at the news of Patroclus's death and shocked when Patroclus appears before him alive. The lad testifies that Jesus is his king and overthrows all kingdoms, and his claim leads to immediate professions of faith from three of Nero's chief men: Barsabas Justus, Urion, and Festus, said to be "soldiers of the great king."[35] Nero imprisons them with plans to torment them and put them to death. Paul is brought before him, bound; the allegiance of other prisoners has led Nero to deduce that Paul is their leader. The apostle testifies to the most powerful ruler in the world: "If thou submit and entreat him, thou shalt be saved."[36]

In this account Nero orders the burning of the four servants and the beheading of Paul, and he proceeds to slay many Christians without legal hearing, so that the people call for him to stop. When two guards, Longus and Cestus, offer to free Paul when it seems their duty is to execute him, Paul refuses: "I am not a deserter of Christ, but a lawful solder of the living God."[37] To both these new converts and to the emperor, the apostle testifies that he will come back to life if beheaded. Two new soldiers do not take to the gospel, so Paul faces the east, lifts his hands to heaven, and prays in Hebrew. His decapitation leads to milk discharging from his neck onto the soldiers' cloaks. About the ninth hour, Paul appears to Nero and pronounces judgment against him. The emperor is greatly troubled and reacts by freeing the soldiers of Christ.

Another account, the Acts of the Holy Apostles Peter and Paul, relates how, after Paul seeks an audience with Nero, who refuses, Paul is banned from Italy and goes into hiding. Paul's lack of imprisonment, his freedom of movement, and Jewish fears of his power of persuasion makes this quite a different situation from the account of the biblical Acts. This work includes a second trip to Rome, after some interlude that could include travel to Spain. From Sicily, Paul comes to Rome, where he evangelizes and disciples. Simon Magus conspires with Jews against both Peter and Paul, who are arrested, and their supposed dialogue with Nero is recorded. After judgment, both are led away, and Paul is beheaded on the Ostian Road.[38]

The present book has demonstrated how it is difficult to rely historically on the apocryphal Acts. Yet all of the traditions around Paul's death are located exclusively at key spots in Italy and Rome, making it likely that this aspect of the Acts of Paul is historically rooted. McDowell notes that by the

---

35. Acts of Paul 10.2 (James, 294).
36. Acts of Paul 10.3 (James, 295).
37. Acts of Paul 10.4 (James, 295).
38. Acts of Peter and Paul (ANF 8:477–85).

time the Acts of Paul was composed, the tradition of his death in Rome was undeniably accepted.[39] Litfin remarks about the Acts of Paul: "Though it is full of fantastic legends and heroic episodes in the life of Paul, the martyr- dom narrative probably preserves an accurate historical core of a trial before Nero's court."[40]

A legendary account attributed to a late medieval travel guide relates that upon decapitation, Paul's head bounced three times. With each bounce, the head spoke the word "Jesus," and fountains sprang up from the earth at each spot.[41] From this legend, the Roman Abbey of Three Fountains, commemo- rating his martyrdom spot, gained its name, as well as a Roman memorial in Trastevere of three flowing fountains. Interestingly, an estate is referenced in the fourth-century Acts of Peter and Paul manuscript tradition that bears the name Aquae Salvias, "saving waters"; the street leading into the Abbey of Three Fountains in Rome bears this name today.[42] Another story relates that a one-eyed woman named Perpetua provided a handkerchief to Paul en route to his death. When it was returned, her other eye was restored, the guards believed and were martyred, and Nero's sister-in-law was converted by an imprisoned Perpetua before both lost their lives.

In the Acts of Andrew and Paul, Andrew finds himself blocked by Jews from a city where he has disembarked from a ship, after "Paul had plunged into the sea to visit the underworld."[43] The text lacks geographical context prior to Andrew and Paul's parting, besides naming the city Amente, which may be allegorical. These fantastic encounters evidence no historical basis. One fragment of the Acts of Peter and Paul records that Paul was "condemned to the mines in an unknown place."[44]

Spain Ministry

In his Letter to the Romans, Paul writes around 57 that he hopes to visit Spain (Rom. 15:24, 28). Scholars have long debated whether he realized this hope, since Acts does not advance the apostle after his arrival at Rome. The Iberian Peninsula would not have been out of reach for Paul. The Romanized

39. McDowell, *Fate of the Apostles*, 110.
40. Litfin, *After Acts*, 176.
41. Marvels of the City of Rome 1.5, cited in Litfin, *After Acts*, 193n17.
42. Story of Perpetua (*ANF* 8:485). This account from the Acts of Peter and Paul should not be confused with the third-century story of Perpetua and Felicitas sharing a similar name.
43. Acts of Andrew and Paul (James, 472).
44. Acts of Paul 6 (James, 287).

region would have taken only seven days of travel to reach by land, according to Pliny, while a boat to Tarraco would have taken only four days.[45] In fact, Spain could have been viewed as the outer boundary of the Roman Empire at that time, making it as symbolically significant for the spread of the gospel under the apostles as the capital of Rome was for Paul (Rom. 15:15–21). The Muratorian Fragment claims that when Luke wrote Acts, he omitted Paul's going to Spain after a sojourn in Rome.[46]

According to Eusebius, it was said that after a trial in Rome, Paul set out to preach again before his return to Rome, at which time he was martyred.[47] All of these evidences support the possibility that his fourth missionary journey, to Rome, was not the end of his quest. Clement of Rome also says that Paul received glory "having taught righteousness to the whole world and having reached the farthest limits of the west."[48] Otto Meinardus remarks that this "phrase often used by Roman writers to refer to Spain, could only mean the Iberian peninsula."[49] In the Acts of Peter, Paul disappears from the narrative, having left for Spain.[50] Jerome speaks of Paul's journey to Spain after his imprisonment.[51]

Meinardus also reports that Tortosa, a Roman colony in Spain, hosts a local tradition that Paul founded a church there and consecrated the son of Simon of Cyrene, Rufus, as bishop of the city. Yet Meinardus also remarks that none of the local Spanish traditions originate prior to the eighth century, most emerging in later centuries.[52]

If Paul traveled to Spain, it is a mystery to us how and why he returned to Rome in correspondence with the tradition of his martyrdom there. Festus says to Agrippa that he is surprised by the types of charges the Jews are bringing against Paul (Acts 25:14–21), centering on religion. Jews from Asia also stir up sentiment against him (Acts 21:27–36). It is reasonable to imagine that either the complaints of Jews in Spain or the reach of Jews in Rome led to his being rearrested and returned for trial. While we cannot be certain that he journeyed to Spain, we can be certain of his eventual trial and execution in Rome, 64–66, which is an indelible part of his image.

45. Litfin, *After Acts*, 164.
46. Muratorian Fragment 2 (*ANF* 5:603). Scholars range in dating this document from the late first to the early fourth century.
47. Eusebius, *Hist. eccl.* 2.22.2.
48. 1 Clement 5.7 (Holmes, 53).
49. Meinardus, "Paul's Missionary Journey to Spain," 61.
50. Acts of Peter 3.1 (James, 304).
51. Jerome, *On the Perpetual Virginity of the Blessed Mary* 4 (Hritzu, 13).
52. Meinardus, "Paul's Missionary Journey to Spain," 63. He remarks, "It is possible, therefore, that the tradition of Paul's mission to Spain is a mere extension of an intent" (61–62).

Image of Paul

F. F. Bruce comments, "Paul's pre-eminent contribution to the world has been his presentation of the good news of free grace."[53] There is no apostle like Paul. While he was not an original member of the Twelve, or of the Seventy, or even among the five hundred witnesses to the resurrection, his lack of participation in the earthly ministry of Jesus did not inhibit his ministry, deprive him of zeal, or undermine his credibility as an apostle. The tenacity of Paul made him evangelize even in the face of accusations of inferiority due to his lack of experience. In particular, he was a pioneer in expanding the faith beyond the fulfillment of Jewish expectations to the inclusion of gentiles. His greatest contribution is likely his service as apostle to the gentiles.

In honor of the two thousandth anniversary of Paul's birth, Pope Benedict XVI declared June 2008 through June 2009 the "Year of Paul." This included a special indulgence for all who make a pilgrimage to Rome or holy places dedicated to the apostle.[54] Several sites of pilgrimage were identified, notably the Basilica of St. Paul, where his tomb is said to be located.

Symbolism and Image Construction

Paul's death by sword provides the most common of his symbols. His beheading may not be the only reason for the symbol, however, since his contribution to the formation of the New Testament is evoked by his language for the word of God as "the sword of the Spirit" (Eph. 6:17). Although later Europeans employed an ax for beheading, Sean McDowell is right to recognize that Roman beheading usually involved a sword as a symbol of power.[55] Another symbol for the apostle is a scroll or book, associating him with the writing of Scripture. Paul stands for other components of early Christianity, though, that speak to the formation of the faith.

Apostle to the Gentiles

Paul is known as the apostle to the gentiles, a title he himself employs to represent his ministry efforts (Rom. 11:13; 1 Tim. 2:7). While the other apostles are grappling with the Jews and within themselves to understand the application of the gospel among the gentiles, Paul senses a calling to minister to them. Paul's reputation as pro-gentile is further enhanced by his being thought of as anti-Jewish, part of an internal conflict in the early church.

53. Bruce, *Paul*, 18.
54. Eastman, *Paul the Martyr*, 1.
55. McDowell, *Fate of the Apostles*, 111–12.

This conflict can be easily misrepresented, leading to the idea of Paul as a negative force. Tom Bissell, for example, provides excessively negative commentary about Paul's efforts to bring gentiles into the fold. For example, on the content of the Ascent of James, Bissell says: "A figure probably intended to be Paul attacks and badly wounds James on the steps of the Temple. The story . . . further establishes the toxicity of later Jewish Christian feelings toward Paul."[56] This assessment is extreme.

"Inventor" of Christianity

Analysis of Paul's image must include his contribution to Christian doctrine. His authorship of a number of New Testament epistles certainly means that Paul is a teacher of generation after generation of Christians. Even the legend of his execution by beheading that includes milk spewing forth on the cloaks of his executioners can be seen as a reminder of his role as instructor in the faith. Candida Moss believes the event reiterates his words in 1 Corinthians 3:2, "I gave you milk to drink, not solid food," a symbol of his instruction to the church.[57]

Critical biblical scholars often maintain that Paul was responsible for the invention of Christian doctrine, taking the work of a Galilean fisherman and developing a set of doctrines around his legacy, ranging from the nature of the resurrection to prescribing the role of women in the church. A critical theologian himself, Friedrich Nietzsche remarks: "In Paul was embodied the antithetical type of the 'bringer of glad tidings,' the genius of hatred, of the vision of hatred, of the inexorable logic of hatred. What did this dysangelist not sacrifice to his hatred! The redeemer above all; he nailed him to his Cross."[58]

As a result of Paul's contribution to shaping early Christian doctrine, he emerges as apostle extraordinaire, preserved as an early church icon of the faith. The oldest complete form of the liturgy in the East, the Liturgy of St. James, names "Peter and Paul, Andrew, James, John" along with the other disciples. Noteworthy is the prominence of Paul in a list of apostles, worthy to displace James and John in the second slot.[59]

Model for Suffering

Paul describes without hubris his suffering for the gospel:

56. Bissell, *Apostle*, 71.
57. Moss, *Ancient Christian Martyrdom*, 97.
58. Nietzsche, *Antichrist*, 154.
59. Hills, 14.

Three times I was beaten with rods, once I was stoned, three times I was ship-wrecked, a night and a day I have spent in the deep. *I have been* on frequent journeys, in dangers from rivers, dangers from robbers, dangers from *my* countrymen, dangers from the Gentiles, dangers in the city, dangers in the wilderness, dangers on the sea, dangers among false brethren; *I have been* in labor and hardship, through many sleepless nights, in hunger and thirst, often without food, in cold and exposure. Apart from *such* external things, there is the daily pressure on me of concern for all the churches. (2 Cor. 11:25–28)

The Epistle of the Apostles captures the church's second-century perspective on Paul. In the work Jesus tells the other apostles about Paul: "He will be strong among the nations; he will preach, and he will teach many, and they will be delighted to hear him and many will be saved. Then he will be hated and delivered into the hand of the enemy, and he will testify to me before transitory kings. Upon him will be the perfection of my testimony."[60] Paul mentions his sufferings in several places in his letters.[61] In his farewell address to the church at Ephesus, he remarks, "The Holy Spirit solemnly testifies to me in every city, saying that bonds and afflictions await me" (Acts 20:23).

The early church could have used all of the disciples as models for perseverance, but Paul was a favored example. In his Letter to the Philippians, the second-century elder Polycarp marshals Paul and others as a model "to obey the teaching about righteousness and to exercise unlimited endurance."[62] In the generation after him, Clement of Rome uses the martyred apostles as exemplars, especially Paul and Peter. He calls them "those champions who lived nearest to our time" and "the noble examples which belong to our own generation." They are both viewed as victims: "Because of envy and jealousy the most righteous pillars [of the church] were persecuted, and fought to the death." They are worth the exhortation "Let us set before our eyes the illustrious apostles."[63] Tertullian presents Paul as a model martyr in a milieu of church suffering.[64] When Ignatius was facing his own martyrdom, he encouraged his followers by claiming Paul as a model in this regard.[65]

Calvin Roetzel sees suffering as thematic for Paul: "Paul's letters name suffering and death as his constant companions."[66] Roetzel also describes how

---

60. Ep. Apos. 31 (Hills, 59–60).
61. E.g., see 2 Cor. 6:4–5; 11:23–29; 12:10; Rom. 8:35; 1 Cor. 4:9–13; 2 Cor. 4:7–12.
62. Polycarp, *Letter to the Philippians* 9.1–2 (Holmes, 291).
63. 1 Clement 5.1–3 (Holmes, 51).
64. Tertullian, *Prescription against Heretics* 24 (*ANF* 3:254); Tertullian, *Scorpiace* 15:5–6 (*ANF* 3:648).
65. Ignatius, *Letter to the Ephesians* 12.2.
66. Roetzel, *Paul*, 170.

Paul's suffering would be instrumental in the narrative of the early church: "Only the grave was to grant Paul almost a generation of peace as an awkward silence hovered over him until Luke rescued him from obscurity by devoting over half of his Acts to Paul the missionary with wonder working powers."[67]

Tomb and Patronage

The image of Paul is most widely promoted at the site of what is said to be his tomb, the Basilica of St. Paul Outside the Walls. During the early centuries of persecution, the bones of Paul and Peter may have moved along the Appian Way at the Catacombs of St. Sebastian, where another cultic spot arose for the two of them. Under Constantine, they were likely relocated to their original, historical spots. According to the *Liber Pontificalis*, Constantine built a basilica where he buried Paul.[68]

The tomb and the basilica rest along the Ostian Road, which ran southwest from Rome to its dominant port at Ostia. Theodosius expanded the church in scope and size beginning in 386. A fire that destroyed much of the basilica in 1823 revealed two marble slabs with the inscription "To Paul the apostle and martyr," dated from Constantine to the early fifth century. In 2002 the Vatican Museum excavated the burial area, leading to the discovery of a marble sarcophagus dating to the late fourth century, linking the legend of the return of Paul's bones to this spot. In 2009 Pope Benedict announced that archaeological investigation of the sarcophagus revealed bone fragments and precious linen. Chains supposedly of Paul's imprisonment linger over his tomb to enhance its authenticity.

With at least the apostle Paul's tomb likely in view, Jerome remarks about the cult of the martyrs, "Where else [but in Rome] do [Christians] so enthusiastically rush in droves to the churches and martyrs' tombs?"[69] Part of the skull of Paul is said to be contained in a bust above the papal altar in the Basilica of St. John Lateran.[70] Two churches in Rome commemorate where Paul was supposedly under house arrest, St. Paul in Regola and St. Mary in Via Lata (Acts 28:30). Both are close to the former Jewish community area. The Abbey of the Three Fountains in Rome honors Paul's execution site; its sanctuary contains a pillar to which he was supposedly tied when martyred. In Valletta, Malta, St. Paul's Shipwreck Church remembers his sojourn on its island and claims to have a wrist bone resting in its reliquary. There is also a

67. Roetzel, *Paul*, 152.
68. Eastman, *Paul the Martyr*, 25.
69. Jerome, *Commentary on Galatians* 2.proem (Cain, 131).
70. Thelen, *Saints in Rome and Beyond*, 80–81.

pillar to which Paul was supposedly bound when executed.[71] The Mamertine Prison promotes Paul's imprisonment in a dungeon adjacent to the Roman Forum, where a sanctuary contained a pillar to which he was supposedly chained. It was recently moved to the museum.

Paul's feast day is June 29, together with Peter. Paul is the patron saint of authors, writers, editors, and publishers because of his authorial contribution to early Christianity and the New Testament. Additionally, his patronage extends to laborers, tentmakers, basket makers, swordsmen, and theologians. He is invoked against sea storms and snakebites and for rain and crops.[72] Numerous orders and societies bear his name.

71. Thelen, *Saints of Rome and Beyond*, 191.
72. Jöckle, *Encyclopedia of Saints*, 352.

✳ 15 ✳

The Discovery

And what marvel, saith one, if they were moderate in their wishes, since they were fishermen and tentmakers? Yes! Fishermen and tentmakers they were; but they had in a moment mounted even to the height of heaven, and had become more honorable than all earthly kings, being deemed worthy to become the companions of the Lord of the world, and to follow Him whom all beheld with awe.

John Chrysostom, *Homilies on St. John*[1]
early fifth century, Constantinople

This quest for the historical apostles has led us from Jerusalem across three continents. The journey required an understanding of the sources that took us beyond the reaches of the Roman Empire, examining and sifting the writings of the ancient world. The early church fathers and their medieval successors reported the apostles' journeys, shaping the path that we have tried to reconstruct here. Once we reviewed all the available information on each apostle and the dots from their journey could no longer be connected, we examined the image of each apostle in symbols, tombs and relics, liturgy, and art that capture and perpetuate his legacy. This process has hopefully provided the reader with appreciation for the individual apostolic traditions, both in historical form and in the development of theological imagery.

Each apostle took a different path in ministry, faced obstacles to his mission, encountered death, and was succeeded by an inheritance of disciples

1. *NPNF*[2] 14:109.

and images. Amid the conflicting traditions that accompany a quest for the historical apostles, at times it becomes clear that we work in a mixture of fact and tradition that cannot always be distinguished. François Bovon remarks: "Even if the final version of those texts is the editorial result of authors, I suppose that those authors, not separated from communities of faith, were eager to convey or rearrange traditional material."[2] It is hoped that readers view the effort here as commendable and fair, and that the apostles shine through this historical reconstruction.

The Paths of the Historical Apostles

For the purpose of summary and application, the legacy of the apostles will be reviewed here in ways that can help the church to understand and even to perpetuate the gospel initiative that the apostles began, linking the past to the faith of the present. A summary of the findings of each apostle is followed by a brief consideration of each apostle's simple but profound contribution to the church.

Peter

In the legacy of the apostles, no one's influence is like that of Peter. His discipleship in the Gospels paints a picture of an imperfect person whose flaws are eclipsed by an eagerness and willingness to believe. His desire to walk on water, his resisting Jesus's arrest by taking up arms and chopping off a servant's ear, his anxious denial of Jesus, and his response to Christ's postresurrection questions about love mark Peter as a unique and inspirational disciple. His leadership in Acts is powerful, providing a sound rock for the growth of the church, especially in the transition from historic Judaism to free association with gentiles in obedience to the Messiah. Martin Hengel remarks: "Based on this mass of vastly different indicators, one can assume, not only that Peter's heart was concerned to make sure that the missionary proclamation went forward, but that his concern extended to matters of development, structure, and unified activity of the admittedly very different communities."[3]

Peter ministered in Jerusalem, Samaria, Antioch, and Rome. There is significant evidence that he was martyred by crucifixion on Vatican Hill. Spiritual warfare, especially against Simon Magus, characterizes his ministry in

2. Bovon, "Canonical and Apocryphal Acts of Apostles," 166.
3. Hengel, *Saint Peter*, 90.

apocryphal works. Vatican City, with its enormous basilica in his name, is a prominent location of Christian worship alongside the bones of Peter. Atheist Tom Bissell states profoundly: "Christianity begins with a missing body. Today one of its oldest and most federal expressions bases its legitimacy on the remains of an existing one."[4] From fisherman to papal figure, the image of Peter is complex but powerful for the identity of Christianity.

Andrew

The apostle Andrew is overshadowed by Peter so frequently in the New Testament that he is commonly described as being Peter's brother. Among the top tier of disciples, the ministry, travels, and martyrdom of Andrew are least certain. In the Gospels, Andrew is noted for his intermediary role, particularly at the miraculous feeding of the crowd and in some Greeks' request to see Jesus. In the dispersion of the apostles, Andrew journeyed to Scythia, possibly Anatolia, Macedonia, and then to Greece. His ministry in Achaea led to his martyrdom in the city of Patras, where a cathedral commemorates his service and lays claim to part of his body. While a church in Kiev, Ukraine, also claims his ministry legacy, his real mark is on the culture of Scotland, where the saltire supposedly of his crucifixion is on the national flag and the country hails him as its patron saint. His martyrdom story is stirring as he confronts and greets the cross that will bring his death. His boldness in promoting Jesus to Peter and in facing his death combine for rousing first and last stories of his commitment to the gospel.

James

The brother of John represents the ministry of the apostles in the early days of Jerusalem. While little is said of his individual contribution, his death is a harbinger of the fate of the rest of the apostles. When Herod takes James's life suddenly (Acts 12:1–2), his ministry is complete, and his martyrdom alone among the apostles is recorded in the New Testament.

John

The brother of James appears to be the youngest of the disciples, the last apostle to die, and an important link from the teaching of the apostles to the generations that followed through the rule of faith. The ministry of John centered in Ephesus, where his death also finds a historical anchor. He was entrusted

4. Bissell, *Apostle*, 145.

with the care of Mary the mother of Jesus (John 19:26–27), and for decades they shared a path geographically. Legends depict John suffering in Rome, Patmos, and Ephesus. A Gospel, three epistles, and Revelation bear a tradition of his authorship. With the death of John, the era of the original apostles came to an end.

Philip

The path of the apostle Philip is unclear from the beginning because of confusion between the deacon and the apostle in the New Testament. The proximity of Hierapolis to Ephesus connects Philip and John geographically in southwest Anatolia, where they may have intentionally partnered for ministry. There is also a reasonable tradition of ministry in Greece, with Parthia and Scythia less tenable, and Britain and France least tenable. On a personal note, I, like Philip, nurture several daughters and find inspiration in the repeated testimony of the legacy of their faith.

Bartholomew

Bartholomew has the strongest set of geographically diverse traditions among the apostles. He is noted for overseeing the destruction of pagan idols and for being flayed alive, although that tradition is late in the record. The diverse legends report that Bartholomew was clubbed, skinned alive, or beheaded in Armenia or Parthia; cast into the sea in Africa or Parthia; and crucified or beheaded in India. His travels most likely led him to minister in Anatolia and India before encountering opposition in Parthia, or what is now Armenia, that led to his martyrdom. Sifting these legends, it seems likely that Bartholomew's death occurred in Parthia and involved suffering by some striking weapon.

Thomas

Forever known as the one who doubted Christ's resurrection, Thomas had the disadvantage of being the only apostle not present when the resurrected Christ appeared (John 20:24). Thomas's dilemma is redeemed when he utters one of the most christological confessions of all the apostles, "My Lord and my God!" (20:28). The ministry tradition of Thomas is unique because it solidly records him going beyond the farthest reaches of the Roman Empire, to the land of India. The presence of Thomas's legacy in various parts of India complicates this tradition, yet these traditions also combine to strongly affirm his presence in the region. It is quite possible that he traveled in the Syrian region through Parthia to India, since this theory connects with the strong tradition of his veneration in Edessa.

Matthew

Among the apostles, Matthew stands out for two reasons: his unconditional response when called to be a disciple of Jesus and his writing of a Gospel aiding Jewish Christians in understanding how the Old Testament points to Jesus as Messiah. When a seeming enemy walks away from his vocation to embrace a new order, curiosity is our natural response. This is all the more true when the person leaves behind potentially a great deal of wealth; Jesus himself remarked on the difficulty of a rich man entering the kingdom of heaven (Matt. 19:23). Since Matthew likely engaged in a series of tax abuses against the Jews in occupied Palestine, that he would forsake stability to participate in an itinerant life of faith is all the more radical. This apostle likely ministered and died in Persia, perhaps in the Caspian Sea region named Ethiopia. While the two episodes of his martyrdom cannot be harmonized to form one story, the common naming of Ethiopia as a region of Parthia offers historical support for his ministry there.

James, Son of Alphaeus

The relative obscurity of the path of James the Lesser has contributed to the ease of conflating James the Just, brother of Jesus, with this apostle. Even his symbol is drawn from the martyrdom story of the Just. The New Testament contains not a single episode about or quote from James. When a tenth-century hagiographer made a unique comment about this apostle, it took on weight. The tradition of James's ministry in Persia and his journeys to Egypt are the most likely to be true. It is best to conclude that he ministered in North Africa before working in Parthia, where he was martyred by crucifixion.

Jude, Son of James

A Syriac tradition shows significant promise in support of the historicity of Jude's ministering around Edessa. Ministry activity in Parthia, mainly Mesopotamia and Persia, likely led to his martyrdom by spear or sword. His ministry legends recount an unusual number of exorcisms, including cleansing the temple where he was eventually slain in Persia. His discipleship legacy is unique, as one source testifies to his impact on another evangelist in Jude's sphere of influence. He shares a martyrdom legend and a feast day with Simon.

Simon the Zealot

The records of Simon's travels to North Africa, including Mauretania and Egypt, hold promise of an accurate historical path. After this period he likely ministered in Parthia, where he died alongside James in Persia. The tradition of his travels to Britain is not substantiated, though it may be a remote possibility. He shares a martyrdom legend and a feast day with Jude.

Matthias

Matthias is forever known as the one elected to take the place of the betrayer, Judas Iscariot. His biography, including his early discipleship days and his ministry beyond Acts, is shrouded in ambiguity. His activities concentrate in Scythia and Palestine, with his death likely near modern Georgia. Clement of Alexandria remembers him in the standard way: "Matthias, accordingly, who was not chosen along with them, on showing himself worthy of becoming an apostle, is substituted for Judas."[5] When one considers all the early witnesses of Jesus who turned away, Ellsworth Kalas gets an individual assessment of Matthias right: "Matthias was one of those who stayed."[6] His faith in Jesus and his faithfulness to the cause of the nascent church led to his being awarded apostleship.

Paul

A case can be made that Paul is the most extraordinary of the apostles. His self-declared mission, "I am an apostle of Gentiles" (Rom. 11:13), captures his conviction in contrast to the other apostles. The book of Acts highlights him, reporting his attempts to travel to cities to first dialogue with synagogue leaders before inevitably engaging interested gentiles. His journeys are well known, taking him through Palestine, Cyprus, Syria, Anatolia, Macedonia and Greece, and Italy. The possibility of travel and ministry to Spain is likely, given the evidence of one Roman imprisonment with relative freedom separate from another Roman imprisonment that led to suffering and martyrdom. His contributions to the writing of the New Testament and the shaping of Christian doctrine are unmatched among the apostolic college. Among the tombs of the apostles, perhaps none has as much certainty of authenticity as that of Paul.

The Contribution of the Apostles

This quest has revealed more clearly how the apostles are deeply intriguing. These disciples of Christ offer inspiration by their journeys, their perseverance,

---

5. Clement of Alexandria, *Strom.* 6.13 (*ANF* 2:504).
6. Kalas, *Thirteen Apostles*, 143.

and their faith. The early fifth-century archbishop of Constantinople, John Chrysostom, commented on the martyrs in a way that also represents the apostles. The quote is even more significant when one realizes this orator's eloquence earned him the name "Golden Tongue":

> What need could they have of my tongue? Their own struggles surpass our moral nature. The prizes they won go beyond our powers and understanding. They laughed at the life lived on earth; they trampled underfoot the punishment of the rack; they scorned death and took wing to heaven; they escaped from the storms of temporal things and sailed into a calm harbor; they brought with them no gold or silver or expensive garments; they carried along no treasure which could be plundered, but the riches of patience, courage, and love. Now they belong to Paul's choral band while they still await their crowns, but they find delight in the expectation of their crowns, because they have escaped henceforth the uncertainty of the future.[7]

While the apostles' legacy warrants extensive treatment, only three brief elements of their influence are presented here in closing.

Missional Delivery

The apostles embodied a self-sacrifice that sought to glorify a cause greater than themselves. While the Gospels present these men as imperfect and even deeply flawed individuals, something grander than the men themselves transforms them and invites them on a mission to change the known world. Describing the impossible task of transforming the ancient world, N. T. Wright remarks:

> The truly extraordinary thing is that this belief was held by a tiny group who, for the first two of three generations at least, could hardly have mounted a riot in a village, let alone a revolution in an empire. And yet they persisted against all the odds, attracting the unwelcome notice of the authorities because of the power of the message and the worldview and lifestyle it generated. And whenever we go back to the key texts for evidence of why they persisted in such an improbable and dangerous belief they answer: it is because Jesus of Nazareth was raised from the dead. And this provokes us to ask once more, why did they make this claim?[8]

This apostolic mission was based on a profound reality—represented in the life, death, and resurrection of their Master, Jesus—that shook them

---

7. Chrysostom, *Discourses against Judaizing Christians* 6.6 (Harkins, 148–49).
8. Wright, *Resurrection of the Son of God*, 570.

from lives of professional fishing and tax collecting. Following the event of Pentecost, these unextraordinary men found inspiration to share the message of the gospel with the sacrifice of their own lives. The cause greater than them was the kingdom, inaugurated by Jesus and with application to the individual people they encountered. The apostles went forth with the optimism of Jesus's promises, including his words at the Last Supper: "Truly, truly, I say to you, he who believes in Me, the works that I do shall he do also; and greater *works* than these shall he do; because I go to the Father" (John 14:12). The power the apostles witnessed in Jesus they also witnessed in their own ministries of preaching, healing, and even martyrdom. With each convert, their mission gained momentum. With each beating, their mission continued anyway. With each memory of the work of Jesus, their mission went forth in hope that the presence of God would transform more lives and even society itself.

In a hymn Ephraim long ago presented the result of the apostles' mission. Focusing on the death of Thomas, this monk imagines the mind of Satan: "I stirred up Death to slay the Apostles, that I might be safe from their blows. By their deaths now more exceedingly am I cruelly beaten. The Apostle whom I slew in India is before me in Edessa; he is here wholly and also there. I went there, there was he: here and there I have found him and been grieved. Blessed is the might that dwells in the hallowed bones."[9]

Deposit of Faith

Yet if this study were the end of the collective story of the apostles, the story would be incomplete. Even if this study were combined with all existing studies of the apostles, the current generation of the church would be poorly strengthened by merely learning about their lives and legacies. The legacy of the apostles is found not only in their historical study but also in the very life of the present church itself. Here at the end, appreciation should not lie exclusively with the individual apostolic traditions but in the corporate apostolic tradition.

While the mixture of fact, possible fact, and myth in prior chapters has now been sifted through to result in a fairly clear picture of the legends that the church has inherited, it is the deposit of faith that is the true legacy of the apostles. As Glen Thompson remarks, "We do not dishonor them by not repeating all the legends that were related about them. It was the message, not the messenger, which had the power to change lives."[10] In the era of the early church, Clement of Alexandria extended the ministry and reward of the apostles beyond the first century into every generation of believers:

9. Ephraim, *Nisibene Hymns* 42.1 (*NPNF*[2] 13:205).
10. Thompson, review of *After Acts*, by Litfin, 153.

Not that they became apostles through being chosen for some distinguished peculiarity of nature, since also Judas was chosen along with them. But they were capable of becoming apostles on being chosen by Him who foresees even ultimate issues. . . . Those, then, also now, who have exercised themselves in the Lord's commandments, and lived perfectly and gnostically [wisely] according to the Gospel, may be enrolled in the chosen body of the apostles. Such an one is in reality a presbyter of the Church, and a true minister (deacon) of the will of God, if he will do and teach what is the Lord's; not as being ordained by men, nor enrolled in the presbyterate because righteous. And although here upon earth he be not honored with the chief seat, he will sit down on the four-and-twenty thrones, judging the people, as John says in the Apocalypse.[11]

The writing and use of Scripture they provided, the apostolic tradition, and the sacrificial discipleship they modeled all come to us as a foundation for belief. The church is the church because of the apostles. This influence includes the continual making of disciples that marked their lives. Maurice Dilasser describes the effect of even their symbols in this process:

In a secularized world which is foreign to the transcendent and sacred, since it casts aside all sense of God, the meaning of the great symbols is obliterated along with the ultimate questions about our present existence and the existence of a beyond. Christ, whose life marked the course of history through his words and his witness, can awaken the desire for open-mindedness and meaning which slumbers in all people's hearts. He can have them discover the key to the symbols which humanity has kept alive since its origins, and give them faith in him. It is in the light of Christ that the Scriptures can be deciphered.[12]

Here, at the end of the quest represented by this book, the thirteen apostles' journeys warrant a recognition and celebration of the corporate legacy that these apostles created in perpetuating the kingdom inaugurated by Jesus.

Inspiration for Faith

The lives and legacies of the apostles provide not only substance to the faith but also inspiration for the faith. In the second century Ignatius of Antioch reported: "They too despised death; indeed, they proved to be greater than death."[13] Polycarp, in his *Letter to the Philippians*, lists Ignatius, Paul, and the rest of the apostles as faithful during persecution: "Obey the teaching about

11. Clement of Alexandria, *Strom.* 6.13 (*ANF* 2:504).
12. Dilasser, *Symbols of the Church*, 60.
13. Ignatius, *Letter to the Smyrnaeans* 3.2 (Holmes, 251).

righteousness and . . . exercise unlimited endurance. . . . They are now in the place due them with the Lord, with whom they also suffered."[14] In the fourth century, the Syrian Aphrahat declared: "Great and excellent is the martyrdom of Jesus. He surpassed in affliction and in confession all who were before or after. And after Him was the faithful martyr Stephen whom the Jews stoned. Simon (Peter) also and Paul were perfect martyrs. And James and John walked in the footsteps of their Master Christ. Also (others) of the apostles hereafter in diverse places confessed and proved true martyrs."[15]

While the church fathers regularly promoted the faith through the influence of the church's faithful, it is rare to read of personal influences on the writer himself. Tertullian demonstrates the apostles' effect on him:

> The prisons there, and the bonds, and the scourges, and the big stones, and the swords, and the onsets by the Jews, and the assemblies of the heathen, and the indictments by tribunes, and the hearing of causes by kings, and the judgment-seats of pro-consuls and the name of Caesar, do not need an interpreter. . . . Whenever I read of these occurrences, so soon as I do so, I learn to suffer; nor does it signify to me which I follow as teachers of martyrdom, whether the declarations or the deaths of the apostles, save that in their deaths I recall their declarations also.[16]

Our journey began with explaining the ethos of the work of Albert Schweitzer in *The Quest of the Historical Jesus*. It was written during an era when historical studies sought to win back the subjective, deeply personal effects of the New Testament story that modern theology had stolen from it. After thoroughly considering the tensions of scholarship in this book, Schweitzer's purpose for the Jesus quest can still resonate with our quest for the apostles: "It is no doubt interesting to trace how modern thoughts have found their way into the ancient dogmatic system, there to combine with eternal ideas to form new constructions; it is interesting to penetrate into the mind of the thinker in which this process is at work; but the real truth of that which here meets us as history we experience within ourselves."[17]

That experience is the transformative power of the resurrection that inspired the apostles and strengthened them for their task. It is with the rhetoric of Schweitzer as he closed his *Quest* that we close our own quest. Jesus is the one unknown who comes to us by the lakeside, speaking the same words: "Follow

---

14. Polycarp, *Letter to the Philippians* 9.1–2 (Holmes, 291).
15. Aphrahat, *Select Demonstrations* 21.23 (*NPNF*[2] 13:401).
16. Tertullian, *Scorpiace* 15:5–6 (*ANF* 3:648).
17. Schweitzer, *Quest of the Historical Jesus*, 1.

me." He sets us to the tasks that he has to fulfill for our time, illustrated by the apostles in their time. He commands, and to those who obey him he reveals himself in the toils, the conflicts, and the sufferings that we pass through in his fellowship. Then, as an ineffable mystery, we will learn in our own experience, like the apostles learned in their own experience, who he is.[18]

18. Schweitzer, *Quest of the Historical Jesus*, 402.

Works Cited

Ancient and Medieval Sources

Abdias. *The Apostolic History of Abdias*. In James, 462–69.

———. *The Conflicts of the Holy Apostles*. Translated by Solomon Caesar Malan. London: BiblioLife, 2015.

Acts and Martyrdom of St. Matthew the Apostle. Translated by Alexander Walker. In *ANF* 8:528–34.

Acts of Andrew. In Elliott, 231–83.

Acts of Andrew. In James, 337–63.

Acts of Andrew and Matthias. Translated by Alexander Walker. In *ANF* 8:517–25.

Acts of Andrew and Paul. In James, 472–75.

Acts of John. In Elliott, 303–49; in James, 228–69.

Acts of Mār Mārī the Apostle. Translated by Amir Harrak. Boston: Brill, 2005.

Acts of Paul. In Elliott, 350–89.

Acts of Paul. In James, 277–300.

Acts of Peter. In Elliott, 390–430.

Acts of Peter and Andrew. In James, 458–60.

Acts of Peter and Paul. Translated by Alexander Walker. In *ANF* 8:477–85.

Acts of Philip. Translated by Alexander Walker. In *ANF* 8:497–510; in James, 439–52.

Acts of Philip: A New Translation. Translated by François Bovon and Christopher R. Matthews. Waco: Baylor University Press, 2012.

Acts of Simon and Jude. In Elliott, 525–30.

Acts of the Holy Apostle and Evangelist John the Theologian. Translated by Alexander Walker. In *ANF* 8:560–62.

Acts of the Holy Apostle Thaddaeus. Translated by Alexander Walker. In *ANF* 8:558–59.

Acts of the Holy Apostle Thomas. Translated by Alexander Walker. In *ANF* 8:535–52.

Acts of Thomas. In James, 364–437.

Anselm of Canterbury. *Proslogion*. In *Anselm of Canterbury: The Major Works*, edited by Brian Davies and G. R. Evans, 82–104. New York: Oxford University Press, 2008.

Aphrahat. *Select Demonstrations*. Translated by J. Gwynn. In *NPNF*² 13:345–412.

Apocalypse of Paul. In Elliott, 616–51.

Apocalypse of Peter. In James, 505–21.

Apocalypse of Thomas. In James, 555–63.

Augustine. *Homilies on the Gospel of John*. Translated by John Gibb. In *NPNF*¹ 7:7–452.

Book of the Cock. In James, 150.

Book of John concerning the Falling Asleep of Mary. Translated by Alexander Walker. In *ANF* 8:587–91.

Book of the Resurrection of Christ by Bartholomew the Apostle. In James, 181–86.

Book of Thomas the Contender. Translated by John D. Turner. In Robinson, 199–207.

Chrysostom, John. *Commentary on Galatians*. Translated by Gross Alexander. In *NPNF*¹ 13:1–172.

———. *Discourses against Judaizing Christians*. Translated by Paul W. Harkins. FC 68. Washington, DC: Catholic University of America Press, 1979.

———. *Homilies on the Acts of the Apostles*. Translated by J. Walker, J. Sheppard, and H. Browne. In *NPNF*¹ 11:1–328.

———. *Homilies on the Gospel of St. John*. Translated by Philip Schaff. In *NPNF*¹ 14:1–334.

———. *Homilies on the Gospel of St. Matthew*. Translated by George Prevost. In *NPNF*¹ 10:1–534.

———. *Homily on St. Ignatius*. Translated by W. R. W. Stephens. In *NPNF*¹ 9:135–40.

Cicero. *De Officiis*. Latin text in *A Commentary on Cicero, De Officiis*, edited by Andrew R. Dyck. Ann Arbor: University of Michigan Press, 1999.

Clement of Alexandria. *The Instructor*. Translated by William Wilson. In *ANF* 2:207–96.

———. *Miscellanies*. Translated by William Wilson. In *ANF* 2:299–567.

———. *Who Is the Rich Man That Shall Be Saved?* Translated by William Wilson. In *ANF* 2:591–604.

Clement of Rome. *1 Clement*. In Holmes, 44–131.

Clementine Homilies. Translated by Thomas Smith, Peter Peterson, and James Donaldson. In *ANF* 8:223–346.

Constitutions of the Holy Apostles. Translated by James Donaldson. In *ANF* 7:387–508.

Correspondence of Paul and Seneca. In James, 480–84.

Ephraim. *The Nisibene Hymns*. Translated by J. T. Sarsfield Stopford. In *NPNF*² 13:167–219.

Epiphanius. *Against Heresies*. Translated by Frank Williams. In *The Panarion of Epiphanius of Salamis: Book I*. Boston: Brill, 2009.

Epistle of Clement to James. Translated by Thomas Smith. In *ANF* 8:218–22.

Epistle of the Apostles. Translated by Julian V. Hills. Early Christian Apocrypha 2. Salem, OR: Polebridge, 2009.

Eusebius. *Eusebius' Ecclesiastical History: Complete and Unabridged*. Translated by C. F. Cruse. New updated version. Peabody, MA: Hendrickson, 2000.

———. *Life of Constantine*. Translated by Ernest Cushing Richardson. In *NPNF*² 1:481–559.

Extracts from Various Books concerning Abgar the King and Addaeus the Apostle. Translated by B. P. Pratten. In *ANF* 8:655–56.

First Apocalypse of James. Translated by William R. Schoedel and Douglas M. Parrott. In Robinson, 270–86.

Fragments of Caius. Translated by S. D. F. Salmond. In *ANF* 5:597–604.

Gospel of Philip. Translated by Hans-Martin Schenke. In Schneemelcher, 1:271–78.

Gospel of Pseudo-Matthew. In Elliott, 84–99.

Gospel of Thomas. Translated by Helmut Koester and Thomas O. Lambdin. In Robinson, 124–38.

Gregory of Nazianzus. *Orations*. Translated by Charles Gordon Browne and James Edward Swallow. In *NPNF*² 7:208–434.

Hippolytus. *Commentary on Daniel*. Translated by Maurice Lefèvre. Sources Chrétiennes 14. Paris: Cerf, 1947.

———. *On the Seventy Apostles*. Translated by S. D. F. Salmond. In *ANF* 8:255–56.

———. *On the Twelve Apostles*. Translated by S. D. F. Salmond. In *ANF* 5:254–55.

———. *Refutation of All Heresies*. Translated by J. H. Macmahon. In *ANF* 5:9–153.

Ignatius. *Letter to the Ephesians*. In Holmes, 182–201.

———. *Letter to the Romans*. In Holmes, 224–35.

———. *Letter to the Smyrnaeans*. In Holmes, 248–61.

Infancy Gospel of Thomas. In Elliott, 68–83.

Irenaeus. *Against Heresies*. Translated by Alexander Roberts and W. H. Rambaut. In *ANF* 1:309–567.

———. *Letter to the Romans*. In Holmes, 224–35.

Jerome. *Commentary on Galatians*. Translated by Andrew Cain. FC 121. Washington, DC: Catholic University of America Press, 2010.

———. *Commentary on Matthew.* Translated by Thomas P. Scheck. FC 51. Washington, DC: Catholic University of America Press, 2008.

———. *Lives of Illustrious Men [De viris illustribus].* Translated by Ernest Cushing Richardson. In *NPNF*² 3:359–84.

———. *On the Perpetual Virginity of the Blessed Mary against Helvidius.* Translated by John N. Hritzu, 3–43. FC 53. Washington, DC: Catholic University of America Press, 1965.

Josephus. *The Antiquities of the Jews.* In *The Works of Josephus: Complete and Unabridged,* 27–542. Translated by William Whiston. Updated ed. Peabody, MA: Hendrickson, 1987.

———. *Flavius Josephus against Apion.* In *The Works of Josephus: Complete and Unabridged,* 773–812. Translated by William Whiston. Updated ed. Peabody, MA: Hendrickson, 1987.

———. *The War of the Jews.* In *The Works of Josephus: Complete and Unabridged,* 543–772. Translated by William Whiston. Updated ed. Peabody, MA: Hendrickson, 1987.

Letter of Peter to Philip. Translated by Marvin W. Meyer and Frederik Wisse. In Robinson, 434–37.

Martyrdom of Peter. In Elliott, 426.

Martyrdom of the Holy and Glorious Apostle Bartholomew. Translated by Alexander Walker. In *ANF* 8:553–57.

Muratorian Fragment. In *ANF* 5:603–4.

Origen. *Contra Celsus.* Translated by Frederick Crombie. In *ANF* 4:395–669.

———. *Homilies on Luke.* Translated by Joseph T. Lienhard. FC 94. Washington, DC: Catholic University of America Press, 1996.

Papias. *Fragments.* In Holmes, 732–67.

Pistis Sophia. Translated by Carl Schmidt. In Schneemelcher, 1:250–63.

Polycarp. *Letter to the Philippians.* In Holmes, 280–97.

Socrates Scholasticus. *Ecclesiastical History.* Translated by A. C. Zenos. In *NPNF*² 2:1–178.

Story of Perpetua. Translated by Alexander Walker. In *ANF* 8:485–86.

Tacitus. *The Annals of Imperial Rome.* Translated by Michael Grant. New York: Dorset, 1984.

Teaching of Addaeus the Apostle. Translated by B. P. Pratten. In *ANF* 8:657–65.

Teaching of the Apostles. Translated by B. P. Pratten. In *ANF* 8:667–72.

Tertullian. *Against Marcion.* Translated by Peter Holmes. In *ANF* 3:269–475.

———. *The Prescription against Heretics.* Translated by Peter Holmes. In *ANF* 3:243–67.

———. *Scorpiace.* Translated by S. Thelwall. In *ANF* 3:633–48.

Vincent of Lérins. *A Commonitory for the Antiquity and Universality of the Catholic Faith against the Profane Novelties of All Heresies*. Translated by C. A. Heurtley. In *NPNF*² 11:127–58.

Voragine, Jacobus de. *The Golden Legend of Jacobus de Voragine*. Translated by Granger Ryan and Helmut Ripperger. New York: Arno, 1969.

Modern Sources

Alexander, David C., and Edward L. Smither. "Bauer's Forgotten Region: North African Christianity." In *Orthodoxy and Heresy in Early Christian Contexts: Reconsidering the Bauer Thesis*, edited by Paul A. Hartog, 166–92. Eugene, OR: Wipf & Stock, 2015.

Atkins, J. D. "Twelve Prophets like Moses: The Commissioning of the Apostles in the *Epistula Apostolorum*." Paper presented at the Annual Meeting of the Society of Biblical Literature, San Francisco, November 22, 2011.

Baker, William H. "Acts." In *Evangelical Commentary on the Bible*, edited by Walter A. Elwell, 881–920. Grand Rapids: Baker, 1989.

Bauckham, Richard J. *Jude, 2 Peter*. Word Biblical Commentary 50. Waco: Word, 1983.

———. "The Martyrdom of Peter in Early Christian Literature." In *Aufstieg und Niedergang der römischen Welt: Geschichte und Kultur Roms im Spiegel der neueren Forschung*, part 2, *Principat* 26.1, edited by Hildegard Temporini and Wolfgang Haase. Berlin: de Gruyter, 1992.

Bauer, Walter. *Orthodoxy and Heresy in Earliest Christianity*. Edited by Robert A. Kraft. Translated by Gerhard Krodel. Philadelphia Seminar on Christian Origins. Philadelphia: Fortress, 1971; repr., Mifflintown, PA: Sigler, 1996.

Bayer, Hans. *Jesus' Predictions of Vindication and Resurrection: The Provenance, Meaning and Correlation of the Synoptic Predictions*. Tübingen: Mohr, 1986.

Berger, Peter. *The Sacred Canopy*. New York: Doubleday, 1967.

Bissell, Tom. *Apostle: Travels among the Tombs of the Twelve*. New York: Pantheon, 2016.

Bockmuehl, Markus. "Peter's Death in Rome? Back to Front and Upside Down." *Scottish Journal of Theology* 60 (2007): 1–23.

Bovon, François. "Byzantine Witness for the Apocryphal Acts of the Apostles." In *Apocryphal Acts of the Apostles*, edited by François Bovon, Ann Graham Brock, and Christopher R. Matthews, 87–98. Cambridge, MA: Harvard University Press, 1999.

———. "Canonical and Apocryphal Acts of Apostles." *Journal of Early Christian Studies* 11 (2003): 165–94.

Braake, David. *The Gnostics: Myth, Ritual, and Diversity in Early Christianity*. Cambridge, MA: Harvard University Press, 2010.

Braght, Thieleman J. van. *The Bloody Theater; or, Martyrs Mirror of the Defenseless Christians.* Translated by Joseph F. Sohm. Scottdale, PA: Herald Press, 1950.

Brooks, James A. *Mark.* New American Commentary 23. Nashville: Broadman, 1991.

Brown, Charles Reynolds. *These Twelve: A Study in Temperament.* New York: Century, 1926.

Brown, Jeannine K. *The Disciples in Narrative Perspective: The Portrayal and Function of the Matthean Disciples.* Academia Biblica 9. Atlanta: Society of Biblical Literature, 2003.

Brown, Raymond E., and John P. Meier. *Antioch and Rome: New Testament Cradles of Catholic Christianity.* New York: Paulist Press, 1983.

Brownrigg, Ronald. *The Twelve Apostles.* New York: Macmillan, 1974.

Bruce, F. F. *The Book of Acts.* Rev. ed. New International Commentary on the New Testament. Grand Rapids: Eerdmans, 1997.

———. *The Gospel and Epistles of John.* Grand Rapids: Eerdmans, 1983.

———. *New Testament History.* New York: Doubleday, 1969.

———. *Paul: Apostle of the Heart Set Free.* Grand Rapids: Eerdmans, 1997.

Buchholz, Dennis D. *Your Eyes Will Be Opened: A Study of the Greek (Ethiopic) Apocalypse of Peter.* Atlanta: Scholars Press, 1998.

Buxton, Harold. *The Armenian Church.* London: Spottiswoode, Ballantyne, 1919.

Cairns, Earle. *Christianity through the Centuries: A History of the Christian Church.* 3rd ed. Grand Rapids: Zondervan, 1996.

Callon, Callie. "Sorcery, Wheels, and Mirror Punishment in the *Apocalypse of Peter.*" *Journal of Early Christian Studies* 18 (2010): 29–49.

Carson, D. A., Douglas J. Moo, and Leon Morris. *An Introduction to the New Testament.* Grand Rapids: Zondervan, 1992.

Chadwick, Henry. *The Early Church.* New York: Penguin, 1967.

Chamblin, J. Knox. "Matthew." In *Evangelical Commentary on the Bible*, edited by Walter A. Elwell, 719–60. Grand Rapids: Baker, 1989.

Cole, R. Alan. *Galatians.* TNTC 9. Leicester, UK: Inter-Varsity; Grand Rapids: Eerdmans, 1965. Reprint, 1989.

Collingwood, R. G. *The Idea of History.* New York: Oxford University Press, 1975.

Collins, C. John. *The God of Miracles: An Exegetical Examination of God's Action in the World.* Wheaton: Crossway, 2000.

Criswell, David. *The Apostles after Jesus: A History of the Apostles.* Dallas: Fortress Adonai, 2013.

Culpepper, R. Alan. *John, the Son of Zebedee: The Life of a Legend.* Columbia: University of South Carolina Press, 1994.

D'Andria, Francesco. "Philip's Tomb Discovered—But Not Where Expected." *Biblical Archaeology Review* 38 (January–February 2012): 18.

Daniélou, Jean, and Henri Marrou. *The Christian Centuries*. London: Darton, Longman, & Todd, 1964.

Davis, Stephen J. "A 'Pauline' Defense of Women's Right to Baptize? Intertextuality and Apostolic Authority in the *Acts of Paul*." *Journal of Early Christian Studies* 8 (2000): 453–59.

Di Berardino, Angelo, ed. *Encyclopedia of Ancient Christianity*. 3 vols. Downers Grove, IL: InterVarsity, 2014.

Dilasser, Maurice. *The Symbols of the Church*. Translated by Mary Cabrini Durkin, Madeleine Beaumont, and Caroline Morson. Collegeville, MN: Liturgical Press, 1999.

Eastman, David L. *Paul the Martyr: The Cult of the Apostle in the Latin West*. Atlanta: Society of Biblical Literature, 2011.

Eedle, Arthur, and Rosalind Eedle. *Albion Restored: A Detective Journey to Discover the Birth of Christianity in England*. Morrisville, NC: Lulu, 2013.

Ehrman, Bart D. "Cephas and Peter." *Journal of Biblical Studies* 109 (1991): 463–74.

———. *The New Testament and Other Early Christian Writings: A Reader*. 2nd ed. New York: Oxford University Press, 2004.

Elliott, J. K., ed. *The Apocryphal New Testament: A Collection of Apocryphal Christian Literature in an English Translation*. Oxford: Clarendon, 1993.

Elwell, Walter A., ed. *Evangelical Commentary on the Bible*. Grand Rapids: Baker, 1989.

France, R. T. *Matthew*. TNTC 1. Reprint, Leicester, UK: Inter-Varsity; Grand Rapids: Eerdmans, 1999.

Frederick, G. Marcille. "Doing Justice in History: Using Narrative Frames Responsibly." In *History and the Christian Historian*, edited by Ronald A. Wells, 220–34. Grand Rapids: Eerdmans, 1998.

Frend, W. H. C. *Martyrdom and Persecution in the Early Church: A Study of a Conflict from the Maccabees to Donatus*. New York: New York University Press, 1967.

Funk, Robert, ed. *The Five Gospels*. San Francisco: HarperOne, 1996.

Goulder, Michael D. "Did Peter Ever Go to Rome?" *Scottish Journal of Theology* 57 (2004): 377–96.

Grant, Robert. *Gnosticism and Early Christianity*. Rev. ed. New York: Harper & Row, 1966.

Green, Bernard. *Christianity in Ancient Rome: The First Three Centuries*. London: T&T Clark, 2010.

Gregory, Andrew, and Christopher Tuckett, eds. *The Oxford Handbook on Early Christian Apocrypha*. Oxford: Oxford University Press, 2015.

Grudem, Wayne. *Systematic Theology: An Introduction to Biblical Doctrine*. Grand Rapids: Zondervan, 1994.

Gumerlock, Francis X. "Chromatius of Aquileia on John 21:22 and Rev. 10:11 against a Legend about the Apostle John." In *The Book of Revelation and Its Interpreters: Short Studies and an Annotated Bibliography*, edited by Ian Boxall and Richard Tresley, 53–64. New York: Rowman & Littlefield, 2016.

———. *Revelation and the First Century: Preterist Interpretations of the Apocalypse in Early Christianity*. Powder Springs, GA: American Vision, 2012.

Gundry, Robert H. *The Use of the Old Testament in St. Matthew's Gospel*. Supplements to Novum Testamentum 18. Leiden: Brill, 1967.

Haenchen, Ernst. *The Acts of the Apostles: A Commentary*. Oxford: Blackwell, 1971.

Hagner, Donald A. "James." In *The Anchor Bible Dictionary*, edited by David Noel Freedman, 3:616–18. New York: Doubleday, 1992.

Harrak, Amir. "Introduction." In *The Acts of Mār Mārī the Apostle*, xi–xxxvii. Boston: Brill, 2005.

Hartog, Paul. *Polycarp's "Epistle to the Philippians" and the "Martyrdom of Polycarp": Introduction, Text, and Commentary*. Oxford: Oxford University Press, 2013.

Hengel, Martin. *Saint Peter: The Underestimated Disciple*. Translated by Thomas H. Trapp. Grand Rapids: Eerdmans, 2010.

Henning, Meghan. "*Chreia* Elaboration and the Un-healing of Peter's Daughter: Rhetorical Analysis as a Clue to Understanding the Development of a Petrine Tradition." *Journal of Early Christian Studies* 24 (2016): 145–71.

Hills, Julian V. *The Epistle of the Apostles*. Early Christian Apocrypha 2. Salem, OR: Polebridge, 2009.

Hockney, Mike. *Causation and the Principle of Sufficient Reason*. Miami: Hyperreality, 2014.

Holmes, Michael W., ed. and trans. *The Apostolic Fathers: Greek Texts and English Translations*. 3rd ed. Grand Rapids: Baker Academic, 2007.

Howard, George. "The Textual Nature of an Old Hebrew Version of Matthew." *Journal of Biblical Literature* 105 (1986): 49–63.

James, Montague Rhodes, trans. *The Apocryphal New Testament: Being the Apocryphal Gospels, Acts, Epistles, and Apocalypses*. Oxford: Clarendon, 1924. Reprint, 1972.

Jeffers, James S. *The Greco-Roman World of the New Testament Era: Exploring the Background of Early Christianity*. Downers Grove, IL: InterVarsity, 1999.

Jenkins, Philip. *The Next Christendom: The Coming of Global Christianity*. New York: Oxford University Press, 2002.

Jöckle, Clemens. *Encyclopedia of Saints*. London: Alpine Fine Arts Collection, 1995.

Jones, Brian W. *The Emperor Domitian*. London: Routledge, 1992.

Jowett, George F. *The Drama of the Lost Disciples*. Bishop Auckland, UK: Covenant, 2004.

Kalas, J. Ellsworth. *The Thirteen Apostles*. Nashville: Abingdon, 2002.

Keener, Craig S. *Matthew*. IVP New Testament Commentary 1. Downers Grove, IL: InterVarsity, 1997.

Klauck, Hans-Josef. *The Apocryphal Acts of the Apostles: An Introduction*. Translated by Brian McNeil. Waco: Baylor University Press, 2008.

Koester, Helmut. Introduction to *The Gospel of Thomas*. In *The Nag Hammadi Library: The Definitive Translation of the Gnostic Scriptures Complete in One Volume*, edited by James M. Robinson, translated by Thomas O. Lambdin, 124–26. San Francisco: HarperSanFrancisco, 1990.

Korn, Frank J. *A Catholic's Guide to Rome: Discovering the Soul of the Eternal City*. New York: Paulist Press, 2000.

Lampe, Peter. *From Paul to Valentinus: Christians at Rome in the First Two Centuries*. Minneapolis: Fortress, 2003.

Lapham, Fred. *An Introduction to the New Testament Apocrypha*. New York: T&T Clark, 2003.

Licona, Michael R. *The Resurrection of Jesus: A New Historiographical Approach*. Downers Grove, IL: InterVarsity, 2010.

Liddell, Henry George, and Robert Scott. *A Greek-English Lexicon*. Revised and enlarged by Henry Stuart Jones with Roderick McKenzie. 9th ed. With rev. supplement edited by P. G. W. Glare with A. A. Thompson. Oxford: Clarendon, 1996.

Lightfoot, Joseph Barber. *Ordination Addresses and Counsels to Clergy*. New York: Macmillan, 1890.

Lindars, Barnabas. "Matthew, Levi, Lebbaeus and the Value of the Western Text." *New Testament Studies* 4 (1958): 220–22.

Linnemann, Eta. *Historical Criticism of the Bible: Methodology or Ideology? Reflections of a Bultmannian Turned Evangelical*. Translated by Robert Yarbrough. Grand Rapids: Baker, 1990.

Litfin, Bryan. *After Acts: The Lives and Legends of the Apostles*. Chicago: Moody, 2015.

———. *Early Christian Martyr Stories: An Evangelical Introduction with New Translations*. Grand Rapids: Baker Academic, 2014.

Marshall, I. Howard. *Acts*. TNTC 5. Leicester, UK: Inter-Varsity; Grand Rapids: Eerdmans, 1980.

McBirnie, William Steuart. *The Search for the Twelve Apostles*. Rev. ed. Carol Stream, IL: Tyndale, 2004.

McDonald, Dennis R. *The Acts of Andrew and the Acts of Andrew and Matthias in the City of Cannibals*. Atlanta: Scholars Press, 1990.

McDowell, Sean. *The Fate of the Apostles: Examining the Martyrdom Accounts of the Closest Followers of Jesus*. New York: Routledge, 2015.

Medlycott, Adolphus E. *India and the Apostle Thomas: An Inquiry, with a Critical Analysis of the "Acta Thomae."* London: Ballantyne, 1905.

Meier, John P. *Antioch and Rome. See* R. Brown and Meier.

———. "The Circle of the Twelve: Did It Exist during Jesus' Public Ministry?" *Journal of Biblical Literature* 116 (1997): 635–72.

Meinardus, Otto F. A. "Paul's Missionary Journey to Spain: Tradition and Folklore." *Biblical Archaeologist* 41, no. 2 (1978): 61–63.

Metzger, Bruce M. "St. Paul and the Baptized Lion: Apocryphal vs. Canonical Books of the New Testament." *Princeton Seminary Bulletin* 39, no. 2 (1945): 11–21.

Meyer, Marvin W. Introduction to *The Letter of Peter to Philip*. In *The Nag Hammadi Library: The Definitive Translation of the Gnostic Scriptures Complete in One Volume*, edited by James M. Robinson, translated by Thomas O. Lambdin, 431–33. San Francisco: HarperSanFrancisco, 1990.

Montgomery, John Warwick. *The Shape of the Past: An Introduction to Philosophical Historiography*. Ann Arbor, MI: Edwards Brothers, 1962.

Moreschini, Claudio, and Enrico Norelli. *Early Christian Greek and Latin Literature*. 2 vols. Peabody, MA: Hendrickson, 2005.

Morgan, G. Campbell. *The Acts of the Apostles*. Reprint, Eugene, OR: Wipf & Stock, 2012.

Moss, Candida. *Ancient Christian Martyrdom: Diverse Practices, Theologies, and Traditions*. New Haven: Yale University Press, 2012.

———. *The Myth of Persecution: How Early Christianity Invented a Story of Martyrdom*. New York: HarperOne, 2013.

———. "Roman Imperialism: The Political Context of Early Christian Apocrypha." In *The Oxford Handbook of Early Christian Apocrypha*, edited by Andrew Gregory and Christopher Tuckett, 378–88. New York: Oxford University Press, 2015.

Mullen, Shirley A. "Between 'Romance' and 'True History': Historical Narrative and Truth Telling in a Postmodern Age." In *History and the Christian Historian*, edited by Ronald A. Wells, 23–40. Grand Rapids: Eerdmans, 1998.

Nichols, Terence L. *That All May Be One: Hierarchy and Participation in the Church*. Wilmington, DE: Michael Glazier, 1997.

Nietzsche, Friedrich. *"Twilight of the Idols" and "The Antichrist."* Translated by R. J. Hollingdale. New York: Penguin, 1982.

Pagels, Elaine. *The Gnostic Gospels*. New York: Random House, 1979.

Pao, David W. "Physical and Spiritual Resurrection: The Role of Healing Miracles in the *Acts of Andrew*." In *The Apocryphal Acts of the Apostles*, edited by François Bovon, Ann Graham Brock, and Christopher R. Matthews, 259–77. Cambridge, MA: Harvard University Press, 1999.

Patrick, James. *Andrew of Bethsaida and the Johannine Circle*. New York: Peter Lang, 2013.

Pearcey, Nancy. *Saving Leonardo: A Call to Resist the Secular Assault on Mind, Morals, and Meaning*. Nashville: B&H, 2010.

Perkins, Pheme. *First and Second Peter, James, and Jude*. Interpretation. Louisville: Westminster John Knox, 1995.

Pervo, Richard I. "The Role of the Apostles." In *The Oxford Handbook of Early Christian Apocrypha*, edited by Andrew Gregory and Christopher Tuckett, 306–18. New York: Oxford University Press, 2015.

Peterson, Peter M. *Andrew, Brother of Simon Peter: His History and His Legends*. NovTSup 1. Boston: Brill, 1963.

Pfeifer, Daniel J. "Which Came First, the Symbol or the Referent? A Study of the Historical Twelve." *Bibliotheca Sacra* 172 (2015): 433–49.

Polhill, John B. *Acts*. New American Commentary 26. Nashville: Broadman, 1992.

Propp, Vladimir. *Morphology of the Folk Tale*. 2nd ed. Austin: University of Texas Press, 1968.

Robinson, James M., ed. *The Nag Hammadi Library: The Definitive Translation of the Gnostic Scriptures Complete in One Volume*. San Francisco: HarperSanFrancisco, 1990.

Roetzel, Calvin. *Paul: The Man and the Myth*. Minneapolis: Fortress, 1999.

Rose, Els. *Ritual Memory: The Apocryphal Acts and Liturgical Commentaries in the Early Medieval West (c. 500–1251)*. Boston: Brill, 2009.

Ruffin, C. Bernard. *The Twelve: The Lives of the Apostles after Calvary*. Huntington, IN: Our Sunday Visitor, 1998.

Sanders, E. P., and Margaret Davies. *Studying the Synoptic Gospels*. London: SCM; Philadelphia: Trinity, 1989.

Schaff, Philip. *History of the Apostolic Church: With a General Introduction to Church History*. 12 vols. Peabody, MA: Hendrickson, 2006.

Schmidt, Thomas E. *The Apostles after Acts: A Sequel*. Eugene, OR: Cascade, 2013.

Schmithals, Walter. *The Office of the Apostle in the Early Church*. Nashville: Abingdon, 1969.

Schnabel, Eckhard J. *Early Christian Mission*. Vol. 1, *Jesus and the Twelve*. Downers Grove, IL: InterVarsity, 2004.

Schneemelcher, Wilhelm, ed. *New Testament Apocrypha*. Translated by R. M. Wilson. Philadelphia: Westminster, 1963.

Schweitzer, Albert. *The Quest of the Historical Jesus: A Critical Study of Its Progress from Reimarus to Wrede*. New York: Collier, 1968.

Shelton, W. Brian. "Patristic Heresiology: The Difficulties of Reliability and Legitimacy." In *Orthodoxy and Heresy in Early Christian Contexts: Reconsidering the Bauer Thesis*, edited by Paul Hartog, 193–212. Eugene, OR: Wipf & Stock, 2015.

Sienkiewicz, Henryk. *Quo Vadis: A Classic Story of Love and Adventure*. Chicago: Moody, 1992.

Smith, Carl B. *No Longer Jews: The Search for Gnostic Origins*. Peabody, MA: Hendrickson, 2004.

Smith, Jonathan Z. "Birth Upside Down or Right Side Up?" *History of Religion* 9 (1970): 281–303.

Smith, Joseph, Jr. *The Doctrine and Covenants, Containing Revelations Given to Joseph Smith, Jr., the Prophet*. Rev. ed. Salt Lake City: Deseret Book, 1951.

Smith, William, and Samuel Cheetham, eds. *A Dictionary of Christian Antiquities: Being a Continuation of the Dictionary of the Bible*. New York: Kraus, 1968.

Spencer, F. Scott. *The Portrait of Philip in Acts: A Study of Roles and Relations*. Journal for the Study of the New Testament Supplement Series 67. Sheffield: JSOT Press, 1992.

Starowieyski, Marek. "Bartholomew." In *Encyclopedia of Ancient Christianity*, edited by Angelo Di Berardino, 1:337. Downers Grove, IL: InterVarsity, 2014.

Taylor, Richard. *How to Read a Church: A Guide to Symbols and Images in Churches and Cathedrals*. Mahwah, NJ: Hidden Spring, 2005.

Thelen, Daniel L. *Saints in Rome and Beyond: A Guide to Finding the First Class Relics of the Saints*. Raleigh, NC: Lulu, 2015.

Thomas, Christine M. "The 'Prehistory' of the Acts of Peter." In *Apocryphal Acts of the Apostles*, edited by François Bovon, Ann Graham Brock, and Christopher R. Matthews, 39–62. Cambridge, MA: Harvard University Press, 1999.

Thompson, Glen L. Review of *After Acts: Exploring the Lives and Legends of the Apostles*, by Bryan Litfin. *Wisconsin Lutheran Quarterly* 113 (2016): 150–53.

Titus, Eric L. "The Identity of the Beloved Disciple." *Journal of Biblical Literature* 69 (1950): 323–28.

Topping, Ryan N. S. *Happiness and Wisdom: Augustine's Early Theology of Education*. Washington, DC: Catholic University of America Press, 2012.

Tuzzi, Federica, ed. *Sacred Rome: Guide to Places of Worship amongst Art, Faith, and Spirituality*. Milan: Mondadori, 2012.

Twelftree, Graham H. *In the Name of Jesus: Exorcism among Early Christians*. Grand Rapids: Baker Academic, 2007.

———. *Jesus the Miracle Worker: A Historical and Theological Study*. Downers Grove, IL: InterVarsity, 1999.

Walls, Andrew F. *The Missionary Movement in Christian History: Studies in the Transmission of Faith*. Maryknoll, NY: Orbis Books, 1996.

Ware, Timothy. *The Orthodox Church*. New York: Penguin, 1993.

Wegner, C. Peter. *Apostles Today: Biblical Government for Biblical Power*. Ventura, CA: Regal, 2012.

Whittemore, Carroll E. *Symbols of the Church*. 6th rev. ed. Nashville: Abingdon, 1987.

Williams, Margaret H. "Palestinian Jewish Personal Names in Acts." In *The Book of Acts in Its First Century Palestinian Setting*, edited by Richard Bauckham, 79–113. Grand Rapids: Eerdmans; Carlisle, UK: Paternoster, 1985.

Williams, Michael A. *Rethinking "Gnosticism": An Argument for Dismantling a Dubious Category.* Princeton: Princeton University Press, 1996.

Wilson, Andrew. "Apostle Apollos?" *Journal of the Evangelical Theological Society* 56 (2013): 325–35.

Winter, Bruce W. *Divine Honours for the Caesars: The First Christians' Responses.* Grand Rapids: Eerdmans, 2015.

Witherington, Ben, III. "The Martyrdom of the Zebedee Brothers." *Biblical Archaeology Review* 33 (May–June 2007): 26.

Wright, N. T. *The Resurrection of the Son of God.* Christian Origins and the Question of God 3. Minneapolis: Fortress, 2003.

Yarbrough, Robert W. "The Date of Papias: A Reassessment." *Journal of the Evangelical Theological Society* 26 (1983): 181–91.

Index of Modern Authors

Index of Scripture and Other Ancient and Medieval Sources

Index of Subjects